The Readers' Advisory Guide
to Historical Fiction

ALA READERS' ADVISORY SERIES

The Readers' Advisory Guide to Genre Blends

The Readers' Advisory Guide to Horror

Serving Boys through Readers' Advisory

The Readers' Advisory Guide to Graphic Novels

The Readers' Advisory Guide to Genre Fiction,
second edition

Research-Based Readers' Advisory

The Readers' Advisory Guide to Nonfiction

Serving Teens through Readers' Advisory

The Horror Readers' Advisory:
The Librarian's Guide to Vampires, Killer Tomatoes,
and Haunted Houses

The Science Fiction and Fantasy Readers' Advisory:
The Librarian's Guide to Cyborgs, Aliens,
and Sorcerers

The Mystery Readers' Advisory:
The Librarian's Clues to Murder and Mayhem

The Romance Readers' Advisory:
The Librarian's Guide to Love in the Stacks

The Short Story Readers' Advisory: A Guide to the Best

The Readers' Advisory Handbook

The Readers' Advisory Guide to Street Literature

The Readers' Advisory Guide to Mystery,
second edition

The Readers' Advisory Guide to Historical Fiction

Jennifer S. Baker

An imprint of the American Library Association

Chicago   2015

JENNIFER BAKER earned her master's degree in librarianship at the Universi
Washington and now works at the Seattle Public Library's Reader Services Departme
a reference and readers' advisory librarian. Baker currently serves on the Listen List Aw
committee, sponsored by the Reference and User Services (RUSA) division of the Americ
Library Association, and she has also served on the Reading List Council. She reviews hi
torical suspense for *Booklist*, serves on the consulting team for EBSCO Publishing's Adul
Core Collection, and is the author of several readers' advisory articles in *Library Journal*,
NoveList, and *Reference and User Services Quarterly*.

© 2015 by the American Library Association.

Extensive effort has gone into ensuring the reliability of the information in this book;
however, the publisher makes no warranty, express or implied, with respect to the
material contained herein.

ISBNs: 978-0-8389-1165-5 (paper); 978-0-8389-1245-4 (PDF); 978-0-8389-1246-1 (ePUB);
978-0-8389-1247-8 (Kindle). For more information on digital formats, visit the ALA Store
at alastore.ala.org and select eEditions.

Library of Congress Cataloging-in-Publication Data

Baker, Jennifer S., 1953-
    The readers' advisory guide to historical fiction / Jennifer S. Baker.
      pages cm. — (ALA readers' advisory series)
    Includes bibliographical references and indexes.
    ISBN 978-0-8389-1165-5 (print : alk. paper) — ISBN 978-0-8389-1246-1 (epub) —
ISBN 978-0-8389-1245-4 (pdf) — ISBN 978-0-8389-1247-8 (kindle)
    1. Fiction in libraries—United States. 2. Libraries—United States—Special
collections—Historical fiction. 3. Readers' advisory services—United States.
    4. Historical fiction—Bibliography. I. Title.
    Z711.5.B27 2015
    026'.8088381—dc23   2014018024

Cover image © André Klaassen / Shutterstock, Inc. Text composition by Dianne M. Rooney
in the Palatino and ITC Franklin Gothic typefaces.

Printed in the United States of America

19 18 17 16 15   5 4 3 2 1

♾ This paper meets the requirements of ANSI/NISO Z39.48-1992 (Permanence of Paper).

For my parents

CONTENTS

Series Introduction   ix
Acknowledgments   xi
Introduction   xiii

1 A WALL OF PORTRAITS, A HALL OF DOORS   1

2 TALKING WITH HISTORICAL FICTION READERS   15

3 HISTORICAL FICTION BY TIME PERIOD   27

4 HISTORICAL FICTION BY PLACE   55

5 BIOGRAPHICAL HISTORICAL FICTION   83

6 HISTORICAL FICTION BY SUBJECT   117

7 CULTURE, ETHNICITY, RELIGION, AND GENDER
   IN HISTORICAL FICTION   143

8 HISTORICAL FICTION AND OTHER GENRES   179

9 EXPANDING READERS' ADVISORY SERVICES:
   The Whole-Collection Approach   209

10 KEEPING CURRENT, STAYING RELEVANT   221

APPENDIXES

A. How to Read a Novel in Just Minutes
   by *Georgine Olson*   245

B. Literary Historical Fiction and Classics for Book Groups   *249*

C. Form-Based Readers' Advisory: A List of Libraries
by *Barry Trott*   257

Bibliography   *263*
Appeal/Subject Index   *295*
Author/Title Index   *317*

SERIES INTRODUCTION

Joyce Saricks and Neal Wyatt, Series Editors

In a library world in which finding answers to readers' advisory questions is often considered among our most daunting service challenges, library staff need guides that are supportive, accessible, and immediately useful. The titles in this series are designed to be just that. They help advisors become familiar with fiction genres and nonfiction subjects, especially those they don't personally read. They provide ready-made lists of "need to know" elements such as key authors and read-alikes, as well as tips on how to keep up with trends and important new authors and titles.

Written by librarians with years of RA experience who are also enthusiasts of the genre or subject, the titles in this series of practical guides emphasize an appreciation of the topic, focusing on the elements and features fans enjoy, so advisors unfamiliar with the topics can readily appreciate why they are so popular.

Because this series values the fundamental concepts of readers' advisory work and its potential to serve readers, viewers, and listeners in whatever future space libraries inhabit, the focus of each book is on appeal and how appeal crosses genre, subject, and format, especially to include audio and video as well as graphic novels. Thus, each guide emphasizes the importance of whole collection readers' advisory and explores ways to make suggestions that include novels, nonfiction, and multimedia, as well as how to incorporate whole collection elements into displays and booklists.

Each guide includes sections designed to help librarians in their RA duties, be that daily work or occasional interactions. Topics covered in each volume include:

> The appeal of the genre or subject and information on subgenres and types so that librarians might understand the breadth and scope of the topic and how it relates to other genres and subjects. A brief history is also included to give advisors context and highlight beloved classic titles.

> Descriptions of key authors and titles with explanations of why they're important: why advisors should be familiar with

them and why they should be kept in our collections. Lists of read alikes accompany these core author and title lists, allowing advisors to move from identifying a key author to helping patrons find new authors to enjoy.

Information on how to conduct the RA conversation so that advisors can learn the tools and skills needed to develop deeper connections between their collections and their communities of readers, listeners, and viewers.

A crash course in the genre or subject designed to get staff up to speed. Turn to this section to get a quick overview of the genre or subject as well as a list of key authors and read-alikes.

Resources and techniques for keeping up-to-date and understanding new developments in the genre or subject are also provided. This section will not only aid staff already familiar with the genre or subject, but will also help those not familiar learn how to become so.

Tips for marketing collections and lists of resources and awards round out the tools staff need to be successful working with their community.

As readers who just happen to be readers' advisors, we hope that the guides in this series lead to longer to-be-read, -watched, and -listened-to piles. Our goal is that the series helps those new to RA feel supported and less at sea, and introduces new ideas or new ways of looking at foundational concepts, to advisors who have been at this a while. Most of all, we hope that this series helps advisors feel excited and eager to help patrons find their next great title. So dig in, explore, learn, and enjoy the almost alchemical process of connecting title and reader.

ACKNOWLEDGMENTS

American Library Association (ALA) conferences seem to be the beginning of many great ideas and more than a few book proposals, and this book is no exception. When Neal Wyatt and Joyce Saricks took me aside at a conference hotel, for a "chat," I received their suggestion that I write a readers' advisory guide on historical fiction with surprise and delight. They said they had every confidence in me and hoped I'd agree to it. That confidence in my ability to write *and* finish this book hasn't wavered in the slightest during the three years it has taken me to do so. I can't thank them enough for their hand-holding support, great suggestions, and gentle corrections. Both Joyce and Neal have read and critiqued every draft of every word in this book, and I am so grateful.

Thanks also go to Nancy Pearl, for mentoring me and for kindling the readers' advisory fire in me and in my colleagues. The Reader Services team at the Seattle Public Library has depended heavily on Nancy and owes much to her acute intellect, consulting skills, professional support, and friendship. So many of my colleagues at the library and their excellent and tireless readers' advisory work have been an inspiration to me in so many ways that it's impossible to thank them enough. I thank librarian Paige Chernow, especially, for her help with chapter 4 and with Jewish historical fiction in chapter 7, and Linda Johns, author of the Hannah West children's fiction series, for her constructive suggestions and ongoing enthusiasm for my writing progress.

My thanks go to Georgine Olson and Barry Trott for their generosity in sharing their work (see appendixes A and C, respectively), and also to EBSCO's NoveList, which was used frequently in the writing of this book, for permission to use some of their appeal terminology. Thanks to Duncan Smith personally, who over the years has given me writing encouragement, career advice, and great readers' advisory support. Duncan Smith and Joyce Saricks are the only people whose enthusiasm for appeal characteristics matches my own!

And of course, I owe so much to my family for putting up with my whining about the book and for celebrating each small accomplishment along the way. My mother, Pat Albiston, is my biggest fan and staunchest supporter, who let me camp over at her house for quiet and solitude when I needed it and cheered me on when I most needed cheer. My sister, Catherine Albiston, attorney, author, and professor, gave me practical advice on organizing a project of this size while encouraging me to carry on, as did my daughter, Cailin Baker. Without their help this book would still be masses of sticky notes and lists of titles in random spiral notebooks. And of course my husband, John: thank you for being the best friend and patient support of my life.

Finally, my ALA publisher and editors, J. Michael Jeffers and Jamie Santoro, thank you for waiting so patiently for me to finish this book and for encouraging me along the way.

This book is my work, but without all of you I could never have accomplished it.

INTRODUCTION

This book is intended to help readers' advisors identify the main types of traditional historical fiction and its offspring; to develop a vocabulary for discussing and understanding historical fiction; to understand the particular appeal of historical fiction; to identify some of the benchmark authors and titles in historical fiction; to suggest resources and tools for readers' advisors; and to develop strategies for successful readers' advisory in historical fiction.

In libraries, bookstores, and educational curricula, historical fiction is usually described by time, place, individual name, or topic. These categories have therefore become historical fiction's subgenres. Organization of references about historical fiction, such as Sarah Johnson's excellent book *Historical Fiction II: A Guide to the Genre*, is therefore based on these frames and usually indexed to include biographical references to famous people mentioned or featured.[1] Little readers' advisory advice is available specific to historical fiction, except in the case of Joyce Saricks's *The Readers' Advisory Guide to Genre Fiction* (revised edition), in which the author discusses the elements of historical fiction readers love, the most important of which, according to Saricks, is accurate and interesting historical and geographic detail that give readers an experience of another time and place or a new perspective on a historical figure.[2] Saricks does an admirable job of pinpointing the essential benchmark authors in many genres, including historical fiction, describing their specific appeals, which in turn gives readers' advisors clues about how to talk to readers. This book encompasses both Johnson's and Saricks's approaches, both by presenting important titles and topics and by discussing readers' advisory in historical fiction.

Given the complexity of reader appeal and the many choices of historical time frames available to choose from, how do we identify historical fiction subgenres that make sense apart from other genres that often co-opt elements of historical fiction? Unlike other genres, such as mystery, romance, and science fiction, where distinct subgenres have predictable appeal to select audiences, historical fiction subgenres have less to do with appeal than with intellectual or topical categorization. Readers of paranormal romance, those who like science fiction space opera, and readers of cozy mystery can use specific language to identify their reading tastes. Paranormal romances are usually chilling, sometimes violent, and often erotic. Space opera is usually suspenseful and filled with the technical language of its postulated interstellar world. Cozy mysteries are witty, sometimes hilarious, and suspenseful but never directly violent. This common language helps readers' advisors immensely in conversation with genre readers. In historical fiction such subgenre-identifying, general-appeal language is missing. Categorized by date, place, and subject, historical fiction's appeal is measured title by title, author by author. This requires readers' advisors to work a little harder in conversation with historical fiction readers, to elicit title- or author-specific appeal information.

Long reference books like those of Saricks and Johnson may seem daunting, especially if a reader needs on-the-spot book suggestions. It's easy to lose momentum with readers if you cannot converse enthusiastically about the kind of books they love. Brad Hooper's *Read On . . . Historical Fiction: Reading Lists for Every Taste*, a fun, shorter historical fiction reference, is filled with wonderfully eclectic book lists with titles like "Turbulence and Change," "The Apple and the Apple Tree, or "When the Fabric of State Is Torn," and is organized by broad appeal (setting, character, story, language, mood or atmosphere).[3] It is written to be enjoyed by the reader, especially a reader who knows what formal appeal category he or she enjoys; it might be a good follow-up to a readers' advisory conversation rather than a readers' advisor's tool. Another wonderful, similar readers' reference, *Book Lust*, by Nancy Pearl, is a great book to savor and refer to at leisure—plucking out title gems is its chief delight—but it is not meant to be used as a reference tool. (Though if you read all the books Nancy suggests, you will probably *be* a great readers' advisor!)

Libraries and bookstores are arranged by broad subjects, by author, and by title. Unless we create a special display, we rarely shelve historical fiction separately for readers to browse. When it comes to labeling the books themselves, it's difficult to draw a genre line and say, "This is historical fiction, but this is not." Is Sir Walter Scott's work historical fiction or classics? What about a fantasy book set in Elizabethan England? Is it fantasy or historical fiction? An alternate history book—is it science fiction, fantasy, or historical fiction? We can catalog it as all three, but we have to shelve the item in only one place. It's easiest and most logical to interfile historical fiction with general fiction. In this book, you may notice a few titles and authors cropping up in several different chapters. This is a virtue of a similar issue: many of the best historical fiction books not only blur the line between genres but also manifest multiple appeals. Some histori-cal novels are strongly character-centric or setting focused, while others may have both a strong sense of place and well-developed characters, and be filled with magical realism.

The library catalog is also difficult to use in historical fiction read-ers' advisory. Searching by general keyword for something as simple as historical fiction about the Civil War yields far too many titles to browse through and is infrequently annotated in a manner conducive to quick scanning during reader conversations. Even book lists of Civil War fiction you may have available online or at your desk make great passive read-ers' advisory, but they are not reader specific. Perhaps the most important role of a good readers' advisor is to provide individual readers with good suggestions uniquely suited to their current mood and taste. The trick is to find useful resources that are as available and fast as a library catalog, Amazon, or Google.

Without an understanding of how readers talk about historical fiction and the broad categories of historical fiction available, readers' advisors can flounder. This book focuses on the aspects of historical fiction that draw readers in and how we can identify them quickly enough to make educated suggestions. What tricks can we use to scan unfamiliar materials and identify appeal? How can we remember huge mounds of historical fiction titles and link them for readers? What do we need to know to talk with readers who love certain types of historical fiction?

The chapters in this book establish an appeal vocabulary for historical fiction that works well with all types of fiction and gives a broad descrip-tion of the genre, broken down into subgenres and categories that give readers' advisors a vocabulary to talk with readers.[4] Each subgenre is illustrated with several popular, current title examples and their appeals, along with a few titles for further reading that are similar.

Chapters 1 and 2 of this book discuss appeal characteristics and how readers' advisors can successfully talk with and make good book sugges-tions for historical fiction readers. Chapters 3–7 are devoted to "pure" his-torical fiction: novels and stories in which the action takes place fifty years or more in the past and before the author's recollection. Historical fiction transports the reader into another time period for the purposes of enter-tainment and understanding of a previous time and place and people. Surprisingly, even this simple definition quickly calls into question many other types of fiction most readers assume are historical fiction, such as Holocaust or World War II fiction by authors whose personal experience informs their writing and classic novels like *The Adventures of Huckleberry*

Finn (Twain) and *Jane Eyre* (Brontë). Chapter 8 discusses historical fiction in relation to other genres, literary fiction, and classics.

Chapter 9 proposes efficiency strategies for busy readers' advisors and ideas for virtual readers' advisory and for integrating other parts of your collection, such as nonfiction and other media, into your reading suggestions for historical fiction readers. Finally, chapter 10 suggests resources and ideas for keeping current in historical fiction readers' advisory, including how to create a historical fiction reading plan.

This book can serve as both a self-guided tour of historical fiction, filled with suggestions for readers' advisory practice, and as a reference for use with readers trolling for great new historical fiction suggestions. In addition, I hope readers will find a tantalizing plethora of historical fiction to add to their personal reading lists.

NOTES

1. Sarah L. Johnson, *Historical Fiction II: A Guide to the Genre*, Genreflecting Advisory Series (Santa Barbara, CA: Libraries Unlimited, 2009).
2. Joyce G. Saricks, *The Readers' Advisory Guide to Genre Fiction*, rev. ed. (Chicago: American Library Association, 2009).
3. Brad Hooper, *Read On . . . Historical Fiction: Reading Lists for Every Taste* (Westport, CT: Libraries Unlimited, 2006).
4. While the appeal language used in this book is my own, some overlap of terminology may be found with EBSCO's NoveList databases as a result of popular usage.

1

A WALL OF PORTRAITS, A HALL OF DOORS

A BRIEF HISTORY OF HISTORICAL FICTION

Looking back on the history of historical fiction is like looking at old paintings in a vestibule or above a staircase: you see what and who went before, but you are also aware that things have changed. We appreciate the works of older historical fiction authors, even though they may seem outdated or anachronistic when compared with our current historical knowledge and storytelling preferences. It's worth taking a peek, though, into some of the older authors and titles, not only for familiarity with titles that older readers may mention but also for the sake of understanding how historical fiction has morphed into what we more often read today.

While most of what we consider historical fiction today was written in the twentieth century, storytelling has been an integral part of civilization from our very beginnings. Many of humanity's earliest stories told of heroic feats of the past, but for the purpose of this book, these works are not considered historical fiction, but they are very old! For our purposes, historical fiction is defined as novels (and sometimes short stories) with settings from a historical period at least fifty years prior to the work's publication or occurring before the author's memory. Surprisingly, this definition leaves out a number of titles most people consider historical fiction, such as *Oliver Twist* (Dickens), *The Count of Monte Cristo* (Dumas), *Uncle Tom's Cabin* (Stowe), and many other well-known books set during the authors' lives.

Sir Walter Scott (1771–1832) is generally recognized as the first author of historical fiction as we know it today. His best-known novel, *Ivanhoe*, is a story that encompasses the legend of Robin Hood and the history of the conflict between King Richard I of England and his brother John.

Scott also wrote *Rob Roy* and *Waverly*, which, with *Ivanhoe*, are only three of the nineteen novels in the Waverly oeuvre. *Rob Roy* and *Waverly* were written in 1814 and 1817, about seventy years after the Jacobite rising, the subject of both books, placing them among the first historical novels written in English. Later, other classic authors of the nineteenth century also ventured into the relatively unknown territory of serious historical fiction. Among the more famous are *A Tale of Two Cities* (Dickens), *The Scarlet Letter* (Hawthorne) and *War and Peace* (Tolstoy).

IMPORTANT TWENTIETH-CENTURY HISTORICAL FICTION AUTHORS

Taylor Caldwell (1900–1985)

By the middle of the twentieth century, earlier classic writers like Dickens, Dumas and Scott, were joined by popular fiction writers in creating great stories of historical fiction. Some of the authors of this period wrote novels that readers still enjoy, once a good readers' advisor suggests them. Taylor Caldwell, for instance, had a huge following for her absorbing and unputdownable family sagas about the powerful and wealthy dynasties that built the US economy. Although literary critics panned Caldwell's writing style, readers recognized her excellent storytelling skills and clamored for more. Try *Captains and the Kings* or *Dear and Glorious Physician*, two of Caldwell's best-known novels.

Dorothy Dunnett (1923–2001)

The six novels in the Lymond Chronicles series were published in Britain between 1961 and 1975 and quickly became Dunnett's most famous work. Set in Renaissance Europe and in Russia, each book in the series features Francis Crawford of Lymond, a Scottish nobleman with a nose for adventure and his own moral code, as he comes into contact with powerful figures of the time. Using this pattern as her frame, Dunnett exercises her skill at bringing the time period alive through her delightful protagonist and her twisted and intricate plot strands. Dunnett's work is not as well known in the United States as in the United Kingdom, and readers of historical adventure who love a great story will appreciate hearing about Lymond. Be sure to include Dunnett on your reading plan, too. Start with *Game of Kings*, the first of the series.

Howard Fast (1914–2003)

Older readers will remember Howard Fast's Immigrants series, beginning with *The Immigrants*, if no other of his nearly one hundred published works. They may be surprised to learn that Fast also wrote novels about the ancient world and the American Revolution. All of his novels read at a good clip and feature ordinary people whose circumstances force them to examine their lives in new ways, often with dramatic results. Fast's popular historical fiction is more than just stories—Fast was an idealistic, intelligent man whose life reflected some of the issues with which his characters contend. Immigrant novels are still popular, and readers may enjoy looking at fictional immigrant experiences of the past.

Jean Plaidy (1906–1993)

Beloved of historical fiction readers in the mid-twentieth century and author of 183 books, Jean Plaidy wrote imaginative stories of famous figures from past centuries, bringing them to life for modern readers. While many people were aware that "Jean Plaidy" was a pseudonym, few knew just how many pseudonyms Eleanor Hibbert actually had. As Victoria Holt she became well known for her gothic romance novels; as Philippa Carr, for romantic historical family sagas. She wrote under several other names, too, including her own! As Jean Plaidy, though, Hibbert is still recognized as a prolific author of popular and well-researched historical novels that focus more on women and relationships than on analysis of time periods. Many Plaidy titles have been reprinted in the past decade, so be sure to include them in your readers' advisory repertoire. Sample the Tudor series, beginning with *Uneasy Lies the Head*; the Borgia Duet (*Madonna of the Seven Hills* and *Light on Lucrezia*); or the Queens of England series, beginning with *Myself, My Enemy*. The Tudor and Queens of England series are highlighted in chapter 6 of this book as part of the section on learning history through historical fiction.

Mary Renault (1905–1983)

Known mainly for her sensitive fictional portrayals of famous ancient Greeks, Renault appeals to modern readers on many levels. Though she was not a historian, Renault did her research, and her novels are filled with the details of ancient life and of warfare. She was one of the first few historical fiction authors to write openly about homosexuality among the leaders of ancient Greece. Her characters come to life; their stories are moving and full of humor. Readers who enjoy this time period and haven't read Renault will thank you for starting them out with her Alexander the Great trilogy, beginning with *Fire from Heaven*.

Irving Stone (1903–1989)

Stone characterized his novels as "bio-history"—biographical novels of historical figures.[1] He wrote sixteen novels featuring politicians, scientists, authors, and artists, all of which are well researched, fascinating to read, and deliciously long. Stone was sometimes criticized for always being "upbeat" and for idealizing his characters rather than showing them as real, flawed individuals, but many readers enjoy this approach to famous people they admire and will appreciate Stone's perspective. *The Agony and the Ecstasy*, about Michelangelo, and *Lust for Life*, about Vincent van Gogh, are two of his very best novels.

By the 1980s, as historical fiction increased in popularity, it was often grouped together with literary novels set in historical time periods and with historical romance, adventure, mysteries, and westerns as one genre, to readers' confusion. It became apparent that readers needed clearer genre delineations in general, and that even within each genre there existed nebulous differences between books that went beyond favorite authors and lengthy descriptions of why we enjoyed reading and particular kinds of books. We lacked a common vocabulary to describe reading tastes. It wasn't until 1982, in *Readers' Advisory Service in the Public Library* (Saricks), that the concept of appeal characteristics was created.[2] As library and information science programs and readers' advisory training grew in influence, so did our use of appeal terminology, which is so important in our interactions with readers. Sometimes readers will mention an author they have enjoyed—a good readers' advisor uses appeal terms in these conversations to help readers talk about why they like certain authors or certain types of books. If a reader cannot think of an author's name, readers' advisors can ask leading questions about appeal and then suggest a well-known author and/or title that might coincide with the reader's taste. These well-known authors and/or titles are referred to as benchmarks. Benchmarks can be introduced into the conversation as references for readers, who have probably heard of or read the book, but if not, then you can tell readers about the book, gauge their interest, and suggest starting with the benchmark.

BENCHMARK AUTHORS OF CURRENT HISTORICAL FICTION

Today's benchmark authors have some of the same characteristics in common with the popular historical fiction writers of the twentieth century. Many cover the same time frames—the Middle Ages and the Renaissance, the ancient world—or have a similar style or structure, such as sweeping sagas, historical romance, and adventure. Others are biographical novels about famous people or fictional characters. One characteristic that differentiates current historical fiction from that of the twentieth century is a modern perspective on history. Some of the older titles feature subjects of limited current interest, like Caldwell's biographical novels of Bible figures or Jean Plaidy's novels that highlight famous female figures from history mainly in relation to their connection with powerful men. Sometimes the language used or views expressed by the characters are noticeably outdated. These factors do not necessarily mean readers should or will bypass older historical fiction, but it can seem to date us as readers' advisors if they are the first books we mention or pull off the shelf. We need to keep up with current trends and popular perspectives on history. Well-known newer titles can serve as modern benchmarks—books that represent the historical fiction genre as it is now, in the twenty-first century.

The authors listed here are great current examples of historical fiction writers that readers' advisors can reference in conversations with readers. If you haven't read these current benchmark authors, take the time to review their work and to include some of the titles listed here in your personal reading plan.

Bernard Cornwell

Like Jean Plaidy, Bernard Cornwell traces English history through its leaders. His series include the Warlord Chronicles, about King Arthur, the medieval Grail Quest trilogy, the Saxon Stories, the Starbuck Chronicles, and his well-known Richard Sharpe novels—all twenty-two of them. His stand-alone book, *Agincourt*, is a phenomenal study of human nature under the pressures of war and a great perspective on medieval battle. The Battle of Agincourt, however, was also a definitive one that dramatically changed the balance of power at the time. Cornwell shows readers what the battle was like through the eyes of a commoner—an archer—whose experience is moving and powerful. If you read only one Cornwell book, let this be the one.

Sarah Dunant

Sarah Dunant started as a writer of hard-boiled female detective mysteries, moved into thrillers, and then went to historical fiction, making a name with the now-famous *The Birth of Venus*. Since then she has published such historical novels as *In the Company of the Courtesan* and *Sacred Hearts*, set in sixteenth-century Italy. Her female characters are self-confident, independent, and often unusually placed in society (like a courtesan or an unwilling nun). *In the Company of the Courtesan* is a good choice for those who haven't yet read Dunant's historical fiction. The courtesan Fiametta lives in Rome with her dwarf servant, Bucino, who narrates the story. When the Germans and Spanish attack Rome in 1527, Fiametta and Bucino escape with nothing and start over in Venice with the help of the mysterious blind woman La Draga. The novel is exotic, strange, suspenseful, and full of period details—highly entertaining and among the best in historical fiction set during the Italian Renaissance.

Philippa Gregory

More than any other historical novelist, Philippa Gregory has made it big with stories about risqué young women insinuated or forced into royal households or positions of power. Gregory's strength is her easy familiarity with well-known figures from the past, weaving the personalities of fictional or little-known characters around the events and personalities of the time. Her stories focus on women's lives and relationships, which makes her novels very readable for a number of audiences, especially readers who prefer to focus on characters rather than settings or history. Although *The Other Boleyn Girl*, one of her Tudor novels, is perhaps her best-known title, Gregory has written many other novels. Try her Cousins' War series, beginning with *The White Queen*, for a delectable taste of Gregory's entertaining perspective on fifteenth-century royals behaving badly.

Edward Rutherfurd

Often compared with James Michener for his in-depth coverage of historical topics and the sheer length of the sagas he produces, Edward Rutherfurd excels at drawing out the big-picture stories that rivet readers to their seats. High-adventure and in-depth studies of famous and not-so-famous people, viewed with a wide lens that fits all the historical details together into a fascinating story, infuse every book he's published, from *Sarum* to *Paris*. Any Rutherfurd historical novel gives readers' advisors a taste of his sweeping epic style. Try *New York*, which traces the history of Manhattan from its early days as a Native American village to September 11, 2001, as portrayed by several families over the generations.

Jeff Shaara

Son of Michael Shaara, winner of the Pulitzer Prize for his 1975 Civil War novel *The Killer Angels*, Jeff Shaara began his writing career by writing a prequel and a sequel to his father's book: *Gods and Generals* and *The Last Full Measure*. He has also recently added to this Civil War oeuvre with *A Blaze of Glory* and *A Chain of Thunder*. Shaara's war novels trace American history from the Revolutionary War through World War II. The first in his World War II series is *The Rising Tide*, though these titles stand well on their own and can be read in any order. Shaara's ability to involve the reader in the minute-by-minute experiences and emotions of officers and soldiers in battle is unforgettable. Readers who enjoy historical fiction about war, especially about World War II, will appreciate a readers' advisor familiar with the modern benchmark authors, so if you haven't read Shaara, it's important to include him on your reading list.

Susan Vreeland

Most often compared with Tracy Chevalier for her focus on art and artists, Vreeland explores the relationship between art and life, especially with regard to women and their position in society throughout the centuries. Best known for *The Girl in Hyacinth Blue*, Vreeland has also written about artists as vastly different in style and time period as a baroque painter (*The Passion of Artemisia*); the impressionist Renoir (*Luncheon of the Boating Party*); and Emily Carr (*The Forest Lover*), whose style reflects the influence of Native American peoples of the Pacific Northwest. In *Luncheon of the Boating Party*, Vreeland's lyrical style and ability to bring historical characters to life are featured prominently alongside a moving love story. Read Vreeland to find out how a late-nineteenth-century French impressionist painting came into existence and to familiarize yourself with current authors' focus on art as the subject of historical fiction.

THE APPEAL OF HISTORICAL FICTION

Visualize a huge house with a long, narrow hallway, flanked on both sides by door after door—perhaps something like Harry Potter's Hogwarts—a manor house hallway that never looks the same each time you walk down it. Every door proclaims the same thing: HISTORICAL FICTION—PLEASE ENTER. How do we know which door to open? We intuit what we want but have no idea how to find it, or even what to call it. We rely on labels to break down elements of a genre into recognizable subgenres, style elements, and other appeal factors. The problem with historical fiction is that it isn't like other genre fiction, with its well-recognized subgenres. The romance genre can be easily delineated into subgenres such as Regency romance, paranormal romance, romantic suspense, and contemporary romance. Subgenres of the mystery genre include cozies, private detective stories, police procedurals, and noir. In each case, readers and readers' advisors recognize the characteristics of the subgenre they most enjoy. Many times historical fiction is seen as a subgenre itself of another genre (or genres), such as historical mysteries or historical romance.

Historical fiction doesn't yet have clearly defined subgenres, so it is necessary to make our own distinctions for the purpose of effective readers' advisory, in order to identify subgenres that readers will recognize as definitive of their own approach to historical fiction. More than any other fiction genre, historical fiction lends itself to breakdown by subject: ancient civilizations, medieval Europe, Wars of the Roses, American Revolution, World War I, and so on. Traditionally, historical fiction has also been broken down by time period or eras such as ancient, medieval, Renaissance, and Enlightenment. Since it's easiest to label reading interests this way for historical fiction readers, libraries have traditionally done so. When a reader says that she loves Philippa Gregory's books, we go looking for other novels about the Tudor period. If someone says they enjoy war stories, we ask which war and then seek out other novels about that war.

The fallacy of this system, however, is that it omits the all-important appeal factor: we need to know *why* the first reader loves Gregory's historical fiction and what it is about war stories that the second reader is seeking. It may not simply be a matter of enjoying the incredibly dysfunctional Tudor family. Perhaps the appeal of Philippa Gregory for this reader is her ability to incorporate accurate historical details into the characters' lives that lend immediacy to the historical setting. Some readers might enjoy Gregory's imaginative storytelling style or her characterizations of regular people in relation to royalty. A "war story" can be realistic, surreal, or contemplative; it can be about battles and strategy; and it can introduce us to characters fighting the war or characters at home. So in addition to knowing the benchmark authors of historical fiction, we also need to lead readers in conversation about other elements that influence their enjoyment of historical fiction—these are appeal characteristics.

Nancy Pearl describes these appeal characteristics in terms of doorways—the portals through which readers eagerly step into a story, a life, a situation, a time, or a place.[3] Joyce Saricks, in the revised edition of her *Readers' Advisory Guide to Genre Fiction*, goes beyond the basic appeal characteristics (e.g., story, character, style, setting, tone, pacing), amplifying them with qualifiers such as *historical accuracy, world building, foreboding, introspective, first-person narrative, gritty, family centered, unhurried, mesmerizing, dialect, elegant,* and *formal.*[4] Almost any word we use to describe a book or an author's voice indicates appeal. Each appeal word helps define one reader's "good book." Considering the variety of words we use to describe what we like, appeal is almost infinite: if each appeal is a doorway, then the hallway is very long indeed.

Reviewers often use appeal words to describe historical fiction, and becoming familiar with some of the adjectives repeated in reviews can help us match titles to appeal more quickly. The following is a list of often-used appeal terms used in historical fiction reviews during 2009 and 2010.[5] I have grouped them into eight general categories that make sense to me. The terminology for appeal characteristics is in flux, so we will consider these categories fluid!

> *Language*: beautifully distilled, richly textured, inventive metaphor, lyrical, flawless, elegant, solid, vibrant, readable, artfully related, beguiling, fresh and forthright, colorfully reflective, quietly effective
>
> *Style (which may be seen as more descriptive of the whole rather than the words)*: high drama, a romp, melodrama, glib, charming, amusing, graphic, satisfying high drama, gritty, hybrid quest saga, cinematic, picaresque, keenly perceptive
>
> *Setting or frame*: accurate, authentic, meticulous description, believable, historically grounded, history comes alive, immersive, contemporary resonance, exquisitely detailed, stellar setting, strikingly vivid, accurately rendered, Dickensian

Character: irresistible characters, dishy, emotional depth, rakish, rascally, full-bodied characters

Pace: brisk-paced, laconic, lively, frenetic, unhurried, swashbuckling, fast-paced

Mood and tone: foreboding, atmospheric, pitch perfect, poignant, riveting, rueful, rustic, serious-minded, wry, spellbinding, sympathetic, taut, transporting, tumultuous, warm, absorbing, evocative

Plot or story: labyrinthine, many faceted, masterful storyteller, multilayered, unexpected turns

Emotions: delightful, fresh, horrifying, bittersweet, bleak, shocking, nightmarish, comic, compelling, dark, enthralling, grim, gripping, rousing, powerful, pathos, harrowing, haunting, tearjerker

ORGANIZING THE GENRE

When viewing the overall scope of historical fiction, as noted already, it is far easier to organize titles by subject or by time period and to index them by geographic location, names of famous people involved, and title and author names. This is the approach taken by most subject-based library catalogs when it comes to historical fiction, and it is what makes them less than useful in readers' advisory: it ignores appeal. In her book *Historical Fiction II: A Guide to the Genre*, Sarah Johnson acknowledges this dichotomy and the need to include both subject and appeal in historical fiction readers' advisory first by discussing the "appeal of the past," and then by chronicling what she calls "traditional historical novels" by geographic location, breaking them down into recognizable historical time periods and events. Remaining chapters in this wonderfully informative reference are listed as either offshoots of other genres ("Romancing the Past," "Historical Mysteries," "Historical Thrillers") or as types of literature ("Multi-Period Epics," "Sagas," and "Literary Historical Novels").

Nancy Pearl's pioneering Book Lust series, beginning with *Book Lust*, is organized alphabetically along eclectic subject headings. Each short section is filled with book suggestions in a conversational tone, as if Nancy Pearl herself were sitting down with the reader to talk about books. This approach is not meant to be suitable for direct readers' advisory work, but it is certainly entertaining and informative. It's difficult for instance to remember that an entry about clothes is listed under *D* for its title—"Do Clothes Make the Man (or Woman)?"—or that tearjerkers are called "Three Hanky Reads."[6] The Book Lust series lends itself very well to perusal by readers who love many kinds of books and can spend time making lists of gems to read later.

During conversations with historical fiction fans, readers' advisors need to be aware not only of a title's frame (e.g., time period, geographic location) but also of its appeal characteristics. And further, the term *appeal* is changing to encompass all the adjectives readers use to describe what they enjoy in a book. Check with readers when they use an adjective to describe what they like about a book to make sure you understand their use of the word. Try to equate it with the words you like to use in describing stories to readers.

HONING YOUR SKILLS

Listening to readers talk about historical novels they enjoy will elicit those ever-important descriptors that can help readers' advisors point to other titles with some of the same characteristics. We can practice on ourselves by identifying our own reading preferences. Study the list above and think about how the appeal terms apply to books you've read. Which terms do you gravitate toward, and which do you find less appealing? Identifying the doors to open on the long hallway—those descriptive terms within the larger framework of "appeal" (e.g., story, frame, character, style, tone or mood, pacing) for the types of literature you enjoy is important for developing a personal reading plan you will look forward to completing. Understanding your own appeal preferences is key to better understanding other readers (see chapter 10 on developing a personal reading plan).

The following is a short list of well-known historical novels and appeal terms that have been used by various reviewers to describe them. If you are familiar with any of these titles, check to see if you agree with the reviewers' appeal terminology. Can you think of other ways to describe these books? What do you think is the main appeal of each—the ones you have read and the ones for which you have read the reviews? Can you think of other books you've read with similar appeals?

> *Things Fall Apart*, by Chinua Achebe: quiet dignity, sings with the terrible silence of dead civilizations, builds to a climax of tragic force

Girl with a Pearl Earring, by Tracy Chevalier: elegant, intriguing, splendid, absorbing, tenderhearted, sharp-eyed ramble

The Red Tent, by Anita Diamant: stirring evocation of time and place, touchingly intimate detail, Bible passages come alive, rich with memory, wonderful storytelling

The Pillars of the Earth, by Ken Follett: entertaining, mystifying puzzle, wealth of historical detail, entertaining, moves like a fast freight train

Cold Mountain, by Charles Frazier: rich in evocative historical detail; leisurely, literate narrative; quiet drama; anachronistic

Memoirs of a Geisha, by Arthur Golden: exotic world, sparkling, compelling, rendered with stunning clarity, flat and overlong

The Other Boleyn Girl, by Philippa Gregory: wonderfully vivid, historical romance, complicated narrative, page-turner, absorbing

The Poisonwood Bible, by Barbara Kingsolver: dramatic and forthright, measureless saga of hubris and deliverance, convincing and emotionally resonant, authoritative background detail, a triumph

Snow Flower and the Secret Fan, by Lisa See: intricate, graceful, lush and involving, poignant, haunting, powerful, painful, nuanced, keenly imagined, richly textured

If you were to compare your own list of appeals for specific titles such as these with another reader's list, you might be surprised by the other person's perceptions. In *Girl with a Pearl Earring* (Chevalier), for instance, if you say the pacing is a "sharp-eyed ramble," another reader might say the leisurely pace was less a ramble than a pointless wandering, or that *The Poisonwood Bible* (Kingsolver) is not a "triumph" but a horrific, sad story. All of these readers, yourself included, would be right. This is the essence of appeal characteristics: readers perceive the same book differently, read for different appeals, and judge a book by those appeals—all while perhaps ignoring others. We often hear people say "I loved that book" or "I hated it" of the same title. Tuning in to others' perceptions is an obvious but important aspect of readers' advisory work and a listening skill honed over time.

THE SUBGENRES OF HISTORICAL FICTION

Since there are an infinite number of appeal adjectives that might apply to historical fiction as a whole, the concept of appeal is best applied to individual titles. We are left with masses of historical fiction to organize if we want to be effective in making book suggestions to readers. Since the time period, geographical, topical, and biographical categories are already in use as organizing principles of historical fiction, these stand as the main subgenres in this book. In addition, many readers seek historical fiction based on culture, ethnicity, religion, and gender, so we can group these topics loosely together as another subgenre. This subgenre, which is covered in chapter 7, is slightly different from the topical, or subject, subgenre, since it's about groups of people more than subjects like medicine or war. Finally, there are multitudes of genre "blended" books that include historical fiction, such as romantic historical fiction, time travel, family sagas, and historical fiction set in the US West.

The subgenres as described in this book, therefore, are the following:

- time period historical fiction
- historical fiction set in specific geographic locations
- biographical historical fiction
- topical historical fiction
- historical fiction on culture, ethnicity, religion, or gender
- genre-blended historical fiction

NOTES

1. "Irving Stone," Random House Group, www.randomhouse.co.uk/authors/irving-stone.
2. Joyce G. Saricks, *Readers' Advisory Service in the Public Library* (Chicago: American Library Association, 1982), 4.
3. Nancy Pearl, "Check It Out with Nancy Pearl: Finding the Next Good Book," *Publishers Weekly* online, March 16, 2012, http://www.publishersweekly.com/pw/by-topic/columns-and-blogs/nancy-pearl/article/51109-check-it-out-with-nancy-pearl-finding-that-next-good-book.html.
4. Joyce G. Saricks, *The Readers' Advisory Guide to Genre Fiction*, 2nd ed. (Chicago: American Library Association, 2009), 292–98.
5. Appeal words were taken from a variety of reviews in sources including *Publishers Weekly*, *Library Journal*, *Booklist*, and *Kirkus Reviews*.
6. Nancy Pearl, *Book Lust: Recommended Reading for Every Mood, Moment, and Reason* (Seattle: Sasquatch Books), 75, 236.

2

TALKING WITH HISTORICAL FICTION READERS

Discussing historical fiction with readers can be a very different sort of interaction from conversing with other fiction readers: it's more like a reference interview in some ways. This is both because historical fiction is based on a set of facts and because historical accuracy is nearly always very important to the historical fiction reader. In a readers' advisory interview, listen first for references to historical accuracy. Another appeal area to listen for with historical fiction readers is tone, which can be established partly by the kinds of historical details on which the author focuses. If you hear a reader describe a book as atmospheric or lyrical, you will be sure to include title suggestions with a similar mood or style.

As in any readers' advisory interaction, the reader will tell you about a book he or she enjoyed by telling you the story. Remember, though, finding great historical fiction is only sometimes about matching the subject or time period of the story. In other words, even though catalogs and indexes and other references categorize historical fiction by subject, place and time period, it's a rare reader who insists on reading only Victorian period stories, narratives about cooking through the ages, or novels set in historical Turkey—unless that reader is researching a topic or doing a homework assignment. A topical reference approach to historical fiction is fun and easy, but it is rarely exactly what a reader wants, and it's important to keep that in mind during your conversations with readers. Sometimes the longer you talk with a historical fiction reader, the less definite she might be about desired material and her appeal preferences. If the reader goes on and on talking about details of what happened and never breathes a word about who the characters are (other than what they did), she may be telling you more about the story in a desire to make you understand the book she loved, or to her, the story might be more important than character development. Listen for appeal words to help with this, and check with the reader to make sure you are getting the right message.

This is a great time to start jotting down ideas, reflecting back particular terms you want to explore as the reader describes the plot. Let's say in describing *Agincourt* (Cornwell), she uses the phrase "the way the characters relate to each other under pressure." You might ask a leading question: "For instance?" This will elicit more information about the sort of relationships of greatest interest to the reader, perhaps surprising you with what you learn. You might find out that the reader is talking about the pressures of leadership under seemingly insurmountable odds, or perhaps the common soldier's response to a wounded man during the peak of battle. These varying perspectives on the same book require different approaches when suggesting read-alikes in readers' advisory work.

A reader who loves Cornwell, especially his novel *Agincourt*, probably zeroes in on characters—how they relate to one another and how they change during the course of the book. This reader most likely demands historical accuracy and likes detailed descriptions of the battles: planning, execution, weapons, and technique. Even when it seems obvious what the reader will like, it's necessary to let the reader talk about the book while you listen carefully to make sure you are on track with what appeals to her. She might surprise you.

Perhaps this same reader mentions military strategy. This is a subject term worth exploring in conjunction with appeal terms. Certainly a military strategist is less likely to seek examples of great battle strategies in fiction than in nonfiction; chances are, something about historical fiction augments the reader's understanding of war. It's worth saying, "Tell me about that," to get a larger picture. Nonfiction might be a possibility as a follow-up to *Agincourt*: all genres can be explored. Keep in mind that readers, especially in a library setting, will sometimes try to fit their reading tastes into librarian-speak, subject categories or genres that they think will help us get what they're talking about. For instance, "I want a novel about war," when they really mean "about how soldiers win wars under impossible odds." They may add that they enjoy characters challenged in this way and experiencing extreme conditions through those characters. Getting to the heart of a reader's desired experience is why readers' advisors focus heavily on appeal.

Let's give this imaginary reader some preferences we can work with:

- She liked Bernard Cornwell's *Agincourt*.

- She likes to read about how people behave under pressure.

- She is interested in politics and how public leaders plan for conflict.
- Accuracy and historical details of war are important.
- She likes characters to come alive.

What can you infer from these specific appeals? The famous Battle of Agincourt occurred in 1415 between the army of King Henry V of England and a much larger French army. Shakespeare's play *Henry V* might appeal to our reader because it is another view of Henry's character and his experiences at Agincourt; or perhaps the stirring 1989 film *Henry V*, starring Kenneth Branagh, a modern adaptation of the play that gives Henry a physical presence that augments his fictional character and features thrilling music that subtly affects the audience's mood and makes every action scene even more visceral. Bernard Cornwell is well known for his historical accuracy, an attribute this reader will appreciate, since she is also interested in politics and military strategy, subjects that require solid facts. Cornwell's Grail Quest series, beginning with *The Archer's Tale*, set during the Hundred Years' War (1347) might also appeal to this reader as another medieval war story. The main character of this series, Thomas Hookton, is an archer, a story element that could be of interest since one of *Agincourt's* main characters is an archer. The details of archery, the fast-paced suspense, and the high ideals that drive the characters are all reminiscent of *Agincourt*. Jeff Shaara's World War II series, beginning with *The Rising Tide*, is also a tense portrayal of military strategy and battlefield experience on an individual level; though check with the reader to make sure the time period difference will not matter to her. Taut with suspense, the story also shows the planning and execution of complex strategies as both sides' leaders prepare for and fight decisive battles of World War II. The characters' thoughts and fears are shared with the reader, lending a sense of participation as the events unfold, a "you are there" feeling.

These are just a few suggestions to show how you can connect the subjects and appeals of a particular book with other titles, even stories set in different time periods. As you listen to readers describe a book or story they loved, you can jot down authors and titles to suggest as they occur to you. As you suggest these titles, you will glean more appeal characteristics to move your search in other directions. Perhaps you learn that a reader is more interested in medieval warfare and isn't attracted to Jeff Shaara's World War II series. At this point you might suggest Sharon Kay Penman's Henry II series, beginning with *When Christ and His Saints Slept*, set during the twelfth-century struggles for the English throne. Penman's historical accuracy and attention to details, especially of politics and war-fare, may be of more interest to this reader.

It's a good idea to have several choices in mind as you head for the stacks, because a book listed in the catalog as on the shelf may not actu-ally be on the shelf. Or maybe once the reader sees the book, he decides against it. You can always send a list home with readers after you actually find something for them to read. The point is to take advantage of the way our minds make connections and to draw information from the reader in a fun way. Your enthusiasm and commitment to providing just the right book will serve you well in readers' advisory work and will enhance the reader's enjoyment of literature.

READING MAPS

In *The Mind Map Book*, Tony Buzan calls mind mapping "radiant think-ing."[1] Mind mapping is a way to visually connect ideas, often depicted as interconnected branches that work outward from a single topic or goal. Mind mapping is an old business concept that works very well for readers' advisors. The idea of using this technique was explored by Neal Wyatt in both her series on readers' advisory for *Library Journal* and her book *The Readers' Advisory Guide to Nonfiction*. In her *Library Journal* article, "Re-Defining RA: Reading Maps Remake RA," Wyatt says:

> Reading maps are web-based visual journeys through books that chart the myriad associations and themes of a title via other books, pictures, music, links to web sites, and additional material. Reading maps open up the world of the book for the reader by diagramming the internal life of the book, allowing readers to inhabit the text and its outward connections, and enabling readers to follow threads of interest that stem from any particular part of the work.[2]

She then goes on to describe how to compose a web-based reading map. Naturally, the website reading maps are more dynamic and can include linked audio and video files, links to reviews, and maybe samples from the book, but the concept can also be applied during readers' advisory con-versations. If you train your mind to make conscious connections between books as you read, you will be making mental reading maps. Writing these maps down or entering them into a website is simply another step in the process of making great book suggestions. Doing an on-the-spot reading map during a conversation with a reader is a great way to get your brain going in a situation with a high failure potential.

I don't know about yours, but my brain is fairly random in the way it makes connections, so I find the branching structures and interconnectivity of reading maps very freeing: I can think of connections between books, subjects, and ideas in any order! Mind mapping is a type of educated book association that readers can contribute ideas to without confusing me! The trick is to identify appeal elements of the book you are trying to match and then find suggestions with similar appeals. For every book you enter on the map you should be able to verbally defend your choice, because readers will need the feedback to know whether they will enjoy a book. A reader who enjoyed *The Adventures of Huckleberry Finn* (Twain) for the humor and adventure may not enjoy the haunting atmosphere of *The Runaway* (Kay), even though the story is similar, but he might love the boyhood adventures and jaw-dropping comedy in *Meely LaBauve* (Wells). It's easy to make a list of read-alikes or a reading map showing connections between books when we have no reader standing in front of us contributing ideas as we go along. Except as a teaching exercise, my reading maps are rarely as formal and tidy as the one shown in figure 2.1.

When talking with a reader, it's easiest to draw a reading map on a blank sheet of paper and simply add titles as you think of them. The reading map in figure 2.2 represents my thought process as the reader and I made

Meely LaBauve Ken Wells	*Life on the Mississippi* Mark Twain	*Some Love, Some Pain, Sometime* J. California Cooper
Finn Jon Clinch	*Tom Sawyer* Mark Twain	*My Jim* Nancy Rawles
The Runaway Terry Kay	**The Adventures of Huckleberry Finn** **Mark Twain**	*Once upon a River* Bonnie Jo Campbell
The Last Girls Lee Smith	*Their Eyes Were Watching God* Zora Neale Hurston	*Out of the Night That Covers Me* Pat Cunningham Devoto

FIGURE 2.1

**A simple reading map using *The Adventures*
of Huckleberry Finn as a starting point.**

FIGURE 2.2
A hand-drawn reading map
***A Thread of Grace* as a starting point.**

connections from one book to another, though I admit my original map was much messier! It may help to show how I came up with these titles.

Starting with *A Thread of Grace* (Russell) in the center and working upward in figure 2.2: *Sophie's Choice* (Styron) is another heart-wrenching example of a split-second decision made by a parent about her children; in the same way the parents in Russell's book had to decide who could make it over the mountains to Italy and who would be left behind. This thread continues upward to *In the Memory of the Forest* (Powers), which is a harsh telling of what happened to the Jews in Poland during and after World War II. *The True Story of Hansel and Gretel* (Murphy) is a powerful view of children trying to escape the horror of wartime persecution. From *Sophie's Choice* to the left is an American example of cultural hatred during the war and its effect on children—*When the Emperor Was Divine* (Otsuka)—as is *Hotel on the Corner of Bitter and Sweet* (Ford). While thinking about the war at home in the United States, *The Postmistress* (Blake) occurred to me as a good example of how the everyday lives of women were affected by the war. Also *The Amazing Adventures of Kavalier and Clay* (Chabon) shows the lengths to which Jewish refugees from Europe went to make their way to a new life.

On the theme of the underground resistance, a driven American soldier attempts to help a band of resistance fighters during the Spanish Civil War in *For Whom the Bell Tolls* (Hemingway), much like the Italian citizens undermined the Nazis in Russell's novel. While thinking about those driven soldiers who disappeared to the war and never came home, like the young man in Hemingway's novel, *A Very Long Engagement* (Japrisot) came to mind.

One of the issues Russell explores in *A Thread of Grace* is the Catholic Church's lack of response to the Nazis and their persecution of the Jews. *Hitler's Pope: The Secret History of Pius XII* (Cornwell) explores historical anti-Semitism throughout history leading up to World War II and the part played by the church. This title led me to think about religious life in Germany and whether or not Christian ministers fought anti-Semitism. In *Life Together*, Dietrich Bonhoeffer proves that they did, although many, like him, were martyred for their activities. Novels such as *Stones from the River* (Hegi) vividly show readers what life was like in German villages during the war and the everyday heroism demanded of average citizens. Heroism is also often demanded of Russell's characters. Similarly, in *Invisible Bridge* (Orringer), Andras Lévi and Claire Morgenstern fight to preserve their meager existence in the face of persecution in Hungary. Everyday lives continue—people fall in love, marry, have children—and people are jolted by danger only occasionally, but it is on those occasions when a personal decision has the potential to bring safety or disaster. Orringer and Russell share the ability to bowl readers over with compassion, sorrow, and sympathy—an appeal that may trump all others.

For those left behind in France during the Nazi occupation, a poignant view of collusion and subtle resistance such as that practiced by Renzo Leoni's mother in Russell's book, is shared in *Suite Française* (Nemirovsky), the first of five novels planned by the author, who died in Auschwitz before completing the series. *Five Quarters of the Orange* (Harris) gives readers another view of life in France during the German occupation—the relationship between the soldiers and local children, whose mother keeps track of her experiences in the margins of her cookbook. Both the children's curiosity about Germans and the mother's poignant understanding of reality are incredibly moving and will appeal to readers for whom the mothers in Russell's novel represent a strong "thread of grace."

The long-term effects of World War II are explored in *The Madonnas of Leningrad* (Dean), in which an elderly woman in the early stages of Alzheimer's disappears into her memories of hiding in an art museum during the Siege of Leningrad. *Those Who Save Us* (Blum) follows the life of a German American history professor as she traces her family's involvement with the Nazis during the war. Doriel Waldman is a Polish Jew who was the only one of his family to survive the war and now, at sixty years old, grapples with incipient madness as a result in *A Mad Desire to Dance* (Wiesel).

Nearly as complex as *A Thread of Grace* in its portrayal of the mixed responses of citizens and soldiers in occupied territories is *Corelli's Mandolin* (Louis de Bernières), which gives readers a view of what happened on the Greek island of Cephalonia to individuals caught in the chaos of the Italian occupation during World War II. Likewise caught in chaos, four African American soldiers of the Buffalo Division wind up behind enemy lines in a remote mountain village in Italy and are befriended by the locals in *Miracle at St. Anna* (McBride). Villagers befriend fleeing Jews in the same way, hiding them and saving them from the enemy in Russell's novel, at the cost of their own safety.

A handwritten reading map like the one shown in figure 2.2 bears little resemblance to Wyatt's polished web-based reading maps, but the method is similar: find read-alikes and "read-arounds." Wyatt says, "A read-around starts with a specific initial title and then expands outward to include fiction and nonfiction, read-alikes, and supporting materials such as works that focus on important aspects of the initial title, books that further illuminate central themes, and titles that provide contextual support."[3] One advantage of making a handwritten reading map is that collaboration provides instant readers' advisory, allowing for input from readers and colleagues. You can sketch it out on the spot and be done, and it's a fun way to keep the conversation going. A more formal online reading map, however, can be used repeatedly as a readers' advisory tool—one that readers' advisors and readers may also discover on their own. Recording a reading map online for a popular book or author will also save you the time of re-creating it for the next person who asks for suggestions.

In *The Readers' Advisory Guide to Nonfiction*, Wyatt describes how to make a more formal reading map.[4] You can also find additional reading maps on the *RA for All* blog (http://raforall.blogspot.com/p/reading -maps.html). Also, on the website for the Kanawha, West Virginia Library, explore further reading around topics, people, and authors (www .kanawhalibrary.org/advisory/reading_maps.html). The Pikes Peak Library District website hosts examples of several reading maps that include film trailers, talking mice, author websites, articles of interest online, and visuals from books (http://ppld.org/reading-maps/all). Creating this type of reading map is a fabulous exercise in training one's mind to think of all types of materials in connection with one another, from fiction to nonfiction, book to downloadable book, to movies and even related websites.

Some readers' advisory websites suggest books on the basis of remote user input to make similar title and author suggestions. Sometimes these sites are essentially reading maps, such as Literature Map (www.literature -map.com), a website that makes connections between authors when given another author name. Names closest on the screen to the one entered will be the authors most like the name entered. On this website, I entered "Mary Doria Russell" to see if the website would list some of the same authors I thought of in connection with her work. Very few were the same. When readers' advisory is applied to an author, rather than a title, the suggestions become more generalized depending on how many and what kind of books the author has published. For instance, Russell's read-alike authors would include writers of science fiction and fantasy, to be similar to *The Sparrow* and *Children of God*, which are both about Jesuits visiting another planet and interacting with aliens. Other read-alike authors would be writing about the 1921 Cairo Peace Conference or mapping out the boundaries of Middle Eastern countries, since that is the story's essence in *Dreamers of the Day*. Only a portion would refer back to *A Thread of Grace*. Some suggested titles will be more about Russell's literary style and facility for characterization, and those are the ones most interesting on the automated reading map. For a reader who loved the characters in *A Thread of Grace*, authors like Donna Cross, Ismail Kadare, and Ursula Hegi would be the most useful suggestions. It's likely that a reader would enjoy any one of these rough categories, but exploring all of them probably represents a lot of fruitless searching. Still the Literature Map website is fun to use, and it's interesting to find out how helpful the automated service can be by starting with an author you know well.

Another fun website to experiment with is UK-based WhichBook (www.whichbook.net), a site devoted to suggesting fiction and poetry that readers might not otherwise find. WhichBook enables UK residents to find local libraries owning the suggested titles simply by clicking on the covers. Readers outside the United Kingdom are directed to WorldCat. Rather than comparing authors like Literature Map does, WhichBook's suggestions are based on appeal characteristics chosen by the reader from a list provided. These appeals are quite different from those we have been working with in the ALA Readers' Advisory series, but they are still worth considering. Readers are asked to identify three qualities among twelve they want all title suggestions to have, such as happy or sad, funny or serious, safe or disturbing, optimistic or bleak. Or one can simply ask for main appeals: plot, character, or setting. This is the same kind of process we librarians use to decide which appeals are most important to our readers and which books might be good matches. It's fun and interesting to share these websites with readers when time allows.

What if you draw a blank when a reader asks you for a reading suggestion? This happens all the time to experienced and inexperienced readers' advisors alike. We work with readers to elicit information about the kind of material they most enjoy, consult reference tools, and ask colleagues for help. But sometimes we just don't know, or we can't figure it out on the spot. I try very hard to find something on the shelf for readers to take home and then offer to send them a personalized reading list. This buys me more time, perhaps a day or two, to come up with more suggestions. To create a reading list for a specific reader, I make a list of about five suitable titles; write short annotations, including reasons I think he or she will like each one; and then send the reader that document. Personalized reading lists are time consuming but can be a good option to fall back on when you're flummoxed. A good strategy to prevent going blank is training yourself to be a more versatile readers' advisor. Read several benchmark books in your least familiar genres and know which reference tools can help you in each. Historical fiction is a great place to start!

HONING YOUR SKILLS

1. Here are three popular historical fiction titles, along with a few key appeal characteristics. Using whatever tools you have at hand, suggest two titles that are similar to each author and/or title (hint: print resource called *What Do I Read Next*, or the NoveList database):

    > *The Red Queen*, by Philippa Gregory (character driven, romantic, leisurely pace, detailed descriptions)
    >
    > *The Invisible Bridge*, by Julie Orringer (literary, character driven, emotionally compelling)
    >
    > *New York*, by Edward Rutherfurd (family saga, plot driven, strong sense of setting)

2. Start with a book you know well and think of the different appeals it has for you. Then match other titles with the subject, theme, style, character types, insights, mood, setting, and story of your initial book. There are no rules: you can include nonfiction, fiction, historical genres like historical mystery or alternate history, movies, audiobooks, short stories, graphic novels, or essays. You might end up being your own best readers' advisor!

3. Try making a reading map with a friend or colleague. When you are finished, compare your map with one made by the Literature Map website using the same author as a starting point.

NOTES

1. Tony Buzan, with Barry Buzan, *The Mind Map Book* (New York: Plume, 1996).
2. Neal Wyatt, "Re-Defining RA: Reading Maps Remake RA," *Library Journal*, November 1, 2006, 38; Neal Wyatt, *The Readers' Advisory Guide to Nonfiction* (Chicago: ALA Editions, 2007), 232, 241–54.
3. Wyatt, *Readers' Advisory Guide to Nonfiction*, 233.
4. Ibid., 242–44.

3

HISTORICAL FICTION BY TIME PERIOD

Time period is the element historical fiction readers usually mention first: no historical fiction occurs in a vacuum after all! The first historical fiction subgenre we will look at is time period, and because time is linear, this chapter is organized linearly. For the purposes of this book, which is not meant to be a history text, the time frames are expanded to simplify categorization. For readers' advisors, knowing seven broad categories of history will suffice: prehistory, ancient civilization, the Middle Ages (sixth through fourteenth centuries), the Renaissance (fifteenth through sixteenth centuries), the Age of Enlightenment (seventeenth and eighteenth centuries), and the nineteenth and twentieth centuries. Usually, a library catalog or a tool like NoveList can help you locate the finer subdivisions of historical fiction, such as books set during the High Renaissance, the Second Crusade, or the Spanish Civil War. When in conversation with readers, we really can't expect ourselves to necessarily know, for instance, when the Battle of Hastings occurred or when the Ottoman Empire was at its zenith, so the broader categories will get us in the ballpark. This chapter introduces significant titles for these seven broad time periods, with the goal of giving readers' advisors a strong knowledge base of the best historical fiction, both familiar and new to readers looking for a great read.

When searching for great historical fiction, reference resources like the NoveList Plus database and library catalogs make it easy to search a time period such as Renaissance or a geographic location. The problem is that readers' tastes are more discerning and complex than time period or setting alone. We need to think of appeal more broadly and include subgenre as merely part of the package. In the historical fiction genre, this means we need to look at other elements that readers express in our conversation with them, in addition to what we usually think of as appeals: story, characters, style, mood, and setting. As chapter 1 shows, we cannot separate the concept of a good book, or the perfect doorway, from the desire for subgenres of historical fiction, so it's important to know the basic appeals of different historical fiction authors and titles.[1]

For example, to a reader who loves historical fiction set in the ancient world who is enthusiastic about war stories and the realities of combat, you might suggest David Gemmell's *Lord of the Silver Bow*, about the Trojan War; *Pride of Carthage*, by David Anthony Durham, about Hannibal's march on Rome; or Bernard Cornwell's *Sword Song*, the fourth of his Saxon Stories series, in which battle scenes take place with rapid pace in early medieval London. A person who enjoys reading about the ancient world but is looking for battles of philosophy, politics, or social manipulation might prefer Robert Harris's *Imperium* and *Conspirata*, and the still-great older title *I, Claudius*, by Robert Graves. Getting these individual appeal preferences right, in addition to the focus on time period, will ensure another visit from readers who will want to ask you for suggestions again. For this reason I list appeal characteristics for each title to help you identify the novels that best fit the tastes of different readers. Also included are read-alike titles to help you make connections between books—and to give you more specific title ideas for your readers. Consider adding a few of these significant authors to your personal reading plan (see chapter 10 for suggestions on creating a personal reading plan).

PREHISTORY

> Prehistoricals are more like fantasy fiction than like historical novels. Lack of detail about how ancient societies actually functioned and about provocative relics whose uses can only be surmised allows writers . . . to create intriguing cultures without being bound by facts.[2]

The relative lack of authoritative historical information on prehistoric people usually means the historicity of fiction about this era is based only loosely on facts and more on surmise and conjecture. While some archaeological artifacts inform historical fiction authors on prehistoric cultures of the Near East, North Africa, and Asia, and anthropologists have well-founded theories on the migration of early tribes, these are the sketchy armature upon which these stories hang. Still, prehistory holds a fascination for a great number of readers, and it behooves us as readers' advisors to be familiar with writing set in this period.

Even in novels of early people, readers can tell when an author has taken the time to research available facts and the places in which the stories are set. Since creating a "you are there" feeling—allowing the reader to imagine life in historical times in relation to modern life—is one of the most important qualifications for good historical fiction, writing realistically about early people while inventing personalities and compelling stories can be tricky, but there are some notable writers of historical fiction who have taken up the challenge. Jean Auel's approach to writing about this period in her Earth's Children series is to focus on human relationships rather than on in-depth setting details, eliminating potential historical inaccuracy. Auel set the standard for fiction taking place in "prehistory," and she has been followed since the 1980s by other authors in their fictional portrayal of early humans.

The Clan of the Cave Bear, by Jean Auel

Jean Auel is the most famous author of historical fiction about early people. Beginning with *The Clan of the Cave Bear*, the first of the Earth's Children series, published in 1980, she portrays the adoption of the orphaned Ayla, a Cro-Magnon child, by a tribe of Neanderthals. Eventually she is forced to leave her new tribe, taking her half-breed child with her. The series follows Ayla's life as the world changes and the tribes fight over supremacy. Auel's fully developed characters are compelling, and her well-described, convincing details help readers relate to one author's view of relatively unknown people and to imagine what it might have been like to live during the Ice Age. Readers who enjoy Auel's perspective are drawn to the leisurely pace in which the world building and immersive story are built. Ayla is the well-developed character whose changing experiences drive the action in all six books of this series.

Appeal: character driven, leisurely pace, richly detailed, steamy

FOR FURTHER READING

Readers who enjoy the steamy romance, leisurely pace, adventure, and character development in the Earth's Children series may also like the Earthsong Trilogy by Mary Mackey, beginning with *The Year the Horses*

Came. Morgan Llywelyn's *The Horse Goddess*, about the early Celts of 700 BC, may also appeal, with a similarly detailed setting and romance.

People of the Wolf, by Kathleen and Michael Gear

In *People of the Wolf*, the Gears cover similar ground as Auel: the fully developed protagonists of different tribes are shown in relationship to one another. In addition, the North American settings in each volume are well described, to help readers fully imagine the pristine world in which the characters lived. The First North Americans series is about "first people" so the focus is on the roles played by the people in the clan: the Warriors and the Dreamers, all descendants of two very different brothers. The overarching story traces the paths of these early tribes from the first people who came across the Bering Strait from Siberia to Alaska and Canada, bringing various perspectives on tribal life through different locations and consecutive time periods as the series goes on from book to book. These stories have a specific cultural emphasis for the purpose of illustrating native life and survival skills prior to the incursion of the Europeans. Written over a period of nearly twenty years, from 1990 to 2009, there are eighteen titles in this series, listed in the bibliography.

Appeal: richly detailed, well-developed characters, romantic, immersive

FOR FURTHER READING

Readers who enjoy the First North Americans series but haven't yet read Jean Auel will enjoy her characters and well-presented setting details. They may also like William Sarabande's First Americans series, beginning with *Beyond the Sea of Ice*, for its rich imaginative setting and ties to tribes of the first people in North America. Although his historical fiction is set in the early period of colonization in the United States, the historical novels of James Alexander Thom may also appeal to those interested in Native American culture and history. Thom's novels introduce readers to Native American people individually, from the perspectives of individual settlers. The stories have just the right touch of romance and adventure and need not be read in any particular order. Try *Follow the River* to get the flavor of Thom's storytelling style.

Stonehenge, 2000 BC, by Bernard Cornwell

In another immersive novel of prehistory, *Stonehenge*, Bernard Cornwell produces a very credible explanation for the monumental and mysterious stone circle on the Salisbury Plain. In 2000 BC sibling rivalry and political jockeying for position threaten to destroy the people of Ratharryn as the chief's sons squabble over who will be successor. Amid the everyday trials of familial dissent, human sacrifice, and attacks by neighboring tribes, a powerful sorcerer arises unexpectedly, and a monument to the sun god, Slaol, is erected.

Appeal: complex plot, richly detailed, fast paced, dramatic, suspenseful, gritty

FOR FURTHER READING

James Michener is another author whose stories usually begin with prehistory and explain the roots of a nearly lost culture: *Hawaii* is an entertaining and immersive example of this. Those readers who enjoy thinking about Stonehenge—how and why it was built—might also enjoy Cecelia Holland's view of Stonehenge in *Pillar of the Sky*, for its mystical, descriptive, and dramatic elements. Marion Zimmer Bradley's Avalon series, beginning with *The Mists of Avalon*, enhances the puzzle of Druidic rites by bringing an ethereal atmosphere to the story of King Arthur and those around him. Even though Cornwell's fast-paced, gritty delivery is very different from Bradley's intensely emotional style, the ultimate reward is a complex plot woven into an elemental belief system and the portrayal of human frailty, which some readers will find comparable to Cornwell's *Stonehenge*.

THE ANCIENT WORLD:
TENTH CENTURY BC TO AD FIFTH CENTURY

Historical fiction set in the ancient world is more factually sound than fiction about the prehistoric world, since we have a better archaeological record and written accounts of the time period, politics, and way of life. A civilization can be simply defined as a complex human culture that is advanced in terms of division of labor and use of technology, and that has a written language, science, and government. Most of the easily accessible information about ancient civilizations comes from the early Greek and Roman empires, around 900 BC to about AD 400.

While early cities existed in Egypt, Greece, and in other parts of the ancient world, many historical fiction authors focus on Rome, which was the seat of Western civilization for hundreds of years. Many historical novels set in this period focus solely on Roman life, government leaders, and military achievements, such as Colleen McCullough's Masters of Rome series. Readers who are fascinated by the early Romans will enjoy drawing parallels between Roman philosophy and government and modern governments, especially in the United States, which also places a high value on the rights of citizenship. Other authors focus more on social relationships, wars, and politics.

Generally speaking, readers desiring historical novels about the ancient world are fairly well educated on the period and will be impatient with poor scholarship, inaccurate historical details, or anachronisms in the narrative. They know the type of novel they are seeking and will ask specifically for it: novels about specific leaders or families; novels of daily life, art, and the common citizenry; stories tracing the birth of modern philosophy and education; those of politics and the shift of power; and sometimes those of military strategy. Note that Jewish and Christian historical fiction set in the ancient world are highlighted separately in chapter 7 of this book.

Gates of Fire: An Epic Novel of the Battle of Thermopylae
by Steven Pressfield

Gates of Fire is a well-documented historical novel about the Battle of Thermopylae, which took place in the late summer of 480 BC. Against seemingly impossible odds, the Greeks, under the leadership of the Spartan King Leonidas I, held off the Persian army, under the Great King Xerxes, at a narrow mountain pass for three days. Told in the oral tradition style, this epic has a varied cadence (according to the action taking place) and descriptive language all its own. Battle scenes are gruesome, realistic, and heroic in scope. Readers interested in ancient wars and battle tactics will read with a white-knuckled grip on their chairs, riveted by characters who come alive on the page and who just might mistake them for the enemy! Not many readers ask for books about a particular battle, but they may refer to Pressfield's war stories, asking for similar glue-you-to-the-seat ancient military battle tales.

Appeal: gritty, suspenseful, thought provoking, well researched, moody, elegiac

FOR FURTHER READING

The gritty graphic novel *300* (Miller) is also an excellent view of the Battle of Thermopylae, depicting the gruesome realities of battle and the tensions it provokes. Another heroic figure of the ancient world foments a seemingly impossible battle plan in *Pride of Carthage: A Novel of Hannibal's War*, by David Anthony Durham. Like Pressfield, Durham is adept in using his epic, lyrical storytelling style to simultaneously describe the physical hardships of Hannibal's trek over the Pyrenees and to portray the characters as the heroes they would become during the Second Punic War. Likewise heroic in scope and style is *The Ten Thousand*, by Michael Curtis Ford. This is a richly detailed, grueling story of the defeated Greek mercenary leader Xenophon, who drags his starving, depleted troops out of Persia and across a thousand miles of enemy territory in the dead of winter.

The First Man in Rome, by Colleen McCullough

You will no doubt recognize Colleen McCullough as the author who made it big with her slightly risqué (at the time), sweeping romance *The Thorn Birds.* McCullough has been writing historical fiction for years, and readers who love stories about ancient Rome may mention her Masters of Rome series in describing the kind of "you are there" experience they seek out in historical fiction. In Masters of Rome, beginning with *The First Man in Rome*, McCullough quickly entrenches the reader in battles of two kinds: the fight for a new kind of leadership in a political war zone and physical violence on the battlefields of war. Two brilliant generals vie for political power in a story full of the minutiae of daily life, fashion, and the customs of a highly ritualized society up against big changes. The story takes on the immediacy that most historical fiction lovers crave, and here McCullough does what she does best: portray realistic characters behaving badly for reasons entirely understandable to the modern reader. In any setting, McCullough writes with passion and compassion, and she is most enjoyed by readers who want to settle in with a nice long story that leisurely wends its way through a fascinating historical period.

Appeal: leisurely, well developed characters, storytelling style, thought provoking, immediacy

FOR FURTHER READING

Readers who enjoy McCullough's descriptions of ancient Roman life and the focus on well-developed characters should be sure to try Robert Graves's *I, Claudius* and *Claudius the God and His Wife Messalina*, set in fifth-century Rome. The likable, stuttering Claudius tells his own story in a revealing and witty style that wends its leisurely way around the political intrigue of the royal courts. Manda Scott's Boudica Trilogy, beginning with *Dreaming the Eagle*, is set in the first century, and she shares McCullough's talent for separating historical figures from the legends, placing them in a realistic setting and making them come alive for the reader.

Pompeii, by Robert Harris

Robert Harris, author of several fine suspense thrillers, has more recently focused his attention on the ancient world, to the delight of historical fiction readers. *Pompeii* is the first of his widely acclaimed historical novels, perhaps his best. Harris's talent for suspense plays out marvelously in this story about the most famous volcanic eruption in history: Mt. Vesuvius, in AD 79. Before the actual catastrophe, Marcus Attilius Primus, a Roman civil engineer, travels to the volcano near Pompeii to locate the origin of a faulty aqueduct. Upon arrival, he also discovers the troubling indications of an unsettled earth: sulfur, earthquakes, and ash. Dramatizing one of the most famous eruptions in history, Harris makes meticulous use of the historical record of a corrupt and violent society, weaving together a story of adventure, discovery, and destruction. Harris sustains the suspense of an impending eruption while balancing the rational, objective stance taken by Primus, the *aquarius* (aqueduct engineer), with heart-pounding action.

Appeal: suspenseful, richly detailed, compelling, fast paced

FOR FURTHER READING

Mary Renault also involves readers emotionally with her characters in her richly detailed, suspenseful *The King Must Die*. Theseus takes advantage of an earthquake to take over the kingdom in a story that brings the myth of Theseus and the Minotaur of Crete to life. Umberto Eco's *Baudolino* is similar to Harris's *Pompeii* in the way the author describes the atmosphere of twelfth-century chaos during the Fourth Crusade and its shocking effect on the local populace. Eco is a master at combining the spirit of fast-paced adventure with the more serious, thought-provoking issues raised by religious and class controversies of the time.

THE MIDDLE AGES:
SIXTH CENTURY THROUGH FOURTEENTH CENTURY

For the purposes of this chapter the Middle Ages refers to early, middle, and late medieval times, encompassing all of the sixth through fourteenth centuries, which many historians treat separately. Fiction about the Middle Ages is popular, and readers seem to never tire of novels about the fascinating characters and events of this time period that laid the groundwork for so much of modern society. Sharon Kay Penman's novels of the twelfth and thirteenth centuries, including her Welsh Princes trilogy, beginning with *Here Be Dragons*, and her Henry II trilogy, beginning with *When Christ and His Saints Slept*, are benchmark examples of historical fiction set squarely in the Middle Ages—filled with the coarse realities of life, hand-to-hand combat, the Inquisition, desperate conditions, and long-lasting feuds.

Because some of the art, literature, and historical record of the Middle Ages still exist today and are often covered in schools, most people are at least somewhat familiar with the personalities and events of the period. Readers are fascinated with the societal changes brought about by the fall of the Roman Empire: the violence, the decline of wealth and creature comforts, and the extremes of belief that brought about the early Crusades and religious persecution. We enjoy historical novels about this era that humanize aspects of those changes and portray the realistic circumstances in which people existed. Appeals focus on creating the historical setting using sensual, physical details to help readers understand the period on a basic level and perhaps to imagine themselves in the story. Believable and well-researched historical details, characters who speak without obvious anachronism and whose stories portray the times seamlessly—without authorial explanations or background narrative—are all key appeals for this time period. Readers well versed in the events of this period often know exactly what century, person, or event they want to read more about, so it's good for readers' advisors to become at least somewhat familiar with the Middle Ages.

The Last Kingdom, by Bernard Cornwell

In *The Last Kingdom,* first in Bernard Cornwell's Saxon Stories series, torn loyalties make Uhtred, a young Englishman kidnapped by the pagan Danes, an intriguing and sympathetic character in this fast-paced tale of ninth-century Vikings and the Saxons defending Northumbria (northern England and southeastern Scotland) from invasion. Uhtred, a Saxon nobleman, is captured and raised by the Danish war leader Ragnar the Fearless after the Vikings defeat Alfred the Great, king of Wessex. Under Ragnar's tutelage, Uhtred ironically becomes Northumbria's enemy.

Appeal: fast paced, suspenseful, gritty, immersive

FOR FURTHER READING

Cecilia Holland's Corban Loosestrife novels, beginning with *The Soul Thief,* also bring a tenth-century picture of a capture-and-rescue story, but this time set in Northern Ireland. Holland doesn't skimp on action or the carnage created by the fierce Vikings as she describes the realities of life for the Irish at that time. Edward Rutherfurd's *The Princes of Ireland* is a similar title for its saga storytelling style and its initial setting in the same time period.

The Pillars of the Earth, by Ken Follett

Fast paced and plot driven, *The Pillars of the Earth,* by Ken Follett, set in twelfth-century England, begins with an ambitious plan to build a cathedral. After the death of Henry I, dissension over succession to the throne keeps England on tenterhooks and Kingsbridge under threat of violence as the master builder executes the prior's directions. In this towering epic, filled with abundant subplots, Follett infuses the story with a multitude of historical details and believable, conflicted characters whose individual narratives constitute the larger picture of what it took to build a cathedral during the twelfth century. The story of the fictional town of Kingsbridge and its cathedral continues two centuries later in *World without End.*

Appeal: historical accuracy, richly detailed, plot driven, complex plot, well developed characters

FOR FURTHER READING

Like *The Pillars of the Earth*, Ellis Peters's (the pseudonym of Edith Pargeter) *The Heaven Tree Trilogy* (an anthology with this title) features a family of artisans hired to build a cathedral. The story follows the stone carvers and other commoners, their wealthy patron, and the politics of the first part of the thirteenth century, and it is full of lush, absorbing historical detail. Pargeter, who is always interested in human foibles, gives readers an engaging, romantic story that's unforgettable. Set in the fourteenth century, *The Illuminator*, by Brenda Rickman Vantrease, highlights dissension between the Catholic Church and the followers of John Wycliffe in a story about a widow who takes in a master illuminator who is more than what he seems. Readers who revel in historically accurate details of medieval life will enjoy Vantrease's portrayal of complicated characters trying to stay out of trouble while adhering to a personal moral code. A versatile narrative nonfiction history that also illuminates the fourteenth century in Europe is Barbara Tuchman's *A Distant Mirror*, a fascinating, accessible depiction of religious strife, Black Death, the persecution of the Jews, the Hundred Years' War, and the chaos brought on by all these extreme pressures.

When Christ and His Saints Slept, by Sharon Kay Penman

When Christ and His Saints Slept is set in the twelfth century, during the Nineteen-Year Winter, or the Anarchy, during which Maud (aka Empress Matilda), daughter of Henry I, vies for the throne with her cousin King Stephen of the English. This unsettled period is described in the *Anglo-Saxon Chronicle*, annals of history published throughout the Middle Ages, as the time "when Christ and his saints slept." Penman's Henry II trilogy begins in this time of strife, during which the English people suffered greatly and out of which the teenage Henry, son of Empress Matilda and Geoffrey Plantagenet, Count of Anjou, emerges as heir to the throne. First in the trilogy, this volume sets the stage for the powerful first Plantagenet king of England, Henry II, and his equally formidable consort, Eleanor of Aquitaine.

Appeal: well developed characters, leisurely pace, richly detailed, atmospheric

FOR FURTHER READING

In *The Running Vixen*, Elizabeth Chadwick portrays the battle begun by King Henry I to secure the throne for his daughter Maud. Although women did not normally rule England, Henry's insistence on naming Maud his heir, after his son's death, sets the stage for nearly twenty years of anarchy and civil strife. Chadwick's novel focuses more on romance than history, but she does give readers an excellent perspective on the political unrest during this time. Readers who enjoyed Penman's vivid descriptions, dark deeds, and the distrustful atmosphere of the medieval world will revel in Ariana Franklin's depiction of Jewish persecution and general superstition surrounding the deaths of several children in *Mistress of the Art of Death*. Summoned from her home in Italy by King Henry II to find the murderer, Adelia Aguilar, a forensic physician, uses misdirection and a quick wit to diffuse tensions. The sequels in the series reveal more of Adelia's character and that of her interesting companions in a leisurely fashion that conveys the pacing of the times.

THE RENAISSANCE:
THE FIFTEENTH AND SIXTEENTH CENTURIES

Among readers of historical fiction, perhaps even more popular than fiction featuring the Middle Ages is historical fiction set during the Renaissance, when tempers ran high over the continuing religious conflicts involving Jews, Catholics, and the new Protestant religion. The world was on the cusp of big, explosive change: the pope was no longer solely in charge of morality, powerful people close to royalty were found guilty of treason, and suspected witches were burned at the stake. However, the Renaissance also saw the birth of humanism, first in Florence with Niccolò Machiavelli and later in other areas of Western Europe. In addition, the Renaissance brought about an explosion of new art forms—music, painting, sculpture—and of trade. Well-known authors who write about this time include Sarah Dunant, in *The Birth of Venus*; Hilary Mantel, in *Wolf Hall*; and Philippa Gregory in her Tudor novels, the best known of which is *The Other Boleyn Girl*.

When readers request historical fiction about this time period, they rarely ask for books set during "the Renaissance." For this time period more than any other, readers instead cite titles they have loved, usually historical novels about a famous artist or work of art; a ruler like King Henry VIII; the Medici family of Florence; or famous thinkers of the time, such as Galileo. Readers revel in detailed descriptions of the riches enjoyed by the ruling class, the methods of art and science, and the characters that drove the stories and shaped the times. Since the cultural rebirth of the Renaissance began as early as the fourteenth century in Italy and spread throughout Europe gradually into the seventeenth century, readers are often confused by the demarcations between the Middle Ages, the Renaissance, and the Enlightenment, which have more to do with advancements and changes in art, philosophy, and science than with a strict time line. Readers seeking book suggestions in any of these broad time periods may clump them all together and call them just Middle Ages, so be sure to ask for details.

Agincourt, by Bernard Cornwell

In Cornwell's *Agincourt*, English archer Nicholas Hook—an imperfect, plucky, and likable character rises from poverty and is on the run after attacking a priest. To escape hanging, Hook joins King Henry V's army and, in 1415, fights in the Battle of Agincourt. This war story is packed with raw details of the combat and weaponry, which creates an intense immediacy for readers as a small army equipped with longbows defeats the much larger French forces. The visceral horror of war is offset by the fact that readers grow to care about Hook as well as his love interest, a French novitiate whom he has rescued from raiding troops. Cornwell is in top form in this stand-alone historical novel, highlighting his mastery at bringing the past to life and readers into the action.

Appeal: detailed, well developed characters, adventure, immersive

FOR FURTHER READING

Although Steven Pressfield writes about an earlier time period, fans of Bernard Cornwell won't want to miss men at war seen through Pressfield's eyes. His *Tides of War: A Novel of Alcibiades and the Peloponnesian War* is another immersive adventure filled with realistic characters. William Shakespeare's play *Henry V*—a read-around—teems with the same pathos and drama of Cornwell's *Agincourt*, and readers with patience for Elizabethan English will be similarly carried away. The main character, Renzo, in Mary Doria Russell's novel *A Thread of Grace*, about the Jews who fled from France to northern Italy during World War II, is a hero to rival Henry V whose story will appeal to Cornwell's fans.

Niccolò Rising, by Dorothy Dunnett

Known for her elaborately complex plots and abundance of characters, Dorothy Dunnett shines true to form in her House of Niccolò series, beginning with *Niccolò Rising,* in which a dye-shop apprentice has ideas above his station and successfully convinces his patroness to change her business. The first book in the series introduces the humble and witty prankster Claes, as he begins his career in the merchant trade by using a small mercenary band as a courier service from Bruges to Milan. Claes eventually takes on the more refined version of his name, Niccolò, and his prospects begin to rise as a result of successful business dealings and his unique relationship with his female employer.

Appeal: complex plot, well developed characters, adventure, fast paced, witty, immersive

FOR FURTHER READING

A female version of Niccolò, Fiametta Bianchini is Sarah Dunant's wily and wonderful protagonist, superbly rendered in *In the Company of the Courtesan.* Fiametta's witty dwarf companion, Bucino Teodoli, is absolutely unforgettable. Likewise memorable is *The Angel with One Hundred Wings: A Tale from the Arabian Nights,* by Daniel Horch, a fast-paced, edge-of-your-seat adventure in which the sultan of Baghdad loses an unhappy concubine when she elopes with the Prince of Persia, helped along by the sultan's friend. The complicated escape, the dire consequences of being caught, and the intricate plot make this book a sure bet for Dunnett fans.

Wolf Hall, by Hilary Mantel

Novelists have long been fascinated with charismatic, impulsive Henry VIII and the dramatic events of his reign, including his six marriages and his role in separating the Church of England from the Roman Catholic Church.. In *Wolf Hall,* Hilary Mantel does a masterful job of humanizing the great figures of the time, along with their political and personal ambitions. Although Henry's actions drive the plot in this 2009 Man Booker Prize winner, the main character is not the king himself, but his chief minister, Thomas Cromwell. As a youth, Cromwell fled his abusive father to make his own way in the world, first as a mercenary soldier and eventually as a statesman. He served Cardinal Thomas Wolsey and then made himself indispensible to

Henry VIII, helping to annul the king's marriage to his first wife so that he could marry Anne Boleyn. Cromwell is a complex, ambitious man, astute at navigating the treacherous political waters of Tudor England and manipulating others for his own needs. The cast of characters in this novel is extensive (fortunately a chart is provided), ranging from servants and craftspeople to lawyers, scholars, statesmen, and royalty. The novel focuses less on setting details and more on characters, who are revealed slowly through dialogue, philosophy, and psychological insights. The sequel to *Wolf Hall* is *Bring Up the Bodies*, the second in this projected trilogy.

Appeal: well developed characters, dialogue rich, complex plot, thought provoking, witty, leisurely

FOR FURTHER READING

Readers can choose from a huge variety of books about King Henry VIII and his wives, his court, and his power and influence in political and religious arenas. Few have the insight and literary power of *Wolf Hall*, although the many novels of Philippa Gregory certainly fill in the personality blanks where the Tudor women and their courts are concerned. Gregory's Tudor Novels start with *The Constant Princess*. In 1986 Margaret George published her first novel, *The Autobiography of Henry VIII: With Notes by His Fool, Will Somers*. Using the frame of a newly discovered journal kept by Henry, George brings the king to life—a kinder, gentler, and younger Henry. When suggesting historical fiction about King Henry and his court, consider referring readers to the dramatic HBO series *The Tudors*, available on DVD and starring Jonathan Rhys Meyers as Henry.

THE AGE OF ENLIGHTENMENT:
THE SEVENTEENTH AND EIGHTEENTH CENTURIES

Scholars may disagree over the exact beginning of the Age of Enlightenment, but for our purposes, the era began at the end of the Thirty Years' War in 1648, at the close of a pan-European fight against religious tyranny and for the expansion of kingdoms. This is grossly oversimplified, but again, it is just a general outline of history in reference to the fiction written by authors with a fascination for the period. The Enlightenment was a turbulent time in Western history. Never before had people banded together at this level to rebel against the "right" to rule by the church and aristocracy, and to create a new government run by the people. Philosophers and scientists such as Newton, Kant, and Descartes touted fresh ideas about free will, personal freedom, and reason over blind belief.

In many ways events of this period do not seem particularly "enlightened" to us today. Outbreaks of plague continued to decimate the general population, doctors were powerless to help the victims, the Jews were still persecuted, and witch hunts continued. The business of slavery grew exponentially to support an international economy. Readers might not ask for stories about the Age of Enlightenment per se, though they often ask for novels about the centuries involved.

Historical fiction illustrative of the Enlightenment period tends to focus on one aspect of the larger picture, for example, the French Revolution and what Paris was like at the time. The first book most of us think of when someone mentions the French Revolution is Charles Dickens's *A Tale of Two Cities*, one of the most vivid portrayals of the fear and bloodshed of the revolution. A period benchmark author is James Clavell, whose *Shogun* is a popular story of an English merchant's adventures in seventeenth-century Japan. Tracy Chevalier's *Girl with a Pearl Earring* is also a well-known novel, set during the seventeenth century, and named for a Vermeer painting in the baroque style of this time period. Readers who enjoy historical fiction set in the turbulent years of the Enlightenment may also enjoy New World settings. *The Whiskey Rebels*, by David Liss, takes readers to all echelons of US society during the Revolution, tracing the effects of a liquor tax rebellion from backcountry moonshiners to financial speculators like Alexander Hamilton.

Year of Wonders: A Novel of the Plague
by Geraldine Brooks

Geraldine Brooks writes frankly about a distasteful subject in *Year of Wonders*, and while touching on the agonies of a plague-ridden town, she writes elegantly of charity, love, and kindness in the midst of horror. In this unusual, riveting novel, set in 1666 England, the tiny town of Eyam is nearly decimated by the bubonic plague. Rather than risk spreading the disease to travelers, the people of the town quarantine themselves, allowing no one in or out for fourteen months. Only about a quarter of the residents survive. Brooks brings rich historical detail to this haunting story. Readers who take your advice on reading *Year of Wonders* might have been seeking out novels about pandemics or medical history, but most likely they will tell you they were moved by the selfless courage shown by the characters under enormous pressure in this historical novel.

Appeal: haunting, inspirational, elegant, character driven

FOR FURTHER READING

A title set in the United States that's reminiscent of Brooks's *Year of Wonders* is *The Last Town on Earth*, by Thomas Mullen, the story of the 1916 flu epidemic and one small town in the Pacific Northwest that quarantined itself to contain the disease in much the same manner as the residents of Eyam. Another novel of selfless courage that might appeal to Brooks's readers is *My Name Is Mary Sutter*, by Robin Oliveira. Although the story is set later during the US Civil War, readers will recognize a similar theme and atmosphere: illness and physical suffering, despair, courage, and ultimate hope. In Oliveira's story, young Mary Sutter works as a nurse in an ill-equipped, understaffed hospital, under horrible conditions, where she amputates limbs and cares for the wounded, in a demonstration of exceptional courage and depth of character.

The Fort: A Novel of the Revolutionary War
by Bernard Cornwell

In *The Fort*, Bernard Cornwell writes about the obscure and disastrous Penobscot Expedition of 1779, in which poor planning and clashing personalities destroyed the possibility of victory for the Patriots. The commander of the naval forces holds his ships back at a key moment; the land force is in the hands of a politician; and the artillery commander, Paul Revere, reveals a cowardice of which most Americans have not heard. All the smells and the raucous, violent sounds of battle are here in true Cornwellian style as the largely untrained, new militia fails miserably—an expedition in futility lost by real people who experience real consequences.

Appeal: immersive, detailed, violent, well researched

FOR FURTHER READING

Jeff Shaara's *Rise to Rebellion: A Novel of the American Revolution* is a good companion book to *The Fort*, as it features the Boston Massacre and highlights the personalities of other American patriots, although in contrast to Cornwell's book, all here are heroes. As with every one of Shaara's military novels, he captivates readers from the start with the complex politics and military strategies. *The Hornet's Nest,* by Jimmy Carter, takes a fresh perspective in showing readers the realities of the American Revolution in the South. Carter's take on the war is on a more personal level than Cornwell's, although the feeling readers get of being in the midst of the action is a strongly similar. Newt Gingrich's *Valley Forge,* second in his George Washington trilogy, highlights the grueling winter spent by Washington's ragged and demoralized troops at the point when Baron von Steuben arrives to help. Like Cornwell and Shaara, Gingrich writes great military history, here highlighting the huge difference between Washington's freezing, impoverished troops and British troops' comparative luxury.

The Heretic's Daughter, by Kathleen Kent

Set in seventeenth-century Salem, Massachusetts, *The Heretic's Daughter* shows readers the power of the superstition and malevolence that took hold of a community and drove it to violence against one of its own in the witch hunts. In this novel a compelling act of love saves lives and brings a level of immediacy to the story of a little girl whose mother, Martha Carrier, and brothers are accused of witchcraft and cruelly imprisoned. Sarah witnesses her mother's trial and hanging as neighbors, and even relatives, cheer. The pathos is palpable as the story outlines the real reasons Martha was hanged and why life will continue to be difficult for nine-year-old Sarah. The prequel, *The Wolves of Andover,* is also quite moving. Readers who refer to Kent's novels may be interested in the subject of witchcraft but are also looking for an author who can evoke powerful emotion to help them understand how such superstitions and cruelty could happen.

Appeal: immersive, compelling, moving, well developed characters

FOR FURTHER READING

Megan Chance's *Susannah Morrow* features a newcomer to Salem, Massachusetts, who falls victim to the anti-witchcraft fervor in a compelling portrayal of what life was like for suspected witches in colonial America. In *The Last Witchfinder,* by James Morrow, the witch finder's daughter, Jennet, horrified by her aunt's execution for being a witch, resolves to fight the Parliamentary Witchcraft Act. Both novels immerse readers in seventeenth-century Salem life, and they can experience firsthand the fear and mistrust among the citizenry.

The Whiskey Rebels, by David Liss

David Liss, whose interest in history centers on economics, banking, and commerce, writes in *The Whiskey Rebels* about distillers of Scotch whiskey in the 1790s who refuse to pay excise tax on their product, despite the new laws. This small but important incident may barely register with many modern readers, but those who enjoy stories of early America and its newly formed economic marketplace will be fascinated by the shrewd merchants and politicians jockeying for power during the postrevolutionary years. The novel is constructed around the lives of a former Revolutionary War spy and drunk, Ethan Saunders, and the aspiring novelist and pioneer Joan Maycott.

Appeal: plot driven, suspenseful, well drawn characters, immersive, richly detailed

FOR FURTHER READING

Fans of David Liss are often looking for an informative tone, lots of unusual and interesting detail, and a great story that pulls them in. In *The Rebellion of Jane Clarke*, by Sally Gunning, women's rights are the main theme. Gunning's storytelling style is similar to Liss's, full of detailed descriptions of the people and the times delivered in a matter-of-fact, informative tone. A powerful story line drives the action in both books. In her novel *Sally Hemings*, and its sequel, *The President's Daughter*, author Barbara Chase-Riboud addresses racial discrimination and the rights of African Americans during the American Revolution. Like Liss, Chase-Riboud grabs the reader from the start with an absorbing and historically accurate story.

THE NINETEENTH CENTURY

Major events of the nineteenth century included the collapse of empires and city-states across Europe and Asia, and the rise to power of England, the United States, and Japan. Many new discoveries and inventions emerged from the Industrial Revolution, and people moved away from an agricultural society toward one that technology was making completely different. Slavery and the American Civil War also affected the world economy, as did the world powers' colonization and annexation of smaller countries and principalities. Historical fiction set during the nineteenth and twentieth centuries is often filled with details of these large-scale changes and how people tried to cope in a world in which they no longer felt comfortable. As with the eras already mentioned, readers' advisors should take note of the major events and innovations that had a huge influence on life during this period. Some of the common themes in historical fiction of this era include immigration and diaspora, civil rights and a sense of national identity, nations' exploitation of one another, racism and miscegenation, invention and scientific discovery, and the American Civil War.

Historical fiction richly explores the human experience as people face all of these issues. In *Cold Mountain*, for example, Charles Frazier highlights the hardships of families left behind during the American Civil War and the broken lives of soldiers who deserted and wandered in the wilderness to find their way home. In another riveting battle foray, Jeff Shaara, in *Gone for Soldiers*, set during the War of 1812, introduces a young Robert E. Lee, who is learning battle tactics from experienced leaders. Isabel Allende gives us front-row seats to the adventures and trials of immigrants and prostitutes during days of the California Gold Rush in *Daughter of Fortune*, and Andrea Barrett portrays a naturalist, Erasmus Darwin Wells, whose scientific curiosity compels him to make a journey to the Arctic in search of a lost explorer, Sir John Franklin, in *The Voyage of the Narwhal*.

The March, by E. L. Doctorow

In his engrossing novel *The March*, E. L. Doctorow writes of Major General William Tecumseh Sherman's march to the sea, which cut a swath of destruction from a conquered Atlanta, to the port city of Savannah in November and December 1864. Despite the horrific scenes of violence, cruelty, and sheer greed, the author cleverly also highlights humor, compassion, and love. Nevertheless, lonely trees with railroad ties wrapped around them and the still-upright chimneys of destroyed buildings are Sherman's calling card. Very little is left of recognizable civilization after the Union Army destroys everything in its path. Conditions are horrible for both sides, and the freed slaves, who march alongside the soldiers, have only their service to trade for the hope of freedom. Doctorow moves among his characters with perceptive, open eyes and writes about real people and fictional ones in visual, camera-shot scenes, giving readers one of the best and most heart-wrenching stories about the Civil War since Ken Burns's PBS documentary *The Civil War*.

Appeal: well developed characters, richly detailed, witty, moving

Like Doctorow's atmosphere in *The March*, humor and hope, along with the brutal realities of war, are featured in *A Long, Long Way*, by Sebastian Barry. In this novel, Irishman William Dunn makes it through the Great War but finds the transition back to life at home difficult. John Jakes writes of the Southern women and children struggling to save their plantations in the face of Sherman's march to the sea in *Savannah; or, A Gift for Mr. Lincoln.* Jakes's novel, like Doctorow's, is character driven and sometimes funny, but with a different atmosphere—one of adventure, drama, and romance. While Jakes's novel is written in a more popular fiction style than Doctorow's, the compelling and sympathetic characters give readers a similar experience of the period, and they'll feel like they've seen it firsthand.

Sea of Poppies, by Amitav Ghosh

The Opium Wars, fought in the mid-nineteenth century, came about after trade agreements failed between China and Britain. In *Sea of Poppies*, by Amitav Ghosh, the lead-up to the first Opium War plays out on the commercial ship *Ibis*, among a group of people who represent the variety of nations involved in trading opium and cheap or indentured labor. Ghosh exquisitely portrays cultural and personality differences, which creates a leisurely pace with a promise of adventure and action to come. The author describes a battle over drugs and labor as a commercial problem whose solution would change the balance of political and economic power. The issue, however, is as clouded as the mind of an opium user. It is this prewar confusion that Ghosh brings to the fore, carefully evoking the mood of the times in revealing the widening gap between the users and the used. *Sea of Poppies* and the sequel, *A River of Smoke*, are the first two books in Ghosh's projected Ibis Trilogy.

Appeal: sophisticated language, adventure, suspense, picaresque, complex plot

Less adventure filled and more character driven than *Sea of Poppies* but equally literary is *Ship of Fools*, by Katherine Anne Porter. In this novel, Porter tells of a ship crossing the Atlantic, filled with characters who metaphorically represent prevalent cultures and attitudes in the year 1931, much as Ghosh's characters do for the mid-nineteenth-century cultures. *Middle Passage*, by Charles Johnson, a complex, literary, and sobering portrait of the slave trade and its creation of a wide chasm between classes, is also a very tense evocation of a voyage toward change.

I Should Be Extremely Happy in Your Company, by Brian Hall

One of the best depictions of the personalities involved in the Lewis and Clark Expedition, *I Should Be Extremely Happy in Your Company* is a panoramic tale of imagination, fortitude, and determination. While never downplaying the importance of Lewis and Clark's overland journey, Hall's story is more about the inner thoughts and temperaments of the characters, including the teenage Sacajawea and her owner-husband Jean Baptiste Charbonneau. What drove them to explore the rugged wilderness and continue on to map the terrain and hope for an inside passage? How surprised they were to meet such a wide array of Native Americans!

Appeal: thought provoking, insightful, compelling, well developed characters, lyrical

FOR FURTHER READING

For another perspective on the personal relationships and the hardships of the Lewis and Clark Expedition, readers might enjoy *Stone Heart*, by Diane Glancy, published the same year as Hall's novel. In this book, the Shoshone interpreter and guide Sacajawea journals her experiences. Snippets from Lewis and Clark's journals reveal the wide gap in perspective, as compared to the intimate, melodic tone of Sacajawea's voice as she describes her spiritual responses to the land from which the cartographers seem a step removed. *Stone Heart* is as thought provoking and character revealing as Hall's novel is. *A Sudden Country*, by Susan Fisher, records a man and woman discovering with awe the magnitude and beauty of the land and its inhabitants along the Oregon Trail in 1847, about forty years after the Lewis and Clark Expedition. Fisher's novel is big hearted—with its feel for the vastness of North America when traveled by land and the compelling characters whose courage propelled them across it.

THE TWENTIETH CENTURY

The first two-thirds of the twentieth century fall within our definition of historical fiction (provided that the author did not live during the period he or she writes about), so we can look at a few of the major events in fiction highlighting those sixty-five years. The 1900s were a time of rapid discovery and change: advances in medicine nearly annihilated diseases like polio and smallpox; major wars occurred in which power changed hands on a global scale; society was transformed by electricity, television, space travel, and atomic power. Well-known authors who contribute to our understanding of the twentieth century in a historical context include Louis de Bernières, who showcased the fall of the Ottoman Empire in *Birds without Wings*; E. L. Doctorow, who in *Ragtime* gave us the panoply of people, famous and infamous, who shaped and defined America in the first decade of the 1900s. Ursula Hegi's popular book about the courage of German villagers during World War II, *Stones from the River*, and Tatjana Soli's portrait of a conflicted American photojournalist of the Vietnam War in *The Lotus Eaters* bring us new understanding of the continued cruelty of war perpetuated through time.

While not many survivors of World War II are still alive today, many older readers remember learning about the war from their relatives' firsthand experience and are quite familiar with the history. For older readers, remembering events of the twentieth century through historical fiction is a way to revisit experiences that not everyone shares—sometimes cathartic, other times nostalgic. Reading about events like the Vietnam War or assassinations during the civil rights era can help those who watched the television in horror at the time gain a fuller understanding of how such tragedies came about. Younger readers looking for historical fiction about the twentieth century are often looking for explanations, too—the history of today's conflicts and social issues—and for a way to understand what life was like during prior times of extreme stress. However, the biggest appeal of books set in the twentieth century is the opportunity to identify with the protagonists, to realize that such events (good and bad) can happen again and what it might be like.

City of Thieves, by David Benioff

One of the most moving, entertaining historical adventures, *City of Thieves* by David Benioff, appeals to adult and teen readers alike—the book won the 2009 Alex Award partly for that reason. In 1941, as the

Siege of Leningrad begins, seventeen-year-old Lev has a run-in with Nazis when he's caught looting, and he ends up in prison. He and his cellmate, the deserter Kolya, expect to be executed for their crimes. Instead, a cruel and wicked Nazi officer sends them on a seemingly impossible mission in a starving city: get twelve eggs for the wedding cake of the colonel's daughter. With the task before them, Lev and Kolya begin an adventure that takes them behind enemy lines. Readers will stay glued to the page, fists clenched while cheering on the downtrodden pair as they struggle to survive.

Appeal: fast paced, suspenseful, adventure, engaging, bittersweet

FOR FURTHER READING

For readers who enjoy learning about the experiences of the Russian people caught in the Siege of Leningrad and the emotional damage they incurred, a good match is *The Madonnas of Leningrad*, by Debra Dean. Although the story is different from *City of Thieves*, the wretchedness of people's lives and the tension of waiting are visceral in both books, as are the bittersweet relationships developed in a time of crisis. *Red Sky at Morning*, by Richard Bradford, is a wonderfully witty, coming-of-age adventure set during World War II. The story involves seventeen-year-old Josh, who isn't quite old enough to enlist and instead has to move across the country with his self-absorbed mother. The dangers Josh faces are less acute than those of Lev and Kolya, but the mood, the pace, and the main characters are similar. *Coal Black Horse*, by Robert Olmstead, set during the Civil War, features a teen on the edge of manhood sent behind enemy lines, on the strength of his mother's premonition, to find his father and bring him home. This teen's journey is as suspenseful, adventurous, and engaging as Lev's and will most likely appeal to the same audience, despite the different time periods.

The Postmistress, by Sarah Blake

The poles between naive, upper-class Cape Cod dwellers and the harsh realities of European life during bombings and flight from the Nazis are well illustrated in *The Postmistress*—a poignant novel set during World War II. Frankie, a daring young female war correspondent, broadcasts news on the radio from the midst of chaos in London. In the United States, Iris, the forty-year-old virgin postmistress, and Emma, the lonely wife of Dr. Fitch, hear Frankie's reports as a disconnected story that is taking place in another dimension. As the effects of war become inescapable on both sides of the ocean, each woman is powerfully changed.

Appeal: compelling, suspenseful, moving, romantic, well developed characters

FOR FURTHER READING

In *The Postmistress* Iris withholds an important letter, causing confusion and heartache. In *Gifts of War*, by Mackenzie Ford, a message is also withheld, this time by a World War I British soldier who falls in love with the sender's girlfriend. Ford's novel, like Blake's, is compelling, romantic, and suspenseful. In *The Guernsey Literary and Potato Peel Pie Society*, by Mary Ann Shaffer, a farmer convinces Guernsey islanders to write letters to author Juliet Ashton about their experiences during World War II when Nazis occupied Guernsey, and they formed a "literary" group to gather together without arousing suspicion. Like *The Postmistress*, Shaffer's war story is hopeful, often romantic on the surface, but undergirded by serious issues of war.

Fall of Giants, by Ken Follett

Ken Follett's *Fall of Giants* is the first of the Century trilogy—a sweeping epic tale whose subject is the United States during the twentieth century. The story follows dissimilar families—German, English, American, Welsh, Russian—through the events of the early 1900s. Facing immigration, World War I and brutal trench warfare, coal mining, diplomacy, and women's rights, characters both historical and fictional illuminate our forefathers' paths and trace the growth of the United States. Absorbing, thoroughly detailed, and leisurely paced, this wonderful tome is similar to the generational sagas so popular in the 1970s—only it's better. The Century trilogy continues in *Winter of the World* and *Edge of Eternity*.

Appeal: immersive, compulsively readable, character driven, compelling

FOR FURTHER READING

New York, by Edward Rutherfurd, is perhaps most closely comparable to *Fall of Giants*—it's also a sweeping saga that portrays the history of a place,

New York City, on a human level. While Rutherfurd's book is plot driven, unlike Follett's, the strong sense of place, plot complexity, and compulsive readability make *New York* a good choice for readers who loved *Fall of Giants*. John Jakes, an early pioneer of the "sweeping saga" style, takes on the Civil War in his melodramatic North and South trilogy, which is also an addictive read and a good bet for readers who appreciate Follett's immersive storytelling style and want a compelling story peopled with characters they can relate to. They should start with *North and South*. In her Tea Rose trilogy, beginning with *The Tea Rose*, Jennifer Donnelly uses the meshing of several families in the late nineteenth and early twentieth centuries to tell the epic story of change in America and the immigrants and blue collar workers who made it happen. Donnelly's stories are leisurely paced, character- driven, and romantic.

The Rising Tide, by Jeff Shaara

Jeff Shaara proves himself equally adept at portraying not only the world of the American Revolution and American Civil War, but also World War II, in his World War II Novels series beginning with *The Rising Tide*. In *The Rising Tide*, Shaara sets the stage for the war in Europe as the United States is pulled into the conflict in North Africa and from there to Italy. Through the eyes of ordinary soldiers and from the perspective of famous heroes and villains, readers get a sense of the brutality and power mongering that went on during the conflict. Famous men such as Franklin D. Roosevelt, Eisenhower, Churchill, Montgomery, Marshall, Rommel, and Hitler are brought to life and examined in the critical scope of circumstance and personality. Shaara's style appeals to readers for the sheer realism, the immediacy of his settings, and the quick development of characters in the narrative.

Appeal: immersive, well developed characters, suspenseful, thought provoking

FOR FURTHER READING

The best read-alike for Shaara's World War II Novels series is *Killing Rommel*, by Steven Pressfield, for its suspenseful, character-driven perspective on combat in Africa during the autumn of 1942. Like Shaara, Pressfield is interested in the people involved in the war, although his combat scenes are also vividly described, tense with emotion, and compulsively readable. Peter T. Deutermann's account in *Pacific Glory* of the attack on Pearl Harbor is more action focused than Shaara's trilogy but every bit as emotionally tense and immersive. A movie reminiscent of Shaara's character-focused descriptions of the battlefield is *Saving Private Ryan*, a drama portraying the desperate reality of an attempt to retrieve a missing paratrooper during World War II. Readers may appreciate hearing about this film in conjunction with their historical fiction interests as a good option for expanding their appreciation of Shaara's work.

The Help, by Kathryn Stockett

When Eugenia "Skeeter" Phelan finishes college, she's ready to take on the South in 1960s Jackson, Mississippi, in *The Help*. After watching her white friend's rude behavior toward a black maid, Skeeter concocts a brilliant, brave, nerve-wracking plan to write and publish the stories of local African American women who work in homes and to expose the ongoing racism of the white elite toward those whose help they cannot live without. She initially experiences some reluctance among the women she hopes to interview, which only makes her more determined. *The Help* is a poignant and often amusing portrait of change during the civil rights era in the South, one person at a time.

Appeal: dialogue rich, richly detailed, fast paced, compelling, humorous

FOR FURTHER READING

In *Freshwater Road* by Denise Nicholas, nineteen-year-old Celeste Tyree, a sheltered, light-skinned, educated African American Northerner, travels to Mississippi to help register black voters in 1964. Her task demands courage and more perseverance than she expected, and her experience of Southern racism opens her eyes and strengthens her resolve for equality, much like Skeeter's experience in *The Help*. The tone of Nicholas's book is darker than Stockett's novel, but readers will find it every bit as absorbing and unforgettable. In Clyde Edgerton's book *The Night Train*, two kids focused on music, one black and one white, try to maintain their friendship in the face of racial tension in 1963 North Carolina. *The Night Train*, like *The Help*, is witty and upbeat, dialogue rich, and memorable. Similarly, in *The Summer We Got Saved*, by Pat Cunningham Devoto, two young women are jolted out of complacence in small-town Alabama and into maturity when Aunt Eugenia takes them to an interracial camp where they learn that activism is a way of life for many people. Like *The Help*, *The Summer We Got Saved* is a poignant, often funny coming-of-age story in which the author's affection for her characters is contagious.

CONCLUSION

When suggesting books for readers who love historical fiction, asking what time period they might enjoy reading about is extremely important. The time period subgenre of historical fiction is the one readers mention most often, even though many times their description of a time period might be historically inaccurate! Readers' advisors are cautioned to be at least somewhat familiar with authors who write mainly in one time period, such as Jean Auel, Steven Pressfield, Dorothy Dunnett, Sharon Kay Penman, and Sarah Dunant. Knowing and mentioning these authors will serve as benchmarks for discussions with readers. Authors who write historical fiction set in many different times, such as Jeff Shaara, Bernard Cornwell, and Cecilia Holland, serve as standbys for when you need a book idea right away. Making read-alike connections between authors who cover the same time periods helps readers' advisors broaden their knowledge base.

NOTES

1. Nancy Pearl, "Opening Doors Opening Books" (staff training, Seattle Public Library, March 22, 2011). See also Neal Wyatt, "Redefining RA: An RA Big Think," *Library Journal* 132, no. 12 (July 15, 2007): 43, http://lj.libraryjournal .com/2007/07/ljarchives/lj-series-redefining-ra-an-ra-big-think.
2. Patricia Monaghan, "Song of the River" (Book Review), *Booklist* (94, no. 5, Nov. 1, 1997), 454.

4

HISTORICAL FICTION BY PLACE

Historical fiction with an emphasis on setting is another subgenre to keep in mind when working with historical fiction readers. Students researching the history of an area may ask for historical fiction to augment their factual sources, in order to better understand the people and the feel of a place. Some enlightened instructors assign historical fiction for this purpose and may be the ones asking readers' advisors for suggestions. An interest in current events may focus readers' attention on historical fiction set in Iraq, Iran, Indonesia, the Ukraine, Korea, or China—all places that readers may wish to explore in fiction. Novels are one of the best vehicles for understanding an unfamiliar or exotic culture. In fact, *exotic* is a word many readers use to describe what they want from historical fiction—when they say this, the geographic location is what they mean. Historical fiction set in places of perennial interest, such as Paris and New York City, also features largely in readers' requests.

Part of the readers' advisory interview should include asking about the reader's interest in where the story takes place. Listen for enthusiastic descriptions of specific areas. Readers who are especially interested in a particular place often want suggestions for novels that feature the location and are less concerned about which time period is highlighted. People who are traveling to a particular place most frequently request historical fiction to painlessly help them learn about the history and culture of that place, desiring to steep themselves in the atmosphere of the area. Sometimes the "traveler" is making a journey of the imagination for the same reason, without ever leaving home, simply because of curiosity about a place.

For these readers specifically interested in geography, as well as the many other fans of rich historical fiction settings, it can be difficult to find novels set in a particular location in a specific time period. Think of all the possible combinations of time and place: a novel set in northern Germany in prehistoric times, a book set in the South Pacific during the eighteenth century, a story about Yemen in ancient history. It may not be impossible to find this type of fiction, but it can certainly be a challenge. Because historical fiction readers who seek books that evoke strong images of place are most interested in experiencing the culture and environment of an area, readers' advisors may sometimes have to broaden the scope of suggestions to fiction set in a slightly different time period with similar themes and focus, or to novels with similar settings but belonging to slightly different genres. So, for example, the Jade del Cameron historical mystery series by Suzanne Arruda (the first book is *The Mark of the Lion*), set in Kenya just after World War I, might be a suitable choice for a reader who enjoyed the Courtney Family novels, starting with *When the Lion Feeds* (Smith), which also features an adventurous heroine who never shuns danger but is set in South Africa. A modern read-alike for *Things Fall Apart* (Achebe), about the destruction of native folkways and religion by European colonization, might be *Little Bee* (Cleave)—a novel about the chaos and violence in Nigeria in the wake of the incursion of international oil corporations. These novels all vividly describe places that readers enjoy reading about—even though they aren't set in the same time periods, they are similarly evocative of a place. So when talking with readers, keep in mind that they may be happy to try a different time period or genre if the setting is the same, just as some readers might enjoy novels set in the same time period in different places.

When making reading suggestions, it is important to include some more recent titles, ones that are quickly defining modern conventions of historical fiction and place. Readers' advisors increasingly need to adjust how we talk about benchmarks, because historical fiction is changing rapidly as writers expand their perceptions of history in other areas of the world. Readers' perceptions are changing, too, as they become curious about areas of the world made more familiar by current events. Older readers who cite *Shipping News* (Proulx) as a great "place" book (which it is, by the way) will catch some blank looks from freshly minted historical fiction fans! In this section, as in most others throughout this book, I use benchmark titles that are generally newer and exemplify modern concerns and interests in different geographic locations, and I include other similar suggestions for further reading.

AFRICA

When readers ask for historical fiction about Africa, many mention authors such as Chinua Achebe or Bryce Courtenay (*The Power of One*) when describing what kind of "place" book they are seeking, and although these books are not as recent as historical fiction in other areas, we still consider them benchmarks. Much of the fiction set in historical Africa centers on themes of colonialism, race, economic dominance, and political upheaval. For instance, the racial problems of South Africa can be traced to the incursion of Europeans and their subsequent governance over the native people. Finding historical fiction in English set in Africa is difficult, so for the purpose of this section, I include novels that are largely considered historical fiction by most readers, even though they may have been written about events that occurred during the author's lifetime.

The Power of One, by Bryce Courtenay

In 1989 *The Power of One* rocked readers of English with its powerful message about racial disparity in post–World War II South Africa and a young British boy, Peekay, who grows into his fists boxing and into adulthood as the friend of a black man. Even now, more than twenty years later, this moving story is a popular benchmark for readers who seek a great story that appeals to teens and adults alike, with enough intellectual meat for thought. Many high schools include *The Power of One* on reading lists, and book groups still enjoy discussing Courtenay's perspective on postwar South Africa, its penal system, and apartheid. Readers may also enjoy the 1992 film of the same name, starring Stephen Dorff as Peekay and Morgan Freeman as Giel Peet.

Appeal: dialogue rich, character driven, disturbing, violent, haunting, moving, inspirational, coming of age, fast paced

FOR FURTHER READING

Another fascinating view of South Africa in the postwar years is *The Servant's Quarters* (Freed), the story of a young girl trying to make sense of class distinctions as she grows up under the tutelage of an older man— an uncomfortable, yet touching relationship, like Peekay's with his adult mentor. And of course, the moving classic *Cry, the Beloved Country* (Paton), though not technically a historical novel, gives modern readers a moving perspective on the personal effects of apartheid and the South African criminal justice system. Both character-driven, compelling novels portray innocent lives touched by racism and peaceful characters bewildered by the hatred of others. And even though it's an older title, don't miss *The Covenant*, by James Michener, which traces the course of South Africa's history from the pioneering Afrikaners to the founding of the Zulu nation. It's a sweeping epic of a place and its people written in Michener's signature style—filled with myriad characters and details on the violent, dramatic history of the area.

Things Fall Apart, by Chinua Achebe

One of the best-known novels on the subject of European colonialism in Africa is Chinua Achebe's *Things Fall Apart*. Despite the fact that this book about nineteenth-century Nigerian culture was first published in 1958, it is still a popular choice for book groups and school assignments. Readers refer to it when describing moving and culturally rich novels set in Africa, and it can, therefore, still be considered a benchmark. It is the story of a village, its complex mores and traditions, and the people for whom metaphor and symbolism define human interaction and understanding. Into this setting come European missionaries committed to replacing native beliefs with their own religion, and the military is close behind them, bent on dominance and commercial gain.

Appeal: compelling, lyrical, magical realism, disturbing, atmospheric, thought provoking

FOR FURTHER READING

A modern counterpart to Achebe's classic is *Half of a Yellow Sun* (Adichie), which illustrates the fight for an independent Biafra (part of Nigeria), which was struggling for a new identity in the late 1960s. Ultimately, the separate state was absorbed in the same way so many small villages, including the one in Achebe's book, were lost in the march of the global economy. Similarly, in *The Eye of the Leopard* (Mankell), a young Swedish man visits a mission in newly independent Zambia in the 1960s and winds up staying, eking out an increasingly harsh existence as an egg farmer, never really understanding the culture in which he lives and of which he still cannot be a part. Mankell's novel, more than Adichie's, is tinged with the same sad bewilderment of Africans dealing with the incursion of inscrutable Europeans.

The Poisonwood Bible, by Barbara Kingsolver

The Poisonwood Bible, set in the Belgian Congo at the beginning of the civil war in 1959, also portrays a type of colonialism—that of Christian missionaries set on evangelizing the nations of Africa. Many readers point to this benchmark novel, published in 1998, as a moving and informative story that aptly describes a Western perspective of African culture and its struggles. A self-proclaimed missionary to Africa, Nathan Price drags his family from Georgia to a remote Congolese village, where his four daughters and his wife vainly try to mitigate Price's virulent, outright insulting treatment of the local people and their beliefs. The humid, remote wilderness is utterly foreign to the Prices, and probably to the reader, and so contributes to the sense of inevitable tragedy that runs beneath the story line as Price's personal fundamentalism overcomes his sanity.

Appeal: character driven, richly detailed setting, exotic, lyrical, haunting, violent

FOR FURTHER READING

Readers fascinated by Kingsolver's novel will also enjoy Ronan Bennett's *The Catastrophist*, in which a man moves to the Congo to be with his lover and encounters violence and corruption during the civil unrest of the 1960s. Although Joseph Conrad's classic, *Heart of Darkness*, was not historical fiction when it was published, it is nevertheless an obvious choice for those who enjoy pondering not only the effect of Europeans on native African culture but also the powerful, sometimes frightening effect Africa had on the white intruders. While *Heart of Darkness* is set in the nineteenth century, parallels can be drawn between Kingsolver's portrayal of a rigidly fundamentalist missionary and Conrad's portrait of the crazed Kurtz, absorbed by a culture he is ill equipped to understand.

NORTH AMERICA

James Michener's penchant for tracing the history of a place—from its first geological formation to its first visit by humankind to the years of civilization—set the standard for authors writing historical fiction with a strong sense of place. Who can forget his portrayal of Alaska, in which readers learn what it's like to be a salmon spawning; *Hawaii*, where a native man plucks out his eye in grief for his dead wife; or *Chesapeake*, where the Canadian geese discuss the proper formation with a crabby "Craaaank!" David Guterson's *Snow Falling on Cedars*, about the trial of a falsely accused Japanese American man in the 1950s, brings a realistic sense of the gloppy wet snow that falls during winters on Puget Sound and the huge trees looming overhead, trying to squeeze out humanity. Likewise unforgettable are the drearily chilly miles of wooded land Inman experiences in North Carolina as he escapes from the nightmare of Civil War in *Cold Mountain* (Frazier). These benchmark authors of the past few decades are recognizable to most seasoned historical fiction readers and can still sometimes be referred to in discussions about finding great historical fiction with memorable settings. Here are some of the newer place-appeal titles that readers may also enjoy.

The Well and the Mine, by Gin Phillips

The Moore family lives in an Alabama mining town when the Great Depression hits, and their children are no strangers to hard times; hard work; and tough, bigoted people. Everyone struggles to eke out an existence; sometimes horrible accidents maim or kill townspeople; segregation and racism are everywhere. But when nine-year-old Tess sees a woman throw a baby down a well, she is horrified, and even her supportive family cannot prevent the nightmares that come. Told in alternating first-person narrative by each family member as details of the baby's death come to light, this is a moving depiction of good people just barely hanging on and children learning more than they should about adulthood.

Appeal: character driven, leisurely, strong sense of place, engaging, poignant, heartwarming

FOR FURTHER READING

Tony Earley's short novel *Jim, the Boy* portrays a tightly knit but unusual family in Aliceville, North Carolina. Ten-year-old Jim lives with his widowed mother and his three uncles in this heartwarming coming-of-age story set during the Great Depression that takes readers on a nostalgic journey of growing up in the South—re-creating the smell of a new mitt; the intensity of a first baseball game, of facing down a bully, of a mother's new suitor; and a world experienced at a slower pace in the 1930s. In *Prayers for Sale* Sandra Dallas brings to life the strengths of women during the Depression in the mountain town of Middle Swan, Colorado, and the friendships that provided a life-saving support system for women like Hennie Comfort and Nit Spindle. Readers who loved the vivid setting, leisurely pace, and poignancy of *The Well and the Mine* will also appreciate Dallas's descriptions of a mining town high in the Rocky Mountains.

The Day the Falls Stood Still
by Cathy Marie Buchanan

Just before World War I, Beth Heath's father is fired from his job at the Canadian Niagara Falls hydroelectric plant, and the family faces a hardship they have never before experienced. Beth's sister plunges into depression, they have no income, and the family's only hope is for Beth to marry into money. Beth has other ideas, however, and instead marries the river man Tom Cole, who abhors the effect the hydroelectric plant has on the environment, to which he is almost mystically connected. Eventually, though, Tom does take a job at the plant to support his family. A melancholy atmosphere infuses the novel as the characters experience poverty and personal challenges, but the ultimate message is uplifting. Readers will be impressed by a deadly Niagara River and falls they will not forget.

Appeal: strong sense of place, historical accuracy, nostalgic, elegant style, leisurely, romantic

FOR FURTHER READING

Readers who imagine the freedom and exhilaration of Tom Cole as he navigates Niagara white waters will revel with Sophie Armant Blanchard as she sails in a hot air balloon above Napoléon's France in *The Little Balloonist* (Donn). Like Buchanan, Donn is an expert at describing the setting seamlessly within the context of a compelling and elegant story. Similarly in love with the outdoors and the concept of discovering something wild and free, in *Wild Life* Molly Gloss writes about a single mother of five boys who joins a search party for a missing child in the chill, wet woods of nineteenth-century Washington State. In *Rainwater* (Brown), Ella Barron, a boardinghouse owner and deserted wife, takes on an ailing renter whose quiet support endears him to her during tough times in a drought-stricken, Depression-era Texas town. All these novels emphasize the setting and evoke nostalgia for place and period.

The Whistling Season, by Ivan Doig

Ivan Doig shares with Annie Proulx an ability to bring the landscape to life as a character. His Montana trilogy is well known as a spot-on description of life on the range at the turn of the past century—the sky is huge, the weather is icy, and life is a battle. In a newer benchmark historical novel set in Montana, *The Whistling Season*, Doig waxes eloquent on dust farming as a way of life and on those who raised their families in the early 1900s. The story is heartwarming: a family of boys needs a housekeeper, a housekeeper who can't cook (but doesn't bite) needs a family—and so it goes. The landscape asserts itself, from the stars at night to the chilly ride to school and the hot dust of poverty. *The Whistling Season* is a sure bet for readers with a sense of humor and a yen for the West. (*Work Song* and *Sweet Thunder* are the sequels.)

Appeal: heartwarming, humor, leisurely pace, lyrical, strong sense of place, storytelling

FOR FURTHER READING

Narrated by young Gladys Cailiff, *The Cailiffs of Baghdad, Georgia* (Stefaniak), like *The Whistling Season*, is a model of great storytelling and features a force-to-be-reckoned-with in its latest immigrant, the gifted schoolteacher, Miss Grace Spivey. Miss Spivey, like Rose's brother, Morris Morgan, in *The Whistling Season*, is unconventional, egalitarian, and positively frothing with great teaching ideas in Depression-era Threestep, Georgia. Richard Bradford's *Red Sky at Morning* is set at the beginning of World War II, first in Mobile, Alabama, and then in Sagrado, New Mexico, where seventeen-year-old Josh and his self-absorbed, alcoholic mother move while his father is away at war. To say Sagrado is remote is an understatement—readers will revel in the vividly depicted landscape of New Mexico. Larry McMurtry also has a talent for poignant, unforgettable stories set against a rich Western background. In *Sin Killer*, the first of the Berrybender narratives features Lord and Lady Berrybender and their fourteen children, all of whom tackle the American West as they head to Missouri. The humor, the vast landscape, and the engaging characters will remind readers of *The Whistling Season*.

West of Here, by Jonathan Evison

Historical fiction readers undaunted by a book's heft will be glad to settle in with a lovely long read such as *West of Here*, an epic historical

Historical Fiction Set in New York City

Don't miss these classics...

East Side Story, by Louis Auchincloss

The Amazing Adventures of Kavalier and Clay, by Michael Chabon

World's Fair, by E. L. Doctorow

A Star Called Henry, by Roddy Doyle

Morningside Heights, by Cheryl Mendelson

Martin Dressler, by Steven Millhauser

A Tree Grows in Brooklyn, by Betty Smith

Recent historical fiction set in New York City

Among the Wonderful, by Stacy Carlson

Elizabeth Street, by Laurie Fabiano

Heir to the Glimmering World, by Cynthia Ozick

New York, by Edward Rutherfurd

City of Dreams and *City of Promise*, by Beverly Swerling

Rules of Civility, by Amor Towles

Diamond Ruby, by Joseph Wallace

Classics set in New York City often considered historical

Maggie: A Girl of the Streets, by Stephen Crane

Manhattan Transfer, by John Dos Passos

The Great Gatsby, by F. Scott Fitzgerald

The Street, by Ann Petry

The Chosen, by Chaim Potok

The Godfather, by Mario Puzo

Call It Sleep, by Henry Roth

novel of Washington State set both in the late nineteenth century, in an area perched on the edge of economic progress, symbolized by the erection of a dam, and in 2006, when the decision is made to tear down the dam for environmental reasons. Evison's characters over the generations epitomize the inexorable march of change in their surroundings—a place of fresh beginnings, weird weather, and varied beauty. *West of Here* is an example of an energetic new style found in regional historical fiction.

Appeal: humor, witty, complex plot, thought provoking, strong sense of place, time sweep

FOR FURTHER READING

Fall of Giants (Follett) is similarly epic in scope, with a strong regional flavor, evocative of a changing New York and peopled with a large cast of characters, as in *West of Here*. Both books use characters that aptly represent their setting as the authors trace progress. *A Moment in the Sun* (Sayles) captures the look, feel, and atmosphere of the turn of the twentieth century through key events like the Alaskan Gold Rush and the effects of colonialism worldwide. Sayles's book will appeal to Evison's readers because it is also thought provoking and witty while perfectly describing the setting and spirit of America experiencing rapid economic and political change. Annie Proulx's *That Old Ace in the Hole* is quite different in setting from all three of the books so far described—pig farms in the Texas and Oklahoma panhandles. It's Global Pork Rind versus the local pig farmers of Woolybucket, Texas, or put another way, the old ways fighting the new. Proulx's bucolic read-around is not historical, although it feels like the same time period as these other titles and readers will likely appreciate the suggestion.

Bloodroot, by Amy Greene

Bloodroot brings Tennessee's Appalachia in the 1960s to life in a powerful family saga. The mountainous landscape creates the characters and their culture—hardy, down-to-earth people—sometimes violent, and full of superstitions and inexplicable talents. For instance, "haint"-eyed Myra Lamb, the main character, is charismatic with people and has a strange connection to animals; her grandmother can charm any living creature. These strange abilities cannot, however, prevent bad luck, dire circumstances, and the consequences of poor choices as the family grows and changes. The story is unforgettable and intense, with characters molded by their locale, superstition, and poverty.

Appeal: literary, complex style, multiple perspectives, strong sense of place, family saga, haunting, mystical, fast paced, dialect rich, complex plot

FOR FURTHER READING

In *Fair and Tender Ladies* (Smith), life in Virginia's Appalachia thrives under the pen of young Ivy Rowe, an aspiring writer whose family lives in a rural mountain community in the 1920s and 1930s, much like the Lambs in *Bloodroot* forty years later. While Smith's dialect-rich story brings the people and the landscape to life in a way that Greene's readers will appreciate, the pacing is slower, the tragedy is balanced with humor, and poverty and lack of opportunity are turned on their head by hope and acceptance. In *Cataloochee* (Caldwell), four generations of three families embody the hardscrabble life and close-knit relationships of North Carolina's Smoky Mountains during the years between 1864 and 1928. Again, although the pace is leisurely and the atmosphere captivating rather than intense, the strong sense of a mountain community with its unique dialect and lyrical descriptions make this an appealing suggestion for those moved by *Bloodroot*. Finally, *Meely LaBauve* (Wells), though permeated with humor that sets a different tone, is an unforgettable coming-of-age story about a 1960s Huck Finn and his no-good daddy, set in the Catahoula Bayou in Louisiana. Wells's descriptions of Meely's everyday journeys into the swamp or out to school immerse readers in a setting that, like *Bloodroot*, is evocative of rural communities around the United States.

SOUTH AND CENTRAL AMERICA, MEXICO, AND THE CARIBBEAN

The countries of South and Central America, Mexico, and the Caribbean, have a rich literary tradition, but it can be difficult to find those books in English translation. During the early 1970s political turmoil and wars, sometimes directly involving the United States, beset South American countries. Much of the translated literature by authors from South and Central America has been published in the United States as a result of spreading political awareness of the region.

Most readers' advisors associate the writing style known as magical realism with authors from Latin America and the Caribbean, largely because of the novels of Colombian author Gabriel García Márquez and Chilean writer Isabel Allende. Some of García Márquez's books are historical fiction, but many are not. Historical fiction readers are usually familiar with his work, but if they are not, his representative works are *One Hundred Years of Solitude* and *Love in the Time of Cholera*. Allende's early novel *The House of the Spirits* combines magical realism with the history of the revolution in Chile in the 1970s. As is often the case, these books treat historical subjects within the authors' lifetime and therefore are not "historical fiction" by our definition here. Still, historical fiction readers often use these books as examples when talking about magical realism. Well-known historical fiction authors with roots in Latin America who have a similar literary style are Luis Urrea (*The Hummingbird's Daughter*) and Laura Esquivel (*Like Water for Chocolate*). Some people might argue that an author's inclusion of magical realism excludes a novel as historical fiction, but I maintain that an emphasis on setting is based on a perception of that setting. If a reader enters a magical setting, as long as the facts of history are accurately reported, the setting is no less "real." The best way to test this for yourself is to include some historical novels filled with magical realism on your personal reading list.

The Long Song, by Andrea Levy

The Long Song is set in Jamaica on a sugar plantation in the years surrounding the island's slave rebellion of 1832. Narrated in the beguiling voice of Miss July, a former slave, the novel is a testament to the resilience of a woman and a people. July's mother was a field slave who was raped by a Scottish overseer. As a child, July is taken into the great mansion as a house slave, where she is taught to read so that she can help the English mistress with business matters. After slavery is abolished in Jamaica, Miss July stays on the plantation, where she and other former slaves still face many difficulties. Although the novel describes the atrocities of slavery, it is also laced with humor and wit, and the conversational patois of Miss July brings warmth and richness to the tale.

Appeal: character driven, lyrical, compelling, moving, dialect rich, witty

FOR FURTHER READING

The Book of Night Women (James) is also set on a Jamaican sugar plantation and vividly captures the brutalities of life for slaves and for slave women in particular, in the late eighteenth and early nineteenth centuries. James's novel is narrated in Jamaican Creole as well, and is more graphic than *The Long Song* in depicting the whippings and rapes that lead a group of slave women to plan a rebellion. Readers interested in Levy's descriptions of life after slavery on a plantation will also enjoy *The Polished Hoe* (Clarke), a moving account of slavery's cruel legacy in the West Indies. Mary, an elderly black woman, narrates the novel in her rich, intimate voice. What starts as a confession to the local police sergeant becomes a powerful stream of memories chronicling a lifetime of mistreatment culminating in deadly rage. *The Farming of Bones* (Danticat) follows the story of a Haitian servant, Amabelle Desir, who searches for her lover, murdered in the cane fields at the order of the Dominican Republic's President Rafael Trujillo. Danticat makes use of dreams and symbolism, along with lyrical language like Levy's, that alternates with stark scenes of violence, creating a powerful atmosphere of lush life contrasted with death.

Invisible Mountain, by Carolina de Robertis

This colorful family saga opens on January 1, 1900, in a small village in Uruguay, where a baby, to be named Pajarita, miraculously appears in a tree. Later, as a young bride, Pajarita moves from the countryside to the city, where she supports her family by selling herbal remedies to local women. Her daughter, Eva, is sexually assaulted as a child but eventually turns to a life of art and poetry. In turn, Eva's daughter, Salomé, grows up to be a revolutionary who attempts to overthrow the government. Through the deftly observed lives of three generations of women, the author chronicles the life of a country. Luxuriant descriptions of countryside and cities—especially the sights, sounds, and smells of the capital port city, Montevideo—bring alive the tumultuous history of Uruguay in the twentieth century.

Appeal: family saga, character driven, complex style, richly detailed, lyrical, moving

FOR FURTHER READING

The House of the Spirits, by Isabel Allende, also explores the history of a country by chronicling multiple generations of a family. Set in Chile, the leisurely paced narrative traces the lives of the Trueba clan from the beginning of the twentieth century to the military coup of 1973. Readers who enjoy viewing a country and revolutionary politics through the lives of women will also be interested in *In the Time of the Butterflies* (Alvarez), which is set in the Dominican Republic during Trujillo's presidency. The novel is based on the real Mirabel sisters, four young women known as Las Mariposas (the Butterflies) who were committed to overthrowing their country's dictator. Another epic novel about settlers ruling their own domain that illustrates the violent history and colorful characters of

Mexico in the late nineteenth and early twentieth centuries is *Country of the Bad Wolfes* (Blake). A picaresque saga of three generations of the Wolfe family, whose arrival and success in Mexico was wholly based on economics, this novel has something for everyone: romance, adventure, evil (and good) twins, and many other characters whose personalities and travails influence the changing landscape.

Conquistadora, by Esmeralda Santiago

Santiago employs sensual, colorful descriptions to bring alive the verdant cane fields and wild jungles of early nineteenth-century Puerto Rico in the novel *Conquistadora*. As a young girl from an aristocratic family in Spain, Ana is entranced by accounts written by her ancestor of his travels to the exotic island. When Ana is eighteen years old, she marries Ramón and convinces him and his twin brother to move to Puerto Rico to run the sugarcane plantation they have inherited. Although slavery has been abolished in Spain, it is still in full force on the island and on the Hacienda Los Gemelos estate. Life on the plantation is far different from what Ana had imagined, and she soon contends with disease, natural disasters, a slave revolt, and a love triangle. Santiago's characters are fully developed and complex. Ana is a strong, intelligent woman who in some ways is a sympathetic character, yet she condones (albeit with mixed feelings) the cruelty of slavery.

Appeal: character driven, sensual, storytelling style, complex plot, strong sense of place

FOR FURTHER READING

Ines of My Soul (Allende) also explores Latin American history from the viewpoint of a Spanish *conquistadora*. The novel's narrator, Ines Suárez (based on the sixteenth-century mistress of the first Spanish governor of Chile), flees a stifling life in Spain to seek adventure in the New World. A strong and intelligent woman, Ines nevertheless participates in the atrocities committed against the native people. This novel is clear-eyed in its depictions of the hardships and cruelties of life in the New World and passionate in its description of the beautiful wild landscapes of South America that shine through almost as characters in their own right. Like *Conquistadora*, *Daughters of the Stone* (Llanos-Figueroa) also depicts social conditions on a sugar plantation in Puerto Rico, albeit from the point of view of Fela, an African slave. The horrors of slavery are clearly presented, but the main focus of this sensual tale is the five generations of mothers and daughters who, in a rapidly changing world, are held together by their belief in the rituals and magic of their African past.

The War of the End of the World
by Mario Vargas Llosa

In this epic novel, Nobel Prize–winning Peruvian writer Mario Vargas Llosa delves deeply into a period of violent upheaval in Brazilian history. In the late 1800s, a fanatical religious leader wanders through the drought-stricken rural areas of Brazil, attracting a diverse following of society's outcasts. They settle on land in Canudos, a remote region in northeastern Brazil that rich landholders nevertheless already lay claim to, and try to establish their own republic. They oppose all the trappings of modern government, including money and taxation. The Brazilian government is determined to suppress them, and a cataclysmic battle between government troops and ragtag peasants ensues. The vivid descriptions of bloodshed and grotesque events are not for the faint of heart. A sprawling cast of characters from both sides of the conflict are drawn with deft detail, helping to bring alive a tumultuous and little-known era of history.

Appeal: epic, thought provoking, violent, bleak, well developed characters

FOR FURTHER READING

Not as violent, but like Vargas Llosa's novel, *The Inhabited Woman* (Belli) is peopled with well-developed characters whose commitment to revolutionary change becomes stronger as the story progresses. Lavinia, a well-born architect in Faguas, a fictional country, falls in love with her colleague Felipe, a revolutionary. Belli brings magical realism to bear on Lavinia in the form of an indigenous spirit from the time of the Spanish conquistadors, who convinces her to take part in a coup. Momentous and unsettled in tone, *Our Lives Are the Rivers* (Manrique) portrays the life of Manuela Sáenz, the Ecuadorian mistress and co-revolutionary of Simón Bolívar, known as the Liberator of South America. Manrique's novel is a fast-paced page-turner, epic in proportion, yet it paints passionate characters filled with human flaws and inconsistencies that bring early nineteenth-century South American history to life.

ASIA AND THE MIDDLE EAST

The British Empire's relentless reach for world domination caused a rebellion in Asia and the Middle East similar to that in Africa during the latter nineteenth and early twentieth century. This desire for autonomy and its natural consequence, revolution, is reflected in historical fiction. Paul Scott's *Raj Quartet*, first published between 1966 and 1975, is still a benchmark of historical fiction about British rule in India, as is the Cairo trilogy by the Egyptian Nobel Prize–winner Naguib Mahfouz, about Egypt's long road to independence. Louis de Bernières's 2004 title *Birds without Wings* is a popular benchmark featuring Turkey in the early twentieth century, during the waning Ottoman Empire. One of the most popular novels about Japan and the changes its people experienced mid-twentieth century is told in the coming-of-age story *Memoirs of a Geisha* (Golden). All these titles are still enjoyed by readers of historical fiction and serve as benchmarks, but as the focus of modern historical novels moves from the subject of British colonialism toward an emphasis on philosophy, religion, and individualism, so have readers' interests changed, and newer titles can also function as benchmarks in reference to other historical fiction about Asia and the Middle East.

The Blood of Flowers, by Anita Amirrezvani

As mesmerizing as Scheherazade, in *The Blood of Flowers* a young woman much mistreated by fate and by men tells her story. In the seventeenth-century Persian city of Isfahan, an unnamed girl and her mother are taken on as indentured servants in an uncle's household. The girl surreptitiously learns how to make beautiful Persian rugs, with the goal of freeing herself and her mother. She is, however, forced to make a temporary marriage in which she provides entertainment and sexual favors for money to a man who eventually marries her friend. Amirrezvani's lyrical language, detailed descriptions of rug making, and lush imagery evoke the exotic atmosphere of times long past that many historical fiction readers crave.

Appeal: compulsively readable, steamy, exotic, sensual, lavishly detailed, lyrical

FOR FURTHER READING

Although it is set in Italy, not Persia, *The Birth of Venus* (Dunant) will appeal to those who love the exotic atmosphere and the sensuality of *The*

Blood of Flowers. Dunant's rich details of fifteenth-century Florence and compelling artist Alessandra Cecchi are reminiscent of the world in which Amirrezvani's determined rug maker wove her tales. In *The Painter from Shanghai* (Epstein), fourteen-year-old Pan Yuliang is sold into prostitution by her uncle. Three years later she is rescued by a man who makes her his concubine and sets her up as an artist. Later she scandalizes her audience with her nude paintings. In *The Rice Mother* (Manicka) Lakshmi, a Sri Lankan teen, is tricked into marrying a man twice her age and must make her home with him in Malaysia in the years before World War II. The novel's exotic locale and Manicka's evocation of Lakshmi's coming-of-age during a difficult time in Malaysia make this a gripping story that will appeal to Amirrezvani's audience.

Map of the Invisible World, by Tash Aw

In 1964 in Indonesia, the "year of living dangerously," the country is in turmoil and the failing government, under President Sukarno, is arresting and deporting Dutch citizens, including Karl, sixteen-year-old Adam's adoptive father, which leaves the boy stranded on his own. Adam makes his way from his remote village home to Jakarta and the American professor Margaret Bates, whose tie to Karl is slim but provides hope to the teen. A complicated and disturbing plot brings Adam into contact with more horror than a boy should experience as he and Margaret launch their search to put the family back together in a world bent on ripping them apart.

Appeal: strong sense of place, atmospheric, haunting, complex plot, disturbing, leisurely pace

FOR FURTHER READING

Exiles and expatriates are also featured in *The Russian Concubine* (Furnivall), set in the fictionalized Chinese city of Junchow (based on prerevolutionary Tianjin) in the early twentieth century. Having escaped from Russia, Valentina and her daughter Lydia are living in the International Settlement, barely scraping by when Lydia's lover involves her with a criminal gang. With its complex story, like *Map of the Invisible World*, and an equally atmospheric setting, Furnivall's novel will appeal to readers who enjoy coming-of-age stories about teens wrenched from their childhood in foreign lands. In *The Gift of Rain* (Tan), a young half-British, half-Chinese boy in Malaysia forges close ties to his Japanese aikido master, Endo-san, in the years prior to World War II in an emotionally complicated story of the divisiveness and corruption of war that will appeal to Aw's readers. Readers fascinated by exotic settings that seduce unwary strangers will also be interested in *The Piano Tuner* (Mason), in which the jungle of Burma literally swallows Englishman Edgar Drake, whose obsession with a native woman may be his downfall.

Dreams of Joy, by Lisa See

In this sequel to *Shanghai Girls*, Joy is captivated by a romanticized ideal of Chairman Mao's communist China and by the idea of finding her natural father. She dashes off to China, only to find that the father she seeks is a propaganda artist who is being sent to a rural reeducation camp as a result of the Cultural Revolution. Joy stays at the camp with her father, maintains her belief in the new social system, and marries a local man—though she is instantly sorry after spending the night with him in squalid conditions. Meanwhile her mother Pearl arrives in China to look for Joy. It isn't long before the crops fail and Joy's beautiful dream is belied by a harsh reality. The juxtaposition of city life to rural life and New World to Old World sensibilities make *Dreams of Joy* a good choice for those desiring immersion in the Chinese landscapes of the 1960s and 1970s.

Appeal: historical accuracy, immersive, moving, lyrical

FOR FURTHER READING

In *The Lily Theater* (Wang), Lian goes with a parent to a reeducation camp during the Cultural Revolution, as Joy does in *Dreams of Joy*. Her mother is a history professor who will be retrained in the country but who also has academic friends at the farm who educate Lily and, ironically, given her circumstances, train her to think for herself. Readers who love Lisa See's immersive storytelling, descriptive writing, and compelling characters will likewise enjoy Wang's absorbing story of these two women uprooted and changed by history and landscape. *Balzac and the Little Chinese Seamstress* (Dai) is an enchanting, warm, poignant story of two teenage boys sent to do hard labor in a rural area of China as their "reeducation" as children of well-off families. While the mood of Dai's story is different from that of See, the rural setting and hardship are very much the same. The author Sijie Dai experienced the Cultural Revolution himself, so his novel isn't technically historical fiction, but readers absorbed by Joy's experience of culture shock in rural China may also like *Balzac*. Kazuo Ishiguro's fiction is darker than Lisa See's and the atmosphere of psychological suspense in *When We Were Orphans* is quite different, but fans will see a similarity of thoughtful prose, lyrical style, and compelling characters. In this moving story, Englishman Christopher Banks, a successful and well-known detective during the 1930s, travels to Shanghai in search of his parents who disappeared years before in suspicious circumstances.

AUSTRALIA

Historical fiction set in Australia and available in the United States generally falls into three main categories: early settlements and interaction with Aborigine people, pioneers and convicts of the nineteenth century, and hardship stories of people living in the Outback. While historical time period is sometimes at issue, most often readers are seeking the exotic "Down Under" story that emphasizes the history of this exotic island continent and its people, flora, and fauna. One of the strangest classic novels inspired by the Aborigine people of Tasmania is *Gulliver's Travels* (Swift). It's not historical fiction but is instead a satire and parody of a historical time when the Europeans viewed Australia and its cultures for the first time. Miles Franklin, one of the first female authors in Australia, published *My Brilliant Career* in 1901 (followed by *My Career Goes Bung*), a feminist novel about an independent young woman living in the Outback in the 1890s. Franklin's novel is an example of writing that many now would consider historical fiction—it doesn't fit our formal definition of historical fiction for this book, but it is interesting to note as an example of early Australian literature.

Since a paucity of well-known Australian authors of historical fiction exists in most American libraries, readers' advisors need to be aware of the older authors still popular in this genre today. Matthew Kneale is best known for his Whitbread Award–winning novel *The English Passengers*, about the English settling in Tasmania in the nineteenth century and the destruction and devastation of the Aborigine people. While not widely read, Kneale is still a respected and recognized author in the United States. In 1994 David Malouf published his haunting and powerful *Remembering Babylon*, about a thirteen-year-old boy, Gemmy Fairley, cast ashore in Queensland and raised by Aborigines. Few books of historical fiction set in Australia do as fine a job as this one of bringing to life the landscape and people of northern Australia in the 1840s. A main piece of Australia's character and history is the convict ships sent from England to the penal colony at Botany Bay, in Sydney. Colleen McCullough illustrates this event through Richard Morgan, the protagonist in *Morgan's Run*. Morgan is framed for murder by his criminal boss and is eventually shipped off to Australia, where he starts a new life: his determination and adaptability characterize Australia's eighteenth-century British heritage.

The True History of the Kelly Gang, by Peter Carey

Most readers' advisors are familiar with Peter Carey, the renowned Australian author. His historical novel *The True History of the Kelly Gang*, which won several prizes, including the Man Booker Prize and the Commonwealth Writers' Prize for Best Book, is a suspenseful and compelling story of folk hero Ned Kelly, the nineteenth-century Irish Australian outlaw—a good man forced by circumstances to live a life of crime. Carey uses diary form to relay Kelly's story of a dirt-poor life in the Outback: the vernacular of a young man on the run makes it even more poignant. Kelly has a good deal of popular support and leads the authorities on a manhunt that lasts more than a year and a half. By the end of the story, readers are rooting for him, too. The book has been a popular icon of Australian literature enjoyed by book groups and popular fiction readers alike since it was published in 2001.

Appeal: compelling, engaging, dramatic, character driven, dialect rich

FOR FURTHER READING

Readers who enjoy the casual, vernacular style of Ned Kelly's first-person story may also like *Anything for Billy* (McMurtry). Ben Sippy, writer of dime novels, meets up with Billy Bone, known later as Billy the Kid, and decides to write the Kid's story. Poignant, clever, and fun, this book is a good choice for Ned Kelly fans who enjoyed the dusty Outback and its hard-bitten denizens. *The Return of Little Big Man* (Berger) brings out the same kind of affection for folk heroes that Carey's tale of Ned Kelly does. Little Big Man is what the Cheyenne called Jack Crabbe: his early life story is told in the well-known western classic of the same name. In this sequel Crabbe narrates his life from the grand old age of 112, to set the record straight on his participation in the Old West. Finally, *Gunman's Rhapsody* (Parker) is about Wyatt Earp during his stint as deputy sheriff in Tombstone, Arizona, at the time of the shootout at the OK Corral. Parker's novel will appeal to Carey's readers because the famous men are not quite what they seem—neither all good nor all bad, as legend paints them. Parker's writing style is terser and his characters crustier than Carey's, but the frontier dust tastes the same.

Wanting, by Richard Flanagan

The governor of the 1840s penal colony in Van Dieman's Land (Tasmania), Sir John Franklin, and his wife, Jane, adopt an Aborigine child, Mathinna, when they realize they will have no children of their own. Instead of nurturing and loving Mathinna, Jane sets about a program of betterment for the girl, exposing Jane's racist attitudes and causing irreparable damage to the child. Sir John is later lost on an Arctic expedition and English writer Charles Dickens becomes obsessed with the rumors of cannibalism that drift home. Meanwhile, in contrast to Jane's life Down Under, Dickens's wife is fat and exhausted from bearing and caring for their ten children without help while Charles contemplates infidelity with a lovely young actress. In a deeply moving story, these many forms of "wanting"—of desire and compulsion, of savagery and refinement, of honor and love—are contrasted. *Wanting* earned several awards in Australia: the Queensland Premier's Award for Fiction, the Western Australia Premier's Award for Fiction, and the Tasmania Book Prize.

Appeal: complex plot, atmospheric, descriptive, disturbing, thought provoking

FOR FURTHER READING

Like Flanagan's book *Wanting, The White Earth* (McGahan) is atmospheric and intricately plotted. Set in the arid plains of Queensland, it's the story of a young boy taken in by his crotchety uncle who adamantly opposes the native title laws that would relinquish land originally taken from Aborigines by colonists. *The White Earth,* while not a historical novel (the action takes place in the 1990s), is a good suggestion as a timeless counterpart to *Wanting.* McGahan's moody and suspenseful novel describes the desolate ranch in the Outback and the ongoing racial strife still present today and will appeal to Flanagan's readers. In Andrea Barrett's well-researched adventure *The Voyage of the Narwhal,* the reckless and strong-willed captain, Zechariah Voorhees, leads the crew and naturalist Erasmus Darwin Wells to the Arctic in search of Sir John Franklin's missing expedition. She is so descriptive of life aboard ship and the chilly

North that readers can almost smell the ocean and hear the creaking of the masts. Barrett's book is thought provoking, and the story weaves through the lives of the characters into two main plot strands, like Flanagan does in *Wanting*.

The Lieutenant, by Kate Grenville

In 1788, commissioned naval officer, Daniel Rooke, sets sail on the first fleet bound for Australia to build a penal colony. The reserved and brilliant young man studies under the encouragement of his mentor, but when his dreams of becoming an astronomer falter, he befriends a group of Aborigines and is captivated by their culture and language. Rooke is bewildered by his colleagues' indifference to the Aborigines, and readers will be disappointed in their shortsightedness and insensitivity, too, as the inevitable confrontation approaches. Even Daniel's example of intercultural diplomacy and friendship doesn't stem the tide of greed and false superiority that drowns the chance of amicable relations between the English and the native Australians.

Appeal: lush, lyrical, strong sense of place, storytelling style, character driven

FOR FURTHER READING

A novel in diary form, *One Last Look* (Morrow) features Lady Eleanor, her ailing sister Harriet, and their brother Henry, who has been appointed governor-general in nineteenth-century Calcutta. Like Daniel Rooke in *The Lieutenant*, Eleanor falls in love with her new home and in a similarly lyrical voice tries to capture the gentle Indian culture and landscape she finds so fascinatingly different from her own. An overarching melancholy pervades both novels, as both characters and the reader become aware of an inevitable bitter end. *Out of Africa*, a memoir by Isak Dinesen (Baroness Karen von Blixen-Finecke), is a series of lyrical vignettes that portray the British experience of East Africa. The story of aristocratic society and life on a coffee plantation, Dinesen's lush descriptions of nature and the exotic cultures create an absorbing, magical experience for readers in much the same way that Grenville does, though the book is both nonfiction and set on a different continent. In *The Collector of Worlds* (Trojanow), the life and travels of Sir Francis Burton portray the explorer-spy as a chameleon who absorbs the language and mannerisms of every indigenous culture he visits. The writing is stylistically complex, featuring stories within stories and many changes of location, which will appeal to readers who enjoy Grenville's storytelling style and lush setting descriptions.

EUROPE

Currently two types of historical fiction dominate the market when it comes to books set in Europe: books about World War II and biographical novels about famous leaders and rulers of all time periods, but particularly

---

Historical Fiction Set in Paris

Classics of historical fiction (some are now considered historical fiction)

A Tale of Two Cities, by Charles Dickens

The Three Musketeers, by Alexandre Dumas

A Sentimental Education, by Gustave Flaubert

Les Misérables, by Victor Hugo

The Scarlet Pimpernel, by Baroness Orczy

City of Darkness, City of Light, by Marge Piercy

An American in Paris, by Margaret Vandenburg

Paris, by Émile Zola

Recent historical fiction set in Paris

Lydia Cassatt Reading the Morning Paper, by Harriet Scott Chessman

The Secret Life of Josephine: Napoleon's Bird of Paradise,
     by Carolly Erickson

Pictures at an Exhibition, by Sara Houghteling

A Place of Greater Safety, by Hilary Mantel

The Paris Wife, by Pauline McClain

Abundance: A Novel of Marie Antoinette, by Sena Jeter Naslund

Paris, by Edward Rutherfurd

The Last Time I Saw Paris, by Lynn Sheene

The Coral Thief, by Rebecca Stott

The Book of Salt, by Monique Truong

April in Paris, by Michael Wallner

the Tudors. Novels about World War I are increasing in number, but for the most part, the sweeping historical novels tracing the history of Europe from its very beginnings and up through the centuries, have, for the most part, become things of the past. For instance, *Poland* (Michener) and Edward Rutherfurd's *The Princes of Ireland* and *The Rebels of Ireland* are the products of a previous trend, although readers looking for a full fictional history of these locations will still enjoy them. Other older historical novels that focused on setting, like *The Greenlanders* (Smiley) and *Kristin Lavransdatter* (Undset), which are still read today, portrayed the details of a place and its people in particular time periods. Modern historical novels with a strong geographical setting tend to be less about the history of that place than about the people in relationship living in the place. Stories tend to be less plot driven and more suspenseful, moving, and character oriented, as shown by nearly all of the examples listed in this section.

Skeletons at the Feast, by Christopher Bohjalian

Two desperate groups make an overland journey through war-torn Europe toward the end of World War II: one group flees the incoming Russian army and the other marches toward their own death. As a group of women prisoners slog away from the concentration camp toward cruelty, humiliation, and death, three mismatched individuals cross Germany, heading west hoping to meet up with Allied forces. Anna Emmerich, the aristocratic wife of a German officer (sent to war with their sons); her lover and the Scottish prisoner of war Callum; and Uri, an escaped Jew, are thrown together as they run toward freedom. Increasingly violent, the Nazis dispatch Jews with a vengeance, and the stakes are high for refugees in this lyrical novel of the redeeming power of love.

Appeal: suspenseful, descriptive, lyrical, moving, bleak, character driven, grim

FOR FURTHER READING

Michael Ondaatje, in *The English Patient*, also writes of the brutality of war as expressed through the ravished landscape and the broken wraiths who survived World War II to its end. Lyrical, bleak, and character driven like Bohjalian's book, Ondaatje's novel gives weight to the individual relationships and thoughts of the characters and will appeal to the same readers. In *A Thread of Grace* (Russell), Jewish refugees flee through the mountains of northern Italy to escape the occupying German forces in France. Readers will feel the chill of early mornings and the bitter silence of the landscape awaiting war. Anita Diamant's book *Day after Night* follows four young women who develop a healing relationship in a refugee camp in Palestine following World War II. Diamant relates each character's horrific past, bringing sadness a step toward hope as life begins anew, in a similar fashion to Bohjalian's "skeletons."

The Voyage of the Short Serpent, by Bernard du Boucheron

Told in a stark manner almost as bleak as the fifteenth-century Icelandic landscape, this is the tale of settlers whose physical distance from civilization causes them to revert to pagan ways—even to the point of cannibalism. The *Short Serpent*, a ship sent out by a representative of the Catholic Church, carries Inquisitor Ordinary Bishop Insulomontanus, whose mission is to bring the colony of New Thule back into the fold of Christianity by whatever torturous means necessary. This he does with gusto until the bitter climate forces the bishop to break some of his own rules to survive.

Appeal: haunting, disturbing, compelling, strong sense of place

FOR FURTHER READING

In *The Owl Killers* (Maitland), the medieval English village of Ulewic is ruled by a pagan cabal of men who brutally enforce conformity and will not allow Christianity to infiltrate their way of life. When a group of women choose to live separately from men in their own sanctuary and then crops fail, the Owl Masters take action. In a story as creepy and dangerous as *The Voyage of the Short Serpent*, spiritual battles are fought on a medieval stage surrounded by a physical darkness that's almost palpable. Readers who enjoy the creative violence and excesses of du Boucheron's novel will recognize the geography of evil and the tension of horrors waiting to happen. Similarly, the deeply unsettling and vicious cruelties of life for women healers accused of witchcraft in *Daughters of the Witching Hill* (Sharratt) will resonate with those who are both appalled and fascinated by the endless cruelties humans inflict on one another. Set in seventeenth-century Lancashire, England, Sharratt's novel illuminates the courage of "witches" facing persecution. In *The Mercy Seller* (Vantrease), a priest who sells indulgences falls in love with a Lollard copyist, a follower of John Wycliffe's Christian reformers, in fifteenth-century France. Religious persecution, a grim beheading, and the fearful suspense in this novel will appeal to readers who enjoy the grittier side of medieval life.

Roma: The Novel of Ancient Rome, by Steven Saylor

As mentioned already, few current time-sweep novels on Europe exist, but Saylor's fictional history of Rome is a very notable exception. Covering the years between the founding of Rome and the assassination of Julius Caesar, Saylor aims to familiarize his readers with the history of the great city through generations of two original families and their experiences of the events. The use of authentic details in each of eleven main historical events—including the founding of Rome by Romulus and Remus, Hercules' defeat of Cacus, and Rome's battle with Hannibal and the Carthaginians—helps cement the reader's sense of ancient Rome. The city is the novel's main character; the Potiti and Pinarius families are her audience, and their stories mirror the change of time.

Appeal: strong sense of place, richly detailed, fast paced

FOR FURTHER READING

The Ancient Egypt series (Moran)—*Nefertiti*, *The Heretic Queen*, and *Cleopatra's Daughter*—is the only recent sweeping historical fiction series about the ancient world that compares well to Saylor's *Roma*. The series features Cleopatra of Egypt, but her love affair with Marc Antony of Rome brings the action to Italy. Moran's novels are richly detailed and have a strong setting appeal. As highly biographical novels about influential royalty, they should also appeal to Saylor's fans. Edward Rutherfurd, mentioned several times in this book, is masterful at bringing the history of a place to life. Readers who love Saylor's time-sweep approach in *Roma* will find Rutherfurd's doorstop-length historical fiction sagas fascinating, especially his book *London*. *London* includes the period of the city's Roman history, and all together Rutherfurd squashes about two thousand years of history into one massive volume that, despite its length, scoops up readers into a richly imagined landscape along with its families of characters. Cynthia Harrod-Eagles authored one of the longest generational series around: The Morland Dynasty. The first book in the series, published in 1980, was *The Founding*, set in fifteenth-century England during the Wars of the Roses. *The Winding Road*, a recent installment (number 34), published in 2011, encompasses the Jazz Age and the early years of the Great

Depression. The appeal for Saylor's readers in this series is the sweeping history seen through the eyes of generations down through time, and the firm setting, from Yorkshire, Crimea, and the New World. The Morland Dynasty series will appeal especially to readers who enjoy a touch more romance than Saylor usually includes!

The Religion, by **Tim Willocks**

Set during the 1565 Turkish invasion of Malta, Willocks's deliciously long, dramatic historical novel is the first of a new series featuring the German mercenary soldier Mattias Tannhauser. A disgraced Maltese countess, Carla La Penautier, hires Tannhauser to find her illegitimate teenage son, whom she gave up at birth to keep him safe. Tannhauser accompanies Carla on a sea voyage from Sicily to Malta, but before they locate Carla's son, a suspicious monk tries to sabotage their quest. In addition, though not a religious man, Tannhauser agrees to be military advisor to the Knights of St. John the Baptist of Jerusalem during the siege by the Ottoman emperor Suleiman's forces, known as the Hounds of Hell. Various aspects of this drama are portrayed as if on a large screen: the sensual details of place, the violence, and the romance put readers right onto the set.

Appeal: plot driven, violent, well researched, lush, steamy, dramatic, swashbuckling

FOR FURTHER READING

John Ball imagines the gruesome, dramatic story of the Siege of Malta in *Ironfire*, a similar plot-driven, action-packed, and violent tale of torn loyalties, betrayal, and religious conflict. Ball's is also a novel of brilliant plotting, like *The Religion*, and includes an element of romance and missing children. *Ironfire* is so similar to *The Religion* that it's difficult to imagine a reader who wouldn't like both. *Agincourt* (Cornwell) is likewise gruesome and dramatic, although the action occurred 150 years before the Siege of Malta. King Henry V's forces faced a numerically superior French army at Agincourt and still defeated them. The setting is the English military camp before and the action during the battle, the setting of which mirrors the mood of the characters: dark, misty, stark, and angry—an atmosphere similar to Willocks's. Like Cornwell's action-packed battle scenes and sweeping dramatic moments in *Agincourt*, Spanish writer Arturo Pérez-Reverte's Captain Alatriste adventures are swashbuckling dramas packed with well-researched details; the third in the series, *The Sun over Breda*, is no exception. Readers who revel in the cinematic, visceral battle scenes and drama of lives in the throes of conflict in *The Religion* will appreciate it particularly.

CONCLUSION

By its very definition, historical fiction connotes stories set in a previous time period. For this reason, it is much easier (and perhaps more logical) to index historical novels by time period, major events, or names of famous people. Setting is usually considered ancillary to era, but as this chapter has illustrated, it can be the driving interest for some readers. Those readers who seek stories about a particular place or culture will greatly appreciate a readers' advisor who quickly understands the difference and can find the "right" kind of historical novel. As we read historical fiction, we can learn to earmark where place itself is a strong appeal: lush description, regional dialect, architectural details, nature, and culture distinct to an area.

5

BIOGRAPHICAL HISTORICAL FICTION

Unwritten though they may be, rules do exist for the writing of biography and autobiography, as James Frey discovered when Oprah Winfrey challenged his "memoir," *A Million Little Pieces* (2003), in an embarrassingly painful interview televised on January 26, 2006.[1] One of those rules is that the facts must be true and reasonably verifiable. Frey was aware that he had exaggerated the facts, and in some cases had created "facts" from whole cloth, still he allowed the book's publication as a memoir (rather than fiction) and eventually became known as "The Man Who Conned Oprah." An article in the *Smoking Gun* begins, "Oprah Winfrey's been had."[2] If defining real truth in biography is difficult, then what are the rules for biographical historical fiction?

Historian Alison Weir writes both historical biography and biographical historical fiction. Since 1992 Weir has published more than ten historical biographies, and since 2005 she has alternated her biographies with historical novels about some of the same figures. When asked in an interview with Lucinda Byatt of *Solander* (the magazine of the Historical Novel Society), Weir explained her enthusiasm for writing her first book of biographical historical fiction, *Innocent Traitor*, as an act of creative liberation: "Often when I'm researching, I wonder how the characters felt. But, as a historian, you have to restrict yourself to real facts, to what you can infer legitimately from what you're reading, so it's liberating to make that leap of the imagination and *be* your character." Weir further explained that she had already done the research on the Tudors for her nonfiction, and when creating her novel about Lady Jane Grey, she often used her own book, *The Children of Henry VIII*, as a reference: "All the details that I have learnt about over the years are very helpful when writing a novel. . . . I'd spent time reconstructing past worlds and now I had an opportunity to do it very, very colourfully."[3]

Readers rely on authors to do this research in all historical fiction, but most assiduously in biographical historical fiction. One way readers and readers' advisors can establish the historical accuracy of a novel is the author's inclusion of bibliographies, notes, genealogies, glossaries, photographs, maps, and even footnotes. Not all fiction authors go to these lengths, but curious readers who want to really know about a person from the past will scour these pages. Conversely, many readers who love factual biography are surprised by the depth of insight that comes when authors weave known facts into a fictional narrative.

DEFINING BIOGRAPHICAL HISTORICAL FICTION

Since biographical historical fiction is ostensibly "about" a character (or characters), the character, rather than the time period, is the central appeal of the subgenre. It's worth pointing out that if a person's name appears in the book title, the book's main appeal is most likely character. When seeking further reading suggestions in this subgenre, readers' advisors can first point to other titles about the same character. Readers who want to read about a historical person or family may wish to continue with more books on the same person or novels about the people who knew that person. It's still important, however, for advisors to think about other appeal factors, as we do in every readers' advisory interaction. A reader may be fascinated by Susan Vreeland's *Clara and Mr. Tiffany* and eager to find similar stories. She may describe the book as one in which a talented female artist and her work become subsumed under the name of a famous man. This summary could indicate an overarching interest in historical feminism. The reader enjoys reading about Clara Driscoll, but that is not her main focus. She may be equally absorbed by *The Painter from Shanghai*, by Jennifer Cody Epstein, in which Pan Yuliang reaches her artistic dreams through the auspices of a famous (male) general. Sometimes readers focus on a type of character, such as women artists from the nineteenth century, and other times on different appeals, such as language or atmosphere. We cannot plan for all the variants or combinations of appeal our readers may present, nor can we predict which historical characters future authors will choose to fictionalize. However, we can organize our thoughts around the kinds of biographical historical fiction currently in publication and its appeal. To help do so, consider this list of defining attributes of biographical historical fiction:

- The subject of the biography was a real person (or group of real people).
- Settings are well described and historically accurate.
- At least some of the supporting characters are historical figures.
- At least some of the narrative events actually happened.
- As in all historical fiction, the story is emphasized over the history.
- Where facts are not available, the author can create scenes to further the story, as long as they accurately represent the time period.
- The author can flesh out the characters as long as such personality traits can be legitimately inferred.[4]
- The author can invent interaction between characters and characters' thoughts and motives, as long as they stay true to the character and times.

THE APPEAL OF BIOGRAPHICAL HISTORICAL FICTION

Curiosity about historical figures and the period in which they lived is often the impetus that drives readers to seek biography or a biographical historical novel. We seek vicarious experience through a person's eyes not only to understand that person better but also to more fully realize complex issues and how they might have been understood at the time. Occasionally a work of biographical historical fiction informs readers about the present, providing the opportunity to compare historical characters with public figures readers might admire today. Other types of literature may lead readers to ask for biographical historical fiction, because it augments factual information or other historical fiction of the period and can provide easy access to historical characters introduced in school, in the media, or through research.

Sometimes the appeal for readers is more esoteric, as when a reader makes a connection between historical figures from different time periods on the basis of their personality traits and experience, such as the military leaders Julius Caesar and Dwight D. Eisenhower, the flamboyantly famous Marie Antoinette and Tsarina Alexandra Feodorovna, or the philosophical moralists Mohandas Gandhi and Martin Luther King Jr. In a conversation with readers, a skilled readers' advisor can identify the appeal of a particular biographical novel and match it to other historical biographical novels. Most often, though, readers make and look for connections between similar individuals living in the same time period.

Readers might enjoy a particular author's approach to biographical historical fiction and seek other authors of a similar nature. Philippa Gregory's novels stress matters of the heart and interpersonal relationships more than government or war. Her style is intimate and her characters are passionate and well drawn. When a reader asks for another author whose style and stories are similar, an author like Carolly Erickson makes a better match than the spare, melancholy tone of Hilary Mantel, even though all three write about the Tudors and their court. Perhaps a reader enjoys the military approach to biographical fiction of Conn Iggulden in his Emperor series about Julius Caesar, beginning with *The Gates of Rome*. In this case, while Colleen McCullough's Masters of Rome series most closely follows the action and subject of Iggulden, it may not quite get to the grittier descriptions of battles in progress. A match in pacing and style, though not in subject, might be a good choice: Steven Pressfield's novel of Alexander the Great in battle, *The Virtues of War*, for instance. We shouldn't assume anything about what readers might enjoy and instead offer them several different options.

WELL-KNOWN BIOGRAPHICAL HISTORICAL FICTION

The Other Boleyn Girl, by Philippa Gregory

The Boleyn sisters, Mary and Anne, are sent to Henry VIII's court by their parents in a scheme to catch the king's eye—and maybe even his heart. Luckily for the Boleyns, the king falls hard for Mary, who becomes his mistress and has two children by him. Meanwhile, Anne fashions her own plan to displace both her sister and the queen, Katherine of Aragon, and capture the king for herself. Gregory is a masterful storyteller who gathers up the reader's full attention with engaging characters whose sly machinations lend suspense to a tale whose end we already know. Gregory has a huge following of captivated readers who fall into her books with a happy sigh. This and all Gregory's historical fiction are representative of the biographical historical romance novel, popular since the 1960s.

Appeal: dramatic, romantic, compelling, leisurely, absorbing, well developed characters

FOR FURTHER READING

In the suspenseful *Mademoiselle Boleyn*, by Robin Maxwell, Anne Boleyn and her sister, Mary, are brought to the French court of Louis XII by their father, who tries to use them both as spies. Mary embraces her assignment and seduces the king. Anne, however, decides to order her own destiny, with the help of her allies, one of whom is Leonardo da Vinci. Readers looking for steamy romance and lush descriptions of life in the sixteenth century will enjoy both Gregory's and Maxwell's compelling portrayals of the Boleyns. In *The Queen's Rival*, by Diane Haeger, when Anne arrives in King Henry VIII's English court, she displaces Elizabeth "Bessie" Blount, one of the king's mistresses, even though Bessie is one of the only two women to bear him a son. As does Gregory, Haeger brings the Boleyn sisters to life in this absorbing love story, the third of a trilogy, also including *The Secret Bride* and *The Queen's Mistake*. Vanora Bennett's romantic *Figures in Silk* also features two sisters determined to win in life: one is a widowed businesswoman and the other becomes King Edward IV's mistress. While the story is set in a different time period, the engaging characters and immersive plot make this a good choice for Gregory readers.

Loving Frank, by Nancy Horan

The famous architect Frank Lloyd Wright designs a home for society elites Edwin and Mamah Borthwick Cheney and winds up in a secret affair with Mamah that eventually finds them both abandoning their marriages and children to live on the Continent together. Despite Frank's overpowering will and strong personality, Mamah carves a niche for herself as a translator of feminist writings. Upon returning to the United States, the couple settles in a gorgeous new home designed by Wright, until an almost unbelievable tragedy ends their life together. This literary fictional biography is frequently, avidly discussed by book groups (see appendix B for literary historical fiction and classics for book groups).

Appeal: dramatic, moody, romantic, character driven, intriguing, well researched, literary

Each of four women who loved Frank Lloyd Wright narrate their own story and comment on Wright's incredibly egotistic personality in the character-driven, literary drama *The Women*, by T. C. Boyle. Equally literary and also an interesting discussion group choice, Boyle's is an electrifying novel with a different atmosphere from Horan's but Frank's personality is clearly the same in both books. In *Clara*, by Janice Galloway, Clara Schumann coddles her musical genius husband, Robert, who has bipolar disorder, and still determinedly holds on to her own creative ability and strong self-image. Dramatic, well-researched, and richly detailed, Galloway's *Clara* gives Horan readers another perspective on the egocentric artists and the women who accommodate them. Unlike the other books mentioned here, *Frida*, by Barbara Louise Mujica, portrays the female artist Frida Kahlo, who, similar to Frank Lloyd Wright, was single-minded in pursuit of her art, volatile in her relationships, and (like her artist husband, Diego Rivera) indulged freely in love affairs, insisting on her right to do as she pleased. Sensuous detail, dramatic, and engrossing, this is a biographical novel that Horan's readers will appreciate.

The Conqueror: A Novel of Kublai Khan, by Conn Iggulden

Fifth in the Conqueror series by Iggulden, *The Conqueror* is the story of Kublai Khan's brutal takeover of Genghis Khan's empire in a power play with his three brothers. His kingdom extended over China, Mongolia, and some outlying areas, and he established the Yuan dynasty. Full of great battle details and the gritty realities of nomadic life in thirteenth-century Asia, this high-energy, violent novel is representative of the military and adventure biographical novel.

Appeal: action packed, epic, atmospheric, violent, gritty, lavishly detailed

In ninth-century Britain—an earlier time frame than Iggulden's Kublai Khan story, Danish marauders attempt to take the Saxon throne from King Alfred, but Uhtred defeats them in the gritty, violent, dramatic, and bloody Battle of Farnham, in *The Burning Land*, by Bernard Cornwell. Readers who enjoy Iggulden's portrayal of aggressive power plays will revel in Cornwell's detailed and action-packed battle scenes in this fifth in

Cornwell's Saxon series.[5] Set even earlier in time, during the fifth century, Rome meets the Huns in an attack by Attila on the Eastern Empire and then in the West, where his former friend, Aetius, commands the Roman army, in *Attila: The Scourge of God*, by William Napier. Like Cornwell and Iggulden, Napier focuses on the gritty, violent aspects of battle in a fast-paced biographical novel about Attila, ruler of the vast Hunnic Empire, who nearly conquered the Western and Eastern Roman Empire and was one of the most feared warriors to ever live. The Attila trilogy continues in *Attila: The Gathering Storm* and *Attila: The Judgement*.

The Last Empress, by Anchee Min

Min presents a sympathetic portrait of Empress Dowager Tzu Hsi (first seen in *Empress Orchid*), told in first-person narrative, as she sacrifices her personal life to rule for her young son, Tung Chih, after the emperor dies in 1862. Stereotyped in the Western press as the "Dragon Lady," Tzu Hsi defied the rules of Chinese culture to hold the kingdom together for her family under tremendous pressure.

Appeal: well researched, authentic, detailed, engaging, character driven, feminist

FOR FURTHER READING

In *Empress*, Sa Shan portrays the seventh-century empress Wu Ze Tian, or "Heavenlight." Like Empress Orchid, Wu Ze Tian is a self-sacrificing, politically astute leader who rises from concubine to ruling empress, but she is disliked and vilified by the commoners. Filled with lavish details of court life, this story set in China hundreds of years before *The Last Empress* will appeal to readers who enjoy an engaging story of female leaders unafraid to fight for their position. In *The Commoner*, by John Burnham Schwartz, when the crown prince of Japan chooses a commoner as his wife in 1959, the path to acceptance is long and torturous for Haruko, who endures her mother-in-law's cruelty for love and leaves her family and her ambitions behind. Like Min's book, Schwartz's biographical novel is well researched and filled with details of royal life. Because Haruko is a commoner entering ethereal, complicated palace life, she is perhaps a more sympathetic character than the hard-edged, manipulative empress dowager in *The Last Empress*, although both books are character driven and tragic.

MAJOR HISTORICAL FIGURES

Some figures from the past are more fully explored in historical fiction than others, such as Alexander the Great, Julius Caesar, Cleopatra, Eleanor of Aquitaine, Henry VIII, and Queen Elizabeth I. For the most part, the novels listed in this section are only a few representative titles featuring these and other historical people. It's surprising to note these same names cropping up in biographical historical fiction over the years. In the mid-1900s authors were intrigued by the Tudors, and now many authors again are writing about the Tudors—we even have a television series and movies about them. The royal families of Britain and France, up and down the line from Henry VIII, are quite popular, and fiction about them and their time periods makes up a large portion of the historical fiction genre. For this reason, at least for the time being, readers' advisors can think of historical biography in broad terms rather than strictly by exact time period, which gets us into trouble when we can't remember relationships and birth dates on the spot. I like to think in terms of all the people who came before Henry VIII, then Henry VIII and his carousel of women, relatives and hangers-on, and then all the people who came after Henry VIII, many of whom are well represented in historical fiction, such as Elizabeth I, Joan of Arc, and Marie Antoinette.

Obviously, this is simplistic, but it helps me get a grip on the wide swath of history's important personages and the fictional historical biographies written about them. Biographical historical fiction is becoming very popular, with authors introducing works about new historical figures every year. The titles in this chapter represent readers' continuing interest in certain people from history.

BEFORE HENRY VIII

In roughly chronological order, here are some major historical figures repeatedly featured in historical fiction. Most of these titles and authors are well known and represent some of the best writing in the subgenre. Other biographical fiction may be every bit as deserving of our attention, but we cannot cover them all.

Helen of Troy, by Margaret George

This epic fictional biography is told in first-person narrative by Helen herself, as she is disappointed in her marriage to Menelaus of Mycenae and snaps at a chance for happiness with Paris, of Troy. According to one *Kirkus* reviewer, "the face that launched a thousand ships is supplied with a brain and a voice" in this sympathetic portrait of a beautiful young woman in a world of violent young men.[6]

Appeal: atmospheric, bittersweet, lushly descriptive, absorbing, page turner, elegant style, romantic, violent

FOR FURTHER READING

In Amanda Elyot's *The Memoirs of Helen of Troy*, a middle-age Helen writes her memoirs, in which she describes her early years, her capture by Theseus, her loveless marriage to Menelaus, and her loneliness and rejection at the hands of other women who were jealous of her beauty. Elyot's Helen is a bit more dramatic than George's, although both create equal sympathy in readers, and those who want more of Helen's story—told in an engrossing, almost mythic way—will be pleased with Elyot. An even more mythological novel, *Bring Down the Sun*, by Judith Tarr, introduces the mother of Alexander the Great, as Myrtale, the crowned one, who is the goddess's priestess, full of power and sensuality. Like Helen of Troy she must make her way in a foreign culture.

Fire from Heaven, *The Persian Boy*, and *Funeral Games* by Mary Renault

Mary Renault, in her popular Alexander the Great trilogy, has made Alexander of Macedon, or Alexander the Great, immortal in fiction. Renault explores all aspects of Alexander's life, from his military conquests to his personality and love life, bringing him to life through the eyes of those around him. *Fire from Heaven*, published in 1969, portrays Alexander growing up under the tutelage of Aristotle in the palace of King Philip. *The Persian Boy*, published in 1972, shows him from the perspective of his young captive lover, who had been a favorite of Darius III, the Persian king destroyed by Alexander's army. The final book in the trilogy, *Funeral Games*, addresses Alexander's death and the chaos that ensued as his family and generals scrambled for the throne. Although the first two books of this trilogy were first published about forty years ago, Renault set the standard very high and continues to be a historical fiction benchmark. Mention the whole trilogy to readers thirsty for perceptive, well-researched, detailed biographical historical fiction about Alexander the Great and a portrait of the heroic leader that's as vigorous as he was.

Appeal: character driven, thought provoking, well researched, lavishly detailed

Annabel Lyon brings her characters to life and postulates believable relationships that grab and propel readers through her humanizing story of the nascent talents of young Alexander, son of King Philip of Macedon, as he is guided in is studies by Aristotle, in *The Golden Mean: A Novel of Aristotle and Alexander the Great*. The book offers fascinating, sometimes amusing details about education and the training of young men in ancient Macedon, and it is written in an immersive, clean style that's a joy to read. In *Virtues of War: A Novel of Alexander the Great*, by Steven Pressfield, Alexander narrates his own story as the consummate soldier and military tactician placed squarely in his gritty, sometimes gruesome, battle-ready setting. Pressfield brings this ancient hero to life as a realistic, psychologically astute human being in the role of heroic leader and conqueror.

The First Man in Rome, by Colleen McCullough

The first five books in McCullough's Masters of Rome series feature Julius Caesar's life; the last two are accounts of Marc Antony and Cleopatra. The first book in the series, *The First Man in Rome*, was published in 1990, and the final volume came out in 2007. This series is still popular with readers and is often referred to in conversations about ancient biography. Readers who start with nonfiction biography of the well-known Julius Caesar may also enjoy fictional biography about him. McCullough is known for her ability to insert fascinating historical details gleaned from meticulous research into her skillfully rendered stories, transporting readers to ancient Rome and introducing them to flesh-and-bone characters.

Appeal: dramatic, descriptive, well researched, storytelling style, well developed characters, insightful, page turner, fast paced, complex plot, immersive

Emperor: The Gates of Rome, the first in his Emperor series, Conn Iggulden covers some of the same territory as McCullough: Julius Caesar's rise to power and his years of strong leadership. But in writing style the two series are very different. Iggulden emphasizes the military training and strategic acumen of Julius Caesar and its appeals are more its action-filled battle scenes and dramatic power scheming, in contrast to McCullough's spotlight on personalities, relationships, and intellectual gymnastics. Iggulden's fast-paced, suspenseful series focuses on the time period of Julius Caesar's life covered in the fifth and sixth books of McCullough's Masters of Rome series (*Let the Dice Fly* and *The October Horse*).

Cleopatra's Daughter, by Michelle Moran

Most recent in Moran's Ancient Egypt series, *Cleopatra's Daughter* is narrated by Kleopatra Selene, daughter of Antony and Cleopatra. When Caesar Octavian conquers Egypt, rather than murder the entire royal family, he kidnaps ten-year-old Selene; her twin brother, Alexander; and Ptolemy the Youngest, dragging the orphaned children to Rome, where they must live in the palace of their parents' enemy. Readers will enjoy the foibles and first loves of these teens as they grow into politically savvy adults amid the pomp and splendor of Roman culture and government.

Appeal: strong sense of place, richly detailed, lush, well developed characters

FOR FURTHER READING

Dragged through the streets as prisoner of war, Princess Selene, Cleopatra's daughter keeps her head to save her life and her brothers in *Lily of the Nile*, by Stephanie Dray. Selene becomes a lovely woman, desired of the ruthless Caesar and able to stand her ground against her enemies and their religion. Dray infuses her story with magic—not quite fantasy, but a hint of ancient power that sustains Selene and makes her mysterious, like her mother. Full of lush detail, character driven, and with a strong sense of place, Dray's novel is a good read-alike for Moran's book. The sequel is *Song of the Nile*. Cleopatra herself narrates Margaret George's *The Memoirs of Cleopatra*, in which readers view the ancient splendor of Egypt, Rome, and other Mediterranean areas that the great queen visited in her life, through her own eyes. Like all of George's historical fiction, Cleopatra's tale is full of shrewd observations about the many characters and situations she encounters, and it provides a full, absorbing portrait of a powerful and intelligent ruler. This novel is more reflective, intense, and atmospheric than the previous two about Princess Selene.

To Be Queen: A Novel of the Early Life of Eleanor of Aquitaine by Christy English

Eleanor of Aquitaine narrates her life, describing herself as a political pawn trapped in an unhappy marriage (to France's King Louis VII). Intimate and romantic, English's portrayal of this twelfth-century female dynamo shows us a determined woman who gets a second chance to choose her own future. As Eleanor grows into adulthood, rules as queen of France, becomes a mother, and falls in love with King Henry II of England, she learns how to manipulate her circumstances and bend people to her will.

Appeal: compulsively readable, compelling, romantic, strong sense of place, richly detailed, well developed characters

FOR FURTHER READING

The twelfth-century world that Margaret Ball describes in *Duchess of Aquitaine: A Novel of Eleanor* is perhaps more vividly colorful as she describes it. Eleanor of Aquitaine might not have actually been so passionate and strong willed, but readers well versed in this historical period will be swayed by the author's storytelling style as she traces Eleanor's progress from a spoiled rich girl in France to the assertive, mature queen consort of Henry II of England. Fast paced and immersive, this atmospheric novel compares well with *To Be Queen*. In the opening scene of *The Secret Eleanor*, by Cecelia Holland, Eleanor sets her covetous eyes on Henry of Anjou (King Henry II of England), in a foreshadowing of her later role as consummate manipulator ruled by her heart. Holland's book delves deeply into the pivotal year of Eleanor's life, when her marriage to the king of France dissolved and King Henry II of England became the love of her heart. Alison Weir also writes about Eleanor of Aquitaine in her book *The Captive Queen*. Her perspective on Eleanor and Henry is electric: the drama, the romance, the authenticity of detail, and the suspense compare very well to all the other titles mentioned here.

Lionheart, by Sharon Kay Penman

Penman's talent for intuiting the inner thoughts and feelings of her characters holds strong in this novel about Richard the Lionheart, his political trials, and his warrior's prowess. Richard, the second son of Henry II and Eleanor of Aquitaine, left England shortly after his coronation to gather an army for the Third Crusade. Penman smoothly outlines the instability between England and France and the power wrestling in the Plantagenet family and among their various followers. The microscope is on Richard, however, as he struggles in the Holy Land to best Saladin, a brilliant and worthy opponent. This is the perfect book for the serious historical fiction reader: Penman's research is impeccable, and her hand is sure as she brings her flawed characters to life.

Appeal: gritty, epic, fast paced, well researched, insightful, richly detailed, character driven

FOR FURTHER READING

Despite when they were published, readers still enjoy books by Jean Plaidy, so don't hesitate to suggest her dynamic and involving novels, with the caveat that Plaidy presents a very different Richard from Penman's. Her Richard is mighty in battle, gorgeous to look at, and not too savvy in politics. *The Heart of the Lion*, fifth in Plaidy's Plantagenet Saga, is more dramatic and suspenseful than Penman's *Lionheart.*[7] Like Penman, Cecelia Holland presents a realistic medieval world in which tempers flare, blood is shed, and might is right in *The King's Witch*, where Queen Eleanor sends Edythe, talented healer, along on Crusade with Richard. Although Edythe is accused of witchcraft, she's indispensible. Holland's research is impeccable, her perspective captivating, and her story as gritty and violent as the Crusades themselves. Finally, *Shadow of the Swords: An Epic Novel of the Crusades*, by Kamran Pasha, is not a biographical historical novel, but it does tell a compelling story of a Jewish woman who tips the balance of power in a bloody conflict that neither Richard I nor Saladin can win. Pasha asks readers to reconsider their perspectives on the Crusades in a fast-paced, suspenseful story that, like Penman's and Holland's novels, is gritty, violent, and realistic.

The Maid: A Novel of Joan of Arc, by Kimberly Cutter

A well-known legend comes to life in Cutter's rendition of the protagonist: Jehanne d'Arc. The improbability of a poor French girl marshaling an army to drive the English out of France disappears in an absorbing tale of Christian calling, unwavering faith, and courage. Jehanne becomes more than a tomboy in armor; she engages readers with her energy, devotion, and strong will. Cutter's tale is impossible to put down: a nineteen-year-old girl so vibrant but tragically cut down in a heart-wrenching and unjust charge of heresy.

Appeal: page turner, well researched, heart wrenching, engaging, character driven, violent, gritty

FOR FURTHER READING

Impeccably researched, Mark Twain's classic biographical sketch, *The Personal Recollections of Joan of Arc*, describes Joan of Arc as charismatic, driven, naive, and courageous. Twain's is a work of his heart: witty, not comic; heroic, not melodramatic; and utterly absorbing. Those who fall under the spell of Cutter's Joan will enjoy more of her in Twain's. While historical record of the Celtic warrior queen Boudica is scant, Manda Scott fills in abundant details of first-century East Britain in *Dreaming the Eagle*, in a style similar to Cutter's. She paints a broad picture of Boudica as a strong leader and warrior like Joan of Arc, committed to driving out an invading force. The Boudica series continues in *Dreaming the Bull*, *Dreaming the Hound*, and *Dreaming the Serpent*. Readers looking for more historical information on the historical saint may also want to try a good narrative nonfiction account, *Joan: The Mysterious Life of the Heretic Who Became a Saint*, by Donald Spoto.

The White Queen, by Philippa Gregory

The Wars of the Roses were a thirty-year civil war in the fifteenth century involving two branches of the Plantagenet family, fighting over the throne of England. The Lancastrians and Henry VI (red rose) were against the Yorkists and Edward IV (white rose). In a compelling, fast-paced read, Gregory portrays newly widowed Lancastrian beauty Elizabeth Woodville Grey, whom the Yorkist king Edward IV marries in secret, setting the stage for potential disaster or alliance. Two weeks later, the Yorkists beat the Lancastrians at the Battle of Hexham (May 15, 1464), securing the throne for Edward IV and his queen consort, Elizabeth. A tangle of intrigue and treachery results from changing loyalties, chiefly that of the Earl of Warwick, the king's friend then enemy. Edward and Elizabeth have two sons, Edward (the heir) and Richard, who later mysteriously disappear into the Tower of London. After their father dies, their Uncle Richard III becomes king. Gregory molds these events (and more) into a compelling, suspenseful saga that begins in this first volume of her Cousins' War series.

Appeal: character driven, leisurely, dramatic, romantic, suspenseful, richly detailed, compelling

FOR FURTHER READING

Told in multiple first-person narratives, *The Stolen Crown*, by Susan Higginbotham, is the story of Katherine Woodville, Elizabeth's younger sister. Readers get a unique picture of the blended York and Lancaster families in one household and how the marriage probably affected history. Higginbotham has a knack for character development and romance, which will appeal to Philippa Gregory's fans. Sandra Worth's *Lady of the Roses* is unabashedly romantic, a story of star-crossed lovers on a scale larger than that of Romeo and Juliet. The story features little-known Isobel Ingoldesthorpe, ward of Queen Margaret of Lancaster, who demands the right to marry Yorkist Sir John Neville during the bloody War of the Roses. It's romantic, bittersweet, and more violent than *The White Queen*, but it may still be of interest to Gregory's readers. Sharon Kay Penman weighs in with the romantic *The Sunne in Splendour*, which challenges popular opinion about Richard III by portraying him as a loving husband to Anne Neville and a canny politician who desires the throne but does not murder his nephews or his brother, King Edward IV. Penman's romantic story is compulsively readable, and its leisurely pace allows readers to savor the rich descriptions of the times.

The King's Daughter: A Novel of the First Tudor Queen
by Sandra Worth

Elizabeth of York was the oldest child of King Edward IV and sister to the two princes held in the Tower of London. Meek and shy on the surface, Elizabeth tells her inner longings to readers in a first-person narrative that meshes nicely with the confusing story of her relatives' jockeying for the throne. After nursing an unrequited love for her uncle Richard, at his death she stays behind to marry Henry VII, a Lancastrian, becoming the first Tudor queen of a united England and eventually the mother of King Henry VIII.

Appeal: richly detailed, moving, poignant, engaging, well researched

FOR FURTHER READING

Margaret Campbell Barnes mixes things up in the story of Elizabeth of York, Richard III, and Henry VII in her 1953 novel *The Tudor Rose*, which was recently reissued. Here Richard III (a cold killer) and Henry VII vie for her hand, and once Elizabeth marries Henry, Margaret Beaufort proves a loving, sympathetic mother-in-law. Like *The King's Daughter*, *The Tudor Rose* weaves a complex, engrossing story that may interest Worth's readers. In *The King's Grace*, Anne Easter Smith, a relative newcomer to the Wars of the Roses oeuvre, chooses an illegitimate daughter of King Edward IV, Grace Plantagenet, to witness, investigate, and narrate the drama surrounding the reappearance of the supposedly imprisoned Prince Richard, returned to claim his crown. Grace is a breath of fresh air in the fetid miasma of court intrigue, and readers who want a new perspective will enjoy her story. An older novel by Jean Plaidy, *Uneasy Lies the Head*, portrays a stressed out King Henry VII who is very busy securing the crown and quashing rebellions, marrying a Lancastrian widow, and siring an heir. More suspenseful and dramatic than either Barnes's or Worth's books, this (fictional) biographical treatment of Henry VII will appeal most to readers who enjoy Anne Easter Smith's and Philippa Gregory's royal intrigues.

THE REIGN OF KING HENRY VIII

We arrive at our randomly defined fulcrum of history: the period of the powerful and dreaded King Henry VIII, who demanded loyalty and obedience and punished all who dared defy him. Although Henry wasn't the only ruler whose character can be summed up as tyrannical, he is the one about whom a plethora of historical fiction is written and read. This section introduces important titles of which readers' advisors should be aware, as well as lesser-known but worthy novels to suggest to avid readers with an unslakable thirst for this period of English history.

The Secret Bride: In the Court of Henry VIII, by Diane Haeger

In love with Charles Brandon, the Duke of Suffolk, who was her brother's best friend, Mary Tudor agrees to a state marriage to the much older King Louis XII of France after exacting a promise that she will be free to marry whomever she chooses once Louis dies, proving

The Wives of Henry VIII (1491–1547)

Catherine of Aragon

Married 1509–1533
Mother of Mary I,
　　Queen of England
Divorced

Anne Boleyn

Married 1533–1536
Mother of Elizabeth I,
　　Queen of England
Executed

Jane Seymour

Married 1536–1537
Mother of Edward VI,
　　King of England
Died

Anne of Cleves

Married January–July 1540
Divorced

Katherine Howard

Married 1540–1542
Executed

Katherine Parr

Married 1543–1547
Widowed

that Henry's sister is as conniving and intelligent as he. She marries her lover secretly, after Louis is dead, wisely not trusting her brother to keep his promise. But as everyone knew then—and knows now— King Henry VIII will get his way, and because of the love he expresses for Mary and Charles, his betrayal is even more heinous.

Appeal: lavishly detailed, complex plot, insightful, suspenseful, romantic

FOR FURTHER READING

Henry's treatment of his beloved sister Mary after her unhappy forced marriage to Louis XII and subsequent secret marriage to Suffolk is also featured in a compelling and dramatic book by Jean Plaidy, *Mary, Queen of France*. Plaidy's novel was originally published in 1964, reissued in 2003, and is still read by historical fiction fans. Haeger's readers will find Plaidy's descriptive detail and suspenseful plot similar to *The Secret Bride*.

The Constant Princess, by Philippa Gregory

Gregory's romantic portrait of the infanta Catalina, daughter of King Ferdinand and Queen Isabella, brings Catherine of Aragon's childhood, early marriage, and later heartbreak to the fore. Catalina married and fell in love with Henry Tudor's older brother Arthur, and the author shares how she and Arthur schemed so that, for the good of the people, she would marry Henry when Arthur died. This she does, and she spends nearly thirty years as queen consort. In their early marriage, Henry proves a loving husband and father, showing readers a side of him that perhaps they hadn't known. The story includes the king's obsession with Anne Boleyn and his setting aside of Catherine in a characteristically riveting story of personalities and passions.

Appeal: romantic, suspenseful, richly detailed, character driven, dramatic, compelling

FOR FURTHER READING

Laurien Gardner's *The Spanish Bride* is the first book in a series about Tudor women as described by their closest friends, the portrayal of Catherine of Aragon's move from Spain to England, and her growth from an idealistic girl to a mature woman of prominence. The author details the dramatic events of Catherine's life and of those around her in absorbing detail. Gregory's fans will enjoy seeing the famous Catherine from these unusual perspectives.

Like Gregory in its intimate tone and romantic drama, Norah Lofts's *The King's Pleasure*, published in 1973 and reissued several times since, allows Catherine to share her own thoughts and feelings about Henry's changing loyalties, egotism, and betrayal with Anne Boleyn. Lofts's story is positively spellbinding. Nearly a decade before Lofts, Jean Plaidy published her trilogy on Catherine of Aragon (called Katharine of Aragon). Beginning with *Katharine, the Virgin Queen*, in her immersive and thoroughly researched style, Plaidy covers the queen's entire life in a mesmerizing, sympathetic voice: her story is romantic and compelling. Newcomers to the genre may not be familiar with Plaidy, and this trilogy will guarantee a new readership for this author who popularized the historical fiction genre in the mid-twentieth century.[8]

At the Mercy of the Queen: A Novel of Anne Boleyn
by Anne Barnhill

In *At the Mercy of the Queen*, Anne Barnhill writes parallel stories of Anne Boleyn and Madge Shelton, her fiercely loyal cousin and lady-in-waiting, portraying them both as somewhat conniving women determined to have loving marriages and, in Anne's case, a son and heir. Queen Catherine is losing Henry's attention and respect as years pass without a son, and Anne Boleyn hatches a plan to put Madge in the king's bed. Little does Anne know, however, that Madge is already pledged to another and agonizes over her conflicting loyalties. Barnhill expertly dramatizes the relationships and the motivations of her characters and reveals the famous queen in relation to a little-known character.

Appeal: character driven, dramatic, steamy, richly detailed, romantic

FOR FURTHER READING

Romantic and suspenseful, *A Lady Raised High*, by Laurien Gardner, is another title in her Wives of Henry VIII series. Barnhill's readers will be pleased by the upbeat tone of this story and insightful character traits noted by Frances Pierce, lady's maid to Anny Boleyn. In Sandra Byrd's *To Die For*, the queen's friend Meg Wyatt elects to stay with the condemned Anne and console her, in a richly detailed and dramatic story that delves into Boleyn's likable character more than most historical fiction. However, in *The Queen of Subtleties*, by Suzannah Dunn, the royal confectioner voices a less flattering opinion of Queen Anne. This leisurely, descriptive story centers on a letter Anne writes from prison to her daughter Elizabeth, documenting her life and blaming others for her downfall. Readers avidly seeking novels about Henry's many wives will enjoy reading about Anne Boleyn from these different perspectives, even if they conflict with one another.

The Favored Queen: A Novel of Henry VIII's Third Wife
by Carolly Erickson

It's easy to be the "favored" queen when married for less than a year to one of the most fickle kings in history! Outwardly, Jane Seymour was shy and unassuming, but Erickson creates an underlying personality for her: an astute observer of human nature, a schemer, and a bit of a bully. She was a loyal maid of honor to Queen Catherine, and she worked for Queen Anne, which placed Jane in a position to catch the king's eye. To him she was all sugar and posies, and she delivered to him his one legitimate son, Edward, at the cost of her life. Not for die-hard history sticklers who want accurate detailed stories that "could have" happened according to historical record and authorial logic: Erickson readily admits she stretched some historical facts to fit her story.

Appeal: romantic, suspenseful, dramatic, compelling

FOR FURTHER READING

A gentle, unassuming Jane is the subject of Laurien Gardner's *Plain Jane*. It is clear to readers, though, that this plain Jane is clever and conniving enough to catch and keep King Henry VIII. Not much historical fiction is devoted to Jane Seymour, probably because she died shortly after the birth of her only child, Edward, and was queen for only five months. Nevertheless, Gardner and Erickson give us enough romance and intrigue to make her a compelling character.

The Boleyn Inheritance, by Philippa Gregory

The only member of the Boleyn clan still living, Jane schemes to put her cousin, Katherine Howard, on the throne by discrediting Anne (of Cleves), whom she served as lady-in-waiting. Jane Boleyn, or Lady Rochford, is the evil former sister-in-law to the king. She doomed both her husband and sister to the block, and she is still plotting havoc among the Tudors. Luckily for Anne of Cleves, her marriage to King Henry VIII was annulled, and she never became official consort. Gregory brings out backstabbing and court intrigue, with Henry as the overbearing dupe, but she builds suspense throughout, despite readers' knowledge of the story's end.

Appeal: leisurely, dramatic, compelling, romantic, richly detailed, suspenseful

FOR FURTHER READING

Historical accuracy notwithstanding, Margaret Campbell Barnes's portrait of Anne of Cleves, in *My Lady of Cleves*, is richly imagined and highly entertaining. Anne is described as an intelligent woman who manages both to placate Henry and to get along with all the Tudors. Like Gregory's portrayal of this fourth wife, Barnes's sketch is dramatic and leisurely paced.

The Confession of Katherine Howard, by Suzannah Dunn

Katherine Howard had a little fling to "confess" in this tragic story of a two-year marriage corrupted by hearsay and ending in vengeful beheading. When asked by the king if she was unfaithful to him, she implicates her ex-lover Francis Dereham, who lands in prison. Once again a queen's fate lays in the hands of her lady-in-waiting, in this case Cat Tilney, who knows Katherine's lusty nature. Someone betrays the queen, as readers know already, but is it Cat?

Appeal: dramatic, leisurely, character driven, richly detailed, steamy, gritty

FOR FURTHER READING

A passionate, distractible, naive teenager and pawn of her uncle's ambition, Katherine Howard doesn't stand a chance in fifty-year-old Henry's world of political savvy, intrigue, and power mongering. In *The Queen's Mistake*, the second title in Diane Haeger's Court of Henry VIII series, the rich details of court and the poignant romance will also appeal to Dunn's fans, who will appreciate another view of the girl bride.

The Last Wife of Henry VIII, by Carolly Erickson

Although she flirted with the king at a young age, Catherine Parr married twice before she wedded the more decrepit Henry in his later years. Catherine narrates her own story—one well known to Tudor fans—revealing a cultured, patient nature and an attraction and aversion to Henry that colors both her reluctance to marry him and her love for the dashing Thomas Seymour. According to the story, Catherine understands Henry best, although her marriage to him is not without the perils of rumor and his suspicion of her. Perhaps if Henry had lived longer, Catherine would have met a different fate. Erickson has come under some criticism for historical inaccuracy, but she is a great storyteller.

Appeal: romantic, dramatic, detailed, insightful, fast paced

FOR FURTHER READING

In Suzannah Dunn's *The Sixth Wife*, the last year of Catherine Parr's (Dunn uses an alternate spelling: Katherine) life is narrated by the Duchess of Suffolk, her best friend and confidante—and her worst betrayer—and by Parr's new husband, Thomas Seymour, with whom she had her only natural child, Lady Mary Seymour. Dunn's novel is dramatic and descriptive like Erickson's, but switches a gritty delivery for a romantic one and is leisurely paced.

AFTER HENRY VIII

The Memoirs of Mary, Queen of Scots, by Carolly Erickson

Written in Mary Stuart's voice, her narration delivers a different side of the political picture during the English reign of her cousin, Queen Elizabeth I: Mary sees herself throughout the story as the victim of her circumstances and the wicked machinations of her royal relatives and other enemies. Married at age fifteen to the dauphin of France and queen consort to him upon coronation, her royal position in France was short lived. When King Francis II died not quite six months later, Mary fled France for fear that her mother-in-law, Catherine de Medici, might take the throne of Scotland. The suspicious death of Mary's second husband sets off a scandal from which the queen flees with her third husband, the Fourth Earl of Bothwell.

Appeal: compelling, suspenseful, fast paced, spare, first person narrative

FOR FURTHER READING

In Margaret George's well-researched biographical novel *Mary, Queen of Scotland and the Isles*, Mary Stuart's charming personality offsets her political failure. She's presented as misunderstood and naive, living amid a tangle of plots and villainous treachery hidden by smiles and luxury. In *The Other Queen*, Philippa Gregory portrays Mary as Queen Elizabeth's prisoner in the Derbyshire estate of George Talbot, Earl of Shewsbury, and his conniving wife, Bess of Hardwick. Mary creates a hotbed of intrigue around herself in an effort to escape and wrest the crown from the queen. More dramatic than either George's or Erickson's versions, the romance and the suspense of *The Other Queen* will captivate readers.

The Confessions of Catherine de Medici, by C. W. Gortner

In this sympathetic portrait of a much-maligned woman motivated to put her sons on the throne, Gortner asks readers to consider Catherine's situation and ask themselves if she really was a conniving, manipulative evil queen, as she has been portrayed. Her life certainly wasn't easy—marriage to an unfaithful King Henry II of France, his death, the vulturous de Guise family's maneuvers to gain the throne, and her own ambitions for her three sons. Was she solely responsible for the massacre at St. Bartholomew's, or did extenuating circumstances account for the disastrous results? Gortner's Catherine de' Medici is a passionate woman: loving and driven—a woman who would give up her own well-being for the sake of her sons.

Appeal: intriguing, thought provoking, well researched, richly detailed

FOR FURTHER READING

Jeanne Kalogridis portrays Catherine as a shrewd, superstitious, sometimes ruthless woman buffeted by circumstances in *The Devil's Queen.* The Medici queen is a somewhat sympathetic figure as queen consort, kept out of the limelight until the death of her third son. The story is well researched, like all of Kalogridis's titles, and dramatic and steamy with barely controlled passion. In a more interior character focus, Jean Plaidy shows Catherine as an introvert who swallows hurt, pride, and ambition to gain the power and love she knows she deserves, in *Madame Serpent.* More suspenseful and dramatic than the other two titles listed here about Catherine de' Medici, this older novel will intrigue readers interested in this mysterious woman. Plaidy's trilogy Catherine de' Medici continues in *The Italian Woman* and *Queen Jezebel.*

Abundance: A Novel of Marie Antoinette, by Sena Jeter Naslund

Readers will be familiar with the story of a pampered Austrian princess forced to marry the dauphin of France at age fourteen and ended up meeting Madame Guillotine during the French Revolution. Marie Antoinette is often portrayed as clueless and overly attached to expensive clothing. Naslund reinterprets the hard evidence by showing readers the sumptuous, decadent French court through "Toinette's" well-meaning, naive eyes—a perspective that asks readers to reconsider her negative image and to be awed with her by the beauty of her new surroundings. Perhaps Marie Antoinette was an otherwise affable teenager bored by her indifferent husband and wanting only to please his relations by acting as agreeable as possible. Naslund's Toinette is likeable and compelling, and the story of her life races to a poignant end.

Appeal: lush, lavishly detailed, suspenseful, well developed characters, well researched, moving

FOR FURTHER READING

As she awaits execution, the queen writes of her life and loves in a narrative that reveals her naïveté regarding politics and courtly love in *The Hidden Diary of Marie Antoinette*, by Carolly Erickson. This engaging view of Marie Antoinette is painted with a good deal more melodrama and romance than Naslund's, but it may also be of interest to her readers. *The Queen's Lover*, by Francine du Plessix Gray, is the romantic story of the Swedish Count Axel von Fersen's love for Marie Antoinette. The novel details his passion for civil rights during the years they knew each other. First of a projected trilogy, *Becoming Marie Antoinette*, by Juliet Grey, is a sympathetic novel that covers Marie's early years as the Austrian princess who learns she's to wed the French dauphin and traces her difficult path to her French "rebirth." The second book is *Days of Splendor, Days of Sorrow*.

The Winter Palace: A Novel of Catherine the Great
by Eva Stachniak

Before Catherine the Great's reign, the Empress Elizabeth, daughter of Peter the Great himself, ruled Russia. Queen Elizabeth is a beautiful hedonist less interested in governance than in manipulation. When she deems it time to find a wife for Peter, her nephew and heir, Elizabeth chooses the Prussian Princess Sophie and moves her into the palace. Elizabeth engages a maid, Varvara, whom she also uses to spy on Sophie, now known as Catherine. Clever Varvara spies on both women and reports on their private activities to Chancellor Bestuzhev, a manipulative, cunning, evil man. The new winter palace is under construction throughout the story as Catherine inexorably rises to the throne, serving as a symbol of her mounting power.

Appeal: complex plot, strong sense of place, richly detailed, suspenseful

FOR FURTHER READING

The main protagonist of Rutherfurd's biographical historical novel *Russka* is Russia herself, as portrayed by the families of a small central town over time, from the second century to modern times. Through the generations of these families, the author illustrates how Russian folkways and historical events made the Russian people who they are. This can be a valuable insight for readers who want to understand eighteenth-century Russia and the context for Catherine's rise to power. Rutherfurd takes a leisurely walk through time, weaving an intricate plot and giving readers a richly detailed, strong sense of place. Although *Russka* is not a fictional biography about a particular person, it is definitely a biographical "place" book that readers of Stachniak's novel will appreciate.

TOPICAL FICTIONAL BIOGRAPHIES: ARTISTS

So far our discussion of biographical historical fiction in this chapter has roughly followed the time periods before, during, and after Henry VIII. Biographical characters featured are the ones most popular in this genre. The remaining headings in this chapter also treat well-known characters in historical fiction, but in three different, broad subject groupings: artists, writers, and heroes and villains.

The early 2000s saw an upsurge in historical fiction about art and artists. Books such as *Girl with a Pearl Earring* (Chevalier) and *The Girl in Hyacinth Blue* (Vreeland) gained great popularity with book groups and historical fiction readers. Vreeland continued her success with other books about artists in *The Passion of Artemisia*, *The Forest Lover*, and *Luncheon of the Boating Party*. Writers such as Karen Essex, with *Leonardo's Swans*, and Elizabeth Hickey, with *The Painted Kiss*, also joined the trend.

Some authors created fictional artists in character-driven stories set in historical periods. This type of historical novel may appeal to readers who demand historical accuracy of the artistic setting and do not mind a fictionalized character. These titles can be introduced to readers who are attracted to character-driven fiction set in the past. For instance, the literary novel by Michael Chabon, *The Amazing Adventures of Kavalier and Clay*, features two Jewish cartoonists in 1930s New York City; Sarah Dunant's *The Birth of Venus* is about a young woman encouraged to paint by her husband in Renaissance Florence; *Gould's Book of Fish*, by Richard Flanagan, tells of an art forger in an Australian prison; and *The Portrait*, by Iain Pears, is the story of an art critic sitting for a painting. These titles tie in with biographical fiction because they often include real historical figures in context and authentic historical details, but in this chapter, the focus is on fiction about actual historical figures that reads like biography.

Claude and Camille, by Stephanie Cowell

The beating heart of this moving portrait of the marriage of Claude Monet and his first wife, Camille Doncieux, is the atmosphere in Paris's art community during the 1860s and 1870s and the creative genius of Monet, originator of the impressionist movement. The story follows the first bloom of love as Monet finds his muse in Camille, the disapproval of her father, and the difficulties they face as a couple. Readers will be fascinated by the origins of this popular art style and the aspiring artists who were Monet's contemporaries: Manet, Pissarro, Renoir, and Bazille.

Appeal: lush, lavishly detailed, dramatic, thought provoking, moving, romantic

FOR FURTHER READING

For readers interested in the impressionist painters, Susan Vreeland's short-story collection *Life Studies* is a great suggestion. Each story drops readers into vignettes from the lives of famous artists as seen through the eyes of the people around them. Vreeland's luminous, easy-flowing style and insight into her characters will especially appeal to those who enjoy Stephanie Cowell's writing. Elizabeth Hickey, in *The Wayward Muse*, writes of artists on the other side of the English Channel, in Oxford. In this book, Dante Gabriel Rossetti spies Jane Burden and convinces her to sit for a portrait of Guinevere. They are attracted to each other, although Dante is married and the tragic scene is set. Darker than *Claude and Camille*, *The Wayward Muse* will appeal to Cowell's readers who will be equally moved by Hickey's portrayal of the love story and her lush setting descriptions in this dramatic, memorable novel.

The Painter from Shanghai, by Jennifer Cody Epstein

The story of early twentieth-century artist Pan Yuliang unfolds in her own voice as she describes her life as a teenager in a Shanghai brothel and her surprising rescue by the customs inspector Pan Zanhua, who brings her into his family as a concubine and encourages her to pursue her interest in art. Yuliang was one of the few women of her time to be educated at the Shanghai Art Academy and to gain recognition as a serious painter. Woven throughout her narrative is the story of women's hardships in Chinese society, which adds another dimension to the historical account. With the arrival of the Cultural Revolution, Yuliang flees the country and lives in France for the remainder of her life. Unlike many women portrayed in this type of biographical historical fiction, Yuliang proves herself truly devoted to her work, even above affairs of the heart.

Appeal: elegant style, well researched, intriguing, exotic, fast paced

FOR FURTHER READING

One hundred years before Pan Yuliang, in Edo (Tokyo), Japan, printmaker Hokusai Katsushika, famous for painting censored subjects in the red-light district and for his lovely seascapes, may have had a ghost painter—his daughter Oei—whose talent, unlike Yuliang's, was never acknowledged. Similar to *The Painter from Shanghai*, in *The Printmaker's Daughter*, elements of traditional Japanese culture come out in the story, especially the issue of women's worth and their ability to compete in a man's world. Katherine Govier brings out the angry drama of Oei's existence and focuses on describing everyday life for the lower classes and the driving force of artistic talent. In *Watermark* by Vanitha Sankaran, small-town medieval France bears little resemblance to the Asian settings of the previous two novels, and yet the main character, the mute albino Auda, who assists her father in his papermaking business, has to connect herself with men to practice her art. Sankaran tells a poignant, sometimes heart-wrenching story of a talented young woman who dares to make a life for herself that is out of tune with the times, like Oei and Yuliang, portraying a female character readers won't soon forget.

TOPICAL FICTIONAL BIOGRAPHIES: WRITERS

The trend in historical biographical fiction of highlighting art and artists has been eclipsed by an even more popular trend: stories about famous authors, the people around them, and sometimes even their fictional characters. Especially popular are Jane Austen and the Brontë sisters,

Charlotte, Emily, and Anne. Biographical fiction about poets is also popular, although it seems no particular poet is written about more than others. Outlined here are some representative novels about these authors and poets, as well as their families. Authors such as Daphne du Maurier, Jane Austen, and Charlotte Brontë are sometimes also featured in mystery series as sleuths. Historical mystery is considered a subgenre of mystery, not historical fiction, so it is not included in this section, but it is featured briefly in chapter 8 on genre blending. Only biographical historical fiction about writers' lives is included in this section.

Charlotte and Emily: A Novel of the Brontës, by Jude Morgan

The title of this accurate, moving novel is somewhat misleading, as Morgan introduces all the Brontës as part of the story, even though Charlotte and Emily and their works are in the limelight. It is aptly made clear that the Brontë sisters were able to write from their isolated village perched on the Yorkshire moors is nearly miraculous. It's astonishing that relatively poor young women could write about characters whose lives were so different from their own; incorporate the dreary, moody atmosphere of the landscape in which they lived; and succeed as authors in a man's world. Morgan paints a moving portrait of the three sisters, all doomed to die young; their brother, Bramwell, a young man who wastes his life; and their father, who was blind to his wastrel son's shortcomings.

Appeal: well developed characters, literary, strong sense of place, moving, bleak

FOR FURTHER READING

In *Romancing Miss Brontë*, Juliet Gael explores Charlotte Brontë's early crush on a married professor in Brussels; her love for her publisher; and later, after a long spinsterhood, her brief marriage to her father's curate. Gael deftly fits her biographical subject into her troubled family and the remote Haworth in this intriguing, moving story of Charlotte, told from an unusual perspective. In *Emily's Ghost*, Denise Giardina imagines an Emily Brontë who sees ghosts and roams the moors alone at night, in a passionate and romantic portrait of the woman who wrote *Wuthering Heights*, loved the same curate her sisters did, and died young. Readers curious about the Brontë sisters will want to dig further into their personalities in these two insightful novels.

The Lost Memoirs of Jane Austen, by Syrie James

The fictional diary of Jane Austen, found in an attic, tells the story of what happened during four years of previously undocumented time in the lives of the Austen family members. James posits a decline in the family fortunes, a move to Bath, and a loss of social status. In her diary Jane bemoans her spinsterhood and shares with her readers a love relationship that ultimately ends in a broken engagement. James movingly takes on the voice of Jane and her well-known, understated wit.

Appeal: first-person narrative, suspenseful, romantic, engaging, witty, well researched, moving

FOR FURTHER READING

Another author who imagines Austen's voice is Nancy Moser. In *Just Jane*, Jane's interior monologue speaks of religion, romance, and familial relationships in diary form, accurately outlining the author's adult life. Jane's sister, Cassandra, narrates the story of their bad luck in romance and the special bond between the sisters growing up at the bottom of the social ladder, in *Cassandra and Jane*, by Jill Pitkeathley. Both novels insightfully portray Jane's close bond with her sister and the hopes of both for romance despite their dire social misfortunes.

TOPICAL FICTIONAL BIOGRAPHIES: HEROES AND VILLAINS

Heroes can be anyone who is a rescuer or is admired by someone, and here we will look at historical heroes who are revered by some, reviled by others, and remembered by many. A variety of readers might enjoy western settings or folk heroes from other areas of the United States, though they may not have specifically asked for them. Outlaws and villains appear in genre western novels, usually as the "bad guys" in plot-based stories. Historical fiction focuses more closely on the character development of famous and infamous people from history, often portraying villains in a compelling light, and sometimes questioning the actions and motives of heroes. Readers who enjoy westerns will probably also enjoy biographical historical fiction about people from the Wild West in the United States and from Australia.

Readers of genre westerns and the novels of Cormac McCarthy and Larry McMurtry will all appreciate a readers' advisor who is knowledgeable about both biographical historical fiction in general and biographical historical novels of the Wild West in particular. (Chapter 8 more thoroughly discusses the genre blending of westerns with historical fiction.) Most biographical historical fiction in this subgenre is set in North America; creative readers' advisors can find these types of characters in other countries as well.

Etta, by Gerald Kolpan

Etta Place was beloved of Harry Alonzo Longabaugh, better known as the Sundance Kid. In Gerald Kolpan's *Etta*, the young socialite leaves Philadelphia when her disgraced father dies and makes her way west with the intention of becoming a Harvey Girl, one of a cadre of contracted servers employed in cafés and hotels along the railway in the American West. Etta is captivated by Longabaugh and his adventurous way of life, and she earns a place in his gang with her riding and shooting skills (being beautiful and sophisticated didn't hurt). In a fast-paced story that draws readers into the spirit of danger and camaraderie, *Etta* is fun to read. Readers might also enjoy the 1969 movie *Butch Cassidy and the Sundance Kid*, starring Paul Newman, Robert Redford, and Katharine Ross, which compares well with Kolpan's novel.

Appeal: storytelling style, engaging, fun, dramatic, romantic, detailed

FOR FURTHER READING

Executed for horse thievery and murder in 1880 in Australia, Ned Kelly is one of the most revered folk heroes down under, much like Butch Cassidy and the Sundance Kid. In *The True History of the Kelly Gang*, Peter Carey brings out Kelly's rare combination of good intentions and ingrained devilry in a saga told in letters written by the semiliterate Kelly to his baby daughter whom he will never meet. Readers will be moved by the harshness of the Kelly gang's existence and amazed that they eluded capture for two years, with the help of common people who accepted them and cheered them on. Billy the Kid is similarly loved as a folk hero and pursued by officials for his participation in criminal activities. *Lucky Billy*, by John Vernon, begins with Billy's bold jailbreak in New Mexico in 1881 and then flashes back to his earlier involvement in the Lincoln County War and revenge killings. Like Kelly, the Kid was forced into violence by his circumstances, and Vernon brings out the unique personality and pathos of a bad guy who became a hero in perpetuity.

Doc, by Mary Doria Russell

Doc, by Mary Doria Russell, explores Doc Holliday's witty, charismatic personality and his tough life as friend to the Earp brothers, as well as his ongoing battle with tuberculosis and his abiding love for Big Nose Kate (Mary Katherine Horony). Few authors can match Russell's eye for personality and understanding of motive. Holliday was an intelligent Southern gentleman and dentist who moved to the Texas frontier for his health and became a gambler and a gunman.

Appeal: moving, strong sense of place, richly detailed, descriptive, character driven, humorous, insightful, heart wrenching

FOR FURTHER READING

One of Doc Holliday's best friends from Dodge City was Wyatt Earp, and in *Gunman's Rhapsody*, by Robert B. Parker, the Earp brothers join Doc in a murder investigation in Tombstone, Arizona. Parker's style is spare and gritty—you can feel the dust in your pores and taste it in your mouth—the tone is witty and will appeal to Russell's fans who are accustomed to her dry humor. In *The Whip*, Karen Kondazian imagines the life of a broken-hearted widow who dares to wed a black man, loses him, and then spends her life as a man—swearing, smoking, and driving a stagecoach. These are the kind of people on the side of good in the Wild West who, like Doc Holliday, faced harsh reality with a set jaw.

The Ballad of Tom Dooley, by Sharyn McCrumb

North Carolina native Sharyn McCrumb pleads not guilty on behalf of Tom Dula, who was hanged for (allegedly) killing one of his lovers, in *The Ballad of Tom Dooley*. Tom returns from his stint as a Confederate soldier to find his beloved married to another man, although that doesn't prevent him from continuing a relationship with her. In the meantime two more lovers enter the scene, and in this tangled mass of relationships, one woman dies. McCrumb's perspective on guilt and innocence reflect also on the Civil War itself in this famous historical murder drama.

>   ***Appeal:*** well researched, violent, absorbing, dramatic, romantic, moving

FOR FURTHER READING

Allan Pinkerton has many secrets according to Eric Lerner's *Pinkerton's Secret*, although the biggest one is his love affair with his new operative, Kate Warne—the first female detective in what will become a very famous investigative agency. Suspenseful, romantic, and fast paced, this book, with its view of Pinkerton and Warne, is fresh, witty, and surprising, and it's bound to appeal to McCrumb's fans. Max McCoy's *I, Quantrill* is also a surprising portrait of a well-known Civil War personage. William Clarke Quantrill, a guerilla warrior for the South who fights under his own flag, tells his story of violence and brutality, exposing his thoughts and opinions about the war and humanizing a folk hero (and villain) who gave his life for the Confederate cause.

CONCLUSION

When confronted with the wide range of biographical historical fiction and an avid reader looking for suggestions, the savvy readers' advisor will first ask readers whether they are seeking a book about the same person they just read about. Usually readers want something similar, or perhaps a biographical novel about people who lived at the same time or in the same place. As always, it's useful to establish what kind of a story a reader enjoys, such as a first-person narrative, a suspenseful romantic book, or an atmospheric novel about an evil character. It can be helpful to keep in mind the key characters about which most biographical historical fiction has been written: Julius Caesar, Cleopatra, Eleanor of Aquitaine, Henry VIII and his court, Elizabeth I, Mary Queen of Scots, Marie Antoinette, and Catherine the Great. Remember the subcategories of historical biographical fiction devoted to famous artists, authors, and heroes and villains. Once a readers' advisor becomes familiar with the best-known authors of biographical historical fiction, it's easier to match authors to characters and time periods. For instance, knowing that Alison Weir and Philippa Gregory focus mostly on the Tudors and British monarchy; that Conn Iggulden and Colleen McCullough write about the ancient world; and that Susan Vreeland, Irving Stone, and Tracy Chevalier write books about artists can be a great help when you need to quickly pull book titles out for a reader (keeping in mind, of course, that most of these authors also wrote other types of fiction and nonfiction).

Once you've gained confidence—and found amenable readers—try suggesting historical fiction that broadens readers' understanding of the time period in which a historical figure lived. For example, you can suggest a nonfiction biography of the same person or someone that person knew, or pair a biographical historical novel with a more general story of the time period, geographic location, or subject. Mixing and matching in this way is one of the joys of whole-collection readers' advisory, which is covered more fully in chapter 9.

NOTES

1. "Oprah's Questions for James" (interview with James Frey), *Oprah*, www.oprah
   .com/oprahshow/Oprahs-Questions-for-James.
2. "A Million Little Lies: Exposing James Frey's Fiction Addiction," *Smoking Gun*,
   January 26, 2006, www.thesmokinggun.com/documents/celebrity/million-little
   -lies.
3. Lucinda Byatt, "Reviews/Interviews—Alison Weir," *Solander* 10 (November
   2006), *World of Words* (blog), http://textline.wordpress.com/solander/
   reviewsinterviews-alison-weir/.
4. Ibid.
5. Other titles in the Saxon Stories by Bernard Cornwell are *The Last Kingdom*, *The
   Pale Horseman*, *The Lords of the North*, *Sword Song: The Battle for London*, and *Death of
   Kings*.
6. Review of *Helen of Troy*, *Kirkus Reviews*, June 1, 2006, 535.
7. The Plantagenet Saga, by Jean Plaidy, consists of sixteen novels; see chapter 6 of
   this book.
8. Both Lofts and Plaidy spell the queen's name as Katharine, but the conventional
   spelling is Catherine.

6

HISTORICAL FICTION BY SUBJECT

Subjects usually touched on in historical fiction don't always match Library of Congress subject headings, and it can be tricky to find good topical historical fiction quickly. Sometimes, readers who ask for subject-based historical fiction are doing a school assignment; they are required to read a novel about the Revolutionary War or fiction set during the Great Depression. These are repeat assignments; we don't need to look them up every year—we can prepare ourselves ahead of time by finding quality fiction and keeping track of it (for more on how to keep track of what you read, see chapter 10).

Another common circumstance under which a readers' advisor is asked for advice on what to read next is when a historical fiction novel becomes popular. For instance, when the annual Seattle Reads book was *When the Emperor Was Divine,* by Julie Otsuka, readers clamored for more fiction about the World War II internment of Japanese Americans.[1] Recently, *The Help,* by Kathryn Stockett, fired up readers' imaginations and prompted a run on novels about racism and the American civil rights movement of the 1950s and 1960s.

Some lists are easy to put together on the spot, and a few prepared ones are good to have around for reference use and for browsing purposes. Consider making your own subject book lists for those topics you are repeatedly asked about as part of your historical fiction readers' advisory preparedness training! Some specific topics, such as Jewish, African American, Native American, and LGBT historical fiction, are treated in chapter 7. Chapter 8 covers genre-blended historical fiction, such as sea stories and Arthurian legends.

Many readers have one specific question: "Can you suggest a really great novel about the Civil War (or World War II, or another war)?" War is a topic of great interest, and it is highly researched, with an abundance of available literature—so much so that finding the cream of the crop can be difficult, especially with the time constraint of in-person readers' advisory. Most of us are aware of the classic works set during various wars, or at least we can recognize them in a list of titles. But without actually reading them, how can we know which newer books best fit the reader in front of us? We've all had that cringe moment when the only thing we can say is, "This one's quite popular." Compiling one's own lists is an ideal way to familiarize oneself with literature in this area and to begin thinking about appeal characteristics of specific titles. In the meantime, what follows are descriptions of four great current historical novels for each topic, representing different perspectives, for quick reference and helping you compile your personal reading plan. In this chapter I eschew the general practice in chapter 3–5 of suggesting benchmark or important titles with read-alikes or books for further reading in favor of concentrating on great titles on different popular topics that readers repeatedly request. In other words, rather than broadening the scope of books on a topic, the focus here is on paring huge lists down to key titles, with the understanding that readers can easily expand to other books on the same subjects. The main appeals of topical historical fiction are that the subject matter is the same with only slight variation and that the settings are similar, if not identical. Other appeals, while secondary, are mentioned in the following sections and can help readers choose which approach to the topic they will most enjoy.

AMERICAN REVOLUTIONARY WAR

Rise to Rebellion, by Jeff Shaara

Rise to Rebellion begins in 1770 with the Boston Massacre, during which five civilians were shot by British soldiers, setting off the first stirrings of a combative rebellion. Many famous key Patriots are featured in the story, including Thomas Paine, Paul Revere, George Washington, John and Abigail Adams, and Thomas Jefferson. The author is an expert at dramatizing the atmosphere of unease and discontent that preceded the American Revolution. The sequel is *The Glorious Cause*.

Appeal: dramatic, well developed characters, atmospheric, richly detailed

The Rebellion of Jane Clarke, by Sally Gunning

In *The Rebellion of Jane Clarke*, Jane shames her family by refusing to marry the man of her father's choice and goes to Boston instead to care for an ailing aunt. Jane witnesses events leading up to the Boston Massacre and learns the importance of standing on one's principles. A woman's perspective adds much to the reader's view of the altercation, and Gunning's keen eye for human nature lends new understanding.

Appeal: suspenseful, immersive, well researched, moody

Patriot Hearts, by Barbara Hambly

Hambly's portrayal of Martha Washington, Dolley Madison, and Sally Hemings is a compelling perspective on the role of women during the colonial period and how they helped create the beginnings of democracy in America. In contrast to Newt Gingrich's fictional coverage of early America in his George Washington novels, in which high drama and a fast pace move the story, Hambly takes a leisurely, highly detailed character approach to the subject, often featuring an internal battleground, or at least one taking place in the drawing room.

Appeal: compelling, leisurely, detailed, well developed characters

Valley Forge, by Newt Gingrich

In *Valley Forge*, the second of Gingrich's George Washington novels, General Washington and his troops are sorely tested during the winter at Valley Forge. Freezing, starving, and demoralized by their circumstances, the troops nevertheless transform into the grimly disciplined, determined military force that will eventually defeat the British at the Battle of Monmouth. In this fast-paced, tense story, Gingrich compels readers—through character sketches of both famous and unknown characters—to feel the gruesome and gritty nature of battle and the effort and lives it costs. This trilogy will appeal to readers who enjoy detailed descriptions of combat, battle strategy, and dialogue-rich narrative.

Appeal: fast paced, suspenseful, gritty, gruesome, accurate

AMERICAN CIVIL WAR

All Other Nights, by Dara Horn

Jacob Rappaport suffers a moral conundrum: as a Union soldier he's assigned to kill an assassination plotter, one who also happens to be his own uncle, whom he must kill during a holiday visit to his Jewish relatives. In *All Other Nights*, Jacob's life reveals the plight of American Jews during the Civil War: he is committed to the Union cause but also connected by business and family to North and South. Horn's complicated story shows several different perspectives, making it immersive and suspenseful.

Appeal: character driven, fast paced, atmospheric, lyrical, richly detailed, suspenseful

My Name Is Mary Sutter, by Robin Oliveira

Another unusual part of the Civil War is portrayed in *My Name Is Mary Sutter*, the story of a young midwife whose goal in life is to be a doctor. Unfortunately, even with a shortage of doctors, women aren't allowed formal medical training. This doesn't stop the tenacious Mary Sutter, however, who earns her medical experience in a Washington, DC, hospital assisting the chief surgeon. Oliveira's detailed descriptions of patients' suffering and the lack of adequate supplies and sanitation bring out the realities of war in a compelling, often heart-wrenching way.

Appeal: gruesome, gory, heart wrenching, taut, lyrical, compelling

The March, by E. L. Doctorow

In *The March* General Sherman's swath of destruction—his march to the sea—cinematically comes to life. Sixty thousand troops and thousands of former slaves marched through Georgia and the Carolinas in a move so unprecedented and demoralizing to the Confederates that it changed the outcome of the war. Despite the march's brutality and destruction, Doctorow brings his signature wit and talent for great characterization to full play here.

Appeal: character driven, moving, atmospheric, funny, complex style

The Widow of the South, by **Robert Hicks**

In an elegiac story of grief and loss based on a true story, *The Widow of the South* depicts a strong Tennessee woman whose farm is commandeered as an army hospital during the 1864 Battle of Franklin. Hicks perceptively depicts the mental and emotional states of various participants in and around the combat area to show how real people dealt with war after four hard years. In the Battle of Franklin, nine thousand Confederate lives were lost; one thousand of the fallen were buried in a field and then removed to the widow's property to prevent desecration of their graves.

Appeal: elegiac, romantic, compelling, well researched

WORLD WAR II

Note that Holocaust history and the Jewish experience in World War II is covered in chapter 7.

The Time in Between, by **María Dueñas**

Before World War II begins, Siri Quiroga, a seamstress in Madrid, is deceitfully abandoned in Morocco and thus misses the Spanish Civil War and its effect on her home. *The Time in Between* follows Siri as she agrees to return to Madrid, set up a shop there, and work as a spy for the British.

Appeal: fast paced, well researched, romantic, suspenseful

Pacific Glory, by **Peter Deutermann**

Likewise fast-paced, *Pacific Glory* is a big-picture drama about the war in the Pacific and close friends who participate in and endure it. Three main battles are covered in the course of the story: Savo Island, Midway, and Samar. Deutermann infuses his novel with the pathos of love, loss, and betrayal, and compellingly portrays the human side of war.

Appeal: fast paced, dramatic, suspenseful, romantic, moving

Killing Rommel, by Steven Pressfield

In North Africa, Field Marshal Erwin Rommel is poised to conquer Egypt, the Suez, and the Middle East with his Afrika Korps, as the British plan a risky mission to assassinate the Desert Fox, in *Killing Rommel.* The story is told from the perspective of young Lieutenant R. L. Chapman, a tank officer on the special-ops team sent behind enemy lines to complete the mission.

Appeal: fast paced, suspenseful, character driven, dramatic

The Rising Tide, by Jeff Shaara

Jeff Shaara's four-book series on World War II portrays famous battles and the men who planned or fought them, with an uncanny sense for getting into the head of each character. The series first, *The Rising Tide,* begins after the bombing of Pearl Harbor as the United States enters the war. The second book, *The Steel Wave,* describes the Allied D-Day invasion of Europe and its key players on both sides; the third book, *No Less Than Victory* features the Battle of the Bulge from the perspectives of Eisenhower, Patton, Churchill, and Hitler. The fourth book, *The Final Storm,* moves to the Pacific, where the long battle for Okinawa ends the war with nuclear tragedy.

Appeal: fast paced, immersive, richly detailed, dramatic, compelling, atmospheric

THE VIETNAM WAR

The Vietnam War occurred between forty and fifty years ago and all four male authors listed in this section served in Vietnam. So that makes these books not historical fiction, right? Well, yes, that's right—but readers who ask for novels about the Vietnam War–era are usually still asking about "history." They don't know if the author is young enough to not remember the war or is relating a fictional story with the details provided by experience. Since those who read about this war are increasingly younger readers who consider fiction on this topic as genuinely historical, and because these novels written by veteran authors are examples of the best fiction about the war in Vietnam, they are included here.

Matterhorn: A Novel of Vietnam, by Karl Marlantes

This recent popular historical novel set in the Vietnam War tells the story of Lieutenant Waino Mellas, a platoon commander sent into the jungles of Vietnam for a thirteen-month tour. Waino and his fellow marines suffer horrific conditions in the jungle, frequent surprise attacks, and the problems any group of strangers would experience under such pressure. In this bleak, literary, gritty coming-of-age story, the characters learn that danger isn't always recognizable and doesn't always come from the enemy.

Appeal: literary, coming-of-age, bleak, haunting, gritty, violent, richly detailed, suspenseful

Tree of Smoke, by Denis Johnson

A slightly older novel, *Tree of Smoke* (2007) is the haunting story of spy-in-training Skip Sands, his two brothers, their uncle, a nurse, and a Vietnamese spy, all of whom are in-country between 1963 and 1970. Major events occurring during that period are highlighted in relation to the characters in the story, including the assassinations of John Kennedy, Martin Luther King Jr., and Robert Kennedy, as well as the Tet offensive and the fall of Saigon. A *Library Journal* reviewer described the Vietnam era as one of "distinctive psychedelic brutality," an accurate description of this image-rich, bleak, moving, and spare war novel.[2]

Appeal: literary, bleak, moving, richly detailed, thought provoking, complex plot, complex style, haunting, spare

The Quick and the Dead, by Randy Lee Eickhoff

Eickhoff's novel is more adrenaline packed and suspenseful than the Marlantes and Johnson books, and it is suited to readers whose focus is action but who still want to read a smart novel set during the Vietnam War. In this story, the Native American Benjamin "Wingo" Wingfoot, a CIA operative fresh from an upcountry arms raid, is ordered to assassinate the Saigon prostitute Lisa Lee. Lisa dies, but not by Wingo's hand, and Wingo discovers the corruption surrounding his assignment; it can eat his soul if he's not careful. While the novel contains elements of suspense, it is also about a unique set of war horrors and the effect of the constant amorality of superior officers on those around them.

Appeal: suspenseful, action packed, thought provoking

The Lotus Eaters, by Tatjana Soli

Soli's suspenseful, dramatic novel is an unusual story about Helen Adams, a female combat photographer assigned to cover Vietnam. Her scrappy personality brings her to the top of her game and to the attention of a famous photojournalist, Sam Darrow. Soli's message about the complex relationships brought about by war is developed against the atmospheric, eerie setting of war-torn Vietnam.

Appeal: suspenseful, dramatic, poignant, character driven, complex style, richly detailed

WITCHCRAFT

Readers never tire of books about witchcraft and are riveted by the inhumane treatment of those suspected of being witches. Two areas of the world especially affected by the witch-hunt craze were Bavaria, in southeastern Germany, and Puritan settlements along the northeastern coast of the United States, the most famous of which was Salem, Massachusetts. The execution of women accused of witchcraft was rife in Europe in previous centuries as well, but in the United States it was during the seventeenth century that strict religious moral codes among the Puritans stirred up antagonism toward anyone who was different, especially women healers. Listed here are four fictional, historical perspectives on how society dealt with the problem of "witches."

The Hangman's Daughter, by Oliver Pötzsch

Set in seventeenth-century Bavaria, *The Hangman's Daughter* tells the story of hangman Jakob Kuisl, who is faced with finding a true child murderer or executing the supposed witch midwife who delivered his own children. When Jakob's own daughter disappears, the investigation turns personal. The story evokes Old Germany and the fearfulness of superstitious townsfolk. The series continues in *The Dark Monk.*

Appeal: fast paced, plot driven, suspenseful, richly detailed, compelling, strong sense of place

The Last Witchfinder, by James Morrow

In *The Last Witchfinder,* Jennet Stearne is the daughter of a British witch finder who is disgraced and exiled to America. After her own aunt falls prey to the witch hunts, Jennet vows to prove that witchcraft does not exist, thereby bringing down the Parliamentary Witchcraft Act. Her adventures bring her into contact with pirates, the Algonquin, and even Benjamin Franklin.

Appeal: witty, engaging, well researched, literary, thought provoking

The Heretic's Daughter, by Kathleen Kent

The Heretic's Daughter features nine-year-old Sarah Carrier, cruelly imprisoned with her brothers during her mother's trial and hanging in Salem, Massachusetts. Martha Carrier, a sharp-tongued nonconformist disliked by many, was one of the first women executed for witchcraft during the Salem witch hunts.

Appeal: compelling, heart wrenching, atmospheric, lyrical, literary, immersive

Corrag, by Susan Fletcher

In seventeenth-century Scotland, Corrag is accused of witchcraft and of participating in the Massacre of Glencoe. The book named for its protagonist is the account, in her own words, of British treachery at Glencoe and of Corrag's own attempts to save members of the clan. Told in a leisurely style filled with hypnotic descriptions of the lovely Highlands, this atmospheric tale is simply unforgettable.

Appeal: leisurely pace, character driven, immersive, lyrical, dramatic, strong sense of place

THE GREAT DEPRESSION

Often, US history and literature students request novels set during the Great Depression, during the decade between 1930 and (roughly) 1940. Sometimes book groups and individuals request a good read set in the Depression. Most readers' advisors know the classic novels of this time, such as *The Grapes of Wrath* and others by Steinbeck, *Tobacco Road* (Caldwell), and the Albany Trio (Kennedy). These titles aren't historical fiction but in addition to being of enduring value for older readers, they are often used in school assignments, and for good reason: they are excellent novels that realistically depict the time period in the United States. If reading a more recent title is acceptable, readers' advisors might also suggest the historical fiction titles in this section.

Jim, the Boy, by Tony Earley

In *Jim, the Boy*, Jim Glass, age ten, lives a normal, hard life in 1934 North Carolina and isn't ready to take on the adult issues he's slowly becoming aware of. Instead, young Jim rests in the security of his loving home, despite the Great Depression, and revels in childhood milestones as intense as the smell of a new mitt, his first baseball game, and besting a bully. The author's nostalgic tone, understated language, and gentle and contemplative style, descriptive of a world experienced at a leisurely pace, make this short novel a poignant, heartwarming meditation on growing up during this era.

Appeal: nostalgic, homespun, lyrical, reflective, strong sense of place

The Wettest County in the World, by Matt Bondurant

The author based his novel *The Wettest County in the World* on his own family history, which is a quite dramatic one. Set in Virginia during and after Prohibition, the Bondurant brothers, Jack, Forrest, and Howard, run a successful moonshine business, despite the corrupt law officials who want to not only shut them down but also take over their business. Each brother is a memorable character who works with the others to stave off poverty in an era of desperation.

Appeal: suspenseful, action packed, richly detailed, strong sense of place, atmospheric

Bucking the Sun, by **Ivan Doig**

Evocative of both the era and the West, *Bucking the Sun* transports the reader to the Montana boomtown of Fort Peck, over the course of five years in the 1930s, along with the Duff family, who move from their farm hoping to find work on the new Fort Peck Dam. Doig's homespun style and poignant descriptions of the place and its people combine for a funny, adventurous historical novel with a strong sense of setting—an upbeat look at the New Deal.

Appeal: nostalgic, poignant, strong sense of place, witty, lyrical, character driven

Stormy Weather, by **Paulette Jiles**

In contrast to Doig's upbeat *Bucking the Sun*, *Stormy Weather* is the sad story of a family broken and impoverished by the Great Depression. Elizabeth Stoddard and her three daughters return to their abandoned Texas ranch when her oil-prospecting husband dies. The hardscrabble rancher's life of constant debt and poverty, drought, and dust storms is brought to life in these women's stories.

Appeal: richly detailed, character driven, compelling, strong sense of place, gritty

HISTORY OF MEDICINE

Occasionally, readers express an interest in reading a historical novel about medicine or medical practitioners. It's relatively easy to come up with titles about midwives and doctors, but it can be time consuming and tedious to sort out the wonderful and unusual stories about medicine at different time periods. Plenty of Christian and genre western fiction series exist about pioneer doctors, but not all readers are interested in these perspectives on history and medicine. It's also worth noting that Christian fiction and genre westerns are usually more about setting and romance than about other topics, such as medicine, even though they may feature doctors or nurses as part of the story. It's a good idea, therefore, to have at hand a few really great titles to suggest, such as the ones to follow.

The Company of Liars, by Karen Maitland

While bubonic plague, dubbed the Black Death in the fourteenth century, was not confined to the medieval era, the sweep of infection that killed between 30 and 60 percent of Europe's population at that time began a centuries-long fear that still inspires authors to write about it. *The Company of Liars* is a historical suspense novel constructed around a band of nine outcasts who travel across Europe, fleeing from the path of the Black Death, each of whom holds a dire secret unknown to the others. Along the way, Maitland paints a vivid picture of the superstitions, the climate of fear, and the conditions that made Europe ripe for a pandemic.

Appeal: suspenseful, gruesome, bleak, richly detailed

My Name Is Mary Sutter, by Robin Oliveira

By the 1860s things hadn't changed much for women—they still were required to have the mentorship and teaching of male doctors to become more than nursemaids and midwives. Previously mentioned in this chapter as a Civil War novel, Oliveira's novel can also be suggested to readers interested in the history of medicine: it features a young woman whose talents as a midwife are sought after but who longs for the knowledge of surgery. Because the Civil War wounded fill hospitals to the bursting point, Mary Sutter stubbornly goes from one Washington hospital to another until, at the worst one of all, a doctor agrees to let her help—with cleaning. Oliveira vividly describes the vile conditions under which soldiers and the sickly suffer as they wait either to die or to get better. With bulldog tenacity, Mary eventually winds up in surgery with a saw in her hand and compassion in her heart.

Appeal: gritty, gory, compelling, lyrical, detailed

Moloka'i, by Alan Brennert

In the 1890s, Rachel Kalama experiences deep suffering of a different nature in *Moloka'i*, a novel set in the Kalaupapa leper colony on the Hawaiian island of Molokai. Diagnosed early in life, Rachel spends all of her childhood and most of her adult life in Kalama, an insular society and one that few visitors brave. The author compassionately tells the story of the patients' horrible lives as they try treatments from herbal injections to surgery and finally sulfa drugs. Even the beauty of the setting cannot erase the experience of Rachel and her fellow patients.

Appeal: strong sense of place, gritty, heart wrenching, compelling, character driven

A Fierce Radiance, by Lauren Belfer

By World War II, pharmaceutical companies had discovered that curing people doesn't always make money, which sometimes creates an ethical dilemma, as in *A Fierce Radiance.* Photojournalist Clara Shipley covers the story of penicillin's almost miraculous effectiveness in curing infections and its potential as an indirect biological weapon during war: wounded soldiers can revive and return. A mysterious death leads to the discovery that the pharmaceutical companies, in fierce competition with one another, are moving away from mass production of the patent-free green mold medication in an effort to get ahead in the market.

Appeal: well researched, suspenseful, dramatic, romantic

HISTORY OF SCIENCE

Like historical fiction about medicine, historical fiction featuring the progression of science and scientific discovery is specifically requested only occasionally, but a readers' advisor might like to suggest it when talking with someone who perhaps works in a scientific field or is interested in a particular area of science. Having a few titles at hand can make your conversation seamless and much easier. These novels, most of them set in the nineteenth century, or the end of the Age of Enlightenment, track scientific exploration and theories that many readers will find fascinating.

Remarkable Creatures, by Tracy Chevalier

During the early 1800s, fossils became a focus of science as paleontologists discovered and tried to explain the life forms they found engraved in the earth. In *Remarkable Creatures,* the potential drama of everyday life is portrayed by Mary Anning and Elizabeth Philpot, two women whose fossil-hunting forays lead them into the world of formal paleontology. Prior to Darwin, few braved religious disfavor and infamy to theorize about prehistory and human evolution. Anning and Philpot challenge that stance, stirring the embers of feminism in an effort to receive credit for their own discovery.

Appeal: leisurely, dramatic, immersive, reflective, strong sense of place

An Imperfect Lens, by Anne Roiphe

An Imperfect Lens follows Louis Thuillier, a protégé of the famous Louis Pasteur, on a journey to Alexandria, Egypt, to discover the cholera microbe. Forces against him and his team make his already-risky task even more difficult: the city is plague ridden and a colonial war zone. Thuillier, interested in stopping cholera, but also in winning approbation and glory for France, races against his famous German counterpart, Dr. Robert Koch.

Appeal: fast paced, richly detailed, immersive, romantic, literary

Measuring the World, by Daniel Kehlmann

The excitement of discovery and the new scientific method propel two German luminaries at the end of the Age of Enlightenment in *Measuring the World.* Alexander von Humboldt, an energetic explorer, is determined to map every river and lake he encounters in his South American odyssey. Carl Friedrich Gauss, an irascible mathematician, disrupted the scientific world as his personal odyssey of the mind made discoveries that most educated people of his time couldn't understand.

Appeal: character driven, fast paced, witty, poignant, engaging, offbeat

Percival's Planet, by Michael Byers

In *Percival's Planet,* a century after Humboldt and Gauss measure the world, the astronomer Percival Lowell paves the way for the discovery of Pluto by a Depression-era Kansas farm boy, Clyde Tumbaugh. Tumbaugh's naive wonder and excitement about the heavens are played off against the author's sharp observations about human nature—while an unassuming sky observer is thrust into fame. Byers is a skilled storyteller who brings an astronomical discovery into focus in this fascinating portrait of setting and character.

Appeal: romantic, storytelling style, lavishly detailed, reflective, dramatic, engaging, witty, literary

REGIONAL HISTORICAL FICTION

As noted in chapter 4 on geographical historical fiction, travelers, students, and other readers often ask for novels that will help them better understand the history of a particular place. Regional historical fiction evokes the atmosphere of a particular area in the United States, such as the South, the Northeast, the Midwest, or the West. Each region has a unique personality, culture, and landscape, which is reflected in historical fiction. People living in these different regions enjoy reading about their own "neck of the woods," and visitors often like to read novels that describe the history of places they are exploring. We may refer to Southern hospitality or the Texas twang; perhaps to the rugged nature of people in the West; or maybe to the stoic, silent people of the midwestern plains. These are ways we describe the type of regional diversity readers sometimes seek in historical fiction.

The River Wife, by Jonis Agee

Set in the Missouri Bootheel in the 1930s, a flat, remote landscape cut by the Mississippi River, *The River Wife* portrays generations of the Ducharme family and their dark legacy of betrayal and greed. The romantic and haunting story is filled with lavish descriptions of river life, characters who give way to passion and violence, and the sassy river wives who persevere.

Appeal: romantic, haunting, violent, lyrical, lushly detailed

Rainwater, by Sandra Brown

In Gilead, Texas, Ella Barron accepts David Rainwater in her boardinghouse, and with him hope arrives in Rainwater. In the drought-stricken area, a government program forces ranchers to relinquish their starving livestock, which is then shot and buried. Scavengers come to get the meat, setting off a dispute with the meat packers. This gripping story will captivate readers, as will the poignant romance between Ella and David. Brown sets hardship and hate against the bounty of kindness and love in this heartwarming historical novel.

Appeal: suspenseful, violent, poignant, romantic, plot driven, heartwarming, moving

Mudbound, by Hillary Jordan

In *Mudbound*, Henry McAllan buys a farm on the Mississippi Delta when World War II ends and moves his wife and children to foreign territory. The "farm" is muddy; there's no running water or electricity; and worst of all, racial prejudice is violently present—thus begins the downward slide of Laura McAllan's life. As Henry's friends and family come to stay, each person narrates his or her own perception of the events in this sophisticated and complex novel that exudes Southern atmosphere.

Appeal: strong sense of place, plot driven, haunting, moving, compelling, atmospheric

On Agate Hill, by Lee Smith

After the Civil War, the South lay in ruins, and many orphans were homeless, like Molly Petree, in *On Agate Hill*. Molly is taken in by her uncle Junius Hall and lives on his plantation at Agate Hill in North Carolina, until her uncle dies and a benefactor moves her to a boarding school. The author frames the story using an old box of mementos discovered in the house at Agate Hill during a much-later renovation, letters, court documents, and Molly's diary, to tell the sad story of Reconstruction and the patched-up, everyday lives of the war's survivors.

Appeal: strong sense of place, poignant, atmospheric, richly detailed

Bound, by Sally Gunning

In an intriguing, unusual meditation on the nature of freedom, *Bound* tells the story of an immigrant family who came to America in 1756 hoping for a better life. Three family members die aboard ship leaving Alice and her father, who are soon in trouble and in debt. To clear his debts, Alice's father binds her to eleven years of servitude and disappears. When life becomes unbearable, Alice escapes to Cape Cod, only to trade one type of service for another.

Appeal: suspenseful, immersive, bleak, moving, compelling

The Given Day, by Dennis Lehane

At the end of World War I, political unrest, uneasy views toward the future, and rising labor disputes came to a head in the Boston Police Strike of 1919, as shown in *The Given Day*. In this atmosphere of impending change and bloody rioting, Danny Coughlin, a police officer from a powerful family, becomes friends with Luther Lawrence, a former servant in the Coughlin household and now a suspected criminal. Their friendship illustrates a metaphorical bond between classes and America's changing values.

Appeal: literary, intricately plotted, leisurely, atmospheric, compelling, richly detailed

Baker Towers, by Jennifer Haigh

In the late 1930s, in the company-run Pennsylvania mining town of Bakerton, the five Novak children are raised by their Italian mother after their Polish father dies of a massive heart attack. Shown in *Baker Towers*, life after World War II is not an easy time for the poor people in Bakerton, who are literally owned by the mining company—and now the company and its town are in decline. Each Novak child has unexpected ties to Bakerton that prevent the escape to a better life in this melancholy and elegiac portrait of ethnic life in small-town western Pennsylvania. Haigh vividly describes the town—unadorned and unlovely—and brings the characters to life in a similar style to Lee Smith's books set in Appalachia.

Appeal: strong sense of place, melancholy, elegiac, character driven, complex style, moving

New York, by Edward Rutherfurd

New York is a sweeping historical novel about New York City, from its beginnings as an Native American village to the bombing of the World Trade Center on September 11, 2001. In his characteristic compulsively readable style, Rutherfurd takes readers on a journey through time, as the Dutch settle Manhattan, the American Revolution upends the government, the Civil War nearly breaks apart the country, immigrants come in waves, the Industrial Revolution provides a new way of life, and two world wars destroy the world as people know it. Many famous figures make cameo appearances, and characters come and go throughout time, but the main hero of this story is New York City itself.

Appeal: plot driven, complex plot, richly detailed, leisurely, strong sense of place, compulsively readable

A Season of Fire and Ice, by Lloyd Zimpel

In *A Season of Fire and Ice*, Gerhard Prager of the Dakota Territory ekes out an existence on an unforgiving farm with his wife and seven sons. Leo Beidermann, denizen of the same area, thrives and escapes hardship—and it's hard for Prager to tolerate. Zimpel brings out the eggshell-thin balance of interdependence on the prairie, where neighbors matter, in this dialect-rich portrait of midwestern farmers.

Appeal: strong sense of place, character driven, dialect rich, compelling

The Quickening, by Michelle Hoover

Iowa farm wives Enidina Current and Mary Morrow barely tolerate each other, but as closest neighbors—only a day's wagon ride away—they are forced to help and support each other. The isolated lives of women in the Midwest during the early twentieth century is starkly described in this subtle, deceptively dispassionate story told by two women who in other circumstances would never be friends.

Appeal: atmospheric, strong sense of place, lyrical, storytelling style, stark

An Unfinished Season, by Ward Just

In contrast to the lonely life of farming families, in *An Unfinished Season*, Chicago suburban living in the 1950s is dangerous and unsettling. Unions, class struggles, the shift to manufacturing on a large scale, McCarthyism, and abuse of power create a miasma of confusion for nineteen-year-old Wilson Ravan. Social tensions are mirrored in Wils's family as his father, a factory owner, rejects the unionization of his employees. Wils loses his innocence in this dryly funny, insightful story of a time and place in transition.

Appeal: humor, elegant style, atmospheric, poignant, thought provoking

That Old Ace in the Hole, by Annie Proulx

Similarly, *That Old Ace in the Hole* sends the young hog scout Bob Dollar to the tiny Oklahoma panhandle town of Woolybucket, among farmers determined to hold onto their land against the incursion of Bob's employer, Global Pork Rind. Sent to convince farmers to sell their land to be used for enclosed hog facilities, Bob Dollar instead is enchanted with the community and its quirky characters—including Ace Crouch, Jerky Baum, and Freda Beautyrooms—and decides to quit his job. Dialect rich and evocative of the land and its people and their dry wit, this leisurely tale is one to be savored.

Appeal: humor, leisurely, literary, dialect rich, strong sense of place, homespun, engaging

Heyday, by Kurt Anderson

In *Heyday*, after the California Gold Rush began in 1848, people flocked to the West to make their fortunes and reinvent themselves—all kinds of people, like an aristocrat from Britain, Benjamin Knowles; a war-damaged firefighter, Duff Lucking; and his strong-willed "actress" sister, Polly. Like many other questionable characters of the time, their past follows them on the journey west, but in the form of a killer. The suspenseful story of these three adventurers is symbolic of America's nineteenth-century rush toward change.

Appeal: romantic, suspenseful, fast paced, well researched

True Sisters, by Sandra Dallas

Almost a decade after the California Gold Rush started, Mormon converts push handcarts across the desert toward Utah in a 1,300 mile journey of extreme conditions, including a freak Wyoming blizzard, in Dallas's compelling novel *True Sisters*. Nannie, Jessie, Anne, and Louisa find strength in their friendships and faith as they trudge toward Salt Lake City in this unusual pioneer story.

Appeal: moving, compelling, atmospheric, homespun, engaging

The Living, by Annie Dillard

In *The Living*, the wilderness and the seasons come to life in this story of the very first white settlers in Bellingham Bay, Washington. Luckily for these pioneers, unprepared for the elemental moods and hardships before them, the Lummi people are friendly and charitable, despite the mutual distrust present between settlers and First Peoples during the late nineteenth century. The novel follows the two families who started the Whatcom community and their growth over the following generations, in a story embellished with the rich details of natural beauty and adversity overcome.

Appeal: leisurely, strong sense of place, haunting, dramatic, richly detailed, complex style, lyrical

The Whistling Season, by Ivan Doig

In Montana during the early 1900s, homesteaders need the help of a housekeeper and cook while they work the land. In *The Whistling Season*, the Millirons need to hire someone after the death of Mrs. Milliron. Their newspaper want ad leads them to Rose, whose answer leads with "Can't cook but doesn't bite." Rose's dry wit, whistling, and spit-and-polish attitude go far toward healing the Millirons' grief, as does Rose's "brother," a strange character who is conscripted to teach in the one-room schoolhouse. Montana's wild vastness and the people who dare its isolated places come to life in this easygoing read about a time and place sadly passed.

Appeal: heartwarming, strong sense of place, homespun, nostalgic, poignant, lyrical, leisurely

CAN YOU REALLY LEARN HISTORY FROM HISTORICAL FICTION?

One of the reasons many historical fiction readers give for their reading preference is that they can learn history painlessly by reading historical fiction. We've seen in previous chapters that historical fiction generally focuses on certain time periods, geographic location, and particular historical characters. So we can say it's easy to learn history from good historical fiction—up to a point. Some authors, like Philippa Gregory and Carolly Erickson, write mainly about the Tudors, and because they write so prolifically on the subject, reading their oeuvre can help readers form a mental picture of how royalty lived and their day-to-day concerns. However, this approach excludes whole classes of people from a reader's understanding of the era, and while the stories are historically accurate, they omit much of the cultural experience of the time.

Rarely is a readers' advisor asked to outline a swath of history using historical fiction alone. If readers are genuinely interested in learning history by reading fiction, then engaging them with authors whose historicity is accurate and whose material sparks an interest is of value. Readers' advisors should, however, point out the advantages of reading nonfiction material to augment the readers' learning in areas that fiction doesn't pursue. This wide-reading approach, known as whole-collection readers' advisory, in which readers' advisors make use of all media, reading levels, and genres—fiction and nonfiction—is an option to keep in mind when readers mention wanting to learn about a particular historical time period. Using the whole-collection approach to readers' advisory is discussed in chapter 9 of this book. In regard to learning history through historical fiction, by itself, fiction is a pleasurable way to explore history rather than an effective way to truly learn history.

The next section gives examples of how a readers' advisor might suggest a course of reading to people who want to expand their understanding of the sweep of English history. Series historical fiction is a good place to start, because series cover a relatively long period as experienced by the same family, group, or person. This type of fictional study may be taken in parts, such as by topic or event, like the Plantagenet family or the Wars of the Roses, or in a string of novels covering the course of human history (to develop reading lists covering a sweep of history, see chapter 3). Authors such as Conn Iggulden, Bernard Cornwell, Jean Plaidy, and Cecelia Holland are well known for tracking broad chronological histories in their series fiction.

The Queens of England, by Jean Plaidy

The following list includes the series title in chronological order by the book's main events, even though the books were not published in this order.

1. *The Courts of Love* (Eleanor of Aquitaine)
2. *The Queen's Secret* (Katherine of Valois, wife of Henry V)
3. *The Reluctant Queen* (Anne of York, wife of Richard III)
4. *The Lady in the Tower* (Anne Boleyn, wife of Henry VIII)
5. *The Rose without a Thorn* (Catherine Howard, wife of Henry VIII)
6. *In the Shadow of the Crown* (Mary I)
7. *Queen of This Realm* (Elizabeth I)
8. *Myself, My Enemy* (Henrietta Maria, wife of Charles I)
9. *William's Wife* (Mary II, wife of William III)
10. *The Pleasures of Love* (Catherine of Braganza, wife of Charles II)
11. *Victoria Victorious* (Queen Victoria)

ENGLISH HISTORY TRACED IN HISTORICAL FICTION

Queens of England series, by Jean Plaidy

Some readers prefer to read sweeping historical overviews written by one author rather than trying to put together a chronology of stand-alone novels or trilogies. Although her books are older and sometimes may seem dated (especially the covers), Jean Plaidy is perfect for this kind of reader. Her Queens of England series, starting with *The Courts of Love*, is a fascinating way to picture famous women from Eleanor of Aquitaine (1122–1204) to Queen Victoria (1819–1901). More than a Tudor or Plantagenet overview, this series includes queens seldom found in fiction, and it might be a good suggestion for readers of biographical historical fiction, too.

At the risk of viewing the past through a very small lens, a reader can quite easily put Plaidy's other series in chronological order for a great sense of English history. Jean Plaidy is a pseudonym for Eleanor Hibbert, who used several pen names throughout her writing career.

She wrote about two hundred books during her lifetime, ninety of which are under the Plaidy pseudonym.[3] Not all the Plaidy books are in print, although some have been reprinted. Many libraries carry some of the older titles and can order others through interlibrary loan. Some of Plaidy's novels are also available electronically. As the following suggestions illustrate, by inserting into Plaidy's chronology a few additional series by other authors, a fiction reader can cover most of the main recorded historical events of English history.

Appeal: character driven, dramatic, suspenseful, compelling

Saxon Stories, by Bernard Cornwell

The Saxon Stories consist of six novels, beginning with *The Last Kingdom*, which tells the story of Alfred the Great, first king of the West Saxons, who reigned from 871 to 899. Cornwell's style is forthright and fast paced, and his portrayal of Alfred and his men is well drawn and insightful.

Appeal: fast paced, dramatic, suspenseful, gritty, richly detailed

Norman Trilogy, by Jean Plaidy

William the Conqueror, was the first Norman king in England, crowned in 1066 after the Battle of Hastings. This trilogy, beginning with *The Bastard King*, tells his story and that of several other contenders for the throne during the eleventh and twelfth centuries. Plaidy never fails to bring her characters to life and keep them within the bounds of historical accuracy.

Appeal: character driven, dramatic, suspenseful, compelling, richly detailed

Plantagenet Saga, by Jean Plaidy

The Plantagenet rule began with King Henry II in 1054 and ended during the reign of Henry VI, with the Wars of the Roses, a civil war between two branches of the house of Plantagenet: the house of York and the house of Lancaster. The author introduces the key players in this turbulent drama to readers in an understandable and riveting story. Readers should start with *Plantagenet Prelude*.

Appeal: character driven, dramatic, suspenseful, compelling, richly detailed

Rose of York trilogy, by Sandra Worth

Richard III, the last Plantagenet king of England, ruled for only two years, until his defeat by Henry Tudor at the Battle of Bosworth Field in 1485. This trilogy, starting with *Love and War*, tells the story of the disappearance of his nephews in the Tower of London, the rebellions during his reign, and his final battle. Since these novels are more romantic and dramatic than others listed here, suggest them to readers who enjoy romance historical fiction.

Appeal: character driven, romantic, suspenseful, compelling, immersive

Tudor series, by Jean Plaidy

Beginning with the Battle of Bosworth and Henry VII in *Uneasy Lies the Head*, Plaidy's Tudor series relates the ongoing saga of King Henry VIII, his cruel reign, his wives, and the monarchies of his children, Edward, Mary, and Elizabeth. The eleven novels cover just over a century of English history, which Plaidy makes easy to remember through her vivid character portrayals.

Appeal: character driven, dramatic, suspenseful, compelling, richly detailed

Stuart Saga, by Jean Plaidy

Following the death of Queen Elizabeth I, the English throne was ascended by James Stuart, called both James I of England and James VI of Scotland, ruling both countries simultaneously. The Stuart Saga, beginning with *The Murder in the Tower*, tells the story of his difficult reign—and that of Charles I, executed in 1649; his sons Charles II and James II (who was also James VII of Scotland); William III (who was also William II of Scotland) and William's daughter, the well-liked Queen Anne—until 1714 when the Stuart rule ended. Again, Plaidy puts personalities to these confusing names and brings a rocky political scene to light with her ever-accurate historical details.

Appeal: character driven, suspenseful, compelling, richly detailed

Georgian Saga, by Jean Plaidy

Kings George I, II, III, and IV ruled during what we know as the Georgian period in England, from 1714 to 1830. The kings George I through George IV (and George IV's son William IV) were of the German royal dynasty of Hanover. Queen Victoria was the last Hanoverian monarch in the United Kingdom. Each regent in this Hanoverian line is highlighted in this wonderfully imagined series of eleven novels, starting with *The Princess of Celle*.

Appeal: character driven, dramatic, suspenseful, compelling, descriptive

Queen Victoria novels, by Jean Plaidy

Victoria reigned for most of the nineteenth century, and her twenty-eight grandchildren married monarchs and the highborn of many other countries, effectively extending her political reach and giving her the popular appellation "Grandmother of Europe." The author brings the queen to life, integrating the wealth of historical detail available with her fictional insights. The series begins with *The Captive of Kensington*.

Appeal: character driven, dramatic, suspenseful, compelling, descriptive

CONCLUSION

In thinking about topical historical fiction, it's good to keep in mind the kinds of subjects that readers ask about and whether a series might paint a larger picture than a stand-alone novel that occurs during the same time period. Make your own short book lists when you encounter repeat requests or notice new trends, to save yourself from repeating the same exercise the next time someone asks for the same thing. For instance, during 2010, after I read four new historical novels about witches, I began wondering if this would become a trend. In 2011 I noted two good historical novels on the same subject and began gathering titles for the list featured in this chapter, so I could quickly refer to books I have read and can suggest. Similarly, I found quite a few recent novels on the history of medicine and science so I put those lists together. The section on the Great Depression is one I use repeatedly, as novels from this time period are assigned every year in a high school near the library where I work.

Often readers request historical fiction on a particular region, as mentioned in chapter 4 on geographical historical fiction, where we explored the idea of traveling to different areas of the world and being fictionally prepared. In addition to exotic locations worldwide, US regions also have their own literature, history, and atmosphere. Some fiction writers— like Ivan Doig (West), Willa Cather (Midwest), Kaye Gibbons (South), and Sarah Orne Jewett (Northeast)—are associated with the history of a region. Sometimes a particular title will evoke a part of the country so well that it becomes synonymous with that area in readers' minds, such as *The Shipping News* (Proulx) and its Newfoundland setting. Knowing about these regions and the authors who write about them can help immensely in suggesting books for readers whose interest in an area may be part of their identity or merely a passing interest.

My approach to learning history through historical fiction has always been secondary to readers' enjoyment of the story and the characters, so it was interesting here to list series that might actually help one learn the chronology of history. Making your own historical fiction "curriculum" is beneficial for learning which authors have written historical fiction series and which periods and places they most often feature. Remembering these types of authors can make historical fiction suggestions much easier to pinpoint.

NOTES

1. Seattle Reads is an annual event sponsored by the Washington Center for the Book and the Seattle Public Library, during which the works of one literary author are read around the city, and book discussions and programs are held, featuring the author's most famous work.

2. Jim Coan, review of *Tree of Smoke*, *Library Journal* 132, no. 13 (August 15, 2007), 69.

3. Susan Higginbotham, "The Queen of Historical Fiction," *Solander*, November 2007, www.susanhigginbotham.com/subpages/plaidy.html.

7

CULTURE, ETHNICITY, RELIGION, AND GENDER IN HISTORICAL FICTION

Readers' advisors often note being asked repeatedly for historical fiction reading suggestions not only on specific topics, time periods, people and geographic locations but also on cultural and ethnic groups. Avid readers will snap up book suggestions in all areas of historical fiction, but the good readers' advisor also needs to have basic knowledge of cultural and ethnic literature of all types, especially if they work in a community where a more intensive depth of particular knowledge is desirable. The purpose of this chapter is to introduce a variety of historical fiction written about cultural and ethnic groups. Not all cultural and ethnic groups have a corresponding oeuvre of historical fiction written by or about them, nor are all such populations of specific interest to readers at any given time. It is wise to keep an eye on trends and to adjust one's collection (and reading) accordingly.

AFRICAN AMERICAN HISTORICAL FICTION

Not all historical fiction about African Americans is written by African American authors, and readers' advisors should ask if readers prefer to read works written by African Americans. Depending on a reader's preference, you might suggest titles by African Americans but also books like *A Million Nightingales* (Straight), *The Help* (Stockett), and *The Healing* (Odell), all well-known works of fiction about African Americans but written by white authors. It is good to suggest a variety of titles and then zero in on the ones the reader seems to respond to.

The bulk of current African American historical fiction is about slavery and its ongoing effects in society. Novels about slaves—their labor, traditions, and unfair treatment—are often, but not always, straightforward accounts of plantation life and slaves' efforts to gain their freedom. The intent of such books is, first, to tell a great story, and second, to inform readers about the horror of two hundred years of slavery and to vividly portray people experiencing the time period, not only to bring immediacy and understanding of what happened but also sometimes to elicit an emotional response from readers. Slave narratives were the first kind of antislavery books written by slaves; these were factual and told from the slave's perspective, such as *Narrative of the Life of Frederick Douglass, an American Slave, Written by Himself* (Douglass) and *Incidents in the Life of a Slave Girl* (Jacobs). Fictional slave narratives developed from this memoir style, such as *Clotel; or, The President's Daughter: A Narrative of Slave Life in the United States* (Brown) and *The Bondswoman's Narrative* (Crafts), originally written in the mid-nineteenth century and republished by Henry Louis Gates Jr. in 2002. Although these narratives are not historical novels, it's important to recognize the style in which they were written, in order to understand the historical fiction that has developed out of this tradition and how best to describe such works to readers.

A well-rounded knowledge of African American history and its literature should include key novels written during the Harlem Renaissance (1920s and 1930s), such as *Cane* (Toomer), *Passing* (Larsen), and *Their Eyes Were Watching God* (Hurston). These titles provide an entertaining and educational backdrop for a time period about which little African American fiction is otherwise available. Readers frequently request suggestions for fiction written in or set during the Harlem Renaissance and will appreciate knowledge of a specific title. Authors like the ones mentioned here, writing about the African American experience, were writing social commentary, not historical fiction, but like so many other older novels, these books can appeal to modern readers looking back on a historical time.

Likewise, many African American novels are set in the 1950s, 1960s, and 1970s, which for some readers will seem to be historical in nature, such as *Meridian* (Walker), *Freshwater Road* (Nicholas), *A Gathering of Old Men* (Gaines), *Native Son* (Wright), and *Invisible Man* (Ellison). Most of these titles were written about a period within the author's conscious memory.

Wench, by Dolen Perkins-Valdez

Wench dramatizes the complicated relationships between enslaved women and their Southern masters in this story set at an Ohio resort frequented by white slave owners and their black mistresses. While the men vacation, the women form friendships over the years and never dream of escaping, though the opportunity exists, until Mawu expresses her determination to flee her sadistic master. The author shows both the importance of women's friendships and the deep ties formed between master and enslaved mistress and between mother and children of their union.

Appeal: compelling, disturbing, character driven, suspenseful, thought provoking

FOR FURTHER READING

In the same time period, the mid-nineteenth century, former slave Henry Townsend is dying in *The Known World* (Jones). In multilinear glimpses of Townsend's life in a narrative that moves back and forth in time, readers learn of his close ties with his former owner, his purchase of land and treatment of his own slaves, and his choice to maintain the slave-based economy of the South. Thought-provoking, disturbing, and haunting, Jones's exploration of the slaves-owning-slaves issue in *The Known World* is like Perkins-Valdez's in *Wench*: not one character is truly free. *A Mercy* (Morrison) similarly reveals the loss of freedom through the life of a young slave girl, whose mother gives her away to pay her master's debt. The mother thinks relinquishing her daughter to a kinder master is an act of mercy, but Florens forever suffers the sense of betrayal and abandonment, causing her to seek and cling to love. Morrison uses a chorus of distinct characters to tell Florens's story, similar to the women's perspectives shown in *Wench*, in a comparably tragic and moving character-driven story set in the seventeenth century. In *Someone Knows My Name* (Hill) the author portrays a strong slave woman, Aminata, who refuses to relinquish her harrowing memories of capture, transport, and degradation and who never ceases to plan for freedom. She forms alliances, learns and teaches others to read and write, and becomes a midwife—a skill that allows her more freedom. Eventually she escapes and turns her skills to helping others gain independence. Aminata's experience is unusual, and while her story is different from the women's in *Wench*, the suspense and emotional impact are the same.

Some Sing, Some Cry, by Ntozake Shange

> *Some Sing, Some Cry* is an example of the African American family saga—a subset of African American historical fiction. In Shange's book, coauthored with her sister, Ifa Bayeza, seven generations of women represent the major historical events that mark African American history, from the Civil War era to the present time. In settings that range from South Carolina to New York City, seven women not only are the strength and backbone of their families but also represent African American women over time.

> **Appeal:** dramatic, lyrical, moving, atmospheric, suspenseful

FOR FURTHER READING

Sapphire's Grave (Gurley-Highgate) is another excellent example of the African American family saga, covering two centuries of the lives of women in one family, generation by generation. The story begins with Sapphire's capture in Sierra Leone in 1749 and shows the horrible conditions under which she lived and how she taught her descendants to be survivors. The book is powerfully dramatic and lyrical, told in what one reviewer called an "incantatory style,"[1] and this compares nicely with the musical atmosphere in *Some Sing, Some Cry*. Lalita Tademy's family saga *Cane River*, published in 2001, is also similar to *Some Sing, Some Cry* in its portrayal of four generations of strong, tenacious African American women living in an isolated community in central Louisiana. They survive slavery and racism and still maintain tightly knit families with faith and high goals as their legacy. The author draws on her own family history for some of the details in this story and its sequel, *Red River*, and she focuses the reader's eye on her characters in a thought-provoking, moving story.

A Lesson before Dying, by Ernest Gaines

> *A Lesson before Dying* spotlights racial injustice and the meaning of integrity. The protagonist, Jefferson, a young black man of limited intelligence, is found at the scene of a white store owner who was gunned down by black men in small-town Louisiana in the late 1940s. Jefferson was just a frightened witness, but he is arrested, jailed, convicted of murder, and sentenced to die. When his godmother, Miss Emma, observes his panicked, groveling condition, she begs the local black teacher to instruct Jefferson in how to die like a man: with pride,

a clear conscience, and dignity, for the sake of his family and his community.

Appeal: moving, thought provoking, suspenseful, lyrical, character driven, dramatic

FOR FURTHER READING

In 1955 a fourteen-year-old young black man from Chicago goes to spend the summer with his relatives in Money, Mississippi, in *The Sacred Place* (Black). A small act of defiance—refusing to put his change in a white store clerk's hand—sets off a barrage of killing that ultimately causes the previously compliant black community to organize an armed protest against whites' mistreatment of African Americans. In both Gaines's and Black's novels, the issues of integrity and injustice come to the fore. The innocent die because of prejudicial assumptions in both stories, which are dramatic, moving, and evocative of time and place. In *Bombingham* (Grooms), another young man is emotionally traumatized by the effects of violence and injustice. Walter Burke is a soldier in Vietnam trying to write to the parents of his friend who's been killed. Memories of his childhood in "Bombingham," Alabama—with its demonstrations, Martin Luther King Jr., and his mother's illness—come flooding in as he struggles with what to write. Moving, vivid, and violently detailed, this bleak tale moves at the deliberate pace of a somber protest.

ASIAN AMERICAN HISTORICAL FICTION

Much of Asian American fiction is modern: events in the stories occur since 1962 or within the authors' memory, but for most purposes, readers still consider them historical, and so this chapter treats them as such. People from Vietnam and Cambodia arrived in the United States mainly during the 1970s, making their stories more autobiographical fiction than historical fiction. For instance, *The Disappeared* (Echlin) traces the love and separation of a white Canadian woman from her older Cambodian lover, who returns to the killing fields in search of his parents. The story begins in the late 1970s during the Khmer Rouge. *Monkey Bridge* (Cao) is an autobiographical novel about a young Cambodian woman and her mother, airlifted from Saigon in 1975 and struggling with their new life in the United States. A newer book, *The Reeducation of Cherry Truong* (Phan), touches on the events in the Vietnam War, but is mostly about starting over, assimilation, and forgiveness. Most fiction by Indian Americans is also too current to be historical fiction, and if it is authored by an Indian American, the historical setting is often India or England.

Asian American historical fiction, as with most immigrant fiction, frequently references countries of origin and the conditions under which the characters emigrated. Not all Asian immigrants and refugees came to the United States, but the examples here are all about people who immigrated to the Americas. Historical fiction about Asian immigrants to Great Britain from the Indian subcontinent can be elusive but not impossible to find. The results of a search, however, can sometimes yield unusual results. A recent book, *The Thing about Thugs* (Khair), for instance, describes the nineteenth-century practice of phrenology through the story of a young Thugee cult member from India who is brought to England by scientists eager to study his skull size and shape in relation to his violent lifestyle in India. This is not your usual historical fiction, and it's certainly surprising! Likewise, in *The Impressionist* (Kunzru), the illegitimate son of a nineteenth-century Indian woman makes a lonely journey to England by taking on various identities. This book is also atypical of the Indian immigrant experience. Family sagas featuring Indian women forced to marry and immigrate to other cultures, such as *Bitter Sweets* (Farooki) and *The Tree Bride* (Mukherjee), are more representative of the common literary experience, but they aren't always strictly historical fiction, as the generations portrayed in them often follow the characters into current times.

The last category here includes historical novels about Chinese Americans who were instrumental in the growth and economic development of the United States in the nineteenth century, and Japanese Americans, often portrayed in historical fiction during World War II. Chinese Americans were often ill treated as they worked in gold mines, built railroads, and performed other menial labor during the 1800s. Stories of families in culture shock or separated during the 1920s and 1930s, and heart-wrenching stories of interracial love, are also typical of this subgenre. Japanese American historical fiction tends to focus on the tragedy of World War II internment camps in the United States and Canada, and on the huge effect this experience has had on individuals and the community at large. The titles here typify these main categories of Asian American historical fiction. Be sure to also direct readers interested in other Asian Americans' stories from the past to some of the titles mentioned already.

Deep Creek, by Dana Hand

Deep Creek combines elements of surrealism and metaphor in a story of nineteenth-century racism and violence. After finding mutilated bodies floating in the Snake River, police judge Joe Vincent undertakes an investigation and discovers dozens of Chinese gold miners' dead bodies in an Idaho lake. He is accompanied in his search for the killers by Lee Loi, a businessman of the Sam Yup labor exchange, and Grace Sundown, a French Nez Percé mountain guide. The killers are easily found—seven violent white men—and brought to trial, with disappointing results. Dana Hand (a pen name for William Howarth and Anne Matthews) re-creates the atmosphere of racial tension in the remote wilderness, where only scrupulously fair people like Vincent would bother seeking justice for murdered Chinese laborers.

Appeal: strong sense of place, fast paced, violent, suspenseful, complex plot, thought provoking

FOR FURTHER READING

Another gripping story of bigotry and injustice against Chinese immigrants, set in San Francisco during the 1840s, is *Daughter of Joy: A Novel of Gold Rush California* (Levy). Ah Toy's master dies during the ocean journey from China to the United States, and upon arrival Ah Toy has no choice but to become a prostitute. Linked to prostitution were powerful gangs of Chinese men who threatened and sometimes assaulted the "daughters of joy." When a gangster harasses Ah Toy, she takes him to court in an effort to procure justice at a time when injustice for Chinese immigrants was a fact of life. Based on a true story, Levy's novel brings modern readers' attention to bear on a little-known historical episode in Chinese American history, with her vivid characters and strong, descriptive portrayal of old San Francisco. Readers curious about the Chinese American experience during the nineteenth-century Gold Rush will enjoy comparing Hand's rural Idaho story with Levy's urban one. And like *Deep Creek*, *The Celestials*, by Karen Shepard, set in North Adams, Massachusetts, in 1870, also deals with a group of Chinese immigrant workers placed in a hostile environment, though with different results. Desperate to break a workers' strike at his shoe factory, Calvin Sampson brings in seventy-five young Chinese men from San Francisco to replace his angry absent employees. Readers who enjoyed the suspense of Hand's darker story will appreciate the tension and personal trials of the characters in Shepard's novel.

In the Shadow of the Cypress, by Thomas Steinbeck

John Steinbeck's son, Thomas Steinbeck, shares his fascination with local history of Monterey Bay, California, in his book *In the Shadow of the Cypress*. Chinese immigrant fishermen were among the first people to settle the area as far back as the 1850s. A 1906 journal written by a marine biologist, however, describes artifacts found in an old cypress tree that indicate the presence of Chinese explorers in 1422. The plaque and the jade carving disappeared under mysterious circumstances, and in the present time, the rediscovery of the journal sparks a new investigation into whether the Chinese preceded Christopher Columbus's arrival in the Americas.

Appeal: upbeat, thought provoking, strong sense of place, plot driven, leisurely pace, lyrical

FOR FURTHER READING

Similarly slow-paced and gently humorous, *Water Ghosts* (Ryan) is another unusual portrait of Chinese American life in the early twentieth century, this time in central California. The small agricultural community of Locke boasts a comfortable existence for its Chinese Americans, as exemplified by Richard Fong at his Lucky Fortune casino, which is next to Poppy See's house of prostitution. Fong's involvement with two women is cut short by the arrival of three Chinese women, one of whom is his deserted wife. Readers who enjoy Steinbeck's emphasis on language and atmosphere will appreciate Ryan's talent for the language of magic realism and sensuality. *The Hundred Secret Senses* (Tan) also exudes magic realism—in the form of fabulous stories told by Kwan, Olivia's Chinese half sister, who claims that her "yin eyes" enable her to see ghosts. Kwan's ghostly narrative about her past life alternates with Olivia's forward-thinking modernity in a complex and mesmerizing dance that highlights Old World and New World Chinese and Chinese American culture. Tan's charming humor and lyrical style will appeal to Steinbeck's readers.

Shanghai Girls, by Lisa See

In *Shanghai Girls* everything in their sheltered lives changes for Pearl and May Chin in 1937 when the Japanese bomb Shanghai. No more late-night parties or posing for "Beautiful Girls" calendars: they are sold to wealthy American businessmen to cover their father's gambling debts and then sent to the United States to marry strangers. In rich detail, the author describes the harrowing experience of the Angel Island immigrant camp in San Francisco and the stress of assimilating into American culture. As the Chin sisters learn to accept different living standards and the need for them to work, they discover how important it is to hold on to cultural traditions and the connection with each other.

Appeal: moving, lyrical, lavishly detailed, well developed characters, complex plot

FOR FURTHER READING

Inheritance (Chang) is similar to *Shanghai Girls* in several ways: the father gambles away his daughter in marriage, a betrayal severs family ties, and a Japanese invasion separates family members. Readers interested in Chinese life during the 1930s will also enjoy Chang's story, set in Taiwan and the United States, about sisters Junan and Yinan, whose love for the same man begets the next generation. Chang's spare style contrasts with Lisa See's descriptive prose while conveying the depth of emotion and sobering effects of a harsh period for young adults in China. Similarly dramatic is the three-generation story of women in one family as told in *Wild Swans: Three Daughters of China*, by Jung Chang. Chang's autobiographical story begins with her grandmother, who was sold into slavery as a concubine and later fled with her baby daughter, Chang's mother, who grew up to marry a Communist Party official under Mao Tse-tung. During the Cultural Revolution, Chang and her mother were "rehabilitated," and in 1978 the author left China. *Wild Swans* mirrors the same culture shock and dramatic women's story found in *Shanghai Girls*, tracing the changes in Chinese female experience over time and emphasizing individual courage and love.

Hotel on the Corner of Bitter and Sweet, by Jamie Ford

Set in pre–World War II Seattle, *Hotel on the Corner of Bitter and Sweet* by Jamie Ford tells the story of Chinese American Henry Lee, who befriends and eventually falls in love with Keiko Okabe, whom he meets at a prestigious private school. The story begins with Henry as a newly widowed adult hearing about the discovery of personal items left by Japanese Americans on their way to relocation camps in

World War II, found in the Panama Hotel. Henry's mind drifts back to his childhood forty years earlier, taking readers with him on a melancholy journey. The sad tale of forbidden love, of separation, accusations, and the pain of betrayal, as represented by the items left at the Panama—especially the shoes—highlights the injustice and disregard for humanity that prompted the Japanese evacuation.

Appeal: romantic, moving, richly detailed, character driven

FOR FURTHER READING

Likewise in *Obasan* (Kogawa), for Naomi Nakane, found objects spark memories of prewar security, the mysterious disappearance of her mother on a trip to Japan in 1942, and the family's disintegration as members are relocated to what Obasan (grandmother) calls "cesspools." Postwar experiences do not ameliorate the hardships of relocation camps, as the formerly middle-class Vancouver family winds up starting over—beet farming. Ford's readers will appreciate Kogawa's use of metaphor, her spare descriptions that evoke deep feeling, and her moving portrait of wartime loss. In *Bridge of Scarlet Leaves* (McMorris) a talented musician with aspirations to attend the Julliard School chooses to follow her Japanese American husband into relocation camp. Like *Hotel on the Corner of Bitter and Sweet*, this is a moving, richly romantic story not only about a couple daring interracial love but also about their families as they struggle to understand their relationship.

NATIVE AMERICAN HISTORICAL FICTION

Most historical fiction by and about Native Americans falls under one of two major themes: relations between Anglo Americans and Native Americans and issues of identity. Early pioneer novels depicted "Indians" almost universally as enemies: violent, sneaky, and likely to scalp the settler and make off with his woman. Dime novels published in the late 1800s were the beginning of this negative image, which persisted until as late as the 1980s. Novels such as *White Serpent, the Shawnee Scourge; or Indian Heart, the Renegade* (Gardner), published in 1870, revealed popular opinion of Native Americans. An excerpt from the story calls the Shawnee "savages" who gave "fierce yells" as they surrounded and attacked white men.[2]

Other dime novel titles reveal a similar prejudicial attitude: *Redlaw, Half-Breed; or, The Tangled Trail: A Tale of the Settlements* (Badger)[3] and *Glass-Eye, the Great Shot of the West*, by "Bruin" Adams (pseudonym of James Fenimore Cooper Adams),[4] in which a helpless woman is rescued from the Indians by the Great Shot himself, also belie popular thinking about Native Americans of the time. Some dime novels featured Native Americans as noble savages, in much the same manner as the Leatherstocking Tales, by the famous author James Fenimore Cooper, which chronicle the life and adventures of Natty Bumppo, a white man raised by Native Americans, and his Mohican "brother" Chingachgook. In the series both men are heroic warriors and trackers, good friends, and peacemakers—perhaps also an unrealistic portrait.

The age of early western films portrayed Native Americans in much the same manner, as evidenced by *Stagecoach* (1939), in which the Apache were "on the warpath." A 1966 remake of the John Ford film starred John Wayne and perpetuated the myth of Native Americans as savages and civilized people (on the stagecoach) in need of protection from them. In the television show *The Lone Ranger*, the Lone Ranger's faithful sidekick, Tonto, may have been a squeaky-clean nonkiller, but the series that ran from 1949 to 1957 did little to dispel the stereotype, especially as Tonto spoke in pidgin English.

In 1969 N. Scott Momaday's novel *House Made of Dawn* won the Pulitzer Prize. As a result of the critical acclaim and widespread popularity of the book, Native American literature became an entity of its own. *House Made of Dawn* is a literary coming-of-age novel set in the post–World War II United States, still enjoyed by students and book groups today. Also key to the development of Native American historical fiction and similarly a coming-of-age story is Forrest Carter's poignant novel *The Education of Little Tree*, which came out in 1976. Leslie Marmon Silko's book *Ceremony*, published the next year, focuses on the traditions and celebrations of the Navajo and Pueblo Indians, which eased Native American fiction in a slightly different direction. And finally, Louise Erdrich's time-sweep novel *Love Medicine* brought an even more personal perspective on Native American life, with a family story told by several individuals on a North Dakota Ojibwe reservation. These four novels are must-reads for readers' advisors who need to brush up on Native American literature, and they should be included in discussions with readers.

The historical fiction titles that follow represent currently popular novels about Native Americans that reflect a pride in surviving cultural traditions and sadness at what's been lost. Not every book listed is by a Native American author, though an effort has been made to include as much current historical fiction by Native Americans as possible.

Flight, by Sherman Alexie

Flight, by the well-known Native American writer Sherman Alexie, represents the unexpected time and identity shift experienced by a modern teen loser nicknamed "Zits." Unattractive in face and personality, Zits is starting a killing rampage when he is propelled back in time to the life of a mute boy who was silenced by a white man's gun. Time after time (literally) Zits travels on a metaphorical vision quest, learning about Native American history and his father—the hard way—through direct experience. Alexie's historical novel includes time travel, an element of fantasy—but it reveals enough Native American history to be considered in this chapter.

Appeal: funny, character driven, witty, magic realism

FOR FURTHER READING

In *Museum of Human Beings* (Sargent) Baptiste Charbonneau, son of Sacajawea, mixes with many cultures but does not identify with any one in particular. He seeks that identity on the trail, as a fur trapper and prospector, in the army, and among the elite of Europe. Readers who enjoy experiencing the school of hard knocks vicariously, as presented in Sherman Alexie's novels, will also appreciate Baptiste's journey in this darkly humorous, character-driven story. In *Black Hills* Dan Simmons calls even more on magical realism to create mood and a sense of historical importance given to the story of an old Native American man, Paha Sapa, who witnesses the Battle of Bull Run, channels Custer, and helps carve the famous white faces at Mount Rushmore. Paha Sapa represents the ambiguity of Native Americans living in an America transformed from frontier to parkland, and readers will consider his plight as similar to Zits's as he grapples with history. Elements of magical realism, wry humor, and great character development make *Black Hills* a good choice for Alexie's fans.

Caleb's Crossing, by Geraldine Brooks

In a story that skirts romance for another kind of heartache, *Caleb's Crossing* is ostensibly about Caleb Cheeshahteaumauk, the first Native

American to graduate from Harvard. The year is 1665; the story is narrated by a missionary's daughter and friend to Caleb who is refused a college education because she is a woman. Tensions between Native Americans and Christians, between classes of people, sexes, and races, are thoroughly probed.

Appeal: lush, detailed, lyrical, engaging, compelling, well researched, thought provoking

FOR FURTHER READING

Like Caleb, Sacajawea is one Native American in a large company of white people, and as such she is highly visible. *I Should Be Extremely Happy in Your Company* (Hall) re-creates the personalities and inner demons of four people on the Lewis and Clark Expedition: William Clark, Meriwether Lewis, Jean-Baptiste Charbonneau, and Sacajawea—their Shoshone Indian guide. Hall's work shares some of the same attributes as Brooks's: it's well researched, engaging, compelling, and lyrical. Readers who like to imagine the early interactions between Native Americans and representatives of America's traditionally white institutions will enjoy both these authors, as well as Joseph Boyden's novel *Three Day Road*, which tells the story of two reservation-raised Cree Indian boys who enlist to fight in World War I. One of the young men, Elijah, becomes a master sniper, concentrating on killing, and the other, Xavier, grapples with the ethics of killing; both are shunned by their fellow soldiers. Boyden's book is also a good suggestion for Brooks's readers as a detailed, compelling story about courageous Native American men who want to participate in society on their own terms.

Fool's Crow, by James Welch

In an elegy to the bygone Blackfoot way of life, *Fool's Crow* tells the story of how communicable diseases like smallpox, attacks by neighboring tribes, and the constant pressure of white incursions into Blackfeet territory in Montana brought about the demise of tribal life at the end of the nineteenth century. Welch is a master of accurate and sensual detail, and his effortless evocation of individuals communicating with animals and integrating their dreams into waking hours, as well as his descriptions of daily life, capture the reader's imagination.

Appeal: suspenseful, moving, elegiac, magical realism, compelling

FOR FURTHER READING

Another haunting, elegiac novel that will appeal to readers who enjoy *Fool's Crow* is *Pushing the Bear: A Novel of the Trail of Tears*, by Diane Glancy. Many voices narrate the nine-hundred-mile forced march from four Southern states to a reservation in Oklahoma: the Trail of Tears, during the Cherokee Removal of 1838. Maritole, with her husband Knobowtee, loses several family members along the way—in fact, one-quarter of the people died or disappeared on the grueling journey. Maritole describes her trek as "pushing the bear"—a heavy burden of fury, insanity, and pain. Readers will identify this burden as the same one James Welch describes in *Fool's Crow*. Similarly, a band of about eight hundred nomadic Nez Percé, the Lamtama, set out for Canada in an effort to elude the US forces who will force them onto a reservation, in *Aurora Crossing* (Schlesier). The main character is John Seton, half white and half Nez Percé, who joins the trek and experiences many of the traditional ceremonies of the tribe and the visions and signs that are common among the people. Schlesier provides intricate details of Nez Percé life, such as the making and tearing down of camp and the continual search for food, incorporating magic realism in a story as compelling as Welch's and just as likely to appeal to his fans.

A Plague of Doves, by Louise Erdrich

In the way of most Erdrich novels, a young Ojibwe person, here Evelina Harp, learns disturbing facts about her ancestors from an elder—her grandfather. The 1911 slaughter of a farming family in North Dakota and the subsequent lynching of Indians who actually saved an infant are the source of the conflict in *A Plague of Doves*. Like a family feud that lasts down the generations, this incident affects the locals on the reservation, as evidenced by a chorus of narrators eager to relate their story. The complicated interrelationships between the progeny of victims and assailants form the body of the story as the identity of the actual perpetrators gradually becomes known.

Appeal: lavishly detailed, moving, leisurely pace, complex plot, character driven, complex style, thought provoking

FOR FURTHER READING

Another complex, character-driven novel of revenge, *The Color of Lightning* (Jiles), is the story of Britt Johnson, a freed slave whose family has been kidnapped in a Kiowa-Comanche raid in post–Civil War Texas. Jiles's novel is likely to appeal to Erdrich's readers because the characters are real people, not caricatures, with conflicting emotions and complicated motives. In *The Color of Lightning* the kidnapped Johnson children do not want to be rescued: they want to stay with their new Native American family. Another story of revenge against Native Americans is *American by Blood* (Huebner), in which soldiers arrive a day late at the battle scene of Little Big Horn and chase after the Sioux, Cheyenne, and Nez Percé warriors responsible for the massacre of General Custer's troops. Three narrative strands give a compelling and suspenseful account of the skirmishes to follow as the Native Americans try to escape, which is stylistically similar to *A Plague of Doves*, as is the complexity of emotion involved in vengeance seeking.

LATINO AND LATIN AMERICAN HISTORICAL FICTION

Latino historical fiction explores some of the same emotional territory as Native American literature: racial discrimination and bigotry, violence, hardship, and political unrest. Like Native Americans in North America, the indigenous people of Latin America were radically changed by incoming white Europeans eager to settle and exploit the land and the people living on it. Those who immigrated to the United States from Latin America and the Caribbean also write of their homeland (or that of their parents) with passion and longing. Historical fiction by Latino and Latin American authors is a relatively new genre and for that reason fewer examples of well-known authors and titles are included here. The need to translate works originally written in Spanish also slows publication for English readers interested in this topic. Some of the titles suggested here are not by Latino authors but do reflect Latino and Latin American culture and concerns.

Inés of My Soul, Isabel Allende

Inés of My Soul dramatizes the life of Doña Inés Suárez, wife of a sixteenth-century conquistador, told as her memoirs, written in her old age. Left behind in Spain while her husband seeks his fortune in South America, Inés sets off in search of him and, after a grueling journey, discovers he has died. Unruffled, she is determined to stay in the New World and eventually marries Don Pedro de Valdivia, known as the conqueror of Chile and the founder of Santiago. Inés's character is unforgettably passionate, and her fighting skills are legendary.

Appeal: dramatic, character driven, lyrical, leisurely pace,
thought provoking

FOR FURTHER READING

Written in diary form, *Conquistadora* (Santiago) reveals the combative,
determined personality of another Spanish woman in the New World, but
several centuries after Inés. Descended from conquistadors, Ana Cubillas
breaks away from her restricted life in Spain and travels to Puerto Rico in
the company of her husband and his twin brother to take over the family's sugarcane plantation. Ana's driving ambition and passionate nature
are offset by Santiago's lush descriptions and interludes of magic realism. Allende's fans will revel in their dream of becoming landowners,
the social relevance of Ana's life to history, and the legendary strength of
another fighting pioneer woman. In *Malinche*, Laura Esquivel describes the
interactions between late fifteenth- and early sixteenth-century Mexican
Indians and the Spanish explorers under Hernán Cortés. Malinche welcomes Cortés, falsely thinking him Quetzalcoatl incarnate—the one who
was to come and eliminate human sacrifice. Known as "the Tongue,"
Malinche becomes Cortés's interpreter and also his mistress, until she is
disillusioned by the realization that he's a greedy, human man. Allende's
readers will enjoy the lyrical language Esquivel uses to describe the land
and the interaction between characters and Malinche's willingness to step
out of a woman's traditional role in a male-centric, violent world.

The Lacuna, by Barbara Kingsolver

Barbara Kingsolver's *The Lacuna* describes the rich personal and political drama surrounding writer Harrison William Shepherd from the
1930s through the 1950s. While staying at the home of Diego Rivera
and his wife Frida Kahlo, Shepherd turns to communism under Leon
Trotsky, which he later regrets when he is called before the House
Un-American Committee to testify in his own defense. Details of
the period, from World War I to the atomic bomb and censorship
evoke the political climate and point out the lacunae—the errors and
gaps that allow for changes in history—and make a statement out of
Shepherd's story.

Appeal: dramatic, leisurely pace, moody, thought provoking,
richly detailed, strong sense of place

FOR FURTHER READING

Country of the Bad Wolfes (Blake) also features smart energetic men with a keen grasp of the legal and political climate, although the Wolfe twins, Samuel and John Roger, turn these talents to more blatantly illegal and unethical activities than does Harrison Shepherd in *The Lacuna*. The story begins with the capture and execution of Irish pirate Roger Wolfe shortly after the birth of his twin sons—a kind of violence often repeated throughout the book as the brothers flee the United States for the relative safety of Mexico, becoming rich and famous via questionable business practices, from which they must eventually flee. This cycle is repeated for three generations in a story rich in a curious, leisurely adventure, packed with details of era and place and filled with characters who, while not always bad, are inevitably bucking the system. (The sequel to *Country of the Bad Wolfes* is *Rules of the Wolf*.) Kingsolver's readers will enjoy the atmosphere of underlying unease, the subtle humor, and the intricate plot of Blake's story. *The Invisible Mountain* (De Robertis) is a magical novel, sometimes funny, occasionally violent, and always moving. Three generations of women unlucky in love mirror the unsettled nature and ambiguous future of Uruguay in the twentieth century: Pajarita is a healer, Eva's an artist, and Salomé is a communist fighter. Readers who enjoy Kingsolver's individualized dramatic interpretation of the historical events that shaped Mexico and the United States in *The Lacuna* will also appreciate *The Invisible Mountain* and the courageous characters willing to suffer for their beliefs.

In the Time of the Butterflies, by Julia Alvarez

During the last part of Rafael Trujillo's regime in the Dominican Republic, in the late 1930s, an organized underground resistance movement was in place to remove him from power. The movement was organized by the now-legendary Mariposa sisters, Patria, Minerva, María Teresa, and Dede, along with their husbands. *In the Time of the Butterflies* is their story: their Catholic family and childhood, their marriages and children, and how they stood up against one of the most powerful dictators in the world. Each sister narrates part of the story, bringing first-person immediacy to the action and quietly including readers in the personal aspects of a tragic time in political history.

Appeal: character driven, leisurely, atmospheric, poignant, dramatic, suspenseful, compelling, immersive

FOR FURTHER READING

Both loved and reviled, Manuela Sáenz was Simón Bolívar's lover and comrade in the fight for South American independence in the early nineteenth century; *Our Lives Are the Rivers* (Manrique) tells the story of their partnership. While the pacing of the story is quick, unlike *In the Time of the Butterflies*, the reader's affection and respect for the characters grows as the first-person narrative brings Simón and Manuela to life in a bittersweet tragedy like that of Alvarez's novel. In *The News from Paraguay* (Tuck), there are no heroes: a dictator's strength of will and political power are the focus, and his outrageous failure to lead his country into prosperity makes him a legend of a different kind from the Mariposas and Bolívar. In a violent and gripping, fast-paced story, Tuck leads readers from Paris to Paraguay on the trail of Francisco Solano López and his new mistress Ella Lynch, to view his rise to power and his crushing defeat in war with Argentina, Uruguay, and Brazil. Complicated politics and the sheer arrogance of the dictator, and of the passions that drive people's behavior, will resonate with Alvarez's readers. Despite the book's comparatively greater instances of violence, Tuck's story is intense and unforgettable and can confidently be suggested to fans of the Butterflies.

Beautiful María of My Soul, by Óscar Hijuelos

Óscar Hijuelos's *Beautiful María of My Soul* is titled after the song written and made famous by Néstor Castillo in *The Mambo King Plays Songs of Love* (Hijuelos) and features part of the same story, told from the perspective of María as an older woman. As a young, vital woman making her way in Havana in the 1950s, María's fortune rests on her beauty, for which she is famous. When she must choose between the security of her relationship with a local gangster and a questionable future in the United States with Castillo, María chooses security and spends the rest of her life remembering her beloved trumpet player. One of the biggest appeals of this novel is its lush writing: Hijuelos evokes the steamy atmosphere of Havana's jazz-filled bars, the sway of erotic love, and the dangerous undercurrents of revolution.

Appeal: character driven, leisurely pace, bittersweet, nostalgic, thought provoking, romantic, steamy, lyrical, strong sense of place, sensual

FOR FURTHER READING

More noir than literary, *King Bongo* (Sanchez) is set in revolutionary Havana's nightclub scene, where anything can happen—and in this case it does: a bomb goes off on stage at the Tropicana and the main show-girl, the Panther, disappears. Bongo, drummer by night, insurance agent by day, who also happens to be Panther's brother and sometime private investigator, takes off in search of her in a story punctuated by violence and underscored by a dark, threatening atmosphere. As in *Beautiful Maria of My Soul*, the overripeness of a country ready for revolution and the almost frantic celebratory ambience of Havana's nightlife is a backdrop for Sanchez's drama. Although the romance is missing, the sensuality and strong sense of place will carry Hijuelos's readers. Comparisons between *Broken Paradise* (Samartin) and *Beautiful María of My Soul* can be made more in terms of theme than in style, character, or setting. Readers who are curious about what life was like in Havana directly following Fidel Castro's rise to power will be intrigued by this story of two cousins raised in luxury and separated by revolution. Nora's family escaped to the United States as soon as the revolution was inevitable, but Alicia married Tony, a handsome communist who hoped for social reform. As time goes by, Alicia's life deteriorates so much that her husband is imprisoned and she is prostituting herself. This is a gripping, bleak, heartbreaking story—one that could have been that of Hijuelos's María in different circumstances.

CHRISTIAN HISTORICAL FICTION

For our purposes, Christian historical fiction is defined as stories about key events or people in the history of Christianity and stories about fictional Christians living in historical times when the theme or message is Christian in nature. Christian fiction is generally written and intended to support, inform, and entertain Christians. The most important difference between historical fiction written for a Christian audience and historical fiction featuring Christian characters is the specifically Christian message that drives the story. Brenda Rickman Vantrease's *The Illuminator*, for instance, about a scholar, Bible illuminator, and John Wycliffe sympathizer who rents space from a widowed landowner in the fourteenth century, focuses very little on a specifically Christian message and more on what was going on in England at the time. Likewise, the Joanna Stafford novels by Nancy Bilyeau (*The Crown* and *The Chalice*) focus more on political corruption during the reign of Henry VIII than on the nuns' Christian calling and message of peace, though readers' advisors should freely suggest these historical fiction titles and others to readers who enjoy specifically Christian novels, too.

Because Christianity is such a diverse religion with many denominations, sometimes readers prefer novels put out by publishers with which they are familiar. Strict Catholic readers may prefer historical mysteries from Chesterton Press, such as *The Spanish Match* (Pursell); historical fiction from Ignatius Press such as *Theophilos* (O'Brien); and historical fiction classics from Loyola Press, like *The Silver Chalice* (Costain) and *The Shoes of the Fisherman* (West). Evangelical Christians may look for Tyndale House, Waterbrook Multnomah, Thomas Nelson, or Bethany House. These are well-known publishers that readers' advisors should know. A reader who asks for books similar to Deeanne Gist's *The Brides* series may appreciate the suggestion of another amusing Bethany House series, such as Karen Witemeyer's romantic historical novels set in nineteenth-century Texas, *A Short-Straw Bride* and *A Tailor-Made Bride*.

Novels labeled "Christian fiction" that are based on Old Testament stories are sometimes nearly the same stories told in the Jewish and Muslim traditions. These "biblical" stories are of universal value, so readers' advisors should keep them in mind. For example, Tom Gauld's tragic but bleakly funny rendering of the David and Goliath story in *Goliath*, and Francine Rivers's series Sons of Encouragement, which follows the lives of supporting male characters in the Bible, both make use of a biographical style to convey important messages to modern readers. Written in the style of Midrash—telling a story to illustrate a spiritual lesson—novels based on the Christian Old Testament and Jewish Tanakh can be of interest to a wide variety of readers.

Eve: A Novel of the First Woman, by Elissa Elliott

Written from the perspectives of Eve and three of her daughters, this biblical story of the first family on Earth follows the basics of the Genesis account in the Bible but personalizes the traditional tale with realistic details that bring humanity to what is often regarded as myth. Now at the end of her life, Eve remembers the Garden of Eden and the wily serpent, with his ploy that insulted Elohim and caused their expulsion. Gradually, the family dynamics tease out dramas and events that may have occurred along with the well-known biblical stories, and modern readers can gain an understanding of possible backgrounds to events such as Cain's murder of his brother Abel. In addition to its compelling characters, the novel's appeal is in its portrayal of a completely new world experienced for the first time by Adam and Eve and their family.

Appeal: compelling, character driven, sensual, dramatic

FOR FURTHER READING

Adam calls his wife Havah in Tosca Moon Lee's *Havah: The Story of Eve*, and so she is named in this lush, compelling story told by Havah herself as she experiences the innocence and joy of Eden and later the shock of exclusion from the garden, after which she and Adam experience hardship and grief. Like Elliott, Lee draws readers into relationship with her characters as they meet and fall away from their Maker and try to find their way back into his favor. Moving, lyrical, and thought-provoking, *Havah* is a great read-alike for *Eve*. *Infinity in the Palm of Her Hand* (Belli) also brings poetic imagery and immediacy to the well-known tale of a family eking out its existence in the new world. Belli's version portrays a more philosophical Eve, whose discussions with the serpent (Satan) invite readers to ruminate on the sin that separated humanity from God. In *Mary Magdalene* (Taylor), although the character-driven novel features a woman from the New Testament, the reader's experience is very similar to that provided in Elliott's and Belli's novels. Known as "Mad Mary" in her town, Mary Magdalene suffers from mental illness that causes headaches, hallucinations, and seizures, branding her as a freak. When Jesus casts out Mary's demons, he gives her hope and a chance at a new life, in this realistic and moving image of redemption played out in a woman's life.

Sinners and the Sea: The Untold Story of Noah's Wife, by Rebecca Kanner

Kanner casts the biblical Noah's unnamed wife as a strong helpmeet for the six-hundred-year-old man who obeys the God of Adam, builds an ark and fills it with animals, then casts it adrift in the roiling floodwaters. Noah and his wife bring their three sons and daughters-in-law aboard, and in expanding on the well-known story, the author creates a microcosm of society through the relationships among family members. Though sheltered aboard the ark from the sinful people of Sorum, their now-nonexistent home city, Noah's family, as described through his young wife's eyes, remains stubbornly imperfect.

Appeal: well developed characters, dramatic, thought provoking, richly detailed

FOR FURTHER READING

Gods and Kings, by Lynn N. Austin, first in her Chronicles of the Kings series, portrays King Ahaz of Judah about to sacrifice his son Eliab to Molach while Eliab's mother, Abijah, struggles to place her trust in the true God to save Eliab and protect her other son, Hezekiah. Readers who appreciated Noah's wife's willingness to stand up for her sons in *Sinners and the Sea* will enjoy Austin's book as well. In Francine Rivers's novel *Unspoken* (fourth in the series Lineage of Grace), Bathsheba tells the story of her love for King David, her marriage to the warrior Uriah, and the poor choices she and David make to be together. The themes of redemption through repentance, the desire for self-fulfillment, and the character-building strength that comes from suffering will resonate with readers who enjoyed *Sinners and the Sea.* Readers captivated by the story of the Flood and God's call on Noah's life may also enjoy *Heart of a Lion* (Morris), first in the Lions of Judah series, which finds a much-younger Noah yearning after a beautiful Baal worshipper and struggling to remain pure in God's sight.

Sarai, by Jill Eileen Smith

Smith's new Wives of the Patriarchs series begins with the story of Abraham and Sarah. Sarah is humiliated by her barrenness in a world where a woman's worth is measured by the number of sons she bears her husband, and she struggles to believe in Abram's god as Lot's wife encourages her to seek the help of the fertility gods. Adonai has promised Abram a new land and a multitude of descendants, and his faith moves him to journey with his family out of Ur to that land. Readers meet Hagar, Sarah's maid, and the extended family as Sarah's life is propelled toward faith and a miracle.

Appeal: compelling, dramatic, leisurely pace, strong sense of place, engaging, character driven

FOR FURTHER READING

Orson Scott Card's *Sarah* also tells the miraculous story of a woman who gives birth at an advanced age, according to God's promise. Moving along at a leisurely pace, Card's narrative closely follows the biblical story of a loving, beautiful, and smart wife whose devotion to God is a heartwarming inspiration to readers—a good choice for Smith fans who enjoy a compelling read that engages without stretching the biblical version. Marek Halter's book, also entitled *Sarah*, takes more liberty with the biblical text than do Card and Smith as it follows Sarah's journey toward motherhood. Halter portrays Sarah as an impulsive and headstrong young woman who refuses an arranged marriage; takes herbs to stop her menses; and elopes with Abram, her childhood boyfriend. *No Woman So Fair* (Morris), second in the Lions of Judah series, presents Sarah as lovely but quick to anger, although eventually Abraham wins her heart. Morris's rich characterization of Sarah and Abraham is set against an accurately drawn historical background.

Christ the Lord: Out of Egypt, by Anne Rice

With this bold retelling of Jesus of Nazareth's boyhood, Anne Rice helps readers imagine who the young god-boy was as they watch Jesus gradually discover his divinity. At seven years old, Jesus narrates his life—his education, his friends, and his family's move from Egypt back to the Holy Land. His curious nature, questioning mind, and compassion for others marks him as an unusual boy, although Rice allows Jesus to be a human boy in her compelling and reverent portrayal of the Savior in the making.

Appeal: well researched, lyrical, character driven, richly detailed, complex plot, atmospheric, compelling

FOR FURTHER READING

Tim F. LaHaye's Jesus Chronicles bring the apostles' stories to life, beginning with *John's Story: The Last Eyewitness*, in a realistic, dramatic, and believable way that sticks closely to the biblical account. At the end of his life, John is anxious to tell Jesus' story and this is that tale, along with a very human portrait of an old man who knew him well and took his role seriously. In the AD Chronicles, beginning with *First Light*, Bodie Thoene retells the stories of the New Testament, framed by modern characters from the Zion Legacy series (Moshe Sachar and his son Simon) who continue to study biblical scrolls that relate the works of Jesus. Richly detailed and dramatic, these novels also give readers a suspenseful, sometimes gruesomely real portrait of the biblical Yeshua. Grounded in historical facts and describing an intensely human Jesus, Nino Ricci's *Testament* comes close to Anne Rice's character portrayal, although Ricci follows Jesus into adulthood. *Testament* veers away from supernatural explanations such as the virgin birth of Jesus and may be a bit "out there" for some Christian readers, though one *Booklist* reviewer called the author's style "rigorously intelligent" and "fiercely thoughtful."[5]

Love Comes Softly, by Janette Oke

Marty Claridge's husband dies on the overland journey to western Canada and she must rely on God's help and sheer force of will to make it through. Pioneer life is hard on a woman, and almost impossible without a man, so Marty and Clark agree to marry: he for his toddler's sake and she for his protection and a roof over her head. Seasoned romance readers will see the love coming well before Marty does, and Clark's trust in God and gentle patience in wooing Marty is what makes this book (and the series) irresistible to readers—especially those who loved the Little House books by Laura Ingalls Wilder as kids.

Appeal: heartwarming, homespun, inspirational, romantic, engaging

FOR FURTHER READING

In *Sophie's Dilemma* (Snelling) Sophie Knutson discovers that she's not cut out to be a fisherman's wife in dreary, lonely Seattle. When her husband is lost at sea and she travels back to North Dakota, she must trust that her parents will welcome her and the baby on the way. As romantic and heartwarming as *Love Comes Softly*, this prodigal daughter story, second in the Daughters of Blessing series, is perfect for Oke's fans. Jane Kirkpatrick is another good author to suggest for Oke's readers. Her books are grounded in a harsher reality but are equally romantic and evocative of pioneer life. *A Tendering in the Storm*, second in the Change and Cherish series, set in 1850s Washington Territory, finds Emma and Christian Giesy separated from the strict German religious colony they broke away from. When Christian drowns, however, rather than seeking family help or returning

---

Christian Historical Fiction Classics

The Pilgrim's Progress, by John Bunyan
Dear and Glorious Physician, by Taylor Caldwell
The Robe, by Lloyd C. Douglas
Joshua, by Joseph F. Girzone
Two from Galilee, by Marjorie Holmes
The Great Divorce: A Dream, by C. S. Lewis
The Source, by James Michener
Redeeming Love, by Francine Rivers
Quo Vadis, by Henryk Sienkiewicz
Ben-Hur, by Lewis Wallace
The Shoes of the Fisherman, by Morris West
War in Heaven, by Charles Williams

---

to the colony, Emma decides to remain apart, making poor decisions that put herself and her three children in danger. Christian readers who enjoy pioneer love stories won't find better than Oke, Snelling, and Kirkpatrick.

JEWISH HISTORICAL FICTION

Jewish historical fiction is defined as novels set in the past (at least fifty years ago and before the author's memory) and in which Jewish characters, themes, and customs are the primary focus. The authors of these books are not necessarily Jewish, although in most cases they are. It is worth noting that the term *Jewish* is often used in a cultural rather than a religious sense. In other words, the books here are about Jewish people and highlight Jewish culture and traditions, but the outlook of the book (and sometimes the characters themselves) is not necessarily pious or reflective of the religious tenets of traditional Judaism. In fact, themes of Jewish fiction often include the questioning of identity and traditions. Other common themes include family ties, persecution, and immigration.

The tradition of Jewish literature is rich and varied. However, some of the familiar classics of Jewish fiction are not represented in this section because the events of the novels occurred within the author's lifetime and so, for our purposes, are not historical fiction. Our parameters exclude, for example, Sholem Aleichem's fiction about shtetl life in nineteenth-century Russia (*Tevye the Dairyman* and *The Railroad Stories*) and Henry Roth's books about Jewish immigrants on New York's Lower East Side in the early twentieth century, like *Call It Sleep* and his Mercy of a Rude Stream series, which begins with *A Star Shines over Mt. Morris Park*. Similarly, Bernard Malamud's (*The Fixer*) and Chaim Potok's (*The Chosen*) fictional works about the American Jewish experience are set during the authors' life spans. This historical demarcation is especially notable in Holocaust fiction, as novels written by Holocaust survivors are not necessarily considered historical. Some classics of Jewish fiction are found on the list of award winners of the National Jewish Book Awards (in the fiction category), presented annually since 1948 by the Jewish Book Council.[6]

There is a plethora of writing about the varieties of Jewish experience during World War II and the Holocaust. Included here are some representative and strongly literary novels from this horrific period of Jewish history. The titles here are a sampling of fiction from diverse time periods and settings, ranging from ancient times in the Middle East to the Italian Renaissance to nineteenth-century Polish shtetls.

The Dovekeepers, by Alice Hoffman

After the Roman conquest of Jerusalem in the first century CE, more than nine hundred Jews flee to Masada, a fortress overlooking the Dead Sea. Among those seeking refuge are four women whose lives become intertwined as they work together in the dovecotes. The alternating voices of the women—an assassin's daughter, a baker's widow, a warrior, and a practitioner of spells—weave a compelling narrative. Even as Roman soldiers surround Masada, determined to crush the last Jewish stronghold in the desert, the women grow closer through shared secrets and sacrifices. Though strongly grounded in historical detail, *The Dovekeepers* shares with Hoffman's other novels a feminist outlook and a fascination with elements of magic. The main characters are all strong, courageous women. Shirah, rumored to be a witch, learned from her mother the ways of amulets and spells and still worships (in secret) the ancient goddess Ashtoreth.

Appeal: haunting, moving, compelling, suspenseful, bleak, multiple perspectives, feminist

FOR FURTHER READING

The Witch of Cologne (Learner) also focuses on the plight of a strong, mystical Jewish woman facing persecution. Ruth, a rabbi's daughter in seventeenth-century Germany, is a skilled midwife who studies the Kabbalah, a mystical aspect of Judaism. She must defend herself against charges of witchcraft before a sadistic Catholic inquisitor. Although the novel depicts persecution and torture, there is also a sensuous love story. Readers fascinated by women's roles and power in ancient times will also enjoy *The Red Tent* (Diamant). A fictionalized account of Dinah, the daughter of Jacob and Leah in the book of Genesis, the novel highlights the powerful bonds formed among women as they endure hardships in a bleak landscape. The red tent of the title refers to the place where women retreat during their monthly menstrual cycle to share stories and wisdom. This powerful story of Hebrew women may resonate with Jewish readers who appreciate the historical connection of tradition and beliefs, but it will certainly be of interest to other readers, too.

The Fruit of Her Hands, by Michelle Cameron

The Fruit of Her Hands depicts the rising tide of anti-Semitism in medieval Europe through the eyes of Shira, a learned and opinionated Jewish woman. Raised by a widowed rabbi, Shira develops a questioning mind and a love of scholarship. When her father is accused of heresy, Shira finds that she must fight for her faith and family. She eventually marries one of her father's favorite students, the renowned Rabbi Meir ben Baruch, and the couple moves to Paris, hoping to settle in to a life of domestic and scholarly pursuits. However, after the public condemnation and burning of the Talmud in thirteenth-century Paris, the family flees to Germany. This is a captivating tale of persecution, family, faith, love, and learning.

Appeal: character driven, richly detailed, immediacy

FOR FURTHER READING

Maggie Anton also examines the lives of scholarly Jewish women in medieval Europe in her trilogy Rashi's Daughters (the first in the series is *Joheved*). Set in eleventh-century France, Anton's books feature a learned father who secretly teaches Talmud to his three daughters. Although persecution and anti-Semitism arise later in the trilogy, much of Anton's focus is on the details of domestic life, such as herbal remedies, cooking, and midwifery. Roberta Rich's novel *The Midwife of Venice* also features a strong Jewish woman in Europe, albeit a few centuries later. Hannah, a renowned healer in sixteenth-century Italy, faces a dilemma when a highborn Venetian asks her to attend to his laboring wife. Jews are forbidden by papal decree from treating Christians, but the ducats she could earn would pay for her kidnapped husband's ransom. This story is richly detailed with descriptions of daily life and Jewish customs, and it also is a fast-paced adventure.

The Last Jew, by Noah Gordon

During the Spanish Inquisition of the late fifteenth century, Jews were forced to convert to Catholicism or flee the country. Yonah, the fifteen-year-old son of a skilled Jewish silversmith, finds himself alone during this terrifying period after his father and brother are killed. Unable to leave Spain, he changes his name and becomes a wanderer, taking on work as a shepherd, a cathedral laborer, and eventually a physician. Though pretending to be Christian, he strives to keep alive his Jewish faith and the memory of his family. Part adventure story, part personal quest, and part love story, this novel is a moving and colorful depiction of one man's journey through a turbulent and violent era of Jewish history.

Appeal: suspenseful, adventure, well developed characters, storytelling style, engaging

FOR FURTHER READING

Lewis Weinstein's novel *The Heretic* is also set in fifteenth-century Spain. Gabriel's father was killed by an angry mob on the eve of the Inquisition. Gabriel converts to Christianity, but as he grows older, he seeks to learn about the forbidden faith of his father. Filled with realistic details and well-developed characters, *The Heretic* is a captivating read, though perhaps not as fast paced as *The Last Jew*. Both books follow a courageous man's efforts to preserve his faith and cultural heritage during a time of persecution. *By Fire, by Water* (Kaplan) also takes place during the Spanish Inquisition. Luis de Santángel, whose grandfather was forced to convert from Judaism to Christianity, is a financier of Christopher Columbus's journey and chancellor to the king of Aragon. Luis falls in love with a Jewish woman and becomes interested in his own Jewish heritage, thus drawing the menacing attention of the Inquisition. This engrossing tale has well-developed characters and plenty of love, drama, and violence.

The Amazing Adventures of Kavalier and Clay
by Michael Chabon

Set in New York City in 1939, this swaggering saga is the story of two Jewish cousins—Joe, a refugee from the Nazis, and Sammy, a Brooklyn native—who conspire to create the comic-book superhero the Escapist. It is the beginning of the golden age of comics, and the powers of comic-book heroes to vanquish evil strike a deep chord with the American public. Joe is an escape artist himself, having fled Czechoslovakia, but his efforts to free his family from Prague will lead him on a convoluted and epic quest of revenge.

Appeal: character driven, richly detailed, humorous, complex plot, dramatic, atmospheric

FOR FURTHER READING

Amy Bloom's novel *Away* also tells the tale of a young Jewish immigrant separated from family by wartime violence. After Lillian's husband and parents are killed during Russian pogroms of the 1920s, she flees to New York City and gets a job as a seamstress at the Goldfadn Yiddish Theatre. When she learns that her young daughter may still be alive in Siberia, Lillian undertakes an epic journey—encompassing trains and boats, Seattle and the Yukon, prostitution and prison—in a quest to find her daughter. This gracefully written tale has many twists and turns. As in *The Amazing Adventures of Kavalier and Clay*, the rocky relationship between a pair of artistic collaborators in the 1940s is at the center of *Niagara Falls All over Again* (McCracken). After the death of his sister, young Mose leaves his Jewish family in Iowa to join the vaudeville circuit and teams up with the aptly named Rocky. The two remain a comedy pair for many years, with their act moving to radio and then to Hollywood, allowing readers a fascinating glimpse inside the golden years of the US entertainment industry. McCracken's high-spirited, rollicking novel is a study of character and relationships as well as an examination of popular culture.

Gratitude, by Joseph Kertes

Gratitude follows the experiences of a wealthy Jewish family in Budapest during World War II. Told by their son Paul, a lawyer who has been stripped of his credentials, this is a gripping account of a family's struggle to survive. The characters are complex and fully drawn, and the presence of historical characters such as Raoul Wallenberg, the Swede who helped save numerous Hungarian Jews, add realism. The writing style is unadorned, with emphasis on the fast-paced plot and three-dimensional characters. Although Kertes describes gas chambers and other atrocities of the Holocaust, he also includes lighter family scenes and a sense of hope.

Appeal: character driven, moving, suspenseful, spare, fast paced

FOR FURTHER READING

Readers fascinated by the World War II setting in Hungary of *Gratitude* will also be interested in *The Invisible Bridge* (Orringer), which traces the impact of the war on Andras Levi, a young Jewish man from Budapest. It is 1937 and Andras has won a scholarship to study architecture in Paris, where he meets and falls in love with Claire, a ballet teacher nine years his senior. As anti-Semitism grows in Paris, Andras returns to Hungary, where he is forced to work in a labor camp. Orringer's writing style—filled with lyrical, detailed descriptions—is a bit more ornate than that of Kertes. Like *Gratitude, The Invisible Bridge* depicts the horrors experienced by Hungarian Jews and explores themes of love and loyalty. Readers interested in *Gratitude*'s story line about Raoul Wallenberg's efforts to save Hungarian Jews may enjoy Thomas Keneally's classic *Schindler's List*, which tells the story of a German industrialist, Oskar Schindler, who saved more than a thousand Jewish workers at his factory from being sent to Nazi death camps. Keneally interviewed many survivors known as "Schindler's Jews" to research the novel. He writes in a straightforward style, letting the powerful facts speak for themselves. As with *Gratitude*, part of what makes the narrative interesting is that even the heroes are not entirely "good" but rather a complex mixture of qualities.

LGBT AND NONTRADITIONAL GENDER IDENTITY HISTORICAL FICTION

Most historical fiction readers are familiar with Mary Renault's Alexander the Great trilogy—*Fire from Heaven*, *The Persian Boy*, and *Funeral Games*—published in 1969, 1972, and 1981 respectively, in which homosexuality was openly part of the story but not the main emphasis. Renault's trilogy is clearly historical and has been enjoyed for years by readers of all sexual orientations.

Radclyffe Hall's novel featuring a lesbian main character from 1928, *The Well of Loneliness*, though not historical, was one of the only books of its kind at the time and was widely debated in court and in the media for its frank and explicit descriptions of lesbian life. It has also been widely read by a huge diversity of readers. Well-known historical fiction includes some LGBT characters in novels like *My Dream of You* (O'Faolain) and *Corelli's Mandolin* (de Bernières).

As society grows more comfortable with and aware of nontraditional gender identities, more fiction specifically by and about LGBT life becomes available. Since 2005 the LGBT historical fiction subgenre has blossomed, even in genre-blending categories such as historical romantic suspense, romance, westerns, and fantasy. Still, books identified as LGBT, as opposed to literary fiction without emphasis on issues of sexual orientation, tend to be read mostly by a specifically LGBT audience. Whatever one's personal thoughts are on issues of sexual orientation, readers' advisors must be open to suggesting all kinds of novels. Many wonderful LGBT novels are simply not to be missed, and often readers haven't heard of them. This section is an attempt to collect a few great historical novels of interest to the LGBT audience for all readers who might be interested and readers' advisors who will enjoy them and suggest them to readers.

Prevalent themes of LGBT fiction in general are coming out (or not), depression, suicide, disenfranchisement, violence, and bullying. As with all strong historical fiction, LGBT historical novels focus more on history than on relationships. Blended historical LGBT novels, such as historical romance, while not necessarily emphasizing history over the other genre(s), must be set squarely in the past to be considered here.

Master Georgie, by Beryl Bainbridge

Well-to-do Englishman George Hardy volunteers his services as a doctor and amateur photographer on the battlefields of the Crimea.

His homosexuality is deeply closeted—he has a wife and children—
and he's a chronically depressed alcoholic. The story, which covers
the years from 1846 to 1854, is narrated by the three people who think
they know him best: his adoptive sister, Myrtle; his brother-in-law Dr.
Potter; and his scrappy assistant Pompey. Destined to become a classic, *Master Georgie* is a masterpiece of antiwar writing and a commentary on how little people really know about one another.

Appeal: storytelling style, strong sense of place, complex plot

FOR FURTHER READING

Another moving novel about one man's experience at war is *The Absolutist*
(Boyne). Tristan Sadler goes to fight in World War I under the cloud of his
family's disapproval and experiences a tender, intense relationship with
Will Bancroft, who is later shot as a traitor. Tristan narrates the story as
he takes letters to Will's sister and remembers the tragic consequences of
forbidden love. Like *Master Georgie*, *The Absolutist* brims with vivid, sometimes gruesome descriptions of combat; is covered by an atmosphere of
depression; and is poignant and absolutely riveting. In *The Unreal Life of
Sergey Nabokov* (Russell), Sergey, brother of the famous Vladimir Nabokov,
remembers his childhood in Russia and his ill treatment by his family;
recalls his introduction to the Lost Generation authors and artists in
Paris; and reveals his feelings of sexual confusion and inadequacy. Nearly
without self-esteem, this man with a stutter now works in the Reich's
Propaganda Ministry in 1943 Berlin and is constantly in fear of being discovered as a homosexual. Russell portrays a complicated life in a melancholy tone that will remind readers of Bainbridge's atmospheric tale of the
depressive George Hardy.

Tipping the Velvet, by Sarah Waters

Not many authors can pull off a lesbian adventure like *Tipping the
Velvet* with the aplomb of Sarah Waters. Set in Victorian England, this
is the story of oyster girl Nancy, who falls in love with a male imper-
sonator on stage and joins her act when it moves to London. When
her lover marries a man, Nan has to scramble to support herself and
makes a few glaringly poor choices—passing as a man, a hustler, a
tart, and a housekeeper—and finally finding the love she sought all
along. What make this coming-of-age lesbian novel so unusual are
the author's candid and sometimes steamy descriptions of Nan's sex

life, humor, and Nan's picaresque adventures—all of which accurately depict the seamy underbelly of London. Instead of dwelling on descriptions, Waters maintains a fast-paced, fascinating story.

Appeal: character driven, funny, steamy, lush, strong sense of setting

FOR FURTHER READING

Under the Poppy (Koja) is also the story of love, betrayal, danger, and treachery told in the first person by two of the main characters and set in nineteenth-century Brussels, where war is about to break out. The brothel owned by Decca and Robert is called Under the Poppy, and it is here that misfits gather—the prostitutes, the puppet master with his naughty puppets, and the men who frequent the house. Fast-paced, melodramatic, sensual, and a bit strange, Koja's novel is a good choice for Waters's readers. David Leavitt's *The Indian Clerk* is another good read for Waters's fans. Although the story is relaxed in pace and imbued with a sense of regret, the odd and witty situation created by the "Hindu calculator" as he invites himself to work at Cambridge with closeted gay mathematician G. H. Hardy will bring a smile to those who loved the saucy, scrappy Nan in *Tipping the Velvet.*

The Republic of Vengeance, by Paul Waters

When his father is killed at sea by pirates and teenage Marcus is the only survivor, his life is tainted by a burning need for vengeance. He becomes a merchant and then a soldier in Rome's war with Philip of Macedon, taking comfort only in the arms of a Greek athlete, Minexenos. Their relationship is presented as a part of Marcus's story as he matures and learns to find more in life than revenge.

Appeal: leisurely pace, atmospheric, dramatic, lyrical, richly detailed

FOR FURTHER READING

In language that is at times reminiscent of Henry James, Jamie O'Neill tells the moving love story of James and Doyle in *At Swim, Two Boys* and their accidental participation in the 1916 Easter Rising in Dublin. The concept of freedom—political and personal—drives this story, while Waters focuses on vengeance, but the passions and the tragedies meld in a story sure to please Paul Waters's fans that will be similarly moved by O'Neill's writing. *Mandrakes from the Holy Land* (Megged) is another very different story on the surface, which may appeal more to women than men, although the inner battle described is similar to that of the men in O'Neill and Waters. Beatrice Campbell, a repressed, Christian lesbian woman who keeps her sexuality secret, travels to 1906 Palestine on a personal pilgrimage. She suffers an emotional crisis brought on by her efforts to sublimate her love for Virginia Woolf's sister by immersing herself in ecstatic spirituality, not helped by the Freudian psychologist her parents hire to examine her. Readers will find comparisons among Beatrice; the characters in *At Swim, Two Boys* poised on the edge of manhood; and Marcus in *The Republic of Vengeance*, a conflicted, angry young man learning to love.

CONCLUSION

Readers' advisors can make use of ready-made book lists for special audiences, whether from this book or self-created. Merely handing readers book lists, however, or showing them websites does not constitute good readers' advisory and must be combined with a conversation about the different titles on the list and features of the subcategory, to ascertain a reader's interests. Knowing, for example, that many African American readers will consider the term *African American fiction* to mean books by and about African Americans can help us in our approach to suggesting novels with African American–specific themes and when introducing readers to new authors. Also, it is important to remember that a focus on cultural and personal identity are common denominators in historical novels, with ethnic, religious, and cultural themes that can help us as we talk with readers about their preferences.

NOTES

1. Review of *Sapphire's Grave*, by Hilda Hurley-Highgate, *Kirkus Reviews*, November 1, 2002, https://www.kirkusreviews.com/book-reviews/hilda-gurley-highgate/sapphires-grave.
2. Andrew Dearborn (pseudonym of Lewis J. Gardner), *New Dime Novels*, no. 413, 37–41, quoted in Albert Johannsen, "The House of Beadle and Adams and Its Dime and Nickel Novels: The Story of a Vanished Literature" (DeKalb: Northern Illinois University Libraries), www.ulib.niu.edu/badndp/gardner_lewis.html.
3. Joseph E. Badger, *Dime Novels*, no. 210, quoted in Johannsen, "The House of Beadle and Adams," www.ulib.niu.edu/badndp/pn-c.html.

4. Bruin Adams, *Dime Novels*, no. 308 (May 19, 1874), quoted in Johannsen, "The House of Beadle and Adams," www.ulib.niu.edu/badndp/dn-e.html.

5. Brad Hooper, Review of *Testament*, by Nino Ricci, *Booklist Online*, February 15, 2003, www.booklistonline.com.ezproxy.spl.org:2048/Testament-Nino-Ricci/pid=624372.

6. "NJBA Winners," Jewish Book Council, www.jewishbookcouncil.org/awards/njba-list.

8

HISTORICAL FICTION AND OTHER GENRES

As previously noted, historical fiction is often combined with other genres. Sometimes it's difficult to know whether a historical mystery, for instance, is more history than mystery, or the other way around. If the historical aspect of the novel is secondary to the mystery plot, it is historical mystery, but if the historical setting is integral to understanding the mystery, it's historical fiction with mystery. Confusing? The problem is that great stories often defy classification: consider the Dewey decimal system. Melvil Dewey couldn't devise a system that was broad enough to adequately classify nonfiction about families and nonfiction about homosexuality, mathematics and computers, travel guides and cultural history. Historical fiction is the same: it's hard to know when a novel is more historical than mystery, or more historical than fantasy. So we are left to judge whether an individual historical fiction reader who likes suspenseful or romantic stories will enjoy a particular title. In a sense, that's what makes readers' advisory so much fun: it's not cut and dried!

An example of historical fiction with mystery is Sharon Kay Penman's Justin de Quincy mysteries, because without an interest in and understanding of who the queen is, presenting a sleuth as the "queen's man" will hold less meaning for the reader. Eleanor of Aquitaine's twelfth-century society is integral to the ambience of and solution to the murder in each book. Knowing medieval English history is helpful, but knowing who Queen Eleanor was is what makes this series appealing to readers. On the other hand, perhaps it is desirable to understand the twelfth-century anarchy over royal succession between King Stephen and Empress Maud when reading the Brother Cadfael mysteries by Ellis Peters, but it is not critical to understanding the interpersonal relationships in Shrewsbury that foment the murderous results.

Likewise, a familiarity with Victorian England in 1888 is not necessary for thoroughly understanding *How to Tame Your Duke*, by Juliana Gray, the story of Princess Emilie of Holstein-Schweinwald-Huhnhof, who seeks asylum in England disguised as a tutor to a Yorkshire duke's son and winds up falling for the duke. But understanding that Jack the Ripper was on the loose in Whitechapel and murdering prostitutes in 1888 is integral to the story in *Grace Hammer*, by Sara Stockbridge, a genre-blended historical fiction thriller about a young woman in love with a mysterious man who may be the Ripper. Again, if the romance part of a historical romance story would work just as well in a modern setting, then we can assume the book is a romance with historical costumes and scenery. But if readers need to focus on the historical setting and characters to understand the story, no matter how steamy the romance, it's more historical fiction than romance. Yes, this makes a book a blend: fully belonging neither to the one nor the other genre, but when suggesting titles to readers, the emphasis may mean the difference between enthusiasm and a blank stare. Keep in mind, however, that like all readers' advisory, the appeal is in the mind of the reader.

HONE YOUR SKILLS

Consider these genre-blended titles and think about how you might describe them to a reader. Are they historical romance or romantic historical fiction? Historical crime or suspenseful historical fiction?

> *The Tsarina's Daughter*, by Carolly Erickson
>
> *Outlander*, by Diana Gabaldon
>
> *What Happens in London*, by Julia Quinn
>
> *The Wine of Violence*, by Priscilla Royal
>
> *The Spies of Warsaw*, by Alan Furst
>
> *The Dante Club*, by Matthew Pearl

Readers will often branch out gradually from historical fiction to other genre fiction that features historical settings accurately portrayed, or vice versa. For instance, those who enjoy Philippa Gregory's historical Tudor novels, with their rich romantic aspects, may also like historical romances that lean a bit more heavily on the love story, as does Kate Emerson in her historical romance *The King's Damsel*, a story of a young woman who catches King Henry VIII's eye. Historical fiction readers who aren't too concerned with dates and facts may enjoy a historical fantasy with a bit of the paranormal included, such as that of the Merlin the Enchanter series, beginning with *The Crystal Cave* (Stewart). Sometimes historical fiction readers like to read alternate history—a type of "what if" historical fantasy—such as Harry Turtledove's series The War That Came Early (beginning with *Hitler's War*) about a completely fictional World War II—one that might have (but didn't) happen. A reader who enjoys the more literary end of historical fiction might be ready for a classic of historical interest such as *The Country of the Pointed Firs*, by Sarah Orne Jewett, or *Red Sky at Morning*, by Richard Bradford

This chapter presents such blended genre novels for the dual purposes of expanding traditional historical fiction to include blended stories that the same readers may appreciate and to remind readers' advisors that sometimes people think of these types of novels as historical fiction.

ADVENTURE: SEA STORIES

Currently the most popular historical sea stories are set during war times, although some readers prefer an old-fashioned sea adventure novel, such as *The Rope Eater* (Jones), *Pirate Latitudes* (Crichton), *A High Wind in Jamaica* (Hughes), and *Fair Blows the Wind* (L'Amour). Readers are more likely to ask for sea stories of a certain era or a certain type than to hone in on appeal characteristics, and readers' advisors are advised to do the same, since most sea stories have the same appeal characteristics: plot driven, adventure, sailing jargon, and a fast pace. Strictly distinguishing a nineteenth-century sea novel written by a nineteenth-century author from a nineteenth-century sea novel written by a current author is moot when it comes to what readers enjoy. The dilemma over what is and what is not historical fiction is largely a cataloging or shelving problem, and it serves more as a mental guideline than a rule in readers' advisory. We need only make such distinctions to help us understand the historical fiction genre and how it relates to other genres and reader preferences and expectations.

By far the current most popular and prolific historical fiction sea stories are set during the Napoleonic Wars (1803–1815), usually involving ships of the British Royal Navy. The twenty-two-book series by Patrick O'Brian featuring Jack Aubrey and Stephen Maturin is the best-known example of this type. Readers will be thrilled to know that many other similar series exist and that readers' advisors can suggest more series to satisfy their vicarious longing for salty sea air.

In addition to Napoleonic sea stories, old-fashioned sea adventures are still somewhat popular, and readers' advisors need to be aware of them. Herman Melville (*Moby Dick* and *Billy Budd*) and Robert Louis Stevenson (*Treasure Island* and *Kidnapped*) wrote rousing sea adventures, as did Joseph Conrad (*Heart of Darkness* and *The Secret Sharer*), Jack London (*The Sea-Wolf*), Stephen Crane (*The Open Boat*), Ernest Hemingway (*The Old Man and the Sea*), and Rudyard Kipling (*Captains Courageous*).

Most classic novels of the sea include elements of appeal popular with modern readers, but they also may offer universal themes and sophisticated stylistic elements. *Moby Dick* (Melville), for instance, a powerful whaling story, is also symbolic of a larger metaphorical journey into manhood and a sense of purpose in life, and it may be a good choice for readers looking for literary adventure. Robert Louis Stevenson's adventure novel *Kidnapped* is another fun classic to suggest; it holds wide appeal and is filled with the same riveting characters and storytelling panache as his more famous tale, *Treasure Island*. These are great examples of classic fiction that some readers consider historical fiction, even though Melville and Stevenson were writing adventure stories set in their own—or near their own—time.

NAPOLEONIC SEA STORIES

Many readers who love what they think of as the best sea stories are primarily interested in Napoleonic-era (early 1800s) stories of war at sea. Patrick O'Brian is the benchmark author for this sub-subgenre and has a loyal army of fans. Readers' advisors who can suggest other historical stories of fighting under sail make friends quickly among O'Brian fans. Readers who enjoy Napoleonic sea stories are often looking for adventure, stories of military valor, honor and heroism, and lavish details of tall ships and sea battles.

Master and Commander, by Patrick O'Brian

The twenty-two Jack Aubrey and Stephen Maturin novels, mainly published between 1969 and 1999, are what most reviewers consider the golden standard for sea adventure and are still very popular. Filled with all the novelistic traits that appeal to fans of sea stories— impeccably accurate details of life and vessels at sea, action, and high drama—O'Brian's work takes a more involved approach to character development and interaction than most. Captain Aubrey is described in fairly straightforward terms and is in many ways the epitome of the successful British sea captain: competent, active, good looking, and likable. He seems socially inept on land, however, which adds a lighter humorous tone to the narrative in places. His friend and the ship's physician Stephen Maturin, in contrast, is a bit more complex, not at all attractive, and hides his secret role as spy while pursuing several intellectual interests and bearing an unrequited love. The first book in the series, *Master and Commander*, was made into a movie, starring Russell Crowe and Paul Bettany.

Appeal: dramatic, jargon filled, richly detailed, complex style

FOR FURTHER READING

The Charles Hayden novels by S. Thomas Russell—*Battle Won*, *Under Enemy Colors*, and *Take, Burn or Destroy*, feature British naval officer Lieutenant Charles Hayden sailing under the cowardly, tyrannical Captain Hart aboard the decrepit *Themis* in 1793. Humorous in spots and character centered, these novels are sure to appeal to O'Brian's fans. C. S. Forester's Horatio Hornblower series, beginning with *Mr. Midshipman Hornblower*, is similar in style to O'Brian's Aubrey and Maturin novels: they are action-packed swashbucklers, filled with authentic dialogue and realistic details.[1] While Forester's series is more plot driven than character oriented like O'Brian's, readers' advisors can suggest them with impunity. Another amusing, action-packed series by Dudley Pope features British Lieutenant Ramage, who begins the series in *Ramage* by abandoning a sinking ship in his command and then facing court-martial. Finally, O'Brian fans may also enjoy Dewey Lambdin's Alan Lewrie series, with its fast action, ribaldry, and realistic portrayal of the gritty life at sea, in which the main character begins as a spoiled rich boy and changes into a brawny seaman rather quickly. The first book of the series is *The King's Coat*.

Nathaniel Drinkwater series, by Richard Woodman

Although Woodman's series is most often described as swashbuckling, the character of Royal Navy Officer Nathaniel Drinkwater develops and changes over the course of fifteen excellent adventures. A bit lighter than O'Brian's stories and usually more compact in length and style, Woodman's compelling stories are filled with you-are-there details and dialogue, tracing the naval career of a young, wave-tossed man during the revolutionary era of the late eighteenth century. Start with *An Eye of the Fleet*.

Appeal: compelling, gritty, richly detailed, action paced, swashbuckler, well developed characters

FOR FURTHER READING

Seth Hunter's Nathan Peake novels deserve a wider readership than they have so far attracted. Complex in plot, witty, boldly written, and often violent, these stories about a young officer in the Royal Navy at sea and on land are riveting and well grounded in historical detail. Peake is a likable, flawed hero who, while smart and brave, doesn't always succeed or make the best choices. Start with *The Time of Terror*, set during the bloody French Revolution. Likewise gruesome and fast paced, the Kydd Sea Adventures, by Julian Stockwin, beginning with *Kydd*, are unusual in their focus on common seamen rather than officers. The main character, Thomas Paine Kydd, a London wig maker, is pressed into service aboard a blockade ship in the English Channel, where he grudgingly learns the value of fighting for Britain. Jay Worrall infuses his Charles Edgemont novels with action; romance; and enough accurate, realistic detail to satisfy Woodman's fans and slake the thirst of the armchair sea salt. In the first book, *Sails on the Horizon*, sea captain Charles Edgemont establishes himself as a charismatic leader, handsome and charming, and sacrifices his first ship to stall the Spanish fleet. The sequel is *Any Approaching Enemy*. Alexander Kent's Bolitho stories are another option for readers who enjoy Napoleonic swashbucklers. These adventures starring a British naval commander with a thirty-book sailing record need not be read in order. After reading one or two in the series, many readers find this action-packed series addictive. The first book is *Midshipman Bolitho* (aka *Richard Bolitho, Midshipman*).

HISTORICAL FICTION SET IN THE WEST

What is the difference between a historical fiction novel set in the American West and a genre western? Most genre western readers will ask just for a western, and usually they mean novels like those of Louis L'Amour or Zane Grey's: stories about lone brave men bringing justice to the Wild West. These genre novels follow a general story arc (man rides into town, does a job, leaves), and they have a strong sense of place and a satisfying conclusion, with all loose ends firmly tied. Lengthy descriptions of the scenery and complex studies of emotions and relationships are notably absent in westerns. A genre western reader might mention Louis L'Amour's Sackett series, *True Grit* (Portis), or *Riders of the Purple Sage* (Grey), and talk about the story.

Historical fiction readers don't usually ask for "westerns"; they might ask for books about the pioneers or explorers—people whose goal was to conquer and "civilize" the territory. Readers looking for western historical fiction might tell you about *O, Pioneers* (Cather), *The Way West* (Guthrie), or *All the Pretty Horses* (McCarthy). These readers are often looking for what Saricks calls "novels of the West" that "depict the western expansion and emphasize historical details and events."[2] Readers will expect a clear, descriptive picture of the landscape and the people—smells, sounds, costumes, social mores, culture, and dialects. Sometimes, though not always, the writing style leans toward literary: the author may experiment with points of view, time frame, or lyrical language and introduce issues such as slavery, racism, and women's rights. Remember, the most important appeal for most historical fiction readers is historical accuracy and detail. Genre western fans expect accurate detail when it comes to guns and ranching, but generally most westerns lack attention to historical setting and character development usually found in novels of the West and in the historical fiction genre as a whole.

It's likely, however, that both western historical fiction and genre western readers will mention *Lonesome Dove* (McMurtry), a novel that appeals to many different readers. A conversation about why a particular reader likes McMurtry's work (you might mention *All the Pretty Horses* and see what the response is) may clear up some potential confusion about what titles and authors to suggest. This distinction, though, is a less important one than listening carefully for clues about readers' preferences. A good rule of thumb is to offer a range of titles. Like *Lonesome Dove*, other western classics work well with historical fiction readers. Some of these crossover classics are *Little Big Man* (Berger), *The Ox-Bow Incident* (Clark), *Shane* (Schaeffer), and *True Grit* (Portis). Readers' advisors should keep a handful of these benchmark titles in mind as starting points when talking with readers.

The All-True Travels and Adventures of Lidie Newton by Jane Smiley

Smiley's story of twenty-year-old Lidie Newton, tomboyish bride to Thomas Newton, an abolitionist pledged to defend the Kansas

Territory from becoming a slave state, is a fantastically entertaining, thought-provoking literary novel. A feminist before her time, Lidie chafes at the restrictive life of most women before the Civil War. When her husband is killed, she vows to avenge his death, and dressed as a man, "Lyman Arguette," she sets out to do so. Unlike Mattie Ross in *True Grit* (Portis), however, Lidie finds a deeper purpose in life beyond revenge by becoming a fervent abolitionist who puts her beliefs into action.

Appeal: atmospheric, bittersweet, moving, richly detailed, thought provoking, picaresque

FOR FURTHER READING

Another moving story of a woman who dons men's clothes to blend in with men is *Crown of Dust* (Volmer). Alex is running from her past when she arrives in the mining town of Motherlode, California, and is taken under the wing of a feisty innkeeper named Emaline. Once Alex stakes a claim, finds gold, and gains notoriety, she finds maintaining her disguise difficult. The lovely and taut writing, a well-described western atmosphere, and a character-driven story make this thought-provoking novel a good suggestion for Smiley's fans. *Snow Mountain Passage* (Houston) is a well-researched chronicle of the tragic journey of the Donner party from Springfield, Illinois, to California in the winter of 1846–1847, told in alternating narrative voices by James Frazier Reed and his daughter, seventy-five years later. Trapped in the Sierra Nevadas during the winter, the Reed family's tragic experience is bleaker than Smiley's novel but sure to be appreciated by the same readers for its courageous characters and richly described frontier setting. Stephen Harrigan's re-creation of the storming of the Alamo in *The Gates of the Alamo* is a compulsively readable, moving homage to participants on both sides of the battle, told from several different perspectives. Like Smiley, Houston, and Vollmer, Harrigan humanizes a key episode in history through his characters with incredible detail and a suspenseful sense of immediacy.

All the Pretty Horses, by Cormac McCarthy

What could have been a fairly standard coming-of-age story set in post–World War II Texas becomes a work of art in the hands of Cormac

McCarthy. In *All the Pretty Horses,* John Grady Cole leaves the ranch when his grandfather dies and rides across the Mexican border with his friend Rawlins. In epic style, they traverse the lonely, richly described landscape; battle the elements; and have various adventures, one of which occurs on a Mexican hacienda. McCarthy's writing style at times takes on the mesmerizing rhythms of the expansive environment, and by investing meaning into the setting, he brings it more fully to life. In another section his clean, compressed dialogue and occasional bursts of humor keep readers glued to the page. The other titles in the Border Trilogy are *The Crossing* and *Cities of the Plain.*

Appeal: coming of age, character driven, atmospheric, bleak, disturbing, lyrical, complex style

FOR FURTHER READING

Canadian poet Gil Adamson's novel *Outlander,* set in the Canadian wilderness, has some of the same elements of style that McCarthy employs in *All the Pretty Horses*: lean prose alternating with gorgeously described wild settings and an emphasis on character. Mary Boulton is only nineteen when she kills her abusive husband and flees, pursued by her twin brothers-in-law. In 1903 a woman traveling alone is vulnerable, but Mary is helped by several strangers and eludes capture—for a while. Over all the action is a sense that Mary may be just a bit unbalanced and unreliable, which gives the novel a heightened atmosphere of unease. Larry McMurtry's first Berrybender novel, *Sin Killer,* is also highly descriptive and character driven, with pacing like *All the Pretty Horses* and a streak of satirical humor that may catch some readers by surprise. Lord and Lady Berrybender, British aristocrats, along with six of their progeny, steam their way up the Missouri River, and their daughter Tamsin falls for a handsome "sin killer" (religious trapper type). *A Sudden Country* (Fisher) is a powerful, literary novel in which two plot lines converge on the Oregon Trail in 1847. Rather than focusing on the hardships of wagon travel and the dangers of affronted Native Americans, Fisher brings two depressed characters, Lucy Mitchell and James McLaren, together to appreciate the "suddenness" and beauty of the landscape as they make a journey that is more internal than physical. The main character is the country—America as a concept and America as a land. Told in gorgeous imagery, this is a novel to savor.

The Sisters Brothers, by Patrick deWitt

The California Gold Rush is the backdrop for deWitt's unusual literary story that's not quite a western and not really a character study, although the characters of Charlie and Eli Sisters play a leading role. The Sisters are hired guns, contracted to kill a prospector, Hermann Kermit Warm. On their way from Oregon to the Sierra Nevadas, the Sisters brothers enjoy picaresque adventures, meeting strange and improbable characters and one red-coated bear. During the journey, narrated by Eli, the calm and shy brother (Charlie is a brutish drunk), readers are treated to darkly humorous meditations on the assassin's life and the attributes of the Wild West.

Appeal: literary, atmospheric, darkly humorous, thought provoking, violent, gritty

FOR FURTHER READING

God's Country (Everett) is a picaresque satire of the Wild West with a different slant from *The Sisters Brothers*. Everett skewers the concept and practice of Manifest Destiny—the idea that the United States was preordained to expand westward—in a story that's thought provoking and darkly humorous. Because *The Sisters Brothers* pokes subtle fun at the lone-hero justice seeker, readers who enjoyed deWitt will also get a kick out of Everett. In *God's Country*, white men dressed as Native Americans burn Curt Marder's house and kidnap his wife, so he tracks the miscreants with the aid of a former slave named Bubba, in this story filled with oddball humor. *Welcome to Hard Times* (Doctorow) is a parable about violence and survival in the Old West. Hard Times is a tiny mining town in North Dakota Territory whose mayor, Blue, does nothing when a violent sociopath razes the town and kills nearly its entire populace. Blue takes in an orphaned boy and a bitter prostitute and then rebuilds the town's population with strangers who wander in. Written in diary form (from Blue's voice), Doctorow's cautionary tale poses the question, what is the better way to thrive—passively or guns blazing? Mary Doria Russell would say that the gunslinger stands a better chance of sticking up for the town against evildoers, as evidenced in her biographical novel *Doc*, about Doc Holliday, in which Holliday sides with the Earp Brothers against the gun packers and roustabouts of Dodge City. Set well before the debacle of the O.K. Corral, this is a character-centric, deeply moving story of the tubercular dentist, cardsharp, alcoholic gunfighter, and the burgeoning West he grows to love. Violent, darkly humorous, and sharply descriptive, this novel and its hero take no prisoners.

HISTORICAL MYSTERIES

By far the largest group of genre blenders is historical mystery; readers' advisors can suggest a good selection of mysteries set in nearly every major time period. Historical mysteries are different from genre mysteries because of their emphasis on historical accuracy and descriptions of events and people from the past. Many historical fiction readers will sample historical mysteries if the stories have the setting and writing style they enjoy. A plot-based mystery story set in the past is not necessarily a good choice for historical fiction readers, so make sure to keep a few stellar historical mystery authors and their specific appeal characteristics in mind when you venture over the genre line.

Early classic detective mystery stories and novels such as Edgar Allan Poe's "The Murders in the Rue Morgue," *The Hound of the Baskervilles*, and the full Sherlock Holmes oeuvre by Arthur Conan Doyle—as well as Wilkie Collins's 1868 novel, *The Moonstone*—provide a model for both detective fiction structure and the Victorian writing style and setting. Modern writers who place their mysteries in the Victorian era, such as Anne Perry's Thomas and Charlotte Pitt mysteries and D. J. Taylor's Captain McTurk stories (*Kept* and *Derby Day*), successfully capture the attention of historical fiction readers with authenticity of detail and vernacular. To say a story is "Dickensian" or that a detective is "Sherlockian" is high praise indeed to historical fiction fans. Readers often revere golden-age mystery writers like Agatha Christie and Dorothy Sayers, whose detectives Hercule Poirot and Lord Peter Wimsey, respectively, used the Sherlockian method of logic and observation to solve crimes to the astonishment, and often disgust, of the local police. Phryne Fisher, a Melbourne flapper and socialite in a mystery series by Kerry Greenwood, is a good example of an upperclass amateur sleuth both similar to and contemporary with Lord Peter, and equally well loved by readers who enjoy a cozy historical mystery. Of course, only the recent mysteries set in the past are actually historical, since Collins, Doyle, Poe, Christie, and Sayers wrote contemporary mysteries, although they continue to be historically valuable and of potential interest to historical fiction lovers.

Some of the series listed here have been going for many years and continue in popularity, whereas others are newer stand-alone titles. It's interesting to note that many, if not most, historical (and other) mysteries feature the same detectives whose lives readers will follow as avidly as hooked viewers watch a television series. Once readers have consumed the last book in a beloved series, the shrewd readers' advisor will have another similar series in mind to suggest. The historical mystery sub-genre contains many wonderful authors, titles, and series: the smattering of books here provide only a few examples of suggestions for readers' advisors.

Marcus Didius Falco mysteries, by Lindsey Davis

In the first mysterious episode featuring the Roman informer, *The Silver Pigs*, Falco is involved in an elaborate silver-smuggling oper-ation after Sosia leads him to the incontrovertible evidence of the involvement of her uncle, Senator Decimus—a silver-filled lead pig. When Sosia is murdered, Falco takes it upon himself to visit the sil-ver mines of Britain to watch the smugglers at the source while at the same time looking for connections to Sosia's murder. Davis uses a hard-boiled noir trope—detective helps a beautiful woman who leads him right into a beehive of trouble—to great effect in the Roman world of cutthroat politics and shady business. Readers who love a good mystery and are curious about first-century Rome and Britain will appreciate Davis's attention to historical detail. There are twenty books in the series, published between 1989 and 2010.

Appeal: hard boiled, richly detailed, romantic, atmospheric, adventurous

FOR FURTHER READING

Steven Saylor's Roma Sub Rosa mystery series is perfect for readers who want a strong sense of place and an atmosphere of wickedness in ancient Rome. The series begins with *Roman Blood*, published in 1991, featur-ing Gordianus the Finder, whose skill at detection is sought by a young Cicero to investigate an alleged patricide. Saylor has a flair for creating unusual and compelling characters squarely set in their period (80 BC), and readers will be happy to follow them through the entire series. The Libertus Mysteries (Rowe), starting with *The Germanicus Mosaic*, are set in second-century Roman Britain, on the outer reaches of the empire. Rowe introduces Libertus, a freed slave with a slave sidekick of his own, who works as a mosaic maker under auspices of his mentor, Marcus Septimus, who asks him to investigate the murder of a much-despised ex-centurion, Crassus Germanicus. A curious combination of the country-house murder, Sherlock Holmes mystery, and historical crime fiction, the Libertus stories take a leisurely look at people of the time in complexly woven plots that will appeal to historical fiction and mystery readers alike. Ruth Downie's character-driven, witty series stars Gaius Petreius Ruso. The first book, *Medicus*, introduces Ruso, a grumpy army *medicus* assigned to the northernmost military outpost in second-century Britannia, where he finds his new life greatly uncomfortable: it's cold, damp, and filthy, and his commanding officer is abusive. After setting a slave girl's arm, he ensconces her in the local bordello and gets caught up in the murders of two prostitutes. Cozier than the other series listed here, the witty Ruso mysteries view Roman Britain through the eyes of many different characters and their roles in the social hierarchy of the time. They may appeal most to readers who mention Falco's romantic interests in the Lindsey Davis series.

Bernhard Gunther mysteries, by **Philip Kerr**

The Bernie Gunther mysteries begin with *March Violets*, set in 1936, featuring a hard-boiled Berlin detective and finder of missing persons in the midst of a horrible discovery. While investigating the murder of a couple, Gunther begins to realize that the recent government changes are more than the usual political party changeover: two top-level Nazis involved in a scandal and a morgue full of dead Jews bodes ill for the future of Germany. These noir mysteries follow Bernhard Gunther's career through World War II as he attempts to maintain his personal code of ethics in a world gone crazy under the thumbs of thugs.

Appeal: hard boiled, complex plot, atmospheric, bleak, descriptive, witty

FOR FURTHER READING

Dennis Lehane's stand-alone suspense novel *Live by Night* is also a compelling, gritty story of a good man compromised by circumstances. Joe Coughlin is a thinking man who prefers to do business without violence; his business is rum running during the Prohibition era—1926—and his business partners are gangsters. A character-driven story that invokes times past—dark with the pace of a train running out of control—this will appeal to Kerr's readers. William Ryan's series Investigations of Captain Korolev closely matches the Bernie Gunther series, with nearly identical appeal: intricate plot, atmospheric, bleak, and hard boiled. It's 1936, and Stalin's Great Terror has begun: any wrong move can land a citizen in prison camp. Korolev, working in Moscow's Criminal Investigation Division, is required to investigate sticky situations like the body of an American on the altar in a deconsecrated church (*The Holy Thief*) and the apparent suicide death of a party member (*The Darkening Field*). Like Gunther, the deeper Korolev digs, the worse the situation becomes. Likewise, in Jonathan Rabb's Berlin Trilogy, Nickolai Hoffner's career—from detective inspector in post–World War I Berlin (*Rosa*) to chief inspector (*Shadow and Light*) to former employee of the Kriminalpolitzei (*The Second Son*)—mirrors his personal tragedies in true noir fashion. One almost supposes that Gunther and Hoffner may have known each other!

William Monk and Hester Latterly mysteries, by Anne Perry

The William Monk and Hester Latterly series takes place in Victorian London's lowlife crime world; he is a police detective and she's a nurse. Episodes cover the heinous and the vile: kidnapping, pornography, theft, rape, and cold-blooded murder. In the first book, *The Face of a Stranger*, Monk suffers from amnesia and must investigate the murder of a nice young man, Joscelin Gray, the wealthy son of a powerful family. Monk discovers a link between himself and Gray and tries to rule out the possibility that he has suppressed a personal knowledge of the crime. These are dark, moody mysteries, and readers' advisors should note that the William and Charlotte Pitt mysteries, while written by the same author, generally are enjoyed by very different readers from those who prefer the bleak, gritty Monk and Latterly series.

Appeal: character driven, bleak, moody, atmospheric, strong sense of place, richly detailed

FOR FURTHER READING

Some Danger Involved is the first of Will Thomas's Cyrus Barker and Thomas Llewelyn mysteries set in the nineteenth century. The books take a sarcastically witty tone to London streets in the form of Holmesian Cyrus Barker, who advertises for an assistant to help with his "enquiries." In the first in the series, Barker and Llewelyn pursue a killer who crucified a young Jewish scholar. To catch him, they must traverse dank alleyways and secret underground passages, braving the fury of an anti-Semitic hate group. As they work together, the relationship between pugnacious Barker and naive Llewelyn develops into a delightful Holmes-Watson friendship that's both perfunctory and subtly affectionate. Their partnership, like that between Monk and Latterly, serves to illuminate the personality and talents of each character, and like the books in Perry's series, these are dark, atmospheric stories. In *The Yard* (Grecian), first of the Walter Day novels, Detective Inspector Day, of the newly formed London "murder squad," cuts his teeth on the chilling murder of another police detective who is found dead, jammed into a steamer trunk with his eyes and mouth sewn shut. The year is 1889, and the squad is already demoralized by their failure to catch Jack the Ripper, so tempers are short and the mood tense. Grecian masterfully depicts the same dark psychological suspense and grimy streets trodden by Perry's and Thomas's characters. In Jenny White's Kamil Pasha series, beginning with *The Sultan's Seal*, an Englishwoman's body washes ashore in Istanbul. The setting is the azure heat of occupied Turkey in the late nineteenth century rather than the cold fog of London, but tension inhabits each step of the investigation in a city no longer fully Ottoman and not yet a free state. White's perspective on the world is similar to Perry's: nothing is as it seems, and something bad is bound to happen.

Amelia Peabody mysteries, by Elizabeth Peters

Over the course of nineteen books in this series, introduced in 1975 with *Crocodile on the Sandbank*, intrepid Victorian Egyptologist Amelia Peabody; her husband, Emerson (Father of Curses); and their very busy genius son, Ramses, won the heart of mystery readers of all types. The affectionate and competitive relationship between Peabody and Emerson is one of the main elements driving the ongoing plot, usually set on an archaeological dig in Egypt. Small details of English expat life in nineteenth-century Egypt, such as dining at Shepheard's Hotel in Cairo, the family *dahabiyeh* (houseboat), and people's horrified reactions to Amelia's working costume—especially her split skirt and trousers and the rather useful sword-umbrella—contribute to a comfortingly amusing historical setting while providing a contrast to the harsher realities of life for the Egyptian lower classes. Because of Peabody's egalitarian attitude and feminist leanings, she manages in nearly every episode to endanger herself and then, much to her chagrin, requires rescuing, although usually not without landing a few whacks of her umbrella. Readers speak fondly of the series' characters and are enthusiastic when readers' advisors can suggest something similar.

Appeal: character driven, complex plot, cozy, richly detailed, witty, romantic

FOR FURTHER READING

It seems that Tasha Alexander's Lady Emily Ashton channels Amelia Peabody in her unconventional behavior (she smokes cigars and drinks port!) and in her forthright manner and headstrong behavior. Her extreme wealth, left to her by Lord Ashton, who died in Africa six months after their wedding, protects Emily from the riffraff that Peabody rather enjoys, but in many other ways Lady Emily's penchant for antiquities, ancient Greek literature, the dashing Colin Hargreaves, and murder makes her adventures a good choice for Peters fans. This series needs to be read in order, starting with *And Only to Deceive*. Deanna Raybourn's Lady Julia Grey mysteries may also appeal to Peabody and Emerson fans, for their witty interplay between characters and the dashing, hard-edged investigator, Nicholas Brisbane, a mixture of the grumpy Emerson and dramatically moody Heathcliff of *Wuthering Heights*. Lady Julia, at first not particularly put out by her husband's death, changes her tune when she learns it may have been murder, enlisting the aid of Brisbane in the first in the series, *Silent in the Grave*. And even though the Yashim Togalu mysteries (Goodwin) feature a male protagonist, fans of Elizabeth Peters's endless fount of creative storytelling set in a historical foreign culture will appreciate Yashim's investigations in 1836 Istanbul. The sultan's troops had squelched the corrupt Janissaries only ten years before, but the deaths of four New Guard officers may herald their return, and Yashim is asked to find out. The cosmopolitan blend of fascinating characters makes this series, beginning with *The Janissary Tree*, a sheer delight to read.

Sano Ichiro mysteries, by Laura Joh Rowland

The prolific and rightfully popular series Sano Ichiro, by Laura Joh Rowland, is a good example of mysteries set in non-Western cultures and can be a starting place for readers with an interest in Asian history who enjoy a good mystery. Sano Ichiro, a samurai in feudal seventeenth-century Japan, has been given the title "Most Honorable

Investigator of Events, Situations, and People." In this role, Ichiro is sanctioned to snoop among the elite samurai and people connected to or threatening the shogun's family. In one typically compelling episode, the sixth of the series, *Red Chrysanthemum*, the samurai detective finds his pregnant wife lying next to the dead body of the shogun's heir: clearly Sano has a problem on his hands. Readers who follow this series enjoy not only the exotic setting and its historical context but also the characters as they have developed over the years. The first book of the series is *Shinju*.

Appeal: character driven, suspenseful, compelling, richly detailed

FOR FURTHER READING

Sugawara Akitada, a low-level government official, is no samurai warrior; his part-time sleuthing activities afford him a much-appreciated break from the boredom of his clerical job. As he gains a reputation for solving crimes, though, his career flourishes. Set in eleventh-century Japan, the mysteries in I. J. Parker's series, beginning with *The Dragon Scroll*, evoke the exotic culture of medieval Japan with leisurely pacing, attention to character development, and a tense atmosphere. Dale Furutani's Samurai mysteries set in seventeenth-century Japan are darker, even nightmarish, compared to Rowland's series, but they may be of interest to samurai enthusiasts. Elegant and thought provoking, this older trilogy featuring a masterless samurai, or *ronin*, may be hard to find, although some public libraries still have them. *Death at the Crossroads* is the first book. Ian Morson's relatively new series featuring Nick Zuliani, an entrepreneur-turned-investigator, might be of interest to readers who enjoy Rowland's series, although Zuliani's sleuthing occurs in thirteenth-century Mongolia during the reign of Kublai Khan. Still, the exotic setting and character-driven nature of these stories bridge the time gap, and the Asian setting, with a warlord authority figure, make this a likely choice for samurai detective fans. Nick himself is a low-level scammer with a keen eye to a profit—he makes a lively, interesting protagonist. First in the series is *City of the Dead*.

Maisie Dobbs novels, by Jacqueline Winspear

Maisie Dobbs started her career in service, began a university education under the patronage of her former employer, worked as a nurse during the Great War, and started a small investigation business in

London in 1929. Her first case, in *Maisie Dobbs*, starts as a simple investigation into marital infidelity, then leads Maisie to a shady establishment, the Retreat, for disfigured soldiers. Remote and sinister, the veterans' rest home takes soldiers in, absorbs their assets, and never seems to release them—at least not alive. Like the first mystery, volumes to follow highlight serious issues, often the social and psychological consequences of war, but resolve on a generally upbeat note. The Maisie Dobbs series is "safe" in that there's no horrible violence, sex, or foul language, but they are certainly not cozy, and therefore may appeal to a wide variety of readers interested in mysteries set during this period.

Appeal: character driven, leisurely pace, upbeat, engaging

FOR FURTHER READING

Equally uncozy yet safe are the adventures of Jade del Cameron (Arruda) in colonial East Africa during the 1920s, beginning with *Mark of the Lion*. An American rancher's daughter and former frontline ambulance driver in France during the Great War, Jade is more assertive than Maisie but is cut from the same cloth—brave, smart, and stubborn. Readers will appreciate Jade's cheeky personality, and the stories are plot driven, each one filled with wild animals, unusual African cultural tidbits, and lightly-alluded-to prejudices that make the setting even more vivid. The Bess Crawford mysteries, by Charles Todd, starting with *A Duty to the Dead*, are another good choice for Winspear fans, because Bess suffers the nightmare of working as a battlefield nurse in Europe, as did Maisie Dobbs. The action is set during the war, rather than afterward, although tender-hearted and stubborn Bess does spend one Christmas at home in England involved in a murder case in *A Bitter Truth*, the third book of the series. Character driven, slightly melancholy, and issue oriented like the Maisie Dobbs series, these excellent mysteries are not to be missed. Slightly cozier but still in the same vein are the Molly Murphy mysteries (Bowen), set in turn-of-the-century New York City. Details of old New York make the setting nearly as important as the suspenseful and romantic stories of this amateur sleuth who is in love with a cop but not sure she wants to marry him. First in the series is *Murphy's Law*.

ROMANTIC HISTORICAL FICTION

The differences between romantic historical fiction and historical romance, as mentioned previously, are matters of degree. Generally, the historical aspect of a blended novel needs to be emphasized as much as or more than the romance for it to be considered historical fiction. Historical fiction readers may describe stories they most enjoy as a historical novel with a bit of a love story or spice, and quite often they cite Diana Gabaldon's Outlander series as an example of what they mean by "a bit" and "spice." The Outlander series, beginning with *Outlander*, is a good example of great historical detail mixed with compelling, steamy romance. Other romantic historical authors may not include such a rich setting and historical context, but to be of interest to historical fiction readers, a good solid historical setting usually needs to be in the foreground.

The September Queen, by Gillian Bagwell

Disguised as a manservant in the house of Charles II of England, Jane Lane aids the exiled king's cause by helping him escape from Cromwell's forces after the Battle of Worcester in 1651, during the English Civil War. Jane engages in the Royalist escape plan to relieve the boredom of life as a highborn young woman, hoping for a grand adventure. Their escape and Charles's eventual resumption of the monarchy is certainly an adventure; Jane falls deeply in love with the king despite his reputation as a heartbreaker. Bagwell's talent for characterization portrays Charles as the ladies' man he was, and as he captures Jane's heart, readers may also fall under his spell. Details of seventeenth-century life, government, and politics flavor a well-known historical event, and the characters ring true and come alive in the pages of this very romantic story.

Appeal: character driven, complex plot, dramatic, richly detailed, steamy, compelling, witty, immediacy

FOR FURTHER READING

Blue Asylum (Hepinstall) is another character-driven, compelling love story that may appeal to Bagwell's readers, although it's set during the American Civil War. Iris Dunleavy defies her plantation-owner husband by seeking justice for his slaves. He has her committed to a lunatic asylum, where she's rendered powerless under the care of a supposedly enlightened Dr. Cowell. Iris and a Confederate soldier suffering from posttraumatic stress syndrome decide to escape together. Hepinstall, like Bagwell, is a master at characterization and at creating a "you are there" feeling for readers. During World War II many Jews escaped to England on work visas and were engaged as domestic help by wealthy landowners such as Christopher Rivers, in *The House at Tyneford* (Solomons). Having escaped Vienna, Elise Landau finds her domestic service in the countryside of England a welcome, quiet refuge from the grumblings of war in Europe and loves her new life—and the master's son, Kit. More than a fairy-tale love story about an individual, this quietly moving novel pays tribute to the Jewish people dispersed by war. Adriana Trigiani's *The Shoemaker's Wife*, set during World War I, follows the meetings, partings, and reuniting of Enza, a seamstress, and Ciro, a shoemaker, Italian immigrants in New York City. In these lovers, Trigiani traces the lives of many early Italian Americans like them who fought for their country and scraped together new lives in the war's aftermath. Compelling and dramatically romantic, this story of strangers in a new land may also appeal to Bagwell's readers.

The Tea Rose trilogy, by Jennifer Donnelly

Many romantic historical novels, including The Tea Rose trilogy, engage readers in history with richly detailed settings that bring a time and place to life. Beginning with *The Tea Rose*, this engrossing family saga follows the lives of the Finnegan family in London's East End and their move to New York following a heinous betrayal. Vowing revenge for her father's and brother's deaths, Fiona Finnegan immigrates to New York City and builds an import tea business from the ground up: the ground being her drunken uncle's grocery store. Donnelly's romantic historical novels contain complex, sometimes elaborate plots involving characters who may or may not be related, living in recognizable historical areas like Whitechapel, London, and the Five Points district of New York City.

Appeal: complex plot, fast paced, dramatic, romantic, strong sense of place, engaging, richly detailed

FOR FURTHER READING

Jonatha Ceely's *Bread and Dreams*, a sequel to *Mina*, will appeal to Donnelly's readers who enjoy strong European female characters determined to follow their dreams in America. Mina disguises herself as a boy and travels aboard a ship bound for New York in the company of Mr. Serle, a chef and protector who may become more than a friend. *The Nun* (Hornby) also features an unconventional woman, a young Italian nun who falls in love with a man. The story emphasizes the lack of choices open to women alone in nineteenth-century Europe and the amount of courage it takes to defy convention. Like Donnelly's trilogy, this novel's strong setting takes readers to another world. A bit more upbeat, *Dancing at the Chance* (Cameron) is a lavishly detailed story set in the early 1900s about a chorus girl at the rundown Chance Theater, dreaming of Broadway and in love with the owner's son. Pepper McClaire's ambitions among New York's elite crowd may overextend her entertainer's life, but as she dances and dreams, readers are caught up in her story and the wonderful details of old vaudeville.

HISTORICAL FANTASY

The term *historical fantasy* initially seems like an oxymoron: how can a book be both fantasy and historical? Many historical fiction readers won't enjoy fantasy, historical or not, but some might like a well-written historical novel with just a tinge of magic or surrealism. It is, therefore, good to know at least a few great historical fantasy titles to suggest. Like other subgenres of historical fiction, historical fantasy needs to have a recognizable setting complete with characters who talk and act like people living in the time period, as well as events and details of daily life that help readers orient themselves in the past. Elements of fantasy—magic, quests, battles of good and evil, and objects of power—may be folded into the historical tale. Legendary characters like King Arthur, who may or may not have existed, or gods and goddesses of ancient myths, might appear, as they do in *Lavinia* (Le Guin). Visionary dreams from the past may inform a character like Liza in *The Boundless Deep* (Brallier). Metaphysical talents in *Thieftaker* (Jackson) add a surreal tone to the plot but do not ultimately detract from the historical setting.

Under Heaven, by Guy Gavriel Kay

Guy Gavriel Kay infuses his historical fantasies with a surreal atmosphere and takes poetic license in stories like *Under Heaven*, inspired by China's medieval Tang dynasty. The story begins with the main character, Shen Tai, honoring his father's memory at Kuala Nor, where the general and his huge army lost their lives twenty years earlier. Shen

Tai is haunted by the ghosts of dead soldiers and decides to bury their bones. The ghosts reward him by protecting him against an assassin's attempt on his life. Shen Tai himself is honored with a gift of 250 Sardian horses, making him the target of jealousy. The many-stranded plot slowly leads readers through the tense politics of the time, the warring factions battling for control, and the characters who drive the action coming to life. The sequel is *River of Stars*.

Appeal: character driven, leisurely paced, dramatic, moving, romantic, strong sense of place, lyrical, surreal, richly detailed, complex style

FOR FURTHER READING

Another historical fantasy, *The Secrets of Jin-Shei* (Alexander), postulates an alternate history of ancient China, known as Syai, ruled largely by women—in this case a self-centered, dangerous empress. The story line is complex and driven by eight main characters, all "sisters of the heart," or *jin-shei*, who have pledged loyalty to each other though they represent all levels of society. Suspenseful, fast-paced, and richly detailed, this stylistically complex atmospheric fantasy may also appeal to Kay's fans. The Tales of the Otori (Hearn), beginning with *Across the Nightingale Floor*, are lyrical adventure stories set in a fictitious medieval Japan and may interest Kay's readers. Takeo, a young survivor of a raid on his mountain village, grows from naive boy to warrior as he learns more about his heritage and his unique gifts. Simon Elegant's *A Floating Life* takes place during the Tang dynasty, the same time period as *Under Heaven*. In the story, Li Po (or Li Bai), one of China's historically famous poets, regales his shipboard scribe with tall tales and poetry about his life's adventures while journeying to his exile for his part in an attempted eighth-century coup. Readers who love Guy Gavriel Kay's use of language and his rich descriptions of medieval China in *Under Heaven* will want to read this older novel, too.

KING ARTHUR

Many readers know the story of King Arthur and Camelot but may not be aware of the legend's origins. Depending on readers' preferences for lengthy classics, readers' advisors may want to suggest Sir Thomas Mallory's fifteenth-century saga, *Le morte d'Arthur*, for its influence on the King Arthur literary oeuvre. Or it might be a great idea to suggest

T. H. White's Once and Future King series, beginning with *The Sword in the Stone*, first published in 1938, which introduces the boy Arthur living with a foster family and tutored by Merlin the Magician. These funny, engaging modern classics are sure to appeal to readers desiring novels about the legendary king. Likewise, if readers haven't sampled Mary Stewart's series Merlin, the Enchanter, starting with *The Crystal Cave*, these four older novels are still popular with modern historical fantasy readers.

Avalon series, by Marion Zimmer Bradley (and Diana Paxson)

The Mists of Avalon is the best-known and seventh of this eight-book series (Bradley wrote five, and Paxson the other three). The first series book is *The Fall of Atlantis*, which introduces an animistic religion. It's not until *The Mists of Avalon* that the battle between Christianity and the Earth Mother come to a head. *The Mists of Avalon* is based on Arthurian legend, although the story is told from the perspective of Morgaine, or Morgan le Fay, and her role as priestess and defender of the Earth Mother's sovereignty. In a sacred fertility rite, Morgaine is impregnated by her brother Arthur, conceiving the child Mordred. This is the center tragedy of the story, as the mating is fated, not humanly intentional. This is a luscious, leisurely story that goes on for almost nine hundred pages and is still loved by readers today, though first published thirty years ago. The novel stands well on its own, but readers may want to go back and read through the first six books before reading on to *Sword of Avalon*, written by Paxson.

Appeal: atmospheric, dramatic, mystical, romantic, feminist, leisurely, richly detailed

FOR FURTHER READING

Mercedes Lackey, Diana Paxson, and Marion Zimmer Bradley have similar writing styles and a feminist perspective that rejects male-dominated culture and accepts the possibility of magic as part of Earth's natural order. In fact, Lackey was mentored by Bradley and inspired by her to write *Gwenhwyfar: The White Spirit*. Lackey uses as her starting point the Welsh legend that King Arthur actually had three wives, all named Guinevere (or Gwenhwyfar). This is the tale of his last wife, who grows from child queen into a warrior who fights the Saxons with Arthur. Lackey's feminist perspective and atmospheric, almost magical setting will appeal to Bradley's fans. In her Guenevere trilogy Rosalind Miles also takes a feminist perspective on the Arthurian story, re-creating Camelot as a matriarchal society in which women are free to love whomever they choose. Guenevere is pressured to change this, however, by the evil three—Merlin, Malgaunt, and Morgan—until her hero, Arthur, appears to save (and marry) her. Together they try to unite Britain against her Saxon foes until Arthur's death in the trilogy finale, *The Child of the Holy Grail*. Nancy McKenzie's *Queen of Camelot* follows the life of Guinevere from her early days through the love and betrayals of her later marriage to King Arthur. More romantic and suspenseful than Marion Zimmer Bradley's *Mists of Avalon*, this engaging story may appeal to a slightly different audience but is worth mentioning.

ALTERNATE HISTORY

Closely allied to historical fantasy are the "what-if" stories of alternate history. For instance, in *The Plot against America*, Philip Roth builds his story on the premise that Charles Lindbergh defeated Franklin D. Roosevelt in the presidential election and then allied with Adolf Hitler during World War II. Michael Chabon's *The Yiddish Policeman's Union* postulates a Jewish state established after World War II in Alaska rather than Israel. And in Stephen Carter's latest, *The Impeachment of Abraham Lincoln*, the president escapes assassination but is caught in an impeachment charge by radical Republicans, who accuse him of trying to establish martial law. These books are all based on historical fact, then stretched to describe a plausible alternate scenario.

Gettysburg trilogy, by Newt Gingrich

Newt Gingrich postulates a battle at Gettysburg in which the Confederates, under General Robert E. Lee, win the day and push on to attack Washington, DC. The outcome in the first volume of this trilogy, simply titled *Gettysburg*, is the opposite of what actually happened historically, though the author's description is convincing when the Rebel army outfoxes Union forces by swinging around and attacking from the rear. Civil War buffs will appreciate Gingrich's attention to the tiniest detail of equipment, strategy, and visceral gore of battle.

Appeal: plot driven, fast paced, gory, violent, lavishly detailed, compelling

FOR FURTHER READING

If Confederate President Jefferson Davis had sent General Robert E. Lee in aid of General Braxton Bragg at Chattanooga, perhaps the ignominious Confederate defeat could have been avoided. This is the premise of *Lee at Chattanooga: A Novel of What Might Have Been* (McIntire), an alternate history that should be of interest to Gettysburg Trilogy fans for its emphasis on strategic battle planning and realistic interactions between key characters from history. *The Secret Trial of Robert E. Lee*, by historian Thomas J. Fleming, is another realistic novel that postulates a retaliatory act by Charles Dana, assistant secretary of war, on the defeated Confederate general. In this novel radical Republican leader Dana hopes to prosecute and hang Lee for treason, ignoring Grant's terms of surrender—an action that could well keep the Civil War alive for years to follow. Fleming's attention to historical detail and portrayal of realistic characters, all of whom felt the effect of the war deeply, make this a good suggestion for Gingrich's readers. A well-known and popular author of many alternate histories, Harry Turtledove wrote the stand-alone Civil War novel *The Guns of the South*, in which white supremacists travel back in time and equip the Confederates with AK-47 rifles. This is, of course, more fantasy than history, but some readers may find this approach entertaining.

TIME TRAVEL

The concept of time travel was famously explored in fiction by H. G. Wells in *The Time Machine*, and before him by Charles Dickens in *A Christmas Carol* and Mark Twain in *A Connecticut Yankee in King Arthur's Court*. In all these novels characters travel back in time. Some time-travel novels feature characters who travel forward in time, to a parallel universe, or randomly in time, like Henry in *The Time Traveler's Wife* (Niffenegger). Our interest here is stories in which characters move back in time to personally experience events and locations from the past. One well-known example of this type of book is *Time and Again* (Finney), in which Simon Morley participates in a government experiment and goes back to 1880s New York City, where he experiences history, including a memorable sequence in which he sees the Statue of Liberty's first arrival in America. Octavia Butler's *Kindred* is another remarkable novel of time travel in which a modern character travels back to experience slavery in the United States firsthand. These and the following titles allow readers to experience significant moments from the past through characters' modern sensibilities.

Outlander novels, by Diana Gabaldon

No discussion of time travel historical fiction would be complete without highlighting the Outlander series, which features the much-beloved eighteenth-century Scotsman Jamie Fraser and his time-traveling lover and wife, Claire Randall. The first in the eight-book series, *Outlander*, begins with Claire and her modern-day husband in Scotland looking for an ancestor's grave. Claire crosses into a stone circle that is a portal to the past and winds up in the Jacobite rising of 1745, meeting the Randall ancestor (whom she dislikes) and being adopted by another clan and falling in love with Jamie Fraser, a Highland diamond in the rough. Claire brings readers into her adventure to experience a true culture shock with her wise and witty first-person narrative.

Appeal: character driven, fast paced, dramatic, suspenseful, romantic, richly detailed

FOR FURTHER READING

The Doomsday Book (Willis) will also be of interest to Gabaldon's readers because the main character, Kivrin, has much in common with Claire as a healer and as a traveler to Great Britain's past. Kivrin Engles has been prepping for her journey to an Oxford Christmas in 1320 and is ready to leave 2054 just as a flu epidemic hits. The technician succumbs to the flu and, feeling ill, miscalculates the year, landing Kivrin instead in 1348 at the beginning of the Black Death. She becomes trapped, an epidemic of horrible proportion at each end of her time line. Kivrin uses her modern knowledge of sanitary medical practice to help the people of the village, in the same way Claire does in the eighteenth century, involving herself with the people of the time. Willis sustains the suspense in this fast-paced drama that's impossible to put down—something Gabaldon's fans know a lot about. Susanna Kearsley infuses her time-travel or time-slip novels with love stories, historical events, and a strong sense of setting—often Scotland. In *The Winter Sea*, writer Carrie McLelland travels to coastal Scotland for inspiration in writing a historical novel set in the area. As she accustoms herself to the setting, a ruined castle in particular, every night she dreams of the Jacobites who lived there in 1708. Soon Carrie is so immersed in the past she's no longer sure where and when she will awaken. Romantic and vividly described, this is a sure hit with Gabaldon fans. Kearsley's novels all follow the same basic plot structure, but they are absorbing and fun to read in the same way as the Outlander series. Selden

Edwards's leisurely *The Little Book* is driven largely by its characters' dialogue and is funny, unlike Gabaldon and Kearsley, though every bit as compelling. After being attacked, Wheeler Burden is catapulted from 1988 San Francisco to 1897 Vienna, where he encounters people and situations he learned about in prep school. The story is told from many perspectives, and Wheeler meets famous men of the time, including Mark Twain, Sigmund Freud, Gustav Mahler, and Buddy Holly. He also has a chance to see his progenitors at vastly different ages. Thematically, the book is very different from the more romantic novels of Gabaldon and Kearsley, focusing in on the hopes and dreams of turn-of-the-century society in contrast to actual future events, but some of the same readers will be intrigued.

TIME SWEEP

Time-sweep novels, historical fiction written to illuminate history of a place or long period of time, have a particular appeal for those readers who love a complex, multilayered story that never seems to end. Time-sweep benchmark authors James Michener (*Hawaii*) and Edward Rutherfurd (*Sarum* and *Russka*), Ken Follett (*The Pillars of the Earth* and *The Fall of Giants*) and Steven Saylor (*Empire* and *Roma*) are all good suggestions. Many of these time-sweep novels have been described in other chapters as geographical or period stories. Most reviewers call this type of historical fiction "epic," in reference to the book's length and depth of coverage over a long period of time or particular era.

The Islam Quintet series, by Tariq Ali

Topically quite different from most other well-known time-sweep stories and of interest to readers who like series that humanize a larger history, the Islam Quintet, by Tariq Ali, fictionalizes the history of Muslims in snapshots from twelfth-, sixteenth-, nineteenth-century, and current life. The settings are as diverse as Islam: Spain, Jerusalem, Turkey, Italy, Lahore, Beijing, Paris, and London. In the first thought-provoking and dramatic novel of the series, *Shadows of the Pomegranate Tree*, a Muslim family tries to rebuild their life after the fall of Granada in 1492 to Christians and the burning of two million Muslim manuscripts by a misguided and vengeful man of the church. This is a fascinating time-sweep series that explores new territory for many English-language readers.

Appeal: thought provoking, dramatic, lyrical, leisurely, romantic, atmospheric, suspenseful

FOR FURTHER READING

Another time-sweep series that will appeal to Ali's readers is the Haque Family trilogy, beginning with *A Golden Age* and *The Good Muslim*. Tahmima Anam traces the modern history of Bangladesh from its 1971 War of Independence to the rise of radical Islam in the 1980s—all through the experiences of one family over time. While these novels aren't strictly historical fiction, readers who enjoyed the Islam Quintet will enjoy Anam's perspective on modern Islamic history. Louis de Bernières's *Birds without Wings* is a single-volume time-sweep historical novel that portrays the World War I–era fall of the Ottoman Empire and the birth of the Turkish Republic, in what one *Library Journal* reviewer called a "polyvocal epic."[3] The story of harmony between ethnic groups shattered by new ideologies, violence, and the influx of Greek-speaking Muslims from Crete is told from many perspectives, making this a dramatic, gritty, and moving story that will appeal to Ali's readers with its political overtones and Muslim history.

FAMILY SAGA

Family sagas—long, delicious, character-centric stories following several generations of one family line—have been popular for decades and some readers still hearken back to the classics of the early to mid-twentieth century in their descriptions of series they've loved. One such series, Whiteoaks of Jalna, by Mazo de la Roche, set in Ontario, Canada, is a sixteen-book set, originally published between 1929 and 1960, but reissued over the past six years given increased demand. Each book stands on its own, so the series doesn't need to be read in strict order. The story begins with the 1850 arrival of Captain Whiteoak and his wife, Adeline, who establish the town of Jalna on the shores of Lake Ontario, in *The Building of Jalna*. The rest of the series covers the next hundred years of the Whiteoak family, told in a heartwarming, intimate style that highlights key events in each generation, with some carryover characters. Another popular older family series, The Forsyte Saga (Galsworthy), published between 1906 and 1930, is often still mentioned by readers and comprises three novels and two "interludes." In the first book, *The Man of Property*, the main character,

Soames Forsyte, places a high value on possessions, treating his wife as one of the many things he owns, setting the stage for the long, complex family drama.

Wilderness series, by Sara Donati

Some family sagas, like Donati's Wilderness series, while focusing on family relationships, include much more historical background and setting than others like the Forsyte Saga, often tracing a sweep of a place's history through the lives of its characters. Readers who enjoy time-sweep fiction and are looking for something new may branch out to family sagas of this type. The Wilderness series features Englishwoman Elizabeth Middleton, new to eighteenth-century upstate New York, and Nathaniel Bonner, a frontiersman who lives with his Native American family on Hidden Wolf, a mountain above the pioneer town where most of the action in the first book takes place. This is a series to read in order, so as to keep the wonderfully fleshed-out characters straight; the first of the six-book series is *Into the Wilderness*. In this engrossing romantic historical novel, Elizabeth Middleton travels from England to the New York town where her father is the judge to establish a school. To her horror, her father has already made plans to marry her off to the town doctor. Thus begins her struggle to live her own life and claim the right to teach the Native American children alongside the white children. Each successive book in the series brings additional characters into Elizabeth's life, new issues to resolve, and a strong sense of the land and its pioneering people.

Appeal: romantic, character driven, complex plot, leisurely, dramatic, moving, strong sense of place, immediacy

FOR FURTHER READING

Cynthia Harrod-Eagles's Morland Dynasty, starting with *The Founding*, published in 1980, is still going, with thirty-four books to date! The setting is Yorkshire, England, from the fifteenth century to the 1920s. The Morland saga begins during the Wars of the Roses, with young Eleanor Morland, wife of the wealthy Robert Morland and still in love with Richard, Duke of York. Staunch Yorkists, the Morlands are about to enter the Tudor era— Lancastrian rule—which becomes an even bigger threat to the Catholic

Morlands in the third book, *The Princeling*, when Protestantism is on the rise. Harrod-Eagles weaves more history into her family saga than many authors do, making this a good choice for readers who enjoy Donati's Wilderness series. Finally, Jeffrey Archer's projected five-book series, the Clifton Chronicles, beginning with *Only Time Will Tell*, starts in World War I–era Bristol, England, where Harry Clifton, born in poverty, grows into an Oxford University scholar by virtue of his angelic singing voice, which opens the door to opportunity and high-placed friends. Readers who enjoy historical fiction about the American people are bound to also like Archer's fast-paced, twisty stories.

CONCLUSION

When a novel is neither strictly historical fiction nor completely identified as another genre, readers don't stop to ask what to call it. They may assume a title is historical fiction simply because the story is set in the past, or they may think of books they enjoy as simply romance or fantasy or mystery without considering the historical setting. Readers' advisors must familiarize themselves with a few benchmark titles that cross genre lines so they can suggest a wider variety of fiction regardless of its level of historical significance.

It's fairly simple to recognize a historical mystery—the setting is in some way important to solving the murder puzzle. Recognizing an alternate history novel may require a familiarity with the actual historical events, to be able to tell fact from fiction, but there's no question about the historical nature of the story. Other genre blenders may be a bit more difficult, such as romantic historical novels and novels of the West. With difficulties in categorization, it should come down to what readers think they are asking for. A good readers' advisory conversation will clarify any issues and make suggesting genre-blended stories easier. It all boils down to letting go of labels and matching appeals.

NOTES

1. Joyce Saricks, "Patrick O'Brian," *NoveList*, 2002.
2. Joyce Saricks, *The Readers' Advisory Guide to Genre Fiction*, 2nd ed. (Chicago: American Library Association, 2009), 314.
3. Mark Singer, "Birds wthout Wings" (Book Review) *Library Journal* (129, no. 15, Sept. 15, 2004), 48.

9

EXPANDING READERS' ADVISORY SERVICES

The Whole-Collection Approach

Throughout this book nonfiction, graphic, video, and audio formats have been given as suggestions for further reading as an example of how to integrate other materials in the collection with historical (or any) fiction. Considering how other kinds of materials may be of interest to readers opens doorways that can lead to further reading interests and openness to new genres and formats. For readers, this is usually an exciting proposition. Historical fiction readers, as mentioned in chapter 8, might lean toward blended genres such as historical romance or historical fantasy, or they might be intrigued by a suggestion of nonfiction that gives background support to their favorite historical fiction. Readers of fictional historical biographies may appreciate the suggestion of a biography or memoir and/or a nonfiction work of narrative history. Whole-collection readers' advisory—or considering nonfiction, topical and narrative, and nonprint resources and books—is a way to open up possibilities for other, related interests. The same appeal factors come into play no matter what kind of material is suggested.

The section on reading maps in chapter 2 demonstrated the concept of mind mapping used in readers' advisory, along with the thought processes used to arrive at read-alikes and read-arounds.[1] The mind-mapping approach is particularly useful in conversation with readers to explore a variety of materials and why you have chosen them. Making a visual chart, even a rough, hand-drawn one, can help you remember why you chose particular materials and what the connections are between titles. This visual connection also helps readers organize their thoughts around topics, themes, and styles they'd like to explore more thoroughly.

Readers infrequently consider their favorite books in terms of fiction or nonfiction, and nonfiction readers' advisory can be difficult for those of us whose advisory strength is fiction. You can, however, make use of Neal Wyatt's *Readers' Advisory Guide to Nonfiction*, watch for popular narrative nonfiction, and use NoveList Plus to quickly access searchable reviews to help you find read-alikes and read-arounds for those who love nonfiction.[2] Don't hesitate, either, to suggest some great historical fiction that augments good narrative nonfiction favorites. Many readers were captivated by *In the Garden of Beasts: Love, Terror, and an American Family in Hitler's Berlin* (Larson), which pairs easily with fiction and nonfiction titles. In Larson's riveting narrative, US ambassador William E. Dodd and his family witness the Nazi attacks on the Jews, as well as the implementation of strict laws and government censorship during their stay in World War II Berlin. Americans are not exempt from punishment for even the most innocuous violations of the law: not saluting Hitler is punished by beating, no matter who you are. Grim yet insightful, the Dodds' story gives readers a new perspective on World War II Germany. Readers are often drawn to Erik Larson's books for his stylistic ability to quietly and inexorably create psychological tension while adding unusual historical details in new ways.

Readers captivated by the Dodd family's reactions to the Nazi threats and their need to take care in every small action of their daily lives will be attracted to stories of others who took extreme steps to avoid Nazi notice. This is a good opportunity to suggest *My Enemy's Cradle* (Young), the story of a young Polish Jew who takes her cousin's place at the Lebensborn maternity home in Munich, hiding from the Nazis in plain sight. *Sophie's Choice* (Styron) is a heart-wrenching novel readers may also like, for the haunting choice one mother must make to abandon a child to the Nazis to save another child. Viewers who have seen the movie *Sophie's Choice*, based on the book and starring Meryl Streep, will attest to the power of the screen in dramatizing this story of everyday people caught, like the Dodds in Larson's book, in horrific events they cannot control. Larson's readers may also be captivated by the graphic novel *Moving Pictures* (Immonen), the elegant and mature story of an art curator who tries to hide precious art treasures from the Nazis in occupied Paris—until she is found out. The black-and-white line drawings boldly depict the anger of people defending what they hold precious against an enemy who cannot or will not understand. The graphic novel format can augment the reader's experience of a story and make it more powerful. Many readers will appreciate the suggestion.

A reader who enjoys the biographical aspect of *In the Garden of Beasts* may also like Madeleine Albright's memoir, *Prague Winter: A Personal Story of Remembrance and War, 1937–1948*. Another nonfiction account that also evokes the trauma seen and experienced in Larson's book is the audiobook version of *Unbroken: A World War II Story of Survival, Resilience, and Redemption*, by Laura Hillenbrand, read by Edward Herrmann. These titles may all be of interest to the same readers absorbed by *In the Garden of Beasts*, and they serve as reminders to consider the whole collection of materials and genres in readers' advisory.

STRATEGIES FOR BUSY READERS' ADVISORS

Discussion in previous chapters of appeal characteristics, subgenres of historical fiction, and the whole-collection approach culminate in a colorful palate of options to consider in one small readers' advisory encounter. How can we compact all these titles and ideas into a realistic strategy for use on the job? How is it possible to make several suggestions that readers will be enthused about in the space of five minutes or less? Let's get real.

Free yourself of the "read-alike" onus. No book is exactly like another book. We first need to talk to readers to find out what they most appreciate in a great read. Then we can find titles with similar key elements. What are the two most important appeals that a reader mentions most often? What can you think of to find (or use a quick resource to find) these two appeals? Do the titles you find seem to fit what the reader has described? In the space of just a minute, you might consider and discard three or four titles before you hit on one that will work.

Remember the thirty-second booktalk. As you find titles that may be similar, tell readers about them, zeroing in on the appeals they mentioned and using some of the same words they used in their descriptions of great reads. These short booktalks are usually more about appeal than plot (unless, of course, plot is the main appeal!).

Use one key resource for ideas when nothing comes to mind. You are busy and so is the reader; most likely neither of you has time to explore many options. Before dispensing advice, try out specific readers' advisory tools until you find one that works best for you. Maybe you like to use NoveList Plus, because it lists appeals and has book reviews. Perhaps your library catalog works well for you. You might have a print resource to share with the reader. Whatever it is, use it as part of your conversation.

What are some read-around ideas you have? Does the reader want to delve more deeply into a theme or topic? Is she a movie buff? Does he have a long commute and want to listen to audiobooks? You can check subject headings quickly for the books readers mention as favorites for ideas on what to suggest.

Make a list of the titles the reader responds well to. This way you can find them quickly on the shelf. Maybe you can draw a little mind map—it will make readers smile to see your thought processes on paper, and it gives them something they can take home if they don't have time to explore all options at the moment (or if material isn't available). Three titles are probably enough for one visit, but listing a few others lets readers know there are other options and might suggest directions for the next visit.

Keep in contact. Tell readers your name and/or give them your business card and encourage them to come back and tell you what they think of the stories you suggested. Even if a reader doesn't care for a book you have suggested, you've given him or her the option of coming back to talk and find new ones.

Keep track of repeat questions and popular titles. Sometimes readers in a community ask for similar things or like a particular book. Historical fiction titles like *The Help* (Stockett), *The Paris Wife* (McLain), and *Bring Up the Bodies* (Mantel) are repeatedly requested for book groups, for example, and having a quick list of titles you've suggested as read-alikes or read-arounds will help you with the next reader who asks for the same book or something like it. You can also make a more permanent book list for readers to use and print it out or put it on your website.

HONING YOUR SKILLS

1. Find five read-alikes and read-arounds for a reader who loves historical fiction and doesn't care what the time period is, as long as the writing is literary and the characters are well developed. The reader enjoyed *The Postmistress* (Blake), *Middle Passage* (Johnson), and the Border Trilogy (McCarthy).

2. Readers frequently request funny books, saying, "Please make me laugh." Matching humor to readers can be difficult, because everyone

has a different idea about what is funny. Try to find five historical novels with a range of humor types, subgenres, and themes.

3. Find three to five historical novels set in your state or region that might augment a well-known historical novel or nonfiction work of history. For example, in Seattle readers like *Skid Road: An Informal Portrait of Seattle*, by Murray Morgan, for a sense of the city's history. Some historical novels to suggest to the same readers might be *Hotel on the Corner of Bitter and Sweet* (Ford), *City of Ash* (Chance), *The Living* (Dillard), and *Snow Falling on Cedars* (Guterson).

VIRTUAL READERS' ADVISORY

Sometimes readers' advisors provide online reading suggestions, and libraries offer a gamut of virtual services in an effort both to reach new audiences and to promote the library as a great place to find good reading. Readers' advisory services have come late to the online world: some libraries don't yet offer interactive virtual readers' advisory. Most library systems provide passive readers' advisory online, though, in the form of book lists and online access to readers' resources such as NoveList and NoveList Plus. Among services offered by many large public libraries online are reference and readers' advisory chat, form-based readers' advisory, interactive flow charts, library catalogs that encourage reader interaction (tagging, rating, reviewing, following other readers, suggesting similar titles), and Facebook and Twitter readers' advisory.

Online information and readers' advisory services have several advantages for libraries. As mentioned already, online library services can reach people who do not, for whatever reason, come to the library. These services can be offered at any hour by joining a consortium of libraries around the country or the world. Virtual readers' advisory can be offered to a large service base by a small staff from any location. Offering online services from a library website is also a visible way to advertise readers' advisory to those who may think of the library merely as a place to find information, use a computer, or borrow movies and music.

Depending on the virtual tools used, online readers' advisory also has its disadvantages, the largest of which is the potential for communication breakdown. Online chat, for instance, is designed to be quick, but when readers use the chat service to request a good book, sometimes the interaction gets messy and drawn out, and readers are eventually referred to a readers' advisor. Form-based readers' advisory is a bit better at ferreting out readers' preferences, but the results will only be as good as the reader's input, and the lack of direct interaction can make things difficult. Sometimes the time lag between when the form is submitted and the delivery of reading suggestions is frustrating to readers who may have expected a faster response. A readers' advisory "event" on Facebook is even less satisfying if communication is the goal, although sometimes it's fun to just get a quick suggestion and have other people chime in with their comments.

Other types of virtual readers' advisory are passive in the sense that no personal interaction takes place between readers and the readers' advisor, but they can be helpful in sparking interest and encouraging library use. Although they are as traditional as old-time libraries, book lists tailored to current general reading interests are still very popular with online users and can be linked to the library catalog directly from the website. The most useful book lists are annotated, allowing readers' advisors to "talk to" readers, even if not face-to-face, any time a reader consults the list. Annotation writing is a skill every readers' advisor needs to hone. For help writing good annotations and creating book lists, refer to Joyce Saricks's *Readers' Advisory Service in the Public Library*, where you will also find suggestions for topic and book selection, printing advice, and editing and displaying the finished product.[3]

Some library catalogs, such as BiblioCommons, considered enhanced discovery platforms, encourage users to rate and to write reviews and tags for what they read, in much the same manner as Amazon, LibraryThing, and Shelfari. Discovering how to add books to the different "shelves" in one's account (e.g., "Completed," "In Progress," "For Later") and making personal book lists (annotated if you like), if your catalog provides this option, are frosting on the cake. Reader reviews can be quite helpful to readers and readers' advisors alike in choosing titles.

Many libraries host blogs where staff and other readers can share their reading interests, post reviews and book lists, and make comments. In 2012 Salem Press awarded its stamp of approval to the *Eleventh Stack* blog sponsored by the Carnegie Library of Pittsburgh, and in 2011 it endorsed the Cecil County (MD) Public Library's blog as best Public Institution Library Blog. Becky Spratford, readers' advisor extraordinaire, former instructor at Dominican University's library school and blog host of *RA for All* and *RA for All: Horror*, mentions several excellent blogs in her feature "Readers' Advisory Blogs You May Have Missed."[4] Among Spratford's favorites are

Blogging for a Good Book, by Williamsburg (VA) Regional Library (bfgb .wordpress.com); *Shelf Talk,* by the Seattle Public Library (shelftalk.spl .org); and *Missouri Book Challenge,* by Brentwood Public Library (mobook challenge.blogspot.com). Find library blogs that interest you and follow them to see what what's trending in the book world.

Interactive reading flow charts or infographics can be a fun approach to visual mapping for readers, one that is more linear and structured than the kind of "mind map" we might draw while suggesting books to readers. Reading flow charts are relatively new and are increasingly popular and great fun visually. They usually begin with a specific title and pose questions to guide readers toward books according to how they answer the questions. These flow charts can be as simple as "What Should I Read Next? A Hipster Lit Flow Chart"[5] or as complex as the "NPR Top 100 Science Fiction and Fantasy Books" flow chart.[6] If you have the skills and inclination, you might construct a similar chart to help students choose good summer reading, such as "Which Books Should You Read This Summer?"[7] These reading flow charts are based on prechosen books, so they lend themselves more to virtual readers' advisory than to in-person discussions, when it's easier to talk about connections between titles. The Seattle Public Library created the book flow chart in figure 9.1 for its adult summer reading program in 2013.

FORM-BASED READERS' ADVISORY

The phrase "form-based readers' advisory" may be new to some of us, but the concept is certainly not. A form-based service is simply one that asks people to fill out a form to receive a product. In this case, the library asks a reader to fill out a reading profile, either on paper or online; then the reader receives book suggestions on the basis of that profile. The profile can be an intensive survey of the reader's tastes in literature or a simple free-form invitation to tell the readers' advisor about what he or she likes to read. Some readers appreciate an in-depth profile form, as it forces them to think about their reading tastes and to acquire a vocabulary for talking about books with library staff (and others). Other readers prefer not to spend the time filling in a long form and respond positively to the free-form approach—the "EZ" reader profile, so to speak.

Advantages of and reasons for the form-based readers' advisory approach have been discussed for years among researchers and librarians. In his 2006 article "Improving the Model for Interactive Readers'

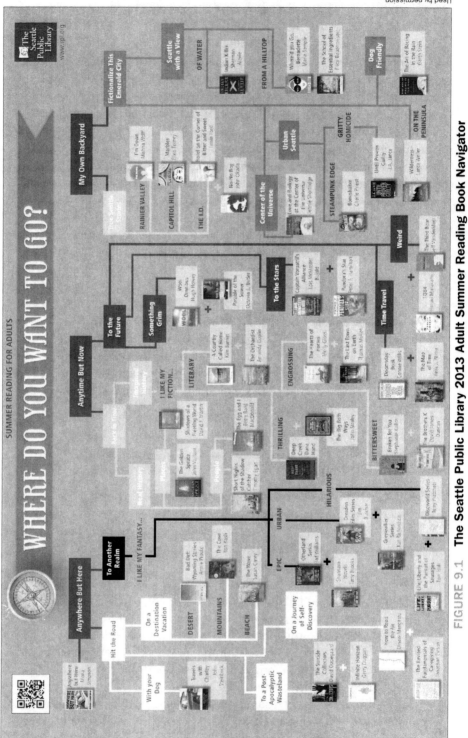

FIGURE 9.1   The Seattle Public Library 2013 Adult Summer Reading Book Navigator

Advisory Service," Neil Hollands suggested that form-based readers' advisory is sometimes more successful in connecting readers with the books they will enjoy than are face-to-face services. Libraries offering only in-person readers' advisory services may be doing their users a disservice by operating under faulty assumptions, including thinking that readers will actually approach a library staff member for reading suggestions, that the person they do approach is the right person to give meaningful suggestions, or that an in-person conversation will elicit enough pertinent information about a reader's tastes.[8] Barry Trott, digital services director at the Williamsburg (VA) Regional Library and editor of *Reference and User Services Quarterly*, expanded on this list of faulty assumptions at the Catholic University of America School of Library and Information Science 2011 symposium, "Bridging the Spectrum." In addition, Trott cites among nine benefits of using the form-based approach to readers' advisory that reader requests can be answered by advisors best suited to the specific profile and that the readers' advisor has the time to more fully respond to requests for reading suggestions.[9]

The Williamsburg (VA) Regional Library uses an in-depth reader-profile form and has good reader response: from 2004 to March 2013, 1,100 forms were completed, according to Barry Trott.[10] The reader-profile form asks for up to ten current and past examples of reading likes and five disliked titles; it requests information on genre and format preferences out of twenty possibilities; it couches eight appeal categories in everyday language and has readers rate them on a scale; and it features the category "peeves and pleasures," or elements readers want to limit or include, such as violence, sexual content, and obscenity. Edmonton Public Library in Alberta, Canada, also offers form-based reading suggestions using a reader-profile questionnaire, but one slightly shorter than Williamsburg's. Text boxes are provided for readers' answers to open-ended questions like "tell us what you want" or "what I like about my favorites." Other topics include format, length, genre, time period, location, and hot-button issues.[11]

The Seattle Public Library has had good success with its form-based virtual readers' advisory service, Your Next 5 Books. Along with virtual reference questions, the Your Next 5 Books service operates from the QuestionPoint reference service platform. Online users click a web button and fill in a short form asking them to describe a book or several books they've enjoyed and why (see figure 9.2). The prompt simply says: "Tell our librarians about a few books and/or authors you've enjoyed, and what you liked about them. Also feel free to tell us about books you

FIGURE 9.2
Your Next 5 Books logo, Seattle Public Library

Used by permission.

haven't liked, and why. What are you in the mood to read next?"[12]

From this profile of 2,500 characters or less, readers' advisors choose five titles that are similar to the ones the reader enjoyed and reply via e-mail. In the e-mail, the readers' advisor describes each of the five titles and why he or she chose it. At the same time, a list of the five items is created in the library catalog and is assigned the QuestionPoint question number and a descriptive title. A link to this list is included in the e-mail, so readers can place holds directly from the list. The added advantage of posting these short lists on BiblioCommons' enhanced discovery catalog is that they can be searched at a later date by title, subject, tags, and staff account lists. For finished examples of saved "Your Next 5 Books" lists, see the Seattle Public Library's catalog, and search under "lists" using "Your Next 5 Books" as the search string.[13]

As of March 2013 approximately one hundred libraries worldwide provide some type of form-based readers' advisory—in Hong Kong, New Zealand, Sweden, Canada, and the United States.[14] But not all libraries have the resources to offer form-based readers' advisory. It is labor intensive and, according to Neal Hollands, even after practice and streamlining, takes between thirty minutes and two hours to complete one reader request.[15] Seattle Public Library reader services librarian David Wright cautions against too much publicity of a personalized book list service, saying, "After an article in the local newspaper we received about 200 requests in two days."[16] The ability to offer such a service requires the technology, available staff time, and commitment on the part of the institution to support the service. There is, however, no doubt that readers appreciate this type of service. Seattle Public Library readers' advisors created approximately 1,500 lists for adults on Your Next 5 Books between July 2011 and April 2013. David Wright and his colleagues keep a running list of "kudos"—the grateful responses of people who have received their "next five books." One of the most poignant was, "I know we aren't friends and that you are just doing your job . . . but this is the best present anyone has ever given me! Thank you a million times!"[17]

PUTTING IT ALL TOGETHER

Using the whole-collection concept in readers' advisory, offering form-based and online readers' advisory, can be both daunting and freeing. Thinking outside genre limits requires effort and practice, but by doing so we are free to imagine similar and supportive stories and information in any genre or format. Virtual real-time readers' advisory on chat, Facebook, or Twitter puts readers' advisors on the spot, as does in-person readers' advisory. By constantly making connections between stories and by talking about our reading with colleagues, however, we can train ourselves to suggest materials from other genres, subject areas, and formats. Readers look to us for suggestions. They are not thinking in categories; they are asking, "What's good?" The more creative matchmaking readers' advisors can do, the more communication lines will stay open with readers. Continually thinking about the books, movies, TV shows, audiobooks, and graphic novels you have enjoyed or are asked about and how to match them with others is a good way to get started in making those links between materials. Use the research tools you have at hand, in print, and online, and talk to your colleagues about how they make whole-collection connections.

NOTES

1. Neal Wyatt, *The Readers' Advisory Guide to Nonfiction* (Chicago: American Library Association, 2007), 233.
2. Ibid.
3. Joyce Saricks, *Readers' Advisory Service in the Public Library*, 3rd ed. (Chicago: American Library Association, 2005), 145–55.
4. Becky Spratford, "Readers' Advisory Blogs You May Have Missed," *RA News*, March 2012, www.ebscohost.com/novelist/novelist-special/readers-advisory -blogs-you-may-have-missed.
5. "The Hipster Lit Flowchart," *Goodreads* (blog), November 27, 2012, www .goodreads.com/blog/show/396-the-hipster-lit-flow-chart.
6. "Flowchart: Navigating NPR's Top 100 Science Fiction and Fantasy Books," *SF Signal*, September 27, 2011, www.sfsignal.com/archives/2011/09/flowchart_for _navigating_nprs_top_100_sff_books/.
7. "Summer Reading Flowchart: What Should You Read on Your Break?" *Teach: Make a Difference* (blog), June 5, 2012, http://teach.com/great-educational-resources/ summer-reading-flowchart.
8. Neil Hollands, "Improving the Model for Interactive Readers' Advisory Service," *Reference and User Services Quarterly* 45, no. 3 (2006): 205–12.

9. Barry Trott, "Form-Based Readers' Advisory Services," presentation at the session "Innovations in Information and Knowledge Services," School of Library and Information Science, Catholic University of America, Washington, DC, February 25, 2011, http://lis.cua.edu/res/docs/symposium/2011-symposium/trott.pdf.

10. "We are actually at just under 1,100 forms completed as of March 2013." Barry Trott, personal communication, April 17, 2013.

11. The Edmonton (Alberta) Public Library personalized book-list service is found at www.epl.ca/services/personalized-book-list.

12. The Seattle Public Library Your Next 5 Books online readers' advisory service is available at www.spl.org/using-the-library/get-help/your-next-5-books.

13. Search for "Your Next 5 Books" lists in the Seattle Public Library's BiblioCommons catalog, using "Your Next 5 Books" and keywords. See examples at http://seattle .bibliocommons.com/search?t=userlist&search_category=userlist&q=your+next +5+books+historical+fiction&commit=Search.

14. See appendix C, taken from an Excel spreadsheet listing libraries currently offering form-based readers' advisory, compiled by Barry Trott, digital services director of Williamsburg (VA) Regional Library.

15. Hollands, "Improving the Model," 205–12.

16. David Wright, "Your Next Five Books: What Form-Based Readers' Advisory Can Do for You," *ALKI* 27, no. 3 (2011): 9–10.

17. Ibid.

10

KEEPING CURRENT, STAYING RELEVANT

MARKETING THE COLLECTION

Once a historical novel is no longer featured in the new books section of a library or bookstore, unless it is hugely popular, like *Wolf Hall* (Mantel) or *Pillars of the Earth* (Follett), or the author is well-known (Philippa Gregory), it is consigned to relative obscurity without readers' advisors as advocates. Hand selling a book to readers is perhaps the most efficient way to suggest books of any kind, but we can reach more people with our great suggestions if we branch out into other types of readers' advisory, such as book lists; displays; posters; programs for readers; and innovative outreach like features in local newspapers, blog posts, comments on others' blog posts, and active participation in online networking of all types (e.g., LinkedIn, Goodreads, LibraryThing, Facebook). "Marketing" any part of your collection takes a conscious effort, and you will be richly rewarded, with readers eager to talk about the books they are reading or ask you in person for reading suggestions.

BOOK LISTS

Book lists are a long-standing tradition for library marketing to patrons but often they seem to be of more use as bookmarks to readers than as informative tools. Also, when you make and print a book list, all the books on that list soon acquire hold lists and people become frustrated when the suggested titles aren't available. Ask yourself a few questions before splurging on book-list printing costs. For instance, which lists might be the most popular for readers browsing in the library? Readers also browse in the online catalog. Can you make book lists in your catalog or link from the catalog to book lists on your webpage?

Do you want to annotate your book lists? In a list of historical novels that are on one topic, are set in the same time period, or are read-alikes for a popular, well-known book, perhaps you don't need to annotate, and a short summary at the top of the list might be all the information readers need to make their choice. In contrast, a list of books with a variety of appeals and topics might be more useful to readers if it is annotated.

Think about strong historical fiction authors. Who is popular, and would a read-alike or while-you-wait (for titles with long hold lists) list alleviate readers' frustration at not finding the exact book they want right now? To keep up with popular demand for fresh new titles and authors, your book lists need to be fast and easy to create. Posting a book list in the catalog or on the website may be the best option for this. Book lists that are of value to readers for at least one or two years could be annotated and printed, but make sure you can support the demand you create with enough copies in your collection.

DISPLAYS

Creating attractive displays is another way to feature a particular collection such as historical fiction, and it is already in wide use. Even if you don't have fancy display shelving, a small table with a few great books makes a big difference for readers needing suggestions. Many readers don't know they will enjoy historical fiction and won't ask for suggestions. Brainstorm some ideas for historical fiction displays, make some quick lists of books to pull from the shelf, and make a small and simple display. Romantic historical fiction is very popular, for example, as are collections of books relating to local festivals or local history. Take advantage of events such as Women's History Month (March) and Black History Month (February), or special dates like Veteran's Day, D-Day, and Independence Day. Change your displays frequently—at least monthly—and every few days rearrange the books to face out new titles for browsers.

OUTREACH, PROGRAMS, AND ONLINE SERVICES

If readers' advisors establish a name for themselves in the reading community, opportunities to speak at local functions often arise, usually from the chamber of commerce, university clubs, churches, senior communities, and library foundation events. This kind of outreach is good publicity for the library, and it gives you a chance to talk about your collection and books you love. Readers will ask for you at the library and assume that the library is the place to go for reading suggestions.

Establishing a name in the community is relatively easy. Here are a few ideas on how to do so:

- Host author readings and events at your library.
- Run several book discussion groups at your library and/or in the community.
- Write regular book reviews for your local paper and library newsletter.
- Post your own staff picks lists on your website and put your picture by it.
- Make "shelf talkers" to advertise books and authors and secure them to the shelf throughout the collection, and be sure to include your name on them.
- Host a fun adult reading program any time of the year, with prizes and special events at which you speak or introduce guest speakers.
- Represent your library at community parades, festivals, and outdoor concerts.

Businesses are increasingly using Twitter to provide on-the-spot customer service, and readers' advisors should take heed and do the same. Linda Johns, a readers' advisor with the Seattle Public Library's social media team, says, "I see all of social media as service—or at least ripe for service potential. We end up answering [reference] questions on Twitter and Facebook, too. There's great potential for doing more—both in terms of RA and reference."[1] Your library system may host blogs, or have a Facebook presence and a Twitter account. If you are involved in representing your library in social media, that's great. If not, now's your chance. Readers' advisors must take advantage of social media as a way to reach readers and increase community awareness of our libraries' relevance.

Plan special Facebook book-suggestion times and invite other readers' advisors to participate. The Seattle Public Library hosts quarterly "Facebook RA Days," when a group of readers' advisors from different locations in our library system gather to invite people to describe what they'd like to read next and receive suggestions—all on Facebook. Each person who asks for a book suggestion receives one or two titles and a brief explanation of why we suggested them. Usually the readers' advisors work as a group in one place with laptops and snacks and then wildly suggest books as fast as they can, generating a camaraderie and enthusiasm for what we do and enjoying readers' excitement at receiving our suggestions. Turnover time from query to answer is about five minutes, and reader response is overwhelmingly positive. We usually suggest books for 100 to 150 readers during each session, which lasts about four to six hours. It's similar to the Your Next 5 Books program mentioned in chapter 9, only much less involved. We usually have a surge of Your Next 5 Books requests following each Facebook RA Day.

If your library can support online chat and/or e-mail reference service, you can integrate a readers' advisory service into the existing online armature. Some questions patrons ask online are more readers' advisory than traditional reference, and that's a chance to offer your personal services. If you don't have library chat or e-mail reference privileges, make a formal proposal to set up an online service. While you wait for approval, find a way to drum up more readers' advisory business using the marketing channels your library has already established. Online readers' advisory is an excellent service that ties busy readers to reading in a fun, easy way that, once set up, is relatively inexpensive to sustain.

Book groups are a long-standing program offered by most libraries, either hosted by staff or by a community member. A good way to expand a book group presence is to offer programs tailored to community book groups: a booktalk in which you offer suggestions for good discussion books, a genre book group just for a season, a meeting for people to come talk about what they are reading, or even a problem-solving session for community book groups.[2] A colleague and I presented a Book Group Tune-Up program, in which we offered solutions for potential book group problems. It was quite popular! Also popular are drop-in events during December, at which readers' advisors give in-person suggestions for books as gifts and have lots of handouts: book lists, program fliers, and free books.

These are just a few of the many ways libraries market themselves and their collections. For each event you plan, emphasize literature and promote the love of reading. Library administrators and foundations have different reasons to extend a hand to the community, and it's up to readers' advisors to talk about books. Putting out fliers and book lists at library events is only a start—we need to talk to readers on a big scale: giving mini-booktalks in the stacks, while great, is only a tiny part of what we can do. If you have the opportunity to get out into the community, host a program or a meeting and incorporate a what-are-you-reading session as part of the agenda.

RESOURCES FOR READERS' ADVISORS

Print Resources

The most effective readers' advisor will read widely and know where to turn for help. Online resources have the advantage of being quick, generally easy to use, and accessible on the spot. Librarians also need to remember some of the wonderful print references that can augment what's available online and sometimes appeal more to readers who prefer to handle a book. The resources listed here are valuable aids to readers' advisors looking for historical fiction suggestions:

Genreflecting: A Guide to Popular Reading Interests, 7th ed. Cynthia Orr and Diana Tixier Herald (Santa Barbara, CA: Libraries Unlimited, 2013).

> An advantage of this print resource is that it serves both readers' advisors and readers directly. Informative text lists and describes the best books in general fiction and in many genres and subgenres, explaining the appeals of each. In addition, an introductory section, aimed at the readers' advisor, gives information about genres and discusses best practices in readers' advisory service.

Historical Fiction II: A Guide to the Genre, Genreflecting Advisory Series, Sarah L. Johnson, ed. (Santa Barbara, CA: Libraries Unlimited, 2009).

> As mentioned in chapter 1 of this book, Johnson's book is most helpful when seeking good historical fiction from particular time periods, events, and geographic locations. Sometimes a list format is an easy way to locate titles, and this is a good reference to keep on hand for complete coverage and quality content on individual titles and topics.

Now Read This III: A Guide to Mainstream Fiction, 3rd ed. Nancy Pearl and Sarah Statz Cords (Santa Barbara, CA: Libraries Unlimited, 2010).

> Pearl and Cords emphasize mainstream fiction, but novels classified as general fiction are sometimes set in historical time periods and may be of interest to historical fiction readers. One advantage of this reference is that it's organized by broad appeal, so once a reader's appeal preferences are established, it's easy to focus on a particular section of the book, according to setting, story, character, or language.

The Readers' Advisory Guide to Genre Fiction, 2nd ed. Joyce G. Saricks
(Chicago: American Library Association, 2009).

Readers' advisors cannot afford to miss this essential self-study guide
to talking with readers about the genres they love. Saricks introduces
fifteen different genres (including historical fiction), lists benchmark
titles and the appeals that entice readers to each genre, and gives suggestions on how to communicate effectively with those readers. Well
indexed and easy to use, this guide is indispensible.

What Do I Read Next? A Reader's Guide to Current Genre Fiction,
Neil Barron (San Francisco: Gale, 2013).

What Do I Read Next? can be useful when seeking older titles as well as
the relatively recent, especially when you keep older editions. Using
this series in your readers' advisory conversation is a good way to
enlist the help and interest of readers on the spot. With many indexing options—such as author, title, subject, time period, geographical
setting, and characters—it's a great browsing tool that makes specific
title suggestions for further reading. Each book entry lists series information, subject headings, a book summary, reviews, other books by
the same author, and five other books you might enjoy. The resource
is also available online.

Online Resources

So many online resources purport to be exactly what readers and readers'
advisors need when seeking read-alikes and book suggestions in general.
It can be truly daunting to sift through them to find the best sites for historical fiction readers' advisory. A few great helps are listed here that are
useful in teaching ourselves about readers' advisory work, and in finding
quick title suggestions, topical book lists, and in some cases, great read-
alike suggestions for specific books. One caution, however, is that in many
cases these wonderful efficient online tools choose "read-alikes" largely
on the basis of subject similarities. Topical matching can be good if readers are interested in the setting details and/or thematic issues, but simply
matching these attributes lacks the appeal factors that make a read-alike
valuable to readers. As a rule of thumb, we should be careful to check
reviews for appeal before suggesting a title.

ADULT READING ROUND TABLE (ARRT)

www.arrtreads.org/home.html

Designed and maintained by Mary Back of Rolling Meadows (IL) Library, this most useful site combines the talents of a steering committee made up of experienced readers' advisors under a common mission. The Adult Reading Round Table (ARRT) mission is "developing Readers' Advisory skills and promoting reading for pleasure through public libraries in the Chicago metropolitan area." Luckily the site is full of useful information and PDF files easily accessible to readers' advisors across the country. Brush up on your genre knowledge with notes from ARRT's genre studies and genre boot camps, check out current annotated reading lists, and keep an eye on the "Resources" tab titled "Common Problems, Uncommon Solutions."

BOOKS AND AUTHORS

http://bna.galegroup.com/bna

Books and Authors is the online version of *What Do I Read Next?* mentioned earlier. It is a free service that asks only that you register your name and e-mail. The site is surprisingly rich with information, though you must click through to it. The homepage opens with "Know What You're Going to Read Next?" and some tempting covers and categories to click on for descriptions. Readers' advisors should look to the left column for genres and subgenres, both fiction and nonfiction. The first page of each genre displays book covers in descending date order: there are 889 pages of historical fiction to "browse" if you like! The left-hand column displays subgenres and topical headings such as "Adventure," "Biblical," "Alternate History," "Gay/Lesbian," "Antebellum American South," and "French Revolution." Numbers of titles listed vary by subject headings— the French Revolution heading lists three pages of titles; "Adventure," twenty; and "World War II," thirty-nine—though many other categories have fewer.

Each title entry includes information about the author and a bibliography of his or her work; a list of characters, time period, and subject headings; edition and format information; book reviews when available; and best of all, read-alikes. Each "recommended similar title" has brief descriptions in addition to links to the full book record.

This site also features "My Reading Room," which allows users to list books they've read and want to read, and to keep track of their own reviews. Not as useful for general fiction, the site nonetheless lists author information and categorizes much of what we might think is "general fiction" into a subgenre—for example, Elizabeth Strout's *The Burgess Boys*, a contemporary story, is categorized as "Family Saga." This is an excellent tool for finding genre reading suggestions and is therefore a strong tool in historical fiction readers' advisory.

EBSCO'S NOVELIST AND NOVELIST PLUS DATABASES
www.ebscohost.com/novelist

If your library subscribes to either version of NoveList, created by Duncan Smith, Roger Rohweder, and John Strickler, you must become familiar with this fabulous readers' advisory tool. NoveList is a great resource for readers' advisors to use for read-alike suggestions, book identification, and reviews, and when seeking books based on appeal characteristics. The basic NoveList database service indexes fiction, and it is completely searchable by keyword, including reviews. NoveList Plus includes both fiction and nonfiction, also completely searchable. Both versions provide tools for readers' advisors, such as feature articles, book discussion guides, award winners, and a readers' advisor's toolbox. The best features of NoveList are its appeals indexing and the read-alikes listed for each title entry, which include brief statements about why the book was chosen as a read-alike, often including the name of the person who chose it.

Subscribe to "NoveList Notes" and "NoveList RA News" for current news and user tips, and take advantage of the other helps accessible from the "How to Use NoveList" button. NoveList also offers NextReads, an e-mail newsletter service that subscribing libraries can offer patrons. More than twenty NextReads newsletters are offered, historical fiction and nonfiction history included. Each topical newsletter lists approximately ten books with meaty descriptions—half new and half older titles of interest.

HISTORICAL NOVELS.INFO
www.historicalnovels.info

This huge website gathers a bit of everything, old and new, and can be a very helpful resource, especially for inclusive lists of titles by time period and geographic location, and for lesser-known historical fiction. Brief annotations give hints at the treasures within, both old and new, well-known and obscure. Readers' advisors should be aware that while this wonderful older website is deep and wide, it's not a quick tool to use in conversation with readers and many titles listed are difficult to find in libraries and bookstores.

HISTORICAL NOVEL SOCIETY

http://historicalnovelsociety.org

The Historical Novel Society website purports to be "the home of histori-cal fiction online." The society has good reason to make this claim, even though many other excellent sites exist. The online magazine boasts 6,673 reviews and 173 feature articles to date. Reviews are keyword searchable and browsable by author, genre, period, century, and publisher. A search for Abraham Lincoln pulled both fiction and nonfiction, so the site is not limited to fiction. This site is a good one for self-educating—to explore and use to keep up with current titles and authors.

Library Websites

It's fun and informative to look at book suggestions from other libraries and librarians. This is, of course, only a small percentage of all the many libraries providing great readers' advisory online. When talking with his-torical fiction readers, you might like to have a few library websites in your toolbox to pull out for specific occasions.

CHARLOTTE MECKLENBURG (NC) PUBLIC LIBRARY

www.cmlibrary.org/readers_club/features/featuresList.asp

The Charlotte Mecklenburg Public Library website is rich with topical lists of books reviewed by staff. Many of the book lists are full of his-torical fiction gems chosen and read by the library staff and linked to other lists, author websites, and author interviews of interest to readers. Readers have an opportunity to comment, making the site even more reader-friendly. The list simply called "Historical Fiction" contains more than one hundred titles and is organized with older titles first, so all the new books are at the end. This is definitely a site to browse, both for read-ers' advisors and for readers, with lists such as "Wild, Wild West," "Sea Stories," "Black History Month," "Alternate History," "Celebrate the First Nations," "Latin American Literature," "Carolina Stories," most of which contain both fiction and nonfiction and will be of interest to historical fic-tion readers.

FICTION_L

www.mgpl.org/read-listen-view/fl/flbooklists/

Sponsored by Morton Grove (IL) Public Library, Fiction_L is a free e-mail service for librarians to share readers' advisory questions and ideas. Book lists created by the group online are compiled and shared on the Morton Grove Library's website. Although many of the book lists date back to the early 2000s, the selection is unparalleled, and the lists include myriad good reads still available in libraries. Some of the gems to explore include "Historical Fiction Not Set in the U.S." (2008), "Civil War Novels" (2011), "Art and Artists in Fiction" (2008), and "King Tut: Ancient Egyptian Fiction" (2005).

HENNEPIN COUNTY (MN) LIBRARY
www.hclib.org/pub/bookspace/FindAGoodBook.cfm?Genre=fiction

Hennepin County Library's website provides a nice selection of up-to-date book lists in many genres, as well as "Bookspace," feature lists created by readers. The historical fiction book list suggests thirty-nine great recent titles, with detailed summaries from the library's catalog. In addition to the historical fiction book list, check out the lists of family sagas, Christian fiction, and adventure novels, all of which include historical novels.

WILLIAMSBURG (VA) REGIONAL LIBRARY
www.wrl.org

Williamsburg Regional Library's website rewards visitors with a wide variety of book lists, from read-alikes to topical, and their handy "100+" lists. These topical book lists, including a great one of historical fiction authors, make a handy and fast tool for on-the-spot readers' advisory without the frills. It's easy to find reviews and blog articles, but not so easy to just get the authors' names. I use huge alphabetical lists like these to jog my memory for good authors to suggest when time is of the essence. Even if you've read a ton of historical fiction, there's nothing like a lunch-hour fly-by reader with an urgent need for a great historical fiction suggestion to make your mind go blank. Thanks to Williamsburg Regional, you need not blank out! This library also hosts the "Looking for a Good Book" personalized reading-list service mentioned in chapter 9.

Readers' Advisory–Related Blogs

Many public libraries host their own blogs. If your library has a blog, be sure to make use of it! The range of book lovers' blogs is wide, and finding genre-specific ones can be difficult. Here are a few to explore that are useful and informative, though this is by no means an exhaustive list. For more information about readers' advisory blogs, read Becky Spratford's article, "Readers' Advisory Blogs You May Have Missed," from the March 2012

EbscoHost/NoveListRANewsnewsletter(www.ebscohost.com/novelist/
novelist-special/readers-advisory-blogs-you-may-have-missed).

BLOGGING FOR A GOOD BOOK

http://bfgb.wordpress.com

Staff members post a book review per day on Williamsburg Regional
(VA) Library's blog. For access to historical fiction postings, click on the
"Historical Fiction," tag or combine words such as "historical fantasy" in
the search box. Frequently reading this blog is a good way to quickly skim
for good, new reading suggestions and ideas.

HISTORICAL-FICTION.COM

http://historical-fiction.com

In "About This Site," blog host Arleigh Johnson, a reviewer for the
Historical Novel Society, explains that she started keeping her historical
fiction reviews on her blog as an indexing and record-keeping exercise.
Readers' advisors are glad she did and still does! Most of the articles and
books reviewed focus on the twelfth through nineteenth centuries and are
about England, Ireland, France, and Italy, so this site is worth keeping in
mind when seeking title suggestions from a certain period, movement, or
war. Using Johnson's categories, finding pertinent titles is quick and easy.
Attempts at keyword searching are less effective, although a search under
the appeal term "humorous" did yield good results. This site is a good
bet for in-depth professional reviews and consistently good title choices.
Blog posts on several topics of interest to historical fiction readers, such as
"Richard III and the Princes in the Tower Novels" and "Versions of Romeo
and Juliet throughout History" are also of interest. In addition to this blog,
Arleigh Johnson hosts a blog at Royal-Intrigue.net (http://royal-intrigue
.net) for Jean Plaidy (aka Philippa Carr, Victoria Holt, et al.) fans, and at
Austenista.com (http://austenista.com), where she keeps track of contin-
uations, retellings, and variations of Jane Austen's fiction.

HISTORICAL FICTION NOTEBOOK

www.historicalfictionnotebook.com

Historical Fiction Notebook is hosted by Katherine Gypson, a journalist and
avid reader and reviewer of historical fiction. The subtitle for the blog is "A
Place for History, Historical Fiction and Other Random Reads"—a good
summary of the site. The site provides good, easily accessible reviews to
help readers' advisors keep current.

READING THE PAST
http://readingthepast.blogspot.com

Reading the Past is historical fiction guru Sarah Johnson's blog, which is not to be missed. Johnson sponsors the blog and invites others to post articles on readers' advisory in historical fiction, author interviews, and book reviews of new and backlist titles. If you want great historical fiction suggestions to consume and share with other readers, this is the blog to watch. A helpful list of other useful blogs is included and the index to reviews and interviews is extensive.

SHELF TALK
http://shelftalk.spl.org

The Seattle Public Library hosts the *Shelf Talk* blog and all staff members are encouraged to contribute posts on anything related to the Seattle Public Library and its collections. The blog features regular columns, such as "Romantic Wednesdays" and "Science Fiction Fridays." Posts about thrillers and historical fiction are also offered on a regular basis and are easily found using keyword searching.

Reviews

All of the blogs listed in this chapter are good places to find reviews outside the usual "review media," such as *Booklist*, *Publishers Weekly*, and the *Washington Post*, which librarians routinely scan for new titles of interest to readers. In addition to blogs that are historical fiction inclusive or focused, it's wise to keep a few more great reviewing websites on your browser's favorites list. These are a few readily accessible online review sites that, while not specific to historical fiction, are good sources for fiction reviews and informative, current information on books and authors.

BOOKBROWSE
www.bookbrowse.com

While BookBrowse encourages membership, which does have its perks (more read-alikes, previews of popular books online, access to advance copies, enhanced searching and sorting capability), much of what's publically available is quite useful. The site offers weekly top picks with descriptions, reviews, and sometimes background information; access to suggested titles by genre and subgenre: BookBrowse annual favorites, and award winners; and author biographies, interviews, and read-alike authors. Visitors can comment on the BookBrowse "Book Talk" online book discussion, and access reading group guides and book club advice.

BOOKLIST ONLINE
www.booklistonline.com

Booklist Online is the online version of the American Library Association's subscription magazine. If your library doesn't subscribe, some content is freely accessible. Book reviews on the main site, however, are not. That said, some feature articles are offered, and if you click on one of the several blogs sponsored by *Booklist*, you can find book discussions and reviews. Three *Booklist* blogs in particular offer topics difficult to find online. The *Book Group Buzz* blog suggests good discussion titles, tips for book group leaders, reading guides, and *Shelf Renewal* reviews and discusses older titles. *Audiobooker* is a good blog to keep up with for reviews and comments on the joys of audiobooks and great "reads." If your library subscribes to Booklist Online, you are in luck—there are more than 160,000 well-indexed book reviews on the site.

BOOKPAGE
http://bookpage.com

BookPage is a good site to follow for substantive and concise book reviews, book lists, and author interviews. The site offers full access to the print edition and online exclusives. Some features are written by guest authors.

BOOK REPORTER
www.bookreporter.com

Be careful to give yourself plenty of time to explore this fun resource for book lovers. You will be tempted to sign up for the site's many e-newsletters, to join contests and give-away drawings, to check out the blog and read reviews, to find out what titles are coming soon, and to learn more about authors in the "News and Interviews" section.

NEW YORK TIMES SUNDAY BOOK REVIEWS
www.nytimes.com/pages/books/review/index.html

It can be tough to find hard copies of this at your public library, because it's a resource many people use to find new titles of interest. Also, it behooves readers' advisors to read it every week, along with your local newspaper's "Books" section. The long, detailed book reviews are quite entertaining and informative.

Awards

Few awards are given specifically for historical fiction, although the wily reader's advisor can locate some historical fiction award winners in lists for other genres, such as those here. Only the most recent award title that's historical fiction is listed here. Full award lists are readily available online.

BLACK CAUCUS OF THE AMERICAN LIBRARY ASSOCIATION AWARDS
www.bcala.org/association/about3.htm

The Black Caucus Award is given to African American authors who have made significant contributions in each award category. Sometimes the winning title is a historical novel. The fiction winner for 2013 was *Freeman*, by Leonard Pitts Jr.

BRITISH CRIME WRITERS ASSOCIATION DAGGER AWARDS
www.thecwa.co.uk/daggers/

Gold Daggers are given for the best crime novels, some of which are historical. The most recent historical fiction Gold Dagger winner was in 2011—a mystery set in the American South, *Crooked Letter, Crooked Letter* (Franklin).

DAVID J. LANGUM, SR. PRIZE FOR AMERICAN HISTORICAL FICTION
www.langumstrust.org/histlit.html

The Langum Charitable Trust awards this annual prize and a $1,000 honorarium for the best novel of American historical fiction that exhibits excellence as great fiction and great history. The 2012 winner was *The Cove*, by Ron Rash.

GOLDEN HEART AWARD
www.rwa.org/p/cm/ld/fid=536

Presented by the Romance Writers of America, winners of this award in the "Historical Romance" category are pertinent to seekers of romantic historical novels. The 2013 Best Historical Romance was *Drawn to the Earl*, by Joanna Shupe.

HISTORICAL NOVEL SOCIETY INTERNATIONAL AWARD
http://historicalnovelsociety.org/hns-award/

This prize of £5,000 and e-publication is awarded for unpublished historical novels. The award winner for 2012–13 is *With Blood in Their Eyes* (Cobb).

JAMES FENIMORE COOPER AWARD

http://sah.columbia.edu/content/information-1

Awarded biennially, on odd-numbered years, this award is sponsored by the Society of American Historians, formed in 1939 to promote biographical and historical literature. The James Fenimore Cooper Award is given to the best novel of American historical fiction that contributes to historical understanding, is historically authentic, and is of high literary caliber. In May 2013, the award went to Stephen Harrigan, for *Remember Ben Clayton*.

NATIONAL JEWISH BOOK AWARD

www.jewishbookcouncil.org/awards/national-jewish-book-award.html

This award is given in honor of outstanding literary fiction that affirms Jewish values. Sometimes the award winners are treasures of Jewish historical fiction. In 2011 Aharon Appelfeld won for his novel *Until the Dawn's Light*.

THE READING LIST

www.ala.org/rusa/awards/readinglist

Sponsored by the Reference and User Services division of the American Library Association, the Reading List comprises the best genre fiction novels each year. Books in eight different genres are honored annually and a short list is also included, which is a great bonus for readers' advisors. Historical fiction is one of the genres on the list; the 2013 winner was *Bring Up the Bodies* (Mantel).

RITA AWARD

www.rwa.org/p/cm/ld/fid=528

The RITA Award goes to excellent romance novels in various categories, including Best Historical Romance. The 2013 historical romance winner was *A Rogue by Any Other Name*, by Sarah MacLean. Other award categories, such as Best First Book, Inspirational Romance, Romance Novella, and Novel with Strong Romantic Elements, may also include historical romance fiction winners.

ROMANTIC TIMES REVIEWERS' CHOICE AWARDS

www.rtbookreviews.com/rt-awards/nominees-and-winners

In 2012 the overall award for historical romance went to Elizabeth Hoyt for *Thief of Shadows*, although *Romantic Times* reviewers give awards in many historical and other categories that may include some historical romance fiction. Award categories for historical romance include but are not limited to First Historical Romance, Historical Love and Laughter, Regency-Set Historical Romance, British Isles-Set Historical Romance, Historical Fantasy/Paranormal and Sensual Historical Romance.

SIDEWAYS AWARD FOR ALTERNATE HISTORY

www.uchronia.net/sidewise/about.html

Novels winning the Sideways Award will be of interest to some historical fiction buffs and some fantasy aficionados. The 2011 Sideways Award for long-form fiction, the most recent year the award was given, went to *When Angels Wept: A What-If History of the Cuban Missile Crisis* (Swedin). The 2011 award for short-form fiction went to Alan Smale, for *A Clash of Eagles*.

THE SOPHIE BRODY AWARD

www.ala.org/rusa/awards/brody

This award is funded by Arthur Brody and the Brodart Foundation to recognize the best in Jewish literature. Many titles are historical, both fiction and nonfiction. One of the honorable mentions for 2013, *I Am Forbidden* (Markovits), is a historical novel, and another, *The Lawgiver* (Wouk), is a creative example of the parallel historical novel—the story of the ancient Moses and that of a modern writer-director and the author himself.

SPUR AWARDS

http://westernwriters.org/spur-awards/

Sponsored by the Western Writers of America, Spur Awards are given in different categories for the best in western fiction. The Spur Award for best long novel in 2013 went to *With Blood in Their Eyes* (Cobb), and the Spur for best short novel to *Tucker's Reckoning* (Compton and Mayo).

WALTER SCOTT PRIZE

www.bordersbookfestival.org/walter-scott-prize

The Walter Scott Prize, sponsored by the Duke and Duchess of Buccleuch, is one of the largest awards in the United Kingdom, given each year since 2010 in mid-June at the Borders Book Festival; the winner of this award for historical fiction receives £25,000. The 2013 winner is Twan Eng Tan, for *The Garden of Evening Mists*.

WESTERN HERITAGE AWARDS (WRANGLER AWARD)
www.nationalcowboymuseum.org/events/wha/WHA_Winners.aspx

Sponsored by the National Cowboy and Western Heritage Museum, this award recognizes top-quality literature, film, television, and music that reflect "the significant stories of the American West."[3] The 2013 winner for best western novel was *Unbroke Horses* (Jackson).

W. Y. BOYD AWARD FOR EXCELLENCE IN MILITARY FICTION
www.ala.org/awardsgrants/wy-boyd-literary-award-excellence-military-fiction

The American Library Association administers this award, in honor of America's veterans, for the best fiction set during a time when the United States was at war. While not all fiction set during a war is historical fiction, the 2013 award book, *Cain at Gettysburg* (Peters), is set during the Civil War.

KEEP TRACK OF WHAT YOU READ: A PERSONAL READING PLAN

Read Outside Your Comfort Zone

To create a personal reading plan for historical fiction, identify your genre weaknesses, and make a plan to familiarize yourself with the best titles in each area of weakness. Your personal reading plan can be as simple or complex as you like. A good online tool to use to make your plan is The Adult Reading Round Table (ARRT) Popular Fiction List, which you can purchase for a nominal fee at the ARRT website (www.arrtreads.org). If you have access to NoveList, you can download the checklist from the database Readers' Advisory Toolbox.

You may need to read benchmark historical fiction titles, or you might be ready to explore specific subgenres to broaden your knowledge of historical fiction. Start with titles containing your favorite appeals so you will be sure to enjoy them. If you want a quick way to read up in the historical fiction genre, you can use the lists later in this chapter, the ARRT Popular Fiction List, or "The Five Book Challenge," an appendix in the second edition of Saricks's *The Readers' Advisory Guide to Genre Fiction*, which offers five book suggestions in each genre fiction category, including historical fiction, that you might like to add to your personal reading plan.[4]

Read the Current "It" Books

Every year, a few books rise to the top of public awareness and become an "it" book: the book that everyone seems to be reading. One of 2013's "it" contenders was Dan Brown's *Inferno*, which is not technically a historical fiction book, but much of it is based on the historical record, in a manner similar to his *The Da Vinci Code*. Another good candidate for what many readers will think of as the "it" historical fiction book in 2013 is Khaled Hosseini's *And the Mountains Echoed*, a family saga that begins in Afghanistan in 1952. A strong knowledge of the current most popular historical fiction is necessary for good readers' advisory. Use the list of online resources in the next section to find the best tool for you to use in keeping current.

Learn to Read and Evaluate Books Quickly

Even the most prolific readers cannot keep up with public demand for book suggestions, and sometimes when you suggest a book to a reader, you won't have read it. Hopefully, however, you will be familiar with it and be able to quickly identify the key features of the story, its genre, and the author. You will probably have found the title using a readers' advisory resource—perhaps one from the list in this chapter—and have scanned a review for key appeal words that match the reader's taste.

The best system for familiarizing yourself with books you haven't the time or inclination to savor is to learn how to "read" a book in just a few minutes. In her readers' advisory classes and at library conferences, Georgine Olson, outreach services manager at Fairbanks (AK) North Star Borough Public Libraries and Regional Center, proposes a "speed-reading" method that works well for busy readers' advisors who want to, but cannot possibly, read all the wonderful novels they suggest. Her handout "Speed Reading Books—or—How to Read a Novel in Just Minutes," lists questions to mentally ask as you peruse an unfamiliar book. Some of the key points ask what you can learn

- from the cover, jacket description, and physical characteristics
- from sampling parts of the text, including reading the first and last chapters
- about appeals, and possible read-alikes and read-arounds
- which readers might enjoy the book[5]

Olson also suggests we set practice goals for ourselves—perhaps to speed-read five books, take notes, and then discuss the books with colleagues who have read the same titles. Whatever system you use, it's smart to find a quick way to identify key elements of unfamiliar books that might be useful in readers' advisory work.

Keep Track of What You Read

GOODREADS
www.goodreads.com

Many librarians keep track of their reading on Goodreads as a matter of course, sharing their comments about books with friends online and reading others' reviews of the books they've read. Goodreads allows you to keep a list of the books you read and when you read them, as well as books you want to read, and to see book descriptions and connect your own reviews to your blog. You can also rate books, write reviews, and see what others think about them. Goodreads will give you book recommendations based on what you've read. One section of the website is devoted to topical book lists, where you can rate the books you've read. This service keeps track of your "friends" and sends frequent e-mails whenever one of your friends rates a book.

LIBRARYTHING
www.librarything.com

LibraryThing was the first social book website and touts itself as both a "book-geekery" and a safe place to catalog one's reading and TBR (to-be-read) lists. Membership is free if you have two hundred or fewer books on your list; if you need more space, membership is inexpensive. Members can participate in the community of book lovers associated with the site as much or as little as they like. It's very similar to Goodreads in how you keep track of your books, rate them, review them, and track other readers' comments.

Create Your Own Book Notes

These websites are great to use in readers' advisory and can help you get in the habit of keeping track of what you've read. You cannot, however, make book notes on these sites, which is an important part of good readers' advisory work, because with good book notes, you can easily write annotations for book lists, make read-alike lists, or write a review later. Neal Wyatt and Joyce Saricks have both developed good formats for book notes.[6]

Essentially, your notes should include pertinent book information that you may need later, when you no longer have the book in hand or the time to look it up. I've devised a simple list that represents what I like to include in my own, usually informal, book notes. My system for keeping track of what I read is sketchier than Saricks's or Wyatt's (as is evident in figure 10.1)!

HISTORICAL FICTION (16TH C) **** (RATING)   6/10

The Heretic's Wife by Brenda Rickman Vantrease
St. Martin's Press, 2010, 416 pp.

Appeal: strong setting, dramatic, sense of foreboding, brutal

Main Characters: John Gough, printer
Kate Gough, his daughter and bookseller
John Frith, beloved of Kate, Tyndale Bible translator

Other Characters: Henry VIII, Cardinal Wolsey, Thomas More

Setting: England, Antwerp, Tudor period

Summary: The Goughs' lives are changed after John is arrested for heresy and Kate falls in love with Frith, a Bible translator. King Henry VIII might be falling away from Catholicism, but the threat to commoners accused of heresy is still very real. If John Frith is caught in England he will be executed. Kate's marriage is a danger to herself and her father, and selling Bibles is a crime.

Notes: Fascinating time capsule of life as it was for common people whose only brush with the rich and powerful was religious beliefs. Makes you think, "What would I do—stick with my beliefs and burn, or recant to save myself and my family?" Hard to tell the good guys from the bad sometimes in the story. Interesting descriptions of printing process, smuggling, clothing, noise, smells. Good historical details. Violent.

Read-alikes: *Watermark* (Sankaran), *Heresy* (Sansom), *By Fire, by Water* (Kaplan)

FIGURE 10.1

Reading record for *The Heretic's Wife*

- Bibliographic information: author, title, date of publication, publisher
- Date I read the book and my overall descriptive rating
- Genre and subject
- Series information with other titles listed (you will be glad you did this)
- Awards, honors, and notes from reviews
- Key characters and brief description (sometimes I draw family trees)
- Summary of story in my own words (or quote and cite)
- Setting, including time frame and location
- Appeal characteristics and strengths
- Read-alikes and read-arounds
- Other comments

A HISTORICAL FICTION READING PLAN: THE ESSENTIAL BOOKS TO CONSIDER READING

If you are inspired to read historical fiction mentioned in the chapters and categories introduced in this book, then you can sample any or all titles on this list. These are the historical novels I have chosen as most representative of each category, and they are highly useful in readers' advisory with historical fiction readers. I encourage you to read all six benchmark titles in the first section.

Must-Read General Historical Fiction Benchmarks

Agincourt, by Bernard Cornwell

In the Company of the Courtesan, by Sarah Dunant

The White Queen, by Philippa Gregory

New York, by Edward Rutherfurd

The Rising Tide, by Jeff Shaara

The Forest Lover, by Susan Vreeland

Focus on Time Period

The March, by E. L. Doctorow
The Pillars of the Earth, by Ken Follett
Wolf Hall, by Hilary Mantel

Focus on Geographic Location

The Blood of Flowers, by Anita Amirrezvani
Skeletons at the Feast, by Chris Bohjalian
The Poisonwood Bible, by Barbara Kingsolver

Biographical Historical Fiction

Emperor: The Gates of Rome, by Conn Iggulden
Abundance, by Sena Jeter Naslund
The Winter Palace, by Eva Stachniak

Historical Fiction by Subject

In the Time of the Butterflies by Julia Alvarez (Latin American)
Life Class, by Pat Barker (World War I)
People of the Book, by Geraldine Brooks (Jewish)
Remarkable Creatures, by Tracy Chevalier (history of science)
The Hearts of Horses, by Molly Gloss (regional: West)
Someone Knows My Name, by Lawrence Hill (African American)
Mudbound, by Hillary Jordan (regional: South)
An Unfinished Season, by Ward Just (regional: Midwest)
The Heretic's Daughter, by Kathleen Kent (witchcraft)
John's Story: The Last Eyewitness, by Tim F. LaHaye (Christian)
The Given Day, by Dennis Lehane (regional: Northeast)
At Swim, Two Boys, by Jamie O'Neill (LGBT)
My Name Is Mary Sutter, by Robin Oliveira (history of medicine)
Shanghai Girls, by Lisa See (Asian American)

Black Hills, by Dan Simmons (Native American)

Half Broke Horses, by Jeannette Walls (regional: Southwest)

Historical Fiction Blended with Other Genres

An Instance of the Fingerpost, by Iain Banks (mystery)

The Mists of Avalon, by Marion Zimmer Bradley (Arthurian)

The Yiddish Policemen's Union, by Michael Chabon (alternate history)

The Madonnas of Leningrad, by Debra Dean (literary)

Into the Wilderness, by Sara Donati (saga or time sweep)

The Tea Rose, by Jennifer Donnelly (romantic historical)

Night Soldiers, by Alan Furst (spy thriller)

Cocaine Blues, by Kerry Greenwood (cozy mystery)

Under Heaven, by Guy Gavriel Kay (historical fantasy)

All the Pretty Horses, by Cormac McCarthy (western)

Master and Commander, by Patrick O'Brian (sea stories)

The Doomsday Book, by Connie Willis (time travel)

CONCLUSION

Readers' advisory work is both challenging and highly rewarding. Learning readers' advisory work is a process—one that you will never fully complete. If you have a working knowledge of historical fiction and readers' advisory resources, develop a reading plan, keep current with what's popular, participate in relevant programs, get involved in marketing and outreach, and actively engage with readers, you are well on your way!

NOTES

1. Linda Johns, reader services librarian, Seattle Public Library, personal communication, June 21, 2013.

2. For great advice on booktalking, see Chapple Langemack, *The Book Talker's Bible: How to Talk about the Books You Love to Any Audience* (Santa Barbara, CA: Libraries Unlimited, 2003).

3. "Western Heritage Awards," National Cowboy and Western Heritage Museum, www.nationalcowboymuseum.org/events/wha/Default.aspx.

4. Joyce G. Saricks, *The Readers' Advisory Guide to Genre Fiction*, 2nd ed. (Chicago: American Library Association, 2009), 335–48.

5. Georgine Olson's handout is available in appendix A of this book.

6. Joyce G. Saricks, *Readers' Advisory Service in the Public Library*, 3rd ed. (Chicago: American Library Association, 2005), 110; Neal Wyatt, *The Readers' Advisory Guide to Nonfiction* (Chicago: American Library Association, 2007), 265.

APPENDIX A

How to Read a Novel in Just Minutes

by Georgine Olson

Basics of Speed "Reading"

1. Select a book to "read"

2. On a card, sheet of paper, or form: record the author, title, genre, series info, call number. As you "read," jot down notes about items listed below that seem pertinent.

3. Hold the book and look at its basic features

   - Is it heavy?

   - When you open it, do the pages lie flat?

   - Look at the typeface, the space between lines, the general layout— How easy to read is it? Is there much white space? Is it densely printed?

4. Look at the cover—What does it tell you about the book (or what the publisher wants you to think about the book)?

5. Read the blurb—Does it give you an idea of the story line; does it tell "everything" (or maybe it doesn't tell you anything)? Is it inviting, teasing, ominous?

6. Read the first chapter—Does it pull you right into the story or is there a slow buildup? If it's a series title, how smoothly does it deliver background info?

7. Skim and read bits and pieces here and there throughout the book— Does it seem to flow? What's your general impression of the book?

8. Read the end (sorry, but this is important!). If it has an epilogue, read a couple of sections before the epilogue. Is there a conclusion or is it

open-ended? Does the ending read like a checklist, wrapping up all loose ends?

9. What can you tell about

> *Style:* humorous; serious; length of sentences, sections, or
> chapters; dialogue
>
> *Pacing:* leisurely or action-oriented
>
> *Format:* straight-line narrative, flashback, single or multiple
> points of view (how smooth are transitions)
>
> *Characters:* many or few; are they a recognizable "type"; does it
> seem character or action-oriented
>
> *Setting:* time; place; integral or wallpaper
>
> *Story line:* character or plot driven
>
> *Genre:* does it follow genre conventions; is it a recognizable
> sub-genre

From the Readers' Advisor's Viewpoint

1. Does this bring to mind any other authors or titles as possible read-alikes?

2. Which readers could enjoy this? Why would they?

3. Think about how you would phrase a recommendation based on speed reading vs. cover-to-cover reading vs. what you might have learned from reviews or other readers.

Becoming Proficient at Speed Reading
(and Learning Its Value and Limitations)

1. Practice; set a goal (3 books an hour; 30 books a week, etc.)

2. Speed read five books you read and enjoyed a long time ago (at least several years). How much comes back to you? How much of what you are "speed reading" reminds you of what you so enjoyed the last time you read the book? Are you getting a "feel" for the book? Does it seem like the same book you read before, or does it seem different?

3. Speed read 5 books that you haven't read, but would be at the top of your "I want to read" list. Then read the books from cover to cover as

you normally would. How different are your impressions of the book: speed reading vs. "regular" reading?

4. Find people (preferably some knowledge of readers' advisory) who read in a genre you do not read. Ask them to select 5 newish books in the genre that they have read and enjoyed. Speed read the 5 books and discuss each with the person recommending the title. How well have you "read" these?

5. Get together with several others and speed read the same book. Have a mini book discussion to compare your impressions and notes. What is similar and different in the various readings of the book? How does this compare with the usual book discussion experience?

APPENDIX B

Literary Historical Fiction and Classics for Book Groups

Like individual readers, a group of readers meeting regularly to talk about literature develops reading tastes, and maybe even consensus, on what they are currently in the mood to read and discuss. Choosing the right book is half the battle of keeping a book group vital and interesting to its members, so it behooves readers' advisors to read and know about literary historical fiction and historical classics that are particularly well suited for discussion, and be prepared to make pertinent suggestions when asked by book club members and facilitators.

In talking with book group members, ask them to describe the group's best and worst discussion titles (a bad discussion doesn't necessarily mean the title was a bad book) to elicit the information you need to make good suggestions. By listening to the responses on the best and worst discussion, you can often glean clues to the group's collective preferences. Perhaps they have read their fill of books about immigrants or don't enjoy deeply metaphorical stories. Maybe they love complex plot lines or character studies. These are valuable clues that can help you make good suggestions that will energize the group and further your relationship with them in the future.

Some of the historical fiction titles listed here are proven book group favorites that have been enjoyed over the years and consistently make for great discussion. I've also included some excellent newer literary historical fiction favorites suitable for book groups. Each entry also contains similar titles good for discussion, if the group has already read and loved these well-known titles.

HHhH, by Laurent Binet

Two stories intertwine in this novel about the partisan killing of Reinhard "the Butcher" Heydrich by Czech agents and the author's chronicle of writing the book.

Also try *A Thread of Grace,* by Mary Doria Russell, and *The Visible World,* by Mark Slouka.

The Amazing Adventures of Kavalier and Clay, by Michael Chabon

Jewish cousins Joe and Sammy collaborate on a superhero comic scheme in 1939 that takes them on the road to success while they also struggle in their personal lives.

Also try *Homer and Langley,* by E. L. Doctorow, and *The Golem and the Jinni,* by Helene Wecker.

The Orchardist, by Amanda Coplin

A troubled fruit grower in early twentieth-century Washington State helps two pregnant girls seeking sanctuary after escaping from their abusive, drug-addled captors.

Also try *Plainsong,* by Kent Haruf, and *The Light between Oceans,* by M. L. Stedman.

Corelli's Mandolin, by Louis de Bernières

During the Italian occupation of the Greek island Cephalonia, Captain Corelli, of the Axis forces, falls in love with islander Pelagia under the cloud of World War II.

Also try *A Very Long Engagement,* by Sebastian Japrisot, and *Miracle at St. Anna,* by James McBride.

The Madonnas of Leningrad, by Debra Dean

Elderly Marina, suffering from Alzheimer's, recalls with clarity the Siege of Leningrad, the time she spent starving in the darkened Hermitage Museum, and the Madonnas that carried her beyond fear.

Also try *Suite Française,* by Irene Nemirovsky, and *City of Thieves* by David Benioff.

A Sudden Country, by Susan Fisher

Lucy Mitchell and James MacLaren meet and fall in love on the Oregon Trail in 1847—on a trip of healing and discovery.

Also try *I Should Be Extremely Happy in Your Company*, by Brian Hall, and *Angle of Repose*, by Wallace Stegner.

Z: A Novel of Zelda Fitzgerald, by Therese Anne Fowler

Fowler paints a moving portrait of the mercurial and talented wife of F. Scott Fitzgerald and her decline and isolation while living in his shadow.

Also try *Guests on Earth*, by Lee Smith, and *Beautiful Fools*, by R. Clifton Spargo.

Sea of Poppies, by Amitav Ghosh

Set during the Opium Wars of 1839 to 1860, a large cast of outcasts come together aboard the *Ibis* in a lyrical novel that's filled with both adventure and insightful social commentary.

Also try *Ship of Fools*, by Katherine Anne Porter, and *The Rope Eater*, by Ben Jones.

City of Women, by David Gillham

Sigrid cannot escape her loveless marriage to a Nazi officer or her wretched mother-in-law, although she can help hide Jews and dream of her Jewish lover in this moving literary novel set in World War II Berlin.

Also try *My Enemy's Cradle*, by Sara Young, and *In the Garden of Beasts*, by Erik Larson.

Flora, by Gail Godwin

After her beloved grandmother dies, ten-year-old Helen spends tense months with her naive cousin Flora during World War II while her father is away doing mysterious military work in North Carolina.

Also try *The Yonahlossee Riding Camp for Girls*, by Anton DiSclafani, and *The Light in the Ruins*, by Chris Bohjalian.

Water for Elephants, by Sara Gruen

As an old man, Jacob Jankowski remembers the Great Depression, which he spent in the circus caring for Rosie, an untrainable elephant.

Also try *Jim, the Boy*, by Tony Earley, and *Seabiscuit*, by Laura Hillenbrand.

Loving Frank, by Nancy Horan

> This is the story of the passionate love between architect Frank Lloyd Wright and feminist Mamah Cheney for which they paid in scandal and heartache.

> Also try *The Women*, by T. C. Boyle, and *The Aviator's Wife*, by Melanie Benjamin.

Train Dreams, by Denis Johnson

> A novel that runs the gamut from joy in partaking in America's expansion to the grief of losing his wife and child, this is Robert Grainier's story—the tale of people in early twentieth-century America distracted by inexorable progress.

> Also try *Bucking the Sun*, by Ivan Doig, and *Bright's Passage*, by Josh Ritter.

The Poisonwood Bible, by Barbara Kingsolver

> Nathan Price drags his wife and four daughters to the Belgian Congo in 1959 hoping to evangelize the natives, but the political upheaval and his insensitivity to African culture tear the family apart.

> Also try *Heart of Darkness*, by Joseph Conrad, and *State of Wonder*, by Ann Patchett.

Transatlantic, by Colum McCann

> Four generations of an Irish American family intersect with famous men who change history at different times: the famous abolitionist Frederick Douglass; early aviators Alcock and Brown; and Senator George Mitchell, who brokered the 1998 Belfast Agreement.

> Also try *Eighty Days: Nellie Bly and Elizabeth Bisland's History-Making Race around the World*, by Matthew Goodman, and *People of the Book*, by Geraldine Brooks.

The Thousand Autumns of Jacob de Zoet, by David Mitchell

> Jacob de Zoet, a clerk in the employ of the Dutch East Indies Company, travels in the nineteenth century to Japan on an assignment to straighten out corrupt business practices, hoping to make his fortune and return home to marry. But he is waylaid by love and its consequences.

Also try *Shogun*, by James Clavell, and *The Stockholm Octavo*, by Karen Engelmann.

The Accursed, by Joyce Carol Oates

An old-fashioned gothic novel complete with hints of the paranormal, this story set at Princeton University in the mid-twentieth century features famous men like Woodrow Wilson, Upton Sinclair, and Grover Cleveland in a tricky tale that's both eerie and socially astute.

Also try *Sleep, Pale Sister*, by Joanne Harris, and *The Little Stranger*, by Sarah Waters.

A Prayer for the Dying, by Stewart O'Nan

When a diphtheria epidemic threatens a small Wisconsin town after the Civil War, the sheriff struggles to protect his community.

Also try *The Last Town on Earth*, by Thomas Mullen, and *Year of Wonders*, by Geraldine Brooks.

The Well and the Mine, by Gin Phillips

Young Tess is plagued by nightmares after watching a woman throw a baby down a well in Depression-era Alabama, where poverty and racism drive good people to commit evil acts.

Also try *The Maytrees*, by Annie Dillard, and *Crooked Letter, Crooked Letter*, by Tom Franklin.

Sarah's Key, by Tatiana de Rosnay

A moving portrayal of the lingering horrors of the Holocaust, in this story an American journalist delves into the history of a Jewish family and a girl who was transported to Auschwitz without her little brother.

Also try *The True Story of Hansel and Gretel*, by Louise Murphy, and *Homecoming*, by Bernard Schlink.

An Atlas of Impossible Longing, by Anuradha Roy

From early childhood Bakul and Mukunda have loved each other, but they are separated as teens to prevent indiscretions, though they later suffer and their feelings never change.

Also try *Consequences*, by Penelope Lively, and *The Cloud Atlas*, by Liam Callanan.

Snow Flower and the Secret Fan, by Lisa See

> In a story both haunting and lovely, the author describes the friendship between Lily and Snow Flower, women of different stations whose lives reflect women's relative insignificance in nineteenth-century rural China.

> Also try *Memoirs of a Geisha*, by Arthur Golden, and *The Buddha in the Attic*, by Julie Otsuka.

The Master, by Colm Toibin

> A poignant and reflective fictional portrait of Henry James and his conflicted emotions when Oscar Wilde receives the public acclamation James craves.

> Also try *Journey in Blue*, by Stig Dalager, and *The Indian Clerk*, by David Leavitt.

The Color Purple, by Alice Walker

> An ugly, harsh life is made beautiful through the love of a sister and a blues singer in this heart-wrenching story of female strength and courage.

> Also try *Song Yet Sung*, by James McBride, and *A Mercy*, by Toni Morrison.

Classic Historical Fiction for Book Groups

Chapter 8 discussed classics of historical fiction. The titles that follow are examples of great discussion books, among both well-known older classics and modern ones:

> *Imperial Woman*, by Pearl S. Buck
>
> *The Leatherstocking Tales*, by James Fenimore Cooper
>
> *The Red Badge of Courage*, by Stephen Crane
>
> *A Tale of Two Cities*, by Charles Dickens
>
> *The Mill on the Floss*, by George Eliot
>
> *Absalom, Absalom!*, by William Faulkner
>
> *Taras Bulba*, by Nikolai Gogol
>
> *I, Claudius*, by Robert Graves

The Western Saga, by A. B. Guthrie

The Scarlet Letter, by Nathaniel Hawthorne

Siddhartha, by Hermann Hesse

Andersonville, by MacKinlay Kantor

The Cairo Trilogy, by Naguib Mahfouz

The Raj Quartet, by Paul Scott

Quo Vadis, by Henryk Sienkiewicz

A Map of Love, by Ahdaf Soueif

Angle of Repose, by Wallace Stegner

War and Peace, by Leo Tolstoy

Johnny Got His Gun, by Dalton Trumbo

The Prince and the Pauper, by Mark Twain

Kristin Lavransdatter, by Sigrid Undset

The Age of Innocence, by Edith Wharton

Musashi, by Eiji Yoshikawa

The Memoirs of Hadrian, by Marguerite Yourcenar

Classics of Historical Interest (Not Historical Fiction) for Book Groups

Things Fall Apart, by Chinua Achebe

My Ántonia, by Willa Cather

Heart of Darkness, Joseph Conrad

Lord Jim, by Joseph Conrad

The Quiet American, by Graham Greene

The Mayor of Casterbridge, by Thomas Hardy

Les Misérables, by Victor Hugo

Their Eyes Were Watching God, by Zora Neale Hurston

The Bostonians, by Henry James

Heat and Dust, by Ruth Prawer Jhabvala

To Kill a Mockingbird, by Harper Lee

Shosha, by Isaac Bashevis Singer

One Day in the Life of Ivan Denisovich, by Aleksandr Solzhenitsyn

The Grapes of Wrath, by John Steinbeck

The Red and the Black, by Roger Stendhal

Vanity Fair, by William Makepeace Thackeray

All the King's Men, by Robert Penn Warren

APPENDIX C

Form-Based Readers' Advisory: A List of Libraries

by Barry Trott

The list in this appendix was extracted from a spreadsheet created by Barry Trott, digital services director at the Williamsburg (VA) Regional Library, to track the libraries in the United States and Canada that provide some type of form-based readers' advisory. Most of these services link to the libraries' websites and are provided online, although a few ask readers to fill in paper forms. The links provided here in most cases allow a visual representation of the form used, but in all cases, the service is for library members only. As of 2014, all links were current.

United States

Acorn (IL) Public Library District: http://acornlibrary.org/pdf/Reader _Questionnaire.pdf

Addison Public Library (IL): www.addisonlibrary.org/readinglist.aspx

Arapahoe (CO) Library District: http://arapahoelibraries.org/ personalized-reading-list-teens-and-tweens

Arlington Heights (IL) Memorial Library: http://ahml.info/content/ book-me

Barrington (IL) Area Library: www.barringtonarealibrary.org/books.html

Beaufort County (SC) Library: www.beaufortcountylibrary.org/ limesurvey/index.php?sid=51812&lang=en

Berkeley (CA) Public Library: http://bancroft.berkeley-public.org/ databases/comments/readers_advisory.php

Bloomingdale (IL) Public Library: www.mybpl.org/ personalizedreadinglist

Boone County (KY) Public Library: www.bcpl.org/forms/reading
-recommendations/

Boulder (CO) Public Library: http://research.boulderlibrary.org/
content.php?pid=32206&sid=2776585

Bullitt County (KY) Public Library: www.bcplib.org/Read/
personalbooklist.html

Canton (MI) Public Library: www.cantonpl.org/may-we-suggest

Cape May County (NJ) Library: www.cmclibrary.org/books-and-more/
book-recommendations

Cecil County (MD) Public Library: www.cecil.ebranch.info/using-your
-library/ask-a-librarian/book-mate/

Central Rappahannock (VA) Regional: www.librarypoint.org/request
_book_match

Chelmsford (MA) Public Library: www.chelmsfordlibrary.org/reading
_room/

City of Mesa (AZ) Public Library: www.mesalibrary.org/forms/
booksforyou.pdf

Clermont County (OH) Public Library: www.clermontlibrary.org/
racprofile.shtml

Columbine Library (CO): http://jefferson.lib.co.us/books-movies
-music/list-for-you

Cuyahoga County (OH) Public Library: www.cuyahogalibrary.org/
What-to-Read/Recommended-Reading.aspx

Delaware County (PA) Library System: www.delcolibraries.org/
nextreads.htm

Delphi (IN) Public Library: www.delphilibrary.org/onlineRAform.html

Denver (CO) Public Library: http://denverlibrary.org/request-reading
-list

Fayetteville(NY)Free Library:https://fflib.org/custom-recommendations

Forbes (MA) Library: https://docs.google.com/forms/d/1X3diN3azyQ
z0o96F6xxO0DWLTgTSEpuGpUzOIucEjd8/viewform?pli=1

Forsyth County (GA) Public Library: www.forsythpl.org/
readersCorner/personalizedReadingSuggestions.aspx

Gail Borden Public Library (Elgin, IL): www.gailborden.info/good
-reads/reading-suggestions/499-need-a-good-read

Gloucester County (NJ) Library: www.gcls.org/ask-us/readers-corner/
need-book

Greenwood (IN) Public Library: www.greenwoodlibrary.us/personallist
.asp

Harker Heights (TX) Public Library: www.ci.harker-heights.tx.us/index
.php/reader-recommendation-service

Harris County (TX) Public Library: www.hcpl.net/form/book-hunters
-your-personal-reading-consultants

Herrick (MI) District Library: www.herrickdl.org/Resources/Books/
readHarmony.aspx

High Plains (CO) Library District: http://highplains.libguides.com/
content.php?pid=58112&sid=634839

Houston (TX) Public Library: www2.houstonlibrary.org/cgi-bin/
services/raform.pl

Indian Prairie (IL) Public Library: http://ippl.info/books-movies-more
-home/1200-personalized-reading-recommendations

Itasca (IL) Community Library: www.itascalibrary.org/good-reads/
personalized-reading-list/

Jacksonville (FL) Public Library: http://jpl.coj.net/lib/readers.html

James V. Brown Library (Williamsport, PA): https://docs.google.com/
spreadsheet/viewform?formkey=dGIxMU5rR3dxNVJsd3VuZXBWU
zEtN2c6MQ#gid=0

Johnson County (KS) Library: www.jocolibrary.org/templates/JCL
_XForm.aspx?id=13669

Jones (MA) Library: www.joneslibrary.org/ref/reading/onlineform.php

Kalamazoo (MI) Public Library: www.kpl.gov/books/now-read-this/

Kent (MI) District Library: www.kdl.org/personalized_lists/new

Lake Oswego (OR) Public Library: https://www.ci.oswego.or.us/
library/webforms/ten-ten-personalized-recommendations

Logan (UT) Library: http://library.loganutah.org/books/
bookrecommendations.cfm

Manhattan (KS) Public Library: www.manhattan.lib.ks.us/index.php/
component/chronoforms/?chronoform=PersonalizedReadingList

Medina County (OH) District Library: http://mcdl.info/index.php
?option=com_content&view=article&id=390&Itemid=60

Memorial Hall Library (Andover, MA): www.mhl.org/read/advice.htm

Meriden (CT) Public Library: http://meridenlibrary.org/adult/what-to
-read-next/

Mesa (AZ) Public Library: www.mesaaz.gov/forms/library/
goodbookprofile.aspx

Mill Valley (CA) Public Library: www.millvalleylibrary.org/Index.aspx
?page=246

Multnomah (OR) County Library: https://multcolib.org/reading
-suggestions

Muskingum County (OH) Library System: www.muskingumlibrary.org/
readadvise.aspx

Naperville (IL) Public Library: www.naperville-lib.org/node/2941

New Albany–Floyde County (IN) Public Library: www.nafclibrary.org/
books-more/looking-for-a-good-book/

Newburyport (MA) Public Library: www.newburyportpl.org/sup/
downloads/Customized_Book_List_for_Adults.pdf

Newport News (VA) Library: www.nngov.com/library/forms/reader

Newton (MA) Free Library: www2.newtonfreelibrary.net/?sec=services
&doc=booksforyou

Northborough (MA) Library: www.northboroughlibrary.org/
northborough/readingsuggestionsform.asp

Omaha (NE) Public Library: www.omahalibrary.org/catalog/reading-list

Orion Township (MI) Public Library: http://orionlibrary.org/your-next
-few-books/

Ottawa (KS) Public Library: http://ottawa.mykansaslibrary.org/
personal-reading-lists

Palatine (IL) Public Library District: www.palatinelibrary.org/books
-movies-music/personalized-book-list

Park County (CO) Public Libraries: http://parkcounty.colibraries.org/
web-forms/book_shopper

Pima County (AZ) Public Library: www.library.pima.gov/contact/read
.php

Pinal County (AZ) Library District: www.pinalcountyaz.gov/Departments/
Library/Pages/PersonalizedReadingList.aspx

Princeton (NJ) Public Library: www.princetonlibrary.org/bookit

Provo (UT) Library: www.provolibrary.com/personalized-reading
-recommendations

Public Library of Bullitt County (KY): www.bcplib.org/Read/
personalbooklist.html

Rampart (CO) Library District: http://rampart.colibraries.org/
ParkCounty/web-forms/book_shopper

Red Wing (MN) Public Library: http://redwing.lib.mn.us/reading
-suggestions-long-for/

Ridgefield (CT) Library: www.ridgefieldlibrary.org/readers_res/pdfs/
ReadingRecommendationPersonalized.pdf

River Forest (IL) Public Library: www.reginalibrary.ca/books4me/

Robert W. Rowe Public Library District (IL): http://rwrlibrary.org/
news/reading-interest-survey

Rogers Memorial Library (NY): https://spreadsheets0.google.com/a/
myrml.org/viewform?formkey=dE1Bbl9CbVFyd1RvN0ZmdjZYMD
hTSXc6MA

Rolling Meadows (IL) Public Library: www.rmlib.org/readers.shtml

Santa Clara County (CA) Library: www.sccl.org/teens/read-this/
personalized-reading-picks-for-teens

Seattle (WA) Public Library: www.spl.org/using-the-library/get-help/
your-next-5-books

Skokie (IL) Public Library: www.surveymonkey.com/s.aspx?sm=YFQLL
a0b_2fsgA47jViEWyvw_3d_3d

St. Charles (IL) Public Library: www.stcharleslibrary.org/rs/whatulike/
index.htm

St. Louis County (MO) Library: www.slcl.org/content/personalized
-reading-list-adults

Syosset (NY) Public Library: www.syossetlibrary.org/books/reading
-recommendations/just-for-me

Tiverton Town (RI) Public Library: http://tivertonlibrary.org/node/
1095

Tulsa City County (OK) Library: www.tulsalibrary.org/your-next-great
-read

Vernon Area Public Library District (IL): http://vapld.wufoo.com/
forms/personalized-reading-lists-for-teens

Virginia Beach (VA) Central Library: www.vbgov.com/government/ departments/libraries/books-and-more/Pages/Your-Personalized -Reading-List.aspx

Wake County (NC) Public Libraries: www.wakegov.com/libraries/ reading/custom/Pages/risadult.aspx

Washington Centerville (OH) Library: www.wclibrary.info/personalized _ra/request.asp

Waukesha (WI) Public Library: http://wpl2.org/contact/booklist.shtml

Wellesley (MA) Public Library: www.surveymonkey.com/s.aspx?sm=ogr opuvPo_2fIn87OYIcw2eg_3d_3d

West Bloomfield Township (MI) Public Library: www.wblib.org/ services/readersadv.php

West Caldwell (NJ) Public Library: http://westcaldwell.bccls.org/ personalized-reading-survey

Westbank Community (TX) Library District: www.westbanklibrary.com/ content/book-connection

Williamsburg (VA) Regional Library: www.wrl.org/books-and-reading/ adults/find-good-book/looking-good-book-reader-profile-forms

Wilmington (MA) Memorial Library: www.wilmlibrary.org/reading -suggestions

Canada

Edmonton (AB) Library: www.epl.ca/services/personalized-book-list/ get-a-fiction-list

Oshawa (ON) Public Libraries: www.oshlib.ca/ReadingIdeas

Red Deer (AB) Public Library: www.rdpl.org/services/readers

Regina (SK) Public Library: www.reginalibrary.ca/books4me

Strathcona County (AB) Library: www.sclibrary.ab.ca/readinglist.htm

Vancouver (BC) Public Library: https://www.vpl.ca/survey/index .php?sid=72586&lang=en

Vaughan (ON) Public Libraries: www.vaughanpl.info/next_reads

BIBLIOGRAPHY

This bibliography includes titles that have been mentioned in the text, as well as other titles with similar appeals that could easily have been included in this book but were left out for the sake of space.

Lyrics Alley, by Leila Aboulea
Mornings in Jenin, by Susan Abulhawa
Things Fall Apart, by Chinua Achebe
Glass-Eye, the Great Shot of the West, by "Bruin" Adams
Outlander, by Gil Adamson
Half of a Yellow Sun, by Chimamonda Ngozi Adichie
The River Wife, by Jonas Agee
Prague Winter: A Personal Story of Remembrance and War, 1937–1948, by
    Madeleine Albright
Tevye the Dairyman and the Railroad Stories, by Sholem Aleichem
The Secrets of Jin-Shei, by Alma Alexander
And Only to Deceive, by Tasha Alexander
Flight, by Sherman Alexie
Shadows of the Pomegranate Tree, by Tariq Ali
Natives and Exotics, by Jane Alison
Daughter of Fortune, *The House of the Spirits*, and *Inés of my Soul*, by Isabel
    Allende
In the Time of the Butterflies, by Julia Alvarez
The Blood of Flowers, by Anita Amirrezvani
A Golden Age and *The Good Muslim*, by Tahmima Anam
Heyday, by Kurt Anderson
Joheved, by Maggie Anton
Only Time Will Tell, by Jeffrey Archer
Mark of the Lion, by Suzanne Arruda
The Clan of the Cave Bear, by Jean Auel
Gods and Kings, by Lynn N. Austin
Map of the Invisible World, by Tash Aw
Redlaw, Half-Breed; or, The Tangled Trail: A Tale of the Settlements,
    by Joseph Badger

The September Queen, by Gillian Bagwell

Master Georgie, by Beryl Bainbridge

Margaret, Duchess of Aquitaine, by Margaret Ball

Life Class, by Pat Barker

My Lady of Cleves, The Tudor Rose, by Margaret Campbell Barnes

At the Mercy of the Queen, by Anne Barnhill

The Voyage of the Narwhal, by Andrea Barrett

A Long, Long Way, by Sebastian Barry

A Fierce Radiance, by Lauren Belfer

Infinity in the Palm of Her Hand and *The Inhabited Woman*,
     by Gioconda Belli

City of Thieves, by David Benioff

The Aviator's Wife, by Melanie Benjamin

The Catastrophist, by Ronan Bennett

Figures in Silk, by Vanora Bennett

Little Big Man and *The Return of Little Big Man*, by Thomas Berger

The Chalice and *The Crown*, by Nancy Bilyeau

The Sacred Place, by Daniel Black

Country of the Bad Wolfes and *The Rules of Wolfe*, by James Carlos Blake

The Postmistress, by Sarah Blake

Away, by Amy Bloom

Those Who Save Us, by Jenna Blum

Skeletons at the Feast, by Chris Bohjalian

The Wettest County in the World, by Matt Bondurant

Life Together: The Classic Exploration of Christian Community,
     by Dietrich Bonhoeffer

Murphy's Law, by Rhys Bowen

Three Day Road, by Joseph Boyden

The Women, by T. C. Boyle

The Absolutist, by John Boyne

Red Sky at Morning, by Richard Bradford

Boundless Deep, by Kate Brallier

Moloka'i, by Alan Brennert

Wuthering Heights, by Emily Brontë

Caleb's Crossing, People of the Book, and *Year of Wonders*,
     by Geraldine Brooks

The Da Vinci Code, Inferno, by Dan Brown

Rainwater, by Sandra Brown

*Clotel; or, The President's Daughter: A Narrative of Slave Life in the United
     States*, by William Wells Brown

The Day the Falls Stood Still, by Cathy Marie Buchanan

Kindred, by Octavia Butler

Percival's Planet, by Michael Byers

To Die For, by Sandra Byrd

Tobacco Road, by Erskine Caldwell

Captains and the Kings, by Taylor Caldwell

Cataloochee, by Wayne Caldwell

Dancing at the Chance, by DeAnna Cameron

The Fruit of Her Hands, by Michelle Cameron

Monkey Bridge, by Lan Cao

Sarah, by Orson Scott Card

The True History of the Kelly Gang, by Peter Carey

The Education of Little Tree, by Forrest Carter

The Hornet's Nest: A Novel of the Revolutionary War, by Jimmy Carter

The Impeachment of Abraham Lincoln, by Stephen Carter

My Ántonia and *O, Pioneers*, by Willa Cather

Bread and Dreams, by Jonatha Ceely

The Amazing Adventures of Kavalier and Clay and *The Yiddish Policeman's
    Union*, by Michael Chabon

The Running Vixen, by Elizabeth Chadwick

City of Ash and *Susannah Morrow*, by Megan Chance

Wild Swans: Three Daughters of China, by Jung Chang

Inheritance, by Lan Chang

The President's Daughter and *Sally Hemings*, by Barbara Chase-Ribaud

Lydia Cassatt Reading the Morning Paper, by Harriet Scott Chessman

Girl with a Pearl Earring, *Remarkable Creatures*, by Tracy Chevalier

The Ox-Bow Incident, by Walter Van Tilburg Clark

The Polished Hoe, by Austin Clarke

Shogun, by James Clavell

Little Bee, by Chris Cleave

With Blood in Their Eyes, by Thomas Cobb

The Moonstone, by Wilkie Collins

Heart of Darkness, *Lord Jim*, and *The Secret Sharer*, by Joseph Conrad

The Leatherstocking Tales, by James Fenimore Cooper

Agincourt, *The Archer's Tale*, *The Burning Land*, *The Fort*, *Heretic*, *The Last
    Kingdom*, *Stonehenge*, *Sword Song*, and *Vagabond*, by Bernard Cornwell

Hitler's Pope: The Secret History of Pius XII, by John Cornwell

The Power of One, by Bryce Courtenay

Claude and Camille, by Stephanie Cowell

The Bondswoman's Narrative, by Hannah Crafts

Maggie: A Girl of the Streets, *The Open Boat*, and *The Red Badge of Courage*, by Stephen Crane

Pirate Latitudes, by Michael Crichton

The Maid, by Kimberly Cutter

Balzac and the Little Chinese Seamstress, by Sijie Dai

True Sisters and *Prayers for Sale*, by Sandra Dallas

Farming of Bones, by Edwidge Danticat

The Silver Pigs, by Lindsey Davis

Birds without Wings and *Corelli's Mandolin*, by Louis de Bernières

The Building of Jalna, by Mazo de la Roche

The Invisible Mountain, by Carolina De Robertis

The Madonnas of Leningrad, by Debra Dean

White Serpent, the Shawnee Scourge; or, Indian Heart, the Renegade, by Andrew Dearborn

Pacific Glory, by Peter Deutermann

The Summer We Got Saved, by Pat Cunningham Devoto

The Sisters Brothers, by Patrick deWitt

Day after Night and *The Red Tent*, by Anita Diamant

A Christmas Carol, *Oliver Twist*, and *A Tale of Two Cities*, by Charles Dickens

The Living, by Annie Dillard

Out of Africa, by Isak Dinesen

The March, *Ragtime*, and *Welcome to Hard Times*, by E. L. Doctorow

Bucking the Sun, *Sweet Thunder*, *The Whistling Season*, and *Work Song*, by Ivan Doig

Into the Wilderness, by Sara Donati

The Little Balloonist, by Linda Donn

The Tea Rose, by Jennifer Donnelly

Narrative of the Life of Frederick Douglass, an American Slave, Written by Himself, by Frederick Douglass

Medicus, by Ruth Downie

The Hound of the Baskervilles, by Arthur Conan Doyle

Lily of the Nile and *Song of the Nile*, by Stephanie Dray

The Voyage of the Short Serpent, by Bernard du Boucheron

The Time in Between, by María Dueñas

The Count of Monte Cristo and *The Three Musketeers*, by Alexandre Dumas

The Birth of Venus and *In the Company of the Courtesan*, by Sarah Dunant

The Confession of Katherine Howard, *The Queen of Subtleties*, and *The Sixth Wife*, by Suzannah Dunn

The Game of Kings and *Niccolò Rising*, by Dorothy Dunnett

Pride of Carthage, by David Anthony Durham

Jim, the Boy, by Tony Earley

Daughter of York and *The King's Grace*, by Anne Easter Smith

The Disappeared, by Kim Echlin

Baudolino and *The Name of the Rose*, by Umberto Eco

The Night Train, by Clyde Edgerton

The Little Book, by Selden Edwards

The Quick and the Dead, by Randy Eickhoff

A Floating Life, by Simon Elegant

Eve, by Elissa Elliott

The Invisible Man, by Harlan Ellison

The Memoirs of Helen of Troy, by Amanda Elyot

The King's Damsel, by Kate Emerson

To Be Queen, by Christy English

The Painter from Shanghai, by Jennifer Cody Epstein

Love Medicine and *A Plague of Doves*, by Louise Erdrich

The Favored Queen; *The Hidden Diary of Marie Antoinette*; *The Last Wife of Henry VIII*; *The Memoirs of Mary, Queen of Scots*; *The Secret Life of Josephine: Napoleon's Bird of Paradise*; and *The Tsarina's Daughter*, by Carolly Erickson

Like Water for Chocolate and *Malinche*, by Laura Esquivel

Leonardo's Swans, by Karen Essex

God's Country, by Percival L. Everett

West of Here, by Jonathan Evison

Bitter Sweets, by Roopa Farooki

The Immigrants, by Howard Fast

Time and Again, by Jack Finney

A Sudden Country, by Karen Fisher

The Great Gatsby, by F. Scott Fitzgerald

Gould's Book of Fish and *Wanting*, by Richard Flanagan

A Sentimental Education, by Gustave Flaubert

The Secret Trial of Robert E. Lee, by Thomas J. Fleming

Corrag, by Susan Fletcher

Ladysmith, by Giles Foden

Fall of Giants, *The Pillars of the Earth*, and *World without End*, by Ken Follett

Hotel on the Corner of Bitter and Sweet, by Jamie Ford

The Clouds beneath the Sun and *Gifts of War* by Mackenzie Ford

The Ten Thousand, by Michael Curtis Ford

Mr. Midshipman Hornblower, by C. S. Forester

The African Queen, by E. M. Forester

Mistress of the Art of Death, by Ariana Franklin

My Brilliant Career and *My Career Goes Bung*, by Miles Franklin

Crooked Letter, Crooked Letter, by Tom Franklin

Cold Mountain, by Charles Frazier

The Servants' Quarters, by Lynn Freed

A Million Little Pieces, by James Frey

The Russian Concubine, by Kate Furnivall

Night Solders and *The Spies of Warsaw*, by Alan Furst

Death at the Crossroads, by Dale Furutani

Outlander, by Diana Gabaldon

Romancing Miss Brontë, by Juliet Gael

A Gathering of Old Men and *A Lesson before Dying*, by Ernest Gaines

Clara, by Janice Galloway

The Man of Property, by John Galsworthy

Love in the Time of Cholera and *One Hundred Years of Solitude*, by Gabriel García Márquez

A Lady Raised High, Plain Jane, and *The Spanish Bride*, by Laurien Gardner

Goliath, by Tom Gauld

People of the Wolf, by Kathleen O'Neal Gear

Autobiography of King Henry VIII: With Notes by His Fool, Will Somers; Elizabeth I; Helen of Troy; Mary, Queen of Scotland and the Isles; and *The Memoirs of Cleopatra*, by Margaret George

Sea of Poppies, by Amitav Ghosh

Emily's Ghost, by Denise Giardina

City of Women, by David Gillham

Gettysburg, Valley Forge, by Newt Gingrich

Hearts of Horses, Pushing the Bear, and *Stone Heart*, by Diane Glancy

The Hearts of Horses, The Jump-Off Creek, and *Wild Life*, by Molly Gloss

Memoirs of a Geisha, by Arthur Golden

The Janissary Tree, by Jason Goodwin

The Last Jew, by Noah Gordon

The Confessions of Catherine de Medici and *The Last Queen*, by C. W. Gortner

The Printmaker's Daughter, by Katherine Govier

Claudius the God and His Wife Messalina and *I, Claudius*, by Robert Graves

The Queen's Lover, by Francine du Plessix Gray

How to Tame Your Duke, by Juliana Gray

The Yard, by Alex Grecian

Bloodroot, by Amy Greene

The Quiet American, by Graham Greene

Cocaine Blues, by Kerry Greenwood

The Boleyn Inheritance, The Constant Princess, The Lady of the Rivers, The Other Boleyn Girl, The Other Queen, The Red Queen, and *The White Queen*, by Philippa Gregory

The Lieutenant, by Kate Grenville

Becoming Marie Antoinette and *Days of Splendor, Days of Sorrow*, by Juliet Grey

Riders of the Purple Sage, by Zane Grey

Bombingham, by Anthony Grooms

Bound and *The Rebellion of Jane Clarke*, by Sally Gunning

Sapphire's Grave, by Hilda Gurley-Highgate

Snow Falling on Cedars, by David Guterson

The Way West, by A. B. Guthrie

The Queen's Mistake, The Queen's Rival, and *The Secret Bride*, by Diane Haeger

Baker Towers, by Jennifer Haigh

I Should Be Extremely Happy in Your Company, by Brian Hall

The Well of Loneliness, by Radclyffe Hall

Haweswater, by Sarah Hall

Sarah, by Marek Halter

Patriot Hearts, by Barbara Hambly

Deep Creek, by Dana Hand

The Gates of the Alamo and *Remember Ben Clayton*, by Stephen Harrigan

Five Quarters of the Orange, by Joanne Harris

Imperium and *Pompeii*, by Robert Harris

The Founding and *The Princeling*, by Cynthia Harrod-Eagles

Plainsong, by Kent Haruf

Across the Nightingale Floor, by Lian Hearn

Stones from the River, by Ursula Hegi

For Whom the Bell Tolls, A Moveable Feast, and *The Old Man and the Sea*, by Ernest Hemingway

Blue Asylum, by Kathy Hepinstall

Siddhartha, by Hermann Hesse

Out of the Dust, by Karen Hesse

The Painted Kiss and *The Wayward Muse*, by Elizabeth Hickey

Widow of the South, by Robert Hicks

The Stolen Crown, by Susan Higginbotham

Beautiful María of My Soul and *The Mambo King Plays Songs of Love*, by Óscar Hijuelos

Someone Knows My Name, by Lawrence Hill

Unbroken, by Laura Hillenbrand

The Dovekeepers, by Alice Hoffman

The King's Witch, *The Pillar of the Sky*, *The Secret Eleanor*, and *The Soul Thief*, by Cecelia Holland

The Quickening, by Michelle Hoover

Loving Frank, by Nancy Horan

The Angel with One Hundred Wings, by Daniel Horch

All Other Nights, by Dara Horn

The Nun, by Simonetta Agnello Hornby

And the Mountains Echoed, by Khaled Hosseini

Pictures at an Exhibition, by Sara Houghteling

Snow Mountain Passage, by James D. Houston

Thief of Shadows, by Elizabeth Hoyt

American by Blood, by Andrew Huebner

A High Wind in Jamaica, by Richard Hughes

The Time of Terror, by Seth Hunter

Their Eyes Were Watching God, by Zora Neale Hurston

The Conqueror: A Novel of Kublai Khan and *Emperor: The Gates of Rome*, by Conn Iggulden

Moving Pictures, by Kathryn Immonen

When We Were Orphans, by Kazuo Ishiguro

Thieftaker and *Unbroke Horses*, by D. B. Jackson

Incidents in the Life of a Slave Girl, by Harriet Jacobs

North and South, *Savannah; or, A Gift for Mr. Lincoln*, by John Jakes

Washington Square, by Henry James

The Book of Night Women, by Marlon James

The Lost Memoirs of Jane Austen, by Syrie James

A Very Long Engagement, by Sébastien Japrisot

The Country of the Pointed Firs, by Sarah Orne Jewett

The Color of Lightning and *Stormy Weather*, by Paulette Jiles

Middle Passage, by Charles Johnson

Tree of Smoke, by Denis Johnson

The Rope Eater, by Ben Jones

The Known World, by Edward P. Jones

Mudbound, by Hillary Jordan

An Unfinished Season, by Ward Just

The Siege, by Ismail Kadare

The Devil's Queen, by Jeanne Kalogridis

Sinners and the Sea, by Rebecca Kanner

By Fire, by Water, by Mitchell Kaplan
River of Stars and *Under Heaven*, by Guy Gavriel Kay
The Runaway, by Terry Kay
The Winter Sea, by Susanna Kearsley
Measuring the World, by Daniel Kehlmann
Schindler's List, by Thomas Keneally
Billy Phelan's Greatest Game, *Ironweed*, and *Legs*, by William Kennedy
Midshipman Bolitho, by Alexander Kent
The Heretic's Daughter, by Kathleen Kent
March Violets, by Philip Kerr
Gratitude, by Joseph Kertes
The Thing about Thugs, by Tabish Khair
The Lacuna and *The Poisonwood Bible*, by Barbara Kingsolver
Captains Courageous, by Rudyard Kipling
A Tendering in the Storm, by Jane Kirkpatrick
The English Passengers, by Matthew Kneale
Obasan, by Joy Kogawa
Under the Poppy, by Kathe Koja
Etta, by Gerald Kolpan
The Whip, by Karen Kondazian
The Impressionist, by Hari Kunzru.
Gwenhwyfar: The White Spirit, by Mercedes Lackey
John's Story, by Tim LaHaye
The King's Coat, by Dewey Lambdin
Fair Blows the Wind and *The Sackett's Land*, by Louis L'Amour
Passing, by Nella Larsen
In the Garden of Beasts, by Erik Larson
Lavinia, by Ursula Le Guin
The Witch of Cologne, by Tobsha Learner
The Indian Clerk, by David Leavitt
To Kill a Mockingbird, by Harper Lee
Havah: The Story of Eve, by Tosca Moon Lee
The Given Day and *Live by Night*, by Dennis Lehane
Pinkerton's Secret, by Eric Lerner
The Long Song, by Andrea Levy
Daughter of Joy, by JoAnn Levy
The Whiskey Rebels, by David Liss
Daughters of the Stone, by Dahlma Llanos-Figueroa
The Horse Goddess, by Morgan Llywelyn
The King's Pleasure, by Norah Lofts

The Sea-Wolf, by Jack London

The Golden Mean, Annabel Lyon

The Wake of Forgiveness, by Bruce Machart

The Year the Horses Came, by Mary Mackey

A Rogue by Any Other Name, by Sarah MacLean

The Cairo Trilogy, by Naguib Mahfouz

The Company of Liars and *The Owl Killers*, by Karen Maitland

The Fixer, by Bernard Malamud

Le morte d'Arthur, by Thomas Mallory

Remembering Babylon, by David Malouf

The Rice Mother, by Rani Manicka

The Eye of the Leopard, by Henning Mankell

Our Lives Are the Rivers, by Jaime Manrique

Bring Up the Bodies, *A Place of Greater Safety*, and *Wolf Hall*,
     by Hilary Mantel

I Am Forbidden, by Anouk Markovits

Matterhorn, by Karl Marlantes

The Piano Tuner, by Daniel Mason

Mademoiselle Boleyn, by Robin Maxwell

Tucker's Reckoning, by Matthew P. Mayo

Miracle at St. Anna and *A Song Yet Sung*, by James McBride

All the Pretty Horses, *Cities of the Plain*, and *The Crossing*,
     by Cormac McCarthy

I, Quantrill, by Max McCoy

Niagara Falls All over Again, by Elizabeth McCracken

The Ballad of Tom Dooley, by Sharyn McCrumb

Caesar: Let the Dice Fly, *The First Man in Rome*, *Morgan's Run*, *The October
     Horse*, and *The Thorn Birds*, by Colleen McCullough

The White Earth, by Andrew McGahan

Lee at Chattanooga, by Dennis P. McIntire

Queen of Camelot, by Nancy McKenzie

The Paris Wife, by Paula McLain

Bridge of Scarlet Leaves, by Kristina McMorris

Anything for Billy, *Lonesome Dove*, and *Sin Killer*, by Larry McMurtry

Mandrakes from the Holy Land, by Aharon Megged

Billy Budd, *Moby Dick*, by Herman Melville

Beneath the Lion's Gaze, by Maaze Mengiste

Alaska, *Chesapeake*, *The Covenant*, *Hawaii*, and *Poland*, by James Michener

The Child of the Holy Grail and *Guenevere: Queen of the Summer Country*,
     by Rosalind Miles

300, by Frank Miller

Empress Orchid and *The Last Empress*, by Anchee Min

The Thousand Autumns of Jacob de Zoet, by David Mitchell

House Made of Dawn, by N. Scott Momaday

Cleopatra's Daughter and *Nefertiti*, by Michelle Moran

Charlotte and Emily, by Jude Morgan

Skid Road: An Informal Portrait of Seattle, by Murray Morgan

Heart of a Lion and *No Woman So Fair*, by Gilbert Morris

A Mercy, by Toni Morrison

One Last Look, by Susannah Morrow

The Last Witchfinder, by James Morrow

City of the Dead and *A Deadly Injustice*, by Ian Morson

Just Jane, by Nancy Moser

Frida, by Barbara Louise Mujica

The Tree Bride, by Bharati Mukherjee

The Last Town on Earth, by Thomas Mullen

The True Story of Hansel and Gretel, by Louise Murphy

Attila: The Gathering Storm, Attila: The Judgement, and *Attila: The Scourge of God*, by William Napier

Abundance, by Sena Jeter Naslund

Freshwater Road, by Denise Nicholas

The Time Traveler's Wife, by Audrey Niffenegger

Maralinga, by Judy Nunn

Master and Commander, by Patrick O'Brian

Theophilos, by Michael O'Brien

My Dream of You, by Nuala O'Faolain

At Swim, Two Boys, by Jamie O'Neill

The Healing, by Jonathan Odell

Love Comes Softly, by Janette Oke

My Name Is Mary Sutter, by Robin Oliveira

Coal Black Horse, by Robert Olmstead

The English Patient, by Michael Ondaatje

The Scarlet Pimpernel, by Emma Orczy

The Invisible Bridge, by Julie Orringer

When the Emperor Was Divine, by Julie Otsuka

The Heaven Tree Trilogy, by Edith Pargeter

The Dragon Scroll, by I. J. Parker

Gunman's Rhapsody, by Robert B. Parker

Heresy, Prophecy, and *Sacrilege*, by S. J. Parris

Shadow of the Swords, by Kamran Pasha

State of Wonder, by Ann Patchett

Cry, the Beloved Country, by Alan Paton

Marion Zimmer Bradley's Sword of Avalon, by Diana Paxson

The Dante Club, by Matthew Pearl

An Instance of the Fingerpost and *The Portrait*, by Iain Pears

Here Be Dragons, Lionheart, The Sunne in Splendour, and *When Christ and His Saints Slept*, by Sharon Kay Penman

The Sun over Breda, by Arturo Pérez-Reverte

Wench, by Dolen Perkins-Valdez

The Face of a Stranger and *No Graves as Yet*, by Anne Perry

Crocodile on the Sandbank, by Elizabeth Peters

The Heaven Tree Trilogy, by Ellis Peters

Cain at Gettysburg, by Ralph Peters

The Street, by Ann Petry

The Reeducation of Cherry Truong, by Aimee Phan

The Well and the Mine, by Gin Phillips

City of Darkness, City of Light, by Marge Piercy

Cassandra and Jane, by Jill Pitkeathley

Freeman, by Leonard Pitts

The Bastard King; The Captive of Kensington; The Courts of Love; The Heart of the Lion; The Italian Woman; Katharine, the Virgin Widow; The Last Kingdom; Light on Lucrezia; Madame Serpent; Madonna of the Seven Hills; Mary, Queen of France; The Murder in the Tower; The Plantagenet Prelude; The Princess of Celle; Queen Jezebel; and *Uneasy Lies the Head*, by Jean Plaidy

"The Murders in the Rue Morgue" (short story), by Edgar Allan Poe

Ramage, by Dudley Pope

Ship of Fools, by Katherine Anne Porter

True Grit, by Charles Portis

The Chosen, by Chaim Potok

The Dark Monk and *The Hangman's Daughter*, by Oliver Pötzsch

In the Memory of the Forest, by Charles Powers

Gates of Fire, Killing Rommel, Tides of War, and *The Virtues of War*, by Steven Pressfield

Shipping News, That Old Ace in the Hole, by Annie Proulx

The Spanish Match, by Brennan Pursell

What Happens in London, by Julia Quinn

Rosa, The Second Son, and *Shadow and Light*, by Jonathan Rabb

The Cove, by Ron Rash

Silent in the Grave, by Joanna Raybourne

Fire from Heaven, Funeral Games, The King Must Die, and *The Persian Boy,*
    by Mary Renault
Testament, by Nino Ricci
Christ the Lord: Out of Egypt and *Christ the Lord: The Road to Cana,*
    by Anne Rice
The Midwife of Venice, by Roberta Rich
Unspoken, by Francine Rivers
An Imperfect Lens, by Ann Roiphe
Sarah's Key, by Tatiana de Rosnay
Call It Sleep and *A Star Shines over Mt. Morris Park,* by Henry Roth
The Plot against America, by Philip Roth
The Germanicus Mosaic, by Rosemary Rowe
Red Chrysanthemum and *Shinju,* by Laura Joh Rowland
Children of God, Doc, Dreamers of the Day, The Sparrow, and *A Thread of
    Grace,* by Mary Doria Russell
The Unreal Life of Sergey Nabokov, by Paul Russell
A Battle Won; Take, Burn or Destroy; and *Under Enemy Colors,*
    by S. Thomas Russell
London, New York, Paris, The Princes of Ireland, The Rebels of Ireland, Russka,
    and *Sarum,* by Edward Rutherfurd
Water Ghosts, by Shawna Yang Ryan
The Darkening Field and *The Holy Thief,* by William Ryan
Broken Paradise, by Cecilia Samartin
King Bongo, by Thomas Sanchez
Watermark, by Vanitha Sankaran
Conquistadora, by Esmeralda Santiago
Beyond the Sea of Ice, by William Sarabande
Museum of Human Beings, by Colin Sargent
A Moment in the Sun, by John Sayles
Empire, Roma, and *Roman Blood,* by Steven Saylor
Shane, by Jack Schaeffer
Aurora Crossing, by Karl H. Schlesier
The Commoner, by John Schwartz
Dreaming the Eagle, Dreaming the Hound, and *Dreaming the Serpent,*
    by Manda Scott
Ivanhoe, Rob Roy, and *Waverly* by Sir Walter Scott
Dreams of Joy, Shanghai Girls, and *Snow Flower and the Secret Fan,*
    by Lisa See
*A Blaze of Glory, A Chain of Thunder, The Final Storm, Gods and Generals,
    The Glorious Cause, The Final Storm, Gone for Soldiers, The Last Full*

Measure, No Less Than Victory, Rise to Rebellion, The Rising Tide, and *The Steel Wave*, by Jeff Shaara

The Killer Angels, by Michael Shaara

The Guernsey Literary and Potato Peel Pie Society, by Mary Ann Shaffer

Henry V, by William Shakespeare

Empress, by Sa Shan

Some Sing, Some Cry, by Ntozake Shange

Daughters of the Witching Hill, by Mary Sharratt

Storm Bay, by Patricia Shaw

The Last Time I Saw Paris, by Lynne Sheene

The Celestials, by Karen Shepard

Ceremony, by Leslie Marmon Silko

Black Hills, by Dan Simmons

Shosha, by Isaac Bashevis Singer

The All-True Travels and Adventures of Lidie Newton and *The Greenlanders*, by Jane Smiley

Sarai, by Jill Eileen Smith

Fair and Tender Ladies, Guests on Earth, and *On Agate Hill*, by Lee Smith

When the Lion Feeds, by Wilbur Smith

Sophie's Dilemma, by Lauraine Snelling

The Lotus Eaters, by Tatjana Soli

The House at Tyneford, by Natasha Solomons

Beautiful Fools, by R. Clifton Spargo

Joan, by Donald Spoto

The Winter Palace, by Eva Stachniak

The Cailiffs of Baghdad, Georgia, by Mary Helen Stefaniak

The Grapes of Wrath, by John Steinbeck

In the Shadow of the Cypress, by Thomas Steinbeck

Kidnapped and *Treasure Island*, by Robert Louis Stevenson

The Crystal Cave, by Mary Stewart

Grace Hammer, by Sara Stockbridge

The Help, by Kathryn Stockett

Kydd, by Julian Stockwin

The Agony and the Ecstasy and *Lust for Life*, by Irving Stone

Uncle Tom's Cabin, by Harriet Beecher Stowe

A Million Nightingales, by Susan Straight

The Burgess Boys, by Elizabeth Strout

Sophie's Choice, by William Styron

The Feast of Roses and *The Twentieth Wife*, by Indu Sundaresan

Gulliver's Travels, by Jonathan Swift

Cane River and *Red River*, by Lalita Tademy

The Hundred Secret Senses, by Amy Tan

The Garden of Evening Mists and *The Gift of Rain*, by Twan Eng Tan

Bring Down the Sun, by Judith Tarr

Derby Day and *Kept*, by D. J. Taylor

Mary Magdalene, by Diana Wallis Taylor

First Light, by Bodie Thoene

Follow the River, by James Alexander Thom

Some Danger Involved, by Will Thomas

The Good Thief, by Hannah Tinti

A Duty to the Dead, by Charles Todd

Cane, by Jean Toomer

The Shoemaker's Wife, by Adriana Trigiani

Collector of Worlds, by Ilija Trojanow

The Book of Salt, by Monique Truong

A Distant Mirror: The Calamitous 14th Century, by Barbara Tuchman

The News from Paraguay, by Lily Tuck

The Guns of the South, by Harry Turtledove

The Adventures of Huckleberry Finn, A Connecticut Yankee in King Arthur's Court, and *The Personal Recollections of Joan of Arc*, by Mark Twain

Kristin Lavransdatter, by Sigrid Undset

The Hummingbird's Daughter, by Luis Urrea

The Heretic's Wife, The Illuminator, and *The Mercy Seller*, by Brenda Rickman Vantrease

The War of the End of the World, by Mario Vargas Llosa

Cutting for Stone, by Abraham Verghese

Lucky Billy, by John Vernon

Crown of Dust, by Mary Volmer

Clara and Mr. Tiffany, The Forest Lover, The Girl in Hyacinth Blue, Life Studies, Luncheon of the Boating Party, and *The Passion of Artemisia*, by Susan Vreeland

Meridian, by Alice Walker

April in Paris, by Michael Wallner

Half Broke Horses, by Jeannette Walls

The Lily Theater, by Lulu Wang

The Republic of Vengeance, by Paul Waters

Tipping the Velvet, by Sarah Waters

The Heretic, by Lewis Weinstein

The Captive Queen, The Children of Henry VIII, Innocent Traitor, and *The Lady Elizabeth*, by Alison Weir

Fool's Crow, by James Welch
The Time Machine, by H. G. Wells
Meely LaBauve, by Ken Wells
The Wedding, by Dorothy West
The Sultan's Seal, by Jenny White
The Sword in the Stone, by T. H. White
A Mad Desire to Dance, by Elie Wiesel
The Doomsday Book, by Connie Willis
The Religion, by Tim Willocks
Maisie Dobbs, Jacqueline Winspear
A Short-Straw Bride and *A Tailor-Made Bride*, by Karen Witemeyer
An Eye of the Fleet, by Richard Woodman
Any Approaching Enemy and *Sails on the Horizon*, by Jay Worrall
The King's Daughter, *Lady of the Roses*, and *Love and War*, by Sandra Worth
The Lawgiver, by Herman Wouk
Native Son, by Richard Wright
My Enemy's Cradle, by Sara Young
The Fall of Atlantis, *The Mists of Avalon*, and *Sword of Avalon*,
      by Marion Zimmer
A Season of Fire and Ice, by Lloyd Zimpel
Paris, by Émile Zola

Series Bibliography

I have included all titles in these series—even when I mention only one or two titles in the text of this book—for the convenience of readers who may wish to quickly discover the other titles of the series, rather than have to look them up elsewhere. All series included here are mentioned in this book. Titles listed under each series name are listed in the order they should be read, not necessarily in publication order.

Lady Emily Ashton Mysteries
by Tasha Alexander

And Only to Deceive
A Poisoned Season
A Fatal Waltz
Tears of Pearl
Dangerous to Know
A Crimson Warning
Death in the Floating City

Islam Quintet
by Tariq Ali

Shadows of the Pomegranate Tree
The Book of Saladin
Night of the Golden Butterfly
The Stone Woman
A Sultan in Palermo

Rashi's Daughters
by Maggie Anton

Joheved
Miriam
Rachel

The Clifton Chronicles
by Jeffrey Archer

Only Time Will Tell
The Sins of the Father
The Best Kept Secret

Jade del Cameron Mysteries
by Suzanne Arruda

Mark of the Lion
The Serpent's Daughter
The Leopard's Prey
Treasure of the Golden Cheetah
The Crocodile's Last Embrace

Chronicles of the Kings
by Lynn N. Austin

Gods and Kings
Song of Redemption
The Strength of His Hand
Faith of My Fathers
Among the Gods

Molly Murphy Mysteries
by Rhys Bowen

Murphy's Law
Death of Riley
For the Love of Mike
In Like Flynn
Oh Danny Boy
In Dublin's Fair City
Tell Me, Pretty Maiden
In a Gilded Cage
The Last Illusion
Bless the Bride
Hush Now, Don't You Cry
The Family Way
City of Dark and Light

Avalon
by Marion Zimmer Bradley
(and Diana Paxson)

The Fall of Atlantis
Ancestors of Avalon (Paxson)
Ravens of Avalon (Paxson)
The Forest House
Lady of Avalon
Priestess of Avalon
The Mists of Avalon
Sword of Avalon (Paxson)

Women of Genesis
by Orson Scott Card

Sarah
Rebekah
Rachel and Leah

The Leatherstocking Tales
by James Fenimore Cooper

The Deerslayer
The First War Path
The Last of the Mohicans
The Pathfinder
The Inland Sea
The Pioneers

The Grail Quest
by Bernard Cornwell

The Archer's Tale
Vagabond
Heretic

Saxon Stories
by Bernard Cornwell

The Last Kingdom
The Pale Horseman
The Lords of the North
Sword Song
The Burning Land
Death of Kings
The Pagan Lord

The Starbuck Chronicles
by Bernard Cornwell

Rebel
Copperhead
Battle Flag
The Bloody Ground

The Warlord Chronicles
by Bernard Cornwell

The Winter King
Enemy of God
Excalibur

Marcus Didius Falco Mysteries
by Lindsey Davis

The Silver Pigs
Shadows in Bronze
Venus in Copper
The Iron Hand of Mars
Poseidon's Gold
Last Act in Palmyra
Time to Depart
A Dying Light in Corduba
Three Hands in the Fountain
Two for the Lions
One Virgin Too Many
Ode to a Banker
A Body in the Bathhouse
The Jupiter Myth
The Accusers
Scandal Takes a Holiday
See Delphi and Die
Saturnalia
Alexandria
Nemesis

Whiteoaks of Jalna
by Mazo de la Roche

The Building of Jalna
Morning at Jalna
Mary Wakefield
Young Renny
Whiteoak Heritage
The Whiteoak Brothers
Jalna
Whiteoaks of Jalna
Finch's Fortune
The Master of Jalna
Whiteoak Harvest
Wakefield's Course
Return to Jalna
Renny's Daughter

Variable Winds at Jalna
Centenary at Jalna

Wilderness
by Sara Donati

Into the Wilderness
Dawn on a Distant Shore
Lake in the Clouds
Fire along the Sky
Queen of Swords
The Endless Forest

The Tea Rose
by Jennifer Donnelly

The Tea Rose
The Winter Rose
The Wild Rose

Gaius Petreius Ruso
by Ruth Downie

Medicus
Terra Incognita
Persona Non Grata
Caveat Emptor

Lymond Chronicles
by Dorothy Dunnett

The Game of Kings
Queen's Play
The Disorderly Knights
Pawn in Frankincense
The Ringed Castle
Checkmate

Immigrants
by Howard Fast

The Immigrants
The Second Generation

The Establishment
The Legacy
The Immigrant's Daughter
An Independent Woman

Hornblower Saga
by C. S. Forester

Mr. Midshipman Hornblower
Lieutenant Hornblower
Hornblower and the Hotspur
Hornblower and the Atropos
Beat to Quarters
Ship of the Line
Flying Colours
Commodore Hornblower
Lord Hornblower
Admiral Hornblower
Hornblower during the Crisis
*The Life and Times of Horatio
    Hornblower*

Samurai Mysteries
by Dale Furutani

Death at the Crossroads
Jade Palace
Kill the Shogun

Outlander
by Diana Gabaldon

Outlander
Dragonfly in Amber
Voyager
Drums of Autumn
The Fiery Cross
A Breath of Snow and Ashes
An Echo in the Bone
Written in My Own Heart's Blood

The Forsyte Saga
by John Galsworthy

The Man of Property
Indian Summer of a Forsyte
In Chancery
Awakening
To Let
The White Monkey
A Silent Wooing
The Silver Spoon
Passers By
Swan Song
One More River (aka Over the River)

George Washington
by Newt Gingrich

To Try Men's Souls
Valley Forge
Victory at Yorktown

Gettysburg
by Newt Gingrich

Gettysburg
Grant Comes East
Never Call Retreat: Lee and Grant,
  the Final Victory

The Joshua Series
by Joseph F. Girzone

Joshua
Joshua and the Children
The Shepherd
Joshua and the Holy Land
Joshua and the City
Joshua, the Homecoming
The Parables of Joshua
Joshua in a Troubled World
Joshua's Family: A Prequel to Joshua

The Brides
by Deeanne Gist

A Bride Most Begrudging
The Measure of a Lady
Courting Trouble
Deep in the Heart of Trouble
A Bride in the Bargain

Yashim Togalu Mysteries
by Jason Goodwin

The Janissary Tree
The Snake Stone
The Bellini Card
An Evil Eye

Phryne Fisher Mysteries
by Kerry Greenwood

Cocaine Blues
Flying Too High
Murder on the Ballarat Train
Death at Victoria Dock
The Green Mill Murder
Blood and Circuses
Ruddy Gore
Urn Burial
Raisins and Almonds
Death before Wicket
Away with the Fairies
Murder in Montparnasse
The Castlemaine Murders
Queen of the Flowers
Death by Water
Murder in the Dark
Murder on a Midsummer Night
Dead Man's Chest
Unnatural Habits

Cousins' War
by Philippa Gregory

The White Queen
The Red Queen
The Lady of the Rivers
The Kingmaker's Daughter
The White Princess

The Tudor Series
by Philippa Gregory

The Constant Princess
The Other Boleyn Girl
The Boleyn Inheritance
The Queen's Fool
The Virgin's Lover
The Other Queen

The Western Saga
by A. B. Guthrie Jr.

The Big Sky
The Way West
Fair Land, Fair Land
These Thousand Hills
Arfive
The Last Valley

The Morland Dynasty
by Cynthia Harrod-Eagles

The Founding
The Dark Rose
The Princeling
The Oak Apple
The Black Pearl
The Long Shadow
The Chevalier
The Maiden
The Flood Tide
The Tangled Thread

The Emperor
The Victory
The Regency
The Campaigners
The Reckoning
The Devil's Horse
The Poison Tree
The Abyss
The Hidden Shore
The Winter Journey
The Outcast
The Mirage
The Cause
The Homecoming
The Question
The Dream Kingdom
The Restless Sea
The White Road
The Burning Roses
The Measure of Days
The Fallen Kings
The Dancing Years
The Winding Road

Tales of the Otori
by Lian Hearn

Heaven's Net Is Wide (prequel)
Across the Nightingale Floor
Grass for His Pillow
The Harsh Cry of the Heron

Corban Loosestrife
by Cecelia Holland

The Soul Thief
The Witches' Kitchen
The Serpent Dreamer
Varanger
The High City
Kings of the North

Nathan Peake
by Seth Hunter

The Time of Terror
The Tide of War
The Price of Glory
The Winds of Folly

Conqueror
by Conn Iggulden

Genghis: Birth of an Empire
Genghis: Lords of the Bow
Genghis: Bones of the Hills
Khan: Empire of Silver, a Novel of the
    Khan Empire
Conqueror: A Novel of Kublai Khan

Emperor
by Conn Iggulden

Emperor: The Gates of Rome
Emperor: The Death of Kings
Emperor: The Field of Swords
Emperor: The Gods of War
The Blood of Gods: A Novel of Rome

Albany Trio
by William Kennedy

Legs
Billy Phelan's Greatest Game
Ironweed

The Bolitho Novels
by Alexander Kent

Midshipman Bolitho (aka Richard
    Bolitho, Midshipman)
Midshipman Bolitho and the Avenger
Band of Brothers
Sword of Honour

The Only Victor
Beyond the Reef
The Darkening Sea
In Gallant Company
Stand Into Danger
For My Country's Freedom
Command a King's Ship
The Inshore Squadron
Sloop of War
Colors Aloft!
With All Dispatch
Form Line of Battle!
A Tradition of Victory
Enemy in Sight!
The Flag Captain
To Glory We Steer
Passage to Mutiny
Cross of St. George
In the King's Name
Heart of Oak
Honor This Day
Signal—Close Action!
Success to the Brave
Relentless Pursuit
Second to None
Man of War
The Mutiny Run

Bernhard Gunther Mysteries
by Philip Kerr

March Violets
The Pale Criminal
A German Requiem
The One from the Other
A Quiet Flame
If the Dead Rise Not
Field Gray
Prague Fatale
A Man without Breath

Change and Cherish
by Jane Kirkpatrick

A Clearing in the Wild
A Tendering in the Storm
A Mending at the Edge

Jesus Chronicles
by Tim LaHaye

John's Story: The Last Eyewitness
Mark's Story: The Gospel according
*   to Peter*
Luke's Story: By Faith Alone
Matthew's Story: From Sinner
*   to Saint*

Alan Lewrie Naval Adventures
by Dewey Lambdin

The King's Coat
The French Admiral
The King's Commission
The King's Privateer
The Gun Ketch
H.M.S. Cockerel
A King's Commander
Jester's Fortune
King's Captain
Sea of Gray
Havoc's Sword
The Captain's Vengeance
A King's Trade
Troubled Waters
The Baltic Gambit
King, Ship, and Sword
The Invasion Year
Reefs and Shoals

The Sackets
by Louis L'Amour

Sackett's Land
To the Far Blue Mountains
The Warrior's Path
Jubal Sackett
Ride the River
The Daybreakers
End of the Curve
Lando
Sackett
War Party
Mojave Crossing
The Sackett Brand
The Sky-Liners
The Lonely Men
Mustang Man
Galloway
Treasure Mountain
Ride the Dark Trail
Lonely on the Mountain

Cairo Trilogy
by Naguib Mahfouz

Palace Walk
Palace of Desire
Sugar Street

The Border Trilogy
by Cormac McCarthy

All the Pretty Horses
The Crossing
Cities of the Plain

Masters of Rome
by Colleen McCullough

The First Man in Rome
The Grass Crown
Fortune's Favorites
Caesar's Women
Let the Dice Fly
The October Horse
Antony and Cleopatra

Arthurian Tales
by Nancy McKenzie

The Child Queen
The High Queen
Grail Prince
Prince of Dreams
Queen of Camelot

Berrybender Narratives
by Larry McMurtry

Sin Killer
The Wandering Hill
By Sorrow's River
Folly and Glory

Lonesome Dove
by Larry McMurtry

Lonesome Dove
Streets of Laredo
Dead Man's Walk (prequel)
Comanche Moon (second prequel)

The Guenevere Trilogy
by Rosalind Miles

Guenevere: Queen of the Summer
 Country
The Knight of the Sacred Lake
The Child of the Holy Grail

Ancient Egypt
by Michelle Moran

Nefertiti
The Heretic Queen
Cleopatra's Daughter

Lions of Judah
by Gilbert Morris

Heart of a Lion
No Woman So Fair
The Gate of Heaven
Till Shiloh Comes
By Way of the Wilderness
Daughter of Deliverance

The Aubrey-Maturin Novels
by Patrick O'Brian

The Golden Ocean (prequel)
Master and Commander
Post Captain
H.M.S. Surprise
The Mauritius Command
Desolation Island
The Fortune of War
The Surgeon's Mate
The Ionian Mission
Treason's Harbour
The Far Side of the World
The Reverse of the Medal
The Letter of Marque
The Thirteen-Gun Salute
The Nutmeg of Consolation
The Truelove
The Wine-Dark Sea
The Commodore
The Yellow Admiral
The Hundred Days
Blue at the Mizzen
21: The Final Unfinished Voyage of
 Jack Aubrey

Love Comes Softly
by Janette Oke

Love Comes Softly
Love's Enduring Promise
Love's Long Journey
Love's Abiding Joy
Love's Unending Legacy
Love's Unfolding Dream
Love Takes Wing
Love Finds a Home

Sugawara Akitada Mysteries
by I. J. Parker

The Dragon Scroll
Rashomon Gate
Black Arrow
Island of Exiles
The Hell Screen
The Convict's Sword
The Masuda Affair
The Fires of the Gods

Henry II Trilogy
by Sharon Kay Penman

When Christ and His Saints Slept
Time and Chance
The Devil's Brood

Justin de Quincy Medieval Mysteries
by Sharon Kay Penman

The Queen's Man
Cruel as the Grave
Dragon's Heir
Prince of Darkness

Welsh Princes
by Sharon Kay Penman

Here Be Dragons
Falls the Shadow
The Reckoning

Captain Alatriste Adventures
by Arturo Pérez-Reverte

Captain Alatriste
Purity of Blood
The Sun over Breda
The King's Gold
The Cavalier in the Yellow Doublet
Pirates of the Levant

Thomas and Charlotte Pitt Mysteries
by Anne Perry

The Cater Street Hangman
Callander Square
Paragon Walk
Resurrection Row
Bluegate Fields
Rutland Place
Death in the Devil's Acre
Cardington Crescent
Silence in Hanover Close
Bethlehem Road
Highgate Rise
Belgrave Square
Farrier's Lane
The Hyde Park Headsman
Traitors' Gate
Pentecost Alley
Ashworth Hall
Brunswick Gardens
Bedford Square
Half Moon Street
The Whitechapel Conspiracy

Southampton Row
Seven Dials
Long Spoon Land
Buckingham Palace Gardens
Treason at Lisson Grove
Dorchester Terrace

William Monk and Hester Latterly Mysteries
by Anne Perry

The Face of a Stranger
A Dangerous Mourning
Defend and Betray
A Sudden, Fearful Death
The Sins of the Wolf
Cain His Brother
Weighed in the Balance
The Silent Cry
A Breach of Promise
The Twisted Root
Slaves and Obsession
Funeral in Blue
Death of a Stranger
The Shifting Tide
Dark Assassin
Execution Dock
Acceptable Loss
A Sunless Sea
Blind Justice

World War I
by Anne Perry

No Graves as Yet
Shoulder the Sky
Angels in the Gloom
At Some Disputed Barricade
We Shall Not Sleep

Amelia Peabody Mysteries
by Elizabeth Peters

Crocodile on the Sandbank
The Curse of the Pharaohs
The Mummy Case
Lion in the Valley
The Deeds of the Disturber
The Last Camel Died at Noon
The Snake, the Crocodile, and the Dog
The Hippopotamus Pool
Seeing a Large Cat
The Ape Who Guards the Balance
Guardian of the Horizon
A River in the Sky
A Falcon at the Portal
He Shall Thunder in the Sky
Lord of the Silent
The Golden One
Children of the Storm
The Serpent on the Crown
Tomb of the Golden Bird

The Brother Cadfael Chronicles
by Ellis Peters

A Morbid Taste for Bones
One Corpse Too Many
Monk's Hood
St. Peter's Fair
The Leper of St. Giles
The Virgin in the Ice
Sanctuary Sparrow
The Devil's Novice
Dead Man's Ransom
The Pilgrim of Hate
An Excellent Mystery
The Raven in the Foregate
The Rose Rent
The Hermit of Eyton Forest

The Confession of Brother Haluin
The Heretic's Apprentice
The Potter's Field
The Summer of the Danes
The Holy Thief
Brother Cadfael's Penance

Catherine de Medici
by Jean Plaidy

Madame Serpent
The Italian Woman
Queen Jezebel

Georgian Saga
by Jean Plaidy

The Princess of Celle
Queen in Waiting
Caroline, the Queen
The Prince and the Quakeress
The Third George
Perdita's Prince
Sweet Lass of Richmond Hill
Indiscretions of the Queen
The Regent's Daughter
Goddess of the Green Room
Victoria in the Wings

Katharine of Aragon Trilogy
by Jean Plaidy

Katharine, the Virgin Widow
The Shadow of the Pomegranate
The King's Secret Matter

Norman Trilogy
by Jean Plaidy

The Bastard King
The Lion of Justice
The Passionate Enemies

Plantagenet Saga
by Jean Plaidy

The Plantagenet Prelude
The Revolt of Eagles
The Heart of the Lion
The Prince of Darkness
The Battle of Queens
The Queen from Provence
*The Hammer of the Scots (previous
   title: Edward Longshanks)*
The Follies of the King
The Vow on the Heron
Passage to Pontefract
The Star of Lancaster
Epitaph for Three Women
Red Rose of Anjou
The Sun in Splendour

Queen Victoria
by Jean Plaidy

The Captive of Kensington
The Queen and Lord M
The Queen's Husband
The Widow of Windsor

Stuart Saga
by Jean Plaidy

The Murder in the Tower
The Wandering Prince
A Health Unto His Majesty
Here Lies Our Sovereign Lord
The Three Crowns
The Haunted Sisters
The Queen's Favourites

Tudor Series
by Jean Plaidy

Uneasy Lies the Head
Katharine, the Virgin Widow
The Shadow of the Pomegranate
The King's Secret Matter
Murder Most Royal
Saint Thomas' Eve
The Sixth Wife
The Thistle and the Rose
Mary, Queen of France
The Spanish Bridegroom
A Favorite of the Queen (previous
    title: Gay Lord Robert)

Lord Ramage
by Dudley Pope

Ramage
Ramage and the Drumbeat
Ramage and the Freebooters
Governor Ramage, R.N.
Ramage's Prize
Ramage and the Guillotine
Ramage's Diamond
Ramage's Mutiny
Ramage and the Rebels
The Ramage Touch
Ramage's Signal
Ramage and the Renegades
Ramage's Devil
Ramage's Trial
Ramage's Challenge
Ramage at Trafalgar
Ramage and the Saracens
Ramage and the Dido

Hangman's Daughter Tales
by Oliver Pötzsch

The Hangman's Daughter
The Dark Monk
The Beggar King
The Poisoned Pilgrim

Berlin Trilogy
by Jonathan Rabb

Rosa
Shadow and Light
The Second Sight

Lady Julia Grey Mysteries
by Deanna Raybourn

Silent in the Grave
Silent in the Sanctuary
Silent on the Moor
Dark Road to Darjeeling
The Dark Enquiry

Alexander the Great Trilogy
by Mary Renault

Fire from Heaven
The Persian Boy
Funeral Games

Lineage of Grace
by Francine Rivers

Unveiled
Unashamed
Unshaken
Unspoken
Unafraid

Sons of Encouragement
by Francine Rivers

The Priest
The Warrior
The Prince
The Prophet
The Scribe

Mercy of a Rude Stream
by Henry Roth

A Star Shines Over Mt. Morris Park
A Diving Rock on the Hudson
From Bondage
Requiem for Harlem
An American Type

The Libertus Mysteries
of Roman Britain
by Rosemary Rowe

The Germanicus Mosaic
A Pattern of Blood
Murder in the Forum
The Chariots of Calyz
The Legatus Mystery
The Ghosts of Glevum
Enemies of the Empire
A Roman Ransom
A Coin for the Ferryman
Death at Pompeia's Wedding
Requiem for a Slave
The Vestal Vanishes
A Whispering of Spies

Sano Ichiro Mysteries
by Laura Joh Rowland

Shinju
Bundori
The Way of the Traitor

The Concubine's Tattoo
The Samurai's Wife
Black Lotus
The Pillow Book of Lady Wisteria
The Dragon King's Palace
The Perfumed Sleeve
The Assassin's Touch
Red Chrysanthemum
The Snow Empress
The Fire Kimono
The Cloud Pavilion
The Ronin's Mistress
The Incense Game

The Investigations
of Captain Korolev
by William Ryan

The Holy Thief
The Darkening Field
The Twelfth Department

Captain Blood
by Rafael Sabatini

Captain Blood
Captain Blood Returns
The Fortunes of Captain Blood

Roma Sub Rosa
by Steven Saylor

The Seven Wonders (prequel)
Roman Blood
The House of Vestals
A Gladiator Dies Only Once
Arms of Nemesis
Catilina's Riddle
The Venus Throw
A Murder on the Appian Way
Rubicon

Last Seen in Massilia
A Mist of Prophecies
The Judgment of Caesar
The Triumph of Caesar

Boudica
by Manda Scott

Dreaming the Eagle
Dreaming the Bull
Dreaming the Hound
Dreaming the Serpent

World War II
by Jeff Shaara

The Rising Tide
The Steel Wave
No Less Than Victory
The Final Storm

Courtney
by Wilbur Smith

When the Lion Feeds
The Sound of Thunder
A Sparrow Falls
The Burning Shore
Power of the Sword
Rage
A Time to Die
Golden Fox
Birds of Prey
Monsoon
The Blue Horizon
The Triumph of the Sun
Assegai

The Daughters of Blessing
by Lauraine Snelling

A Promise for Ellie
Sophie's Dilemma
A Touch of Grace
Rebecca's Reward

Merlin the Enchanter
by Mary Stewart

The Crystal Cave
The Hollow Hills
The Last Enchantment
The Wicked Day

Kydd Sea Adventures
by Julian Stockwin

Kydd
Artemis
Seaflower
Mutiny
Quarterdeck
Tenacious
Command
The Admiral's Daughter
The Privateer's Revenge
Invasion
Victory
Conquest
Betrayal

AD Chronicles
by Bodie Thoene

First Light
Second Touch
Third Watch
Fourth Dawn
Fifth Seal

Sixth Covenant
Seventh Day
Eighth Shepherd
Ninth Witness
Tenth Stone
Eleventh Quest
Twelfth Prophecy

Zion Legacy
by Bodie Thoene

Jerusalem Vigil
Thunder from Jerusalem
Jerusalem's Heart
The Jerusalem Scrolls
Stones of Jerusalem
Jerusalem's Hope

Cyrus Barker and Thomas Llewelyn Mysteries
by Will Thomas

Some Danger Involved
To Kingdom Come
The Limehouse Text
The Hellfire Conspiracy
The Black Hand

Bess Crawford Mysteries
by Charles Todd

A Duty to the Dead
An Impartial Witness
A Bitter Truth
An Unmarked Grave
A Question of Honor

The War That Came Early
by Harry Turtledove

Hitler's War
West and East

The Big Switch
Coup d'état

Kamil Pasha Mysteries
by Jenny White

The Sultan's Seal
The Abyssinian Proof
The Winter Thief

The Once and Future King
by T. H. White

The Sword in the Stone
The Witch in the Wood
The Ill-Made Knight
The Once and Future King
The Book of Merlin

Maisie Dobbs
by Jacqueline Winspear

Maisie Dobbs
Birds of a Feather
Pardonable Lies
Messenger of Truth
An Incomplete Revenge
Among the Mad
The Mapping of Love and Death
A Lesson in Secrets
Elegy for Eddie
Leaving Everything Most Loved

Nathaniel Drinkwater Sea Stories
by Richard Woodman

Nathaniel Drinkwater: Midshipman
    (prequel)
An Eye of the Fleet
A King's Cutter
A Brig of War
The Bomb Vessel

Arctic Treachery
Decision at Trafalgar
Baltic Mission
In Distant Waters
A Private Revenge
Under False Colours
The Flying Squadron
Beneath the Aurora
The Shadow of the Eagle
Ebb Tide

The Rose of York Trilogy
by Sandra Worth

Love and War
Crown of Destiny
Fall from Grace

APPEAL/SUBJECT INDEX

A

absorbing
  The Ballad of Tom Dooley (McCrumb), 113–114
  Helen of Troy (George), 90–91
  The Other Boleyn Girl (Gregory), 86–87
accuracy, historical, 15, 17–18
  The Day the Falls Stood Still (Buchanan), 61
  Dreams of Joy (See), 72–73
  The Pillars of the Earth (Follett), 36–37
accurate
  Valley Forge (Gingrich), 119
action packed
  The Conqueror: A Novel of Kublai Khan (Iggulden), 88–89
  Nathaniel Drinkwater series (Woodman), 183–184
  The Quick and the Dead (Eickhoff), 123–124
  The Wettest County in the World (Bondurant), 126
adventure, 181–184
  Agincourt (Cornwell), 39
  City of Thieves (Benioff), 49–50
  The Last Jew (Gordon), 170–171
  Niccolò Rising (Dunnett), 40
  Sea of Poppies (Ghosh), 47
  The Silver Pigs (Davis), 190–191
Africa
  Half of a Yellow Sun (Adichie), 58
  The Poisonwood Bible (Kingsolver), 59
  The Power of One (Courtenay), 57–58
  Things Fall Apart (Achebe), 58
African American historical fiction, 143–147
Age of Enlightenment

  The Fort: A Novel of the Revolutionary War (Cornwell), 43–44
  The Heretic's Daughter (Kent), 44
  The Whiskey Rebels (Liss), 45
  Year of Wonders: A Novel of the Plague (Brooks), 42–43
alternate history
  Gettysburg trilogy (Gingrich), 202–203
  The Guns of the South (Turtledove), 203
  Lee at Chattanooga: A Novel of What Might Have Been (McIntire), 203
  The Secret Trial of Robert E. Lee (Fleming), 203
American Revolutionary War
  Patriot Hearts (Hambly), 119
  The Rebellion of Jane Clarke (Gunning), 119
  Rise to Rebellion: A Novel of the American Revolution (Shaara), 118
  Valley Forge (Gingrich), 119
ancient world
  The First Man in Rome (McCullough), 33–34
  Gates of Fire: An Epic Novel of the Battle of Thermopylae (Pressfield), 32–33
  Pompeii (Harris), 34–35
annotations, 214
appeal characteristics/terms, xv, 4
  examples of, 11–12
  practice with, 25
Asia
  Dreams of Joy (See), 72–73
  Map of the Invisible World (Aw), 71–72
Asian American historical fiction, 147–152

atmospheric
  All Other Nights (Horn), 120
  All the Pretty Horses (McCarthy),
    186–187
  *The All-True Travels and Adventures of
    Lidie Newton* (Smiley), 185–186
  *The Amazing Adventures of Kavalier
    and Clay* (Chabon), 171
  Avalon series (Bradley), 201–202
  Bernhard Gunther mysteries (Kerr),
    191–192
  Christ the Lord: Out of Egypt (Rice),
    165–166
  The Conqueror: A Novel of Kublai Khan
    (Iggulden), 88–89
  The Given Day (Lehane), 133
  Helen of Troy (George), 90–91
  The Heretic's Daughter (Kent), 125
  In the Time of the Butterflies (Alvarez),
    159–160
  Islam Quintet series, The (Ali),
    205–206
  Map of the Invisible World (Aw), 71–72
  The March (Doctorow), 120
  Mudbound (Jordan), 132
  On Agate Hill (Smith), 132
  Outlander (Adamson), 187
  The Quickening (Hoover), 134
  The Republic of Vengeance (Waters),
    175–176
  *Rise to Rebellion: A Novel of the
    American Revolution* (Shaara), 118
  The Rising Tide (Shaara), 122
  The Silver Pigs (Davis), 190–191
  The Sisters Brothers (deWitt), 188–189
  Some Sing, Some Cry (Shange), 146
  Things Fall Apart (Achebe), 58
  True Sisters (Dallas), 136
  An Unfinished Season (Just), 135
  Wanting (Flanagan), 75–76
  The Wettest County in the World
    (Bondurant), 126
  When Christ and His Saints Slept
    (Penman), 37–38
  William Monk and Hester Latterly
    mysteries (Perry), 192–193

Australia, 73–77
  The Lieutenant (Grenville), 76–77
  The True History of the Kelly Gang
    (Carey), 74–75
  Wanting (Flanagan), 75–76
authentic
  The Last Empress (Min), 89
awards, 234

B
benchmarks, 4
biographical historical fiction
  after Henry VIII, 104–107
  appeal of, 85–86
  attributes of, 85
  before Henry VIII, 90–98
  defining, 84–85
  introduction to, 83–84
  major historical figures and, 90
  on artists, 107–109
  on heroes and villains, 111–114
  on writers, 109–111
  reign of King Henry VIII, 98–104
  well-known, 86–89
bittersweet
  *The All-True Travels and Adventures of
    Lidie Newton* (Smiley), 185–186
  Beautiful María of My Soul (Hijuelos),
    160
  City of Thieves (Benioff), 49–50
  Helen of Troy (George), 90–91
bleak
  All the Pretty Horses (McCarthy),
    186–187
  Bernhard Gunther mysteries (Kerr),
    191–192
  Bound (Gunning), 133
  *Charlotte and Emily: A Novel of the
    Brontës* (Morgan), 110
  The Company of Liars (Maitland), 128
  The Dovekeepers (Hoffman), 168–169
  Matterhorn: A Novel of Vietnam
    (Marlantes), 123
  Skeletons at the Feast (Bohjalian),
    78–79
  Tree of Smoke (Johnson), 123

William Monk and Hester Latterly
   mysteries (Perry), 192–193
blogs, 214–215, 230–232
book groups, 224, 249–256
book lists, 214, 221–222
book notes, 240–241
booktalks, 211

C

character, appeal terms regarding, 10
character driven
   Alexander the Great trilogy
      (Renault), 91–92
   All Other Nights (Horn), 120
   All the Pretty Horses (McCarthy),
      186–187
   The Amazing Adventures of Kavalier
      and Clay (Chabon), 171
   Amelia Peabody mysteries (Peters),
      193–194
   At the Mercy of the Queen: A Novel of
      Anne Boleyn (Barnhill), 101
   Baker Towers (Haigh), 133
   Beautiful María of My Soul (Hijuelos),
      160
   Bucking the Sun (Doig), 127
   Christ the Lord: Out of Egypt (Rice),
      165–166
   The Clan of the Cave Bear (Auel), 29
   The Confession of Katherine Howard
      (Dunn), 103
   Conquistadora (Santiago), 68–69
   The Constant Princess (Gregory), 100
   Corrag (Fletcher), 125
   Doc (Russell), 113
   Eve: A Novel of the First Woman
      (Elliott), 162–163
   Fall of Giants (Follett), 51–52
   Flight (Alexie), 154
   The Fruit of Her Hands (Cameron),
      169–170
   Georgian Saga (Plaidy), 141
   Gratitude (Kertes), 172
   Half of a Yellow Sun (Adichie), 58
   Hotel on the Corner of Bitter and Sweet
      (Ford), 151–152

In the Time of the Butterflies (Alvarez),
      159–160
   Inés of My Soul (Allende), 157–158
   Invisible Mountain (de Robertis),
      67–68
   Killing Rommel (Pressfield), 122
   The Last Empress (Min), 89
   A Lesson before Dying (Gaines),
      146–147
   The Lieutenant (Grenville), 76–77
   Lionheart (Penman), 94–95
   The Long Song (Levy), 66–67
   The Lotus Eaters (Soli), 124
   Loving Frank (Horan), 87–88
   The Maid: A Novel of Joan of Arc
      (Cutter), 95–96
   Maisie Dobbs novels (Winspear),
      195–196
   The March (Doctorow), 120
   Measuring the World (Kehlmann), 130
   Moloka'i (Brennert), 128–129
   Norman Trilogy (Plaidy), 139
   Outlander (Adamson), 187
   Outlander series (Gabaldon), 204–205
   A Plague of Doves (Erdrich), 156–157
   Plantagenet Saga (Plaidy), 139–140
   The Poisonwood Bible (Kingsolver), 59
   The Power of One (Courtenay), 57
   Queen Victoria novels (Plaidy), 141
   Queens of England series (Plaidy),
      138–139
   Rose of York trilogy (Worth), 140
   Sano Ichiro mysteries (Rowland),
      194–195
   Sarai (Smith), 164–165
   A Season of Fire and Ice (Zimpel), 134
   The September Queen (Bagwell),
      197–198
   Skeletons at the Feast (Bohjalian),
      78–79
   Stormy Weather (Jiles), 127
   Stuart Saga (Plaidy), 140–141
   Tipping the Velvet (Waters), 174–175
   The True History of the Kelly Gang
      (Carey), 74–75
   Tudor series (Plaidy), 140

character driven (cont.)
  Under Heaven (Kay), 199–200
  The Well and the Mine (Phillips), 60
  Wench (Perkins-Valdez, Dolen), 145
  The White Queen (Gregory), 96–97
  Wilderness series (Donati), 207–208
  William Monk and Hester Latterly
    mysteries (Perry), 192–193
  Year of Wonders: A Novel of the Plague
    (Brooks), 42–43
  See also well developed characters
Christian historical fiction, 161–167
Civil War, 46
  All Other Nights (Horn), 120
  The Ballad of Tom Dooley (McCrumb),
    113–114
  The March (Doctorow), 120
  My Name Is Mary Sutter (Oliveira),
    120
  The Widow of the South (Hicks), 121
coming of age
  All the Pretty Horses (McCarthy),
    186–187
  Matterhorn: A Novel of Vietnam
    (Marlantes), 123
  The Power of One (Courtenay), 57
compelling
  The Boleyn Inheritance (Gregory),
    102–103
  Bound (Gunning), 133
  Caleb's Crossing (Brooks), 154–155
  Christ the Lord: Out of Egypt (Rice),
    165–166
  The Constant Princess (Gregory), 100
  The Dovekeepers (Hoffman), 168–169
  Eve: A Novel of the First Woman
    (Elliott), 162–163
  Fall of Giants (Follett), 51–52
  *The Favored Queen: A Novel of Henry
    VIII's Third Wife* (Erickson),
    101–102
  Fool's Crow (Welch), 155–156
  Georgian Saga (Plaidy), 141
  Gettysburg trilogy (Gingrich), 202
  The Given Day (Lehane), 133
  The Hangman's Daughter (Pötzsch),
    124–125

The Help (Stockett), 53–54
The Heretic's Daughter (Kent), 44, 125
*I Should Be Extremely Happy in Your
    Company* (Hall), 48
In the Time of the Butterflies (Alvarez),
    159–160
The Long Song (Levy), 66–67
The Memoirs of Mary, Queen of Scots
    (Erickson), 104
Moloka'i (Brennert), 128–129
Mudbound (Jordan), 132
My Name Is Mary Sutter (Oliveira),
    120, 128
Nathaniel Drinkwater series
    (Woodman), 183–184
Norman Trilogy (Plaidy), 139
The Other Boleyn Girl (Gregory),
    86–87
Patriot Hearts (Hambly), 119
Plantagenet Saga (Plaidy), 139–140
Pompeii (Harris), 34–35
The Postmistress (Blake), 50–51
Queen Victoria novels (Plaidy), 141
Queens of England series (Plaidy),
    138–139
The Rising Tide (Shaara), 122
Rose of York trilogy (Worth), 140
Sano Ichiro mysteries (Rowland),
    194–195
Sarai (Smith), 164–165
A Season of Fire and Ice (Zimpel), 134
The September Queen (Bagwell),
    197–198
Stormy Weather (Jiles), 127
Stuart Saga (Plaidy), 140–141
Things Fall Apart (Achebe), 58
*To Be Queen: A Novel of the Early Life of
    Eleanor of Aquitaine* (English), 94
The True History of the Kelly Gang
    (Carey), 74–75
True Sisters (Dallas), 136
Tudor series (Plaidy), 140
The Voyage of the Short Serpent (du
    Boucheron), 79–80
Wench (Perkins-Valdez, Dolen), 145
The White Queen (Gregory), 96–97
The Widow of the South (Hicks), 121

complex plot
  The Amazing Adventures of Kavalier
    and Clay (Chabon), 171
  Amelia Peabody mysteries (Peters),
    193–194
  Bernhard Gunther mysteries (Kerr),
    191–192
  Bloodroot (Greene), 64–65
  Christ the Lord: Out of Egypt (Rice),
    165–166
  Conquistadora (Santiago), 68–69
  Deep Creek (Hand), 149
  The First Man in Rome (McCullough),
    92–93
  The Given Day (Lehane), 133
  Map of the Invisible World (Aw), 71–72
  Master Georgie (Bainbridge), 173–174
  New York (Rutherford), 134
  Niccolò Rising (Dunnett), 40
  The Pillars of the Earth (Follett), 36–37
  A Plague of Doves (Erdrich), 156–157
  Sea of Poppies (Ghosh), 47
  The Secret Bride: In the Court of Henry
    VIII (Haeger), 98–99
  The September Queen (Bagwell),
    197–198
  Shanghai Girls (See), 150–151
  Stonehenge, 2000 BC (Cornwell), 31
  Tea Rose trilogy (Donnelly), 198–199
  Tree of Smoke (Johnson), 123
  Wanting (Flanagan), 75–76
  West of Here (Evison), 62–64
  Wilderness series (Donati), 207–208
  The Winter Palace: A Novel of Catherine
    the Great (Stachniak), 106–107
  Wolf Hall (Mantel), 41
complex style
  All the Pretty Horses (McCarthy),
    186–187
  Baker Towers (Haigh), 133
  Bloodroot (Greene), 64–65
  Half of a Yellow Sun (Adichie), 58
  Invisible Mountain (de Robertis),
    67–68
  The Living (Dillard), 136
  The Lotus Eaters (Soli), 124
  The March (Doctorow), 120

  Master and Commander (O'Brian),
    182–183
  A Plague of Doves (Erdrich), 156–157
  Tree of Smoke (Johnson), 123
  Under Heaven (Kay), 199–200
compulsively readable
  The Blood of Flowers (Amirrezvani),
    70–71
  Fall of Giants (Follett), 51–52
  New York (Rutherford), 134
  To Be Queen: A Novel of the Early Life of
    Eleanor of Aquitaine (English), 94
  See also page-turner
cozy
  Amelia Peabody mysteries (Peters),
    193–194

D
darkly humorous
  The Sisters Brothers (deWitt), 188–189
descriptive
  Bernhard Gunther mysteries (Kerr),
    191–192
  Doc (Russell), 113
  The First Man in Rome (McCullough),
    92–93
  Georgian Saga (Plaidy), 141
  Queen Victoria novels (Plaidy), 141
  Skeletons at the Feast (Bohjalian),
    78–79
  Wanting (Flanagan), 75–76
detailed
  Abundance: A Novel of Marie
    Antoinette (Naslund), 105–106
  Agincourt (Cornwell), 39
  Alexander the Great trilogy
    (Renault), 91–92
  All Other Nights (Horn), 120
  The All-True Travels and Adventures of
    Lidie Newton (Smiley), 185–186
  The Amazing Adventures of Kavalier
    and Clay (Chabon), 171
  Amelia Peabody mysteries (Peters),
    193–194
  At the Mercy of the Queen: A Novel of
    Anne Boleyn (Barnhill), 101
  Avalon series (Bradley), 201–202

detailed (cont.)

The Blood of Flowers (Amirrezvani), 70–71

The Boleyn Inheritance (Gregory), 102–103

Caleb's Crossing (Brooks), 154–155

Christ the Lord: Out of Egypt (Rice), 165–166

The Clan of the Cave Bear (Auel), 29

Claude and Camille (Cowell), 108

Cleopatra's Daughter (Moran), 93

The Company of Liars (Maitland), 128

The Confession of Katherine Howard (Dunn), 103

The Confessions of Catherine de Medici (Gortner), 105

The Conqueror: A Novel of Kublai Khan (Iggulden), 88–89

The Constant Princess (Gregory), 100

Doc (Russell), 113

Etta (Kolpan), 112–113

The Fort: A Novel of the Revolutionary War (Cornwell), 43–44

The Fruit of Her Hands (Cameron), 169–170

Gettysburg trilogy (Gingrich), 202

The Given Day (Lehane), 133

The Hangman's Daughter (Pötzsch), 124–125

The Help (Stockett), 53–54

Hotel on the Corner of Bitter and Sweet (Ford), 151–152

An Imperfect Lens (Roiphe), 130

Invisible Mountain (de Robertis), 67–68

The King's Daughter: A Novel of the First Tudor Queen (Worth), 97–98

The Lacuna (Kingsolver), 158–159

The Last Empress (Min), 89

The Last Wife of Henry VIII (Erickson), 103–104

Lionheart (Penman), 94–95

The Living (Dillard), 136

The Lotus Eaters (Soli), 124

The March (Doctorow), 46–47

Master and Commander (O'Brian), 182–183

Matterhorn: A Novel of Vietnam (Marlantes), 123

My Name Is Mary Sutter (Oliveira), 128

Nathaniel Drinkwater series (Woodman), 183–184

New York (Rutherford), 134

Norman Trilogy (Plaidy), 139

On Agate Hill (Smith), 132

Outlander series (Gabaldon), 204–205

Patriot Hearts (Hambly), 119

People of the Wolf (Gear and Gear), 30

Percival's Planet (Byers), 130–131

The Pillars of the Earth (Follett), 36–37

A Plague of Doves (Erdrich), 156–157

Plantagenet Saga (Plaidy), 139–140

The Poisonwood Bible (Kingsolver), 59

Pompeii (Harris), 34–35

The Republic of Vengeance (Waters), 175–176

Rise to Rebellion: A Novel of the American Revolution (Shaara), 118

The Rising Tide (Shaara), 122

The River Wife (Agee), 131

Roma: The Novel of Ancient Rome (Saylor), 80–81

Sano Ichiro mysteries (Rowland), 194–195

Saxon Stories (Cornwell), 139

The Secret Bride: In the Court of Henry VIII (Haeger), 98–99

The September Queen (Bagwell), 197–198

Shanghai Girls (See), 150–151

The Silver Pigs (Davis), 190–191

Sinners and the Sea: The Untold Story of Noah's Wife (Kanner), 163–164

Stonehenge, 2000 BC (Cornwell), 31

Stormy Weather (Jiles), 127

Stuart Saga (Plaidy), 140–141

Tea Rose trilogy (Donnelly), 198–199

To Be Queen: A Novel of the Early Life of Eleanor of Aquitaine (English), 94

Tree of Smoke (Johnson), 123

Tudor series (Plaidy), 140

Under Heaven (Kay), 199–200

The Wettest County in the World (Bondurant), 126

When Christ and His Saints Slept
(Penman), 37–38

The Whiskey Rebels (Liss), 45

The White Queen (Gregory), 96–97

William Monk and Hester Latterly
mysteries (Perry), 192–193

*The Winter Palace: A Novel of Catherine
the Great* (Stachniak), 106–107

dialect rich

Bloodroot (Greene), 64–65

The Long Song (Levy), 66–67

A Season of Fire and Ice (Zimpel), 134

That Old Ace in the Hole (Proulx), 135

The True History of the Kelly Gang
(Carey), 74–75

dialogue rich

The Help (Stockett), 53–54

The Power of One (Courtenay), 57

Wolf Hall (Mantel), 41

diary

The River Wife (Agee), 131

displays, 221–222

disturbing

All the Pretty Horses (McCarthy),
186–187

Map of the Invisible World (Aw), 71–72

The Power of One (Courtenay), 57

Things Fall Apart (Achebe), 58

The Voyage of the Short Serpent (du
Boucheron), 79–80

Wanting (Flanagan), 75–76

Wench (Perkins-Valdez, Dolen), 145

dramatic

*The Amazing Adventures of Kavalier
and Clay* (Chabon), 171

*At the Mercy of the Queen: A Novel of
Anne Boleyn* (Barnhill), 101

Avalon series (Bradley), 201–202

The Ballad of Tom Dooley (McCrumb),
113–114

The Boleyn Inheritance (Gregory),
102–103

Claude and Camille (Cowell), 108

The Confession of Katherine Howard
(Dunn), 103

The Constant Princess (Gregory), 100

Corrag (Fletcher), 125

Etta (Kolpan), 112–113

Eve: A Novel of the First Woman
(Elliott), 162–163

*The Favored Queen: A Novel of Henry
VIII's Third Wife* (Erickson),
101–102

A Fierce Radiance (Belfer), 129

The First Man in Rome (McCullough),
92–93

Georgian Saga (Plaidy), 141

In the Time of the Butterflies (Alvarez),
159–160

Inés of My Soul (Allende), 157–158

Islam Quintet series, The (Ali),
205–206

Killing Rommel (Pressfield), 122

The Lacuna (Kingsolver), 158–159

The Last Wife of Henry VIII (Erickson),
103–104

A Lesson before Dying (Gaines),
146–147

The Living (Dillard), 136

The Lotus Eaters (Soli), 124

Loving Frank (Horan), 87–88

Master and Commander (O'Brian),
182–183

Norman Trilogy (Plaidy), 139

The Other Boleyn Girl (Gregory),
86–87

Outlander series (Gabaldon),
204–205

Pacific Glory (Deutermann), 121

Percival's Planet (Byers), 130–131

Plantagenet Saga (Plaidy), 139–140

Queen Victoria novels (Plaidy), 141

Queens of England series (Plaidy),
138–139

The Religion (Willocks), 81–82

Remarkable Creatures (Chevalier),
129–130

The Republic of Vengeance (Waters),
175–176

*Rise to Rebellion: A Novel of the
American Revolution* (Shaara), 118

The Rising Tide (Shaara), 122

Sarai (Smith), 164–165

Saxon Stories (Cornwell), 139

dramatic (cont.)

   The September Queen (Bagwell),
     197–198

   *Sinners and the Sea: The Untold Story
     of Noah's Wife* (Kanner),
     163–164

   Some Sing, Some Cry (Shange), 146

   Stonehenge, 2000 BC (Cornwell), 31

   Tea Rose trilogy (Donnelly), 198–199

   The True History of the Kelly Gang
     (Carey), 74–75

   Tudor series (Plaidy), 140

   Under Heaven (Kay), 199–200

   The White Queen (Gregory), 96–97

   Wilderness series (Donati), 207–208

E

elegant style

   The Day the Falls Stood Still
     (Buchanan), 61

   Helen of Troy (George), 90–91

   The Painter from Shanghai (Epstein),
     108–109

   An Unfinished Season (Just), 135

   Year of Wonders: A Novel of the Plague
     (Brooks), 42–43

elegiac

   Baker Towers (Haigh), 133

   Fool's Crow (Welch), 155–156

   *Gates of Fire: An Epic Novel of the
     Battle of Thermopylae* (Pressfield),
     32–33

   The Widow of the South (Hicks), 121

emotions

   appeal terms regarding, 10

engaging

   Caleb's Crossing (Brooks), 154–155

   City of Thieves (Benioff), 49–50

   Etta (Kolpan), 112–113

   *The King's Daughter: A Novel of the
     First Tudor Queen* (Worth), 97–98

   The Last Empress (Min), 89

   The Last Jew (Gordon), 170–171

   The Last Witchfinder (Morrow), 125

   The Lost Memoirs of Jane Austen
     (James), 111

   Love Comes Softly (Oke), 166–167

   The Maid: A Novel of Joan of Arc
     (Cutter), 95–96

   Maisie Dobbs novels (Winspear),
     195–196

   Measuring the World (Kehlmann), 130

   Percival's Planet (Byers), 130–131

   Sarai (Smith), 164–165

   Tea Rose trilogy (Donnelly), 198–199

   That Old Ace in the Hole (Proulx), 135

   The True History of the Kelly Gang
     (Carey), 74–75

   True Sisters (Dallas), 136

   The Well and the Mine (Phillips), 60

English history

   The Courts of Love (Plaidy), 138

   Georgian Saga (Plaidy), 141

   In the Shadow of the Crown (Plaidy),
     138

   The Lady in the Tower (Plaidy), 138

   Myself, My Enemy (Plaidy), 138

   Norman Trilogy (Plaidy), 139

   Plantagenet Saga (Plaidy), 139–140

   The Pleasures of Love (Plaidy), 138

   Queen Victoria novels (Plaidy), 141

   Queens of England series(Plaidy),
     138–139

   The Queen's Secret (Plaidy), 138

   The Reluctant Queen (Plaidy), 138

   Rose of York trilogy (Worth), 140

   The Rose without a Thorn (Plaidy), 138

   Saxon Stories (Cornwell), 139

   Stuart Saga (Plaidy), 140–141

   Tudor series (Plaidy), 140

   Victoria Victorious (Plaidy), 138

   William's Wife (Plaidy), 138

epic

   The Conqueror: A Novel of Kublai Khan
     (Iggulden), 88–89

   Lionheart (Penman), 94–95

   The War of the End of the World
     (Vargas Llosa), 69

Europe

   The Religion (Willocks), 81–82

   Roma: The Novel of Ancient Rome
     (Saylor), 80–81

   Skeletons at the Feast (Bohjalian),
     78–79

The Voyage of the Short Serpent (du
  Boucheron), 79–80
evaluating books, 238–239
exotic
  The Blood of Flowers (Amirrezvani),
    70–71
  The Painter from Shanghai (Epstein),
    108–109
  The Poisonwood Bible (Kingsolver), 59

F

Facebook, 223
family saga, 206–208
  Bloodroot (Greene), 64–65
  Invisible Mountain (de Robertis),
    67–68
  The River Wife (Agee), 131
fast paced
  All Other Nights (Horn), 120
  Bloodroot (Greene), 64–65
  City of Thieves (Benioff), 49–50
  Deep Creek (Hand), 149
  The First Man in Rome (McCullough),
    92–93
  Gettysburg trilogy (Gingrich), 202
  Gratitude (Kertes), 172
  The Hangman's Daughter (Pötzsch),
    124–125
  The Help (Stockett), 53–54
  Heyday (Anderson), 135
  An Imperfect Lens (Roiphe), 130
  Killing Rommel (Pressfield), 122
  The Last Kingdom (Cornwell), 36
  The Last Wife of Henry VIII (Erickson),
    103–104
  Lionheart (Penman), 94–95
  Measuring the World (Kehlmann), 130
  The Memoirs of Mary, Queen of Scots
    (Erickson), 104
  Niccolò Rising (Dunnett), 40
  Outlander series (Gabaldon), 204–205
  Pacific Glory (Deutermann), 121
  The Painter from Shanghai (Epstein),
    108–109
  Pompeii (Harris), 34–35
  The Power of One (Courtenay), 57
  The Rising Tide (Shaara), 122

Roma: The Novel of Ancient Rome
  (Saylor), 80–81
Saxon Stories (Cornwell), 139
Stonehenge, 2000 BC (Cornwell), 31
Tea Rose trilogy (Donnelly), 198–199
The Time in Between (Dueñas), 121
Valley Forge (Gingrich), 119
See also page-turner
feminist
  Avalon series (Bradley), 201–202
  The Dovekeepers (Hoffman), 168–169
  The Last Empress (Min), 89
first person narrative
  The Lost Memoirs of Jane Austen
    (James), 111
  The Memoirs of Mary, Queen of Scots
    (Erickson), 104
flow charts, reading, 215, 216
form-based readers' advisory, 215, 217,
  257–262
frame
  appeal terms regarding, 9
fun
  Etta (Kolpan), 112–113
funny. *See* humorous

G

genre blends, 179–180
gory
  Gettysburg trilogy (Gingrich), 202
  My Name Is Mary Sutter (Oliveira),
    120, 128
  See also violent
Great Depression
  Bucking the Sun (Doig), 127
  Jim, the Boy (Earley), 126
  Stormy Weather (Jiles), 127
  The Wettest County in the World
    (Bondurant), 126
grim
  Skeletons at the Feast (Bohjalian),
    78–79
gritty
  The Confession of Katherine Howard
    (Dunn), 103
  The Conqueror: A Novel of Kublai Khan
    (Iggulden), 88–89

gritty (cont.)
  Gates of Fire: An Epic Novel of the
      Battle of Thermopylae (Pressfield),
      32–33
  The Last Kingdom (Cornwell), 36
  Lionheart (Penman), 94–95
  The Maid: A Novel of Joan of Arc
      (Cutter), 95–96
  Matterhorn: A Novel of Vietnam
      (Marlantes), 123
  Moloka'i (Brennert), 128–129
  My Name Is Mary Sutter (Oliveira),
      128
  Nathaniel Drinkwater series
      (Woodman), 183–184
  Saxon Stories (Cornwell), 139
  The Sisters Brothers (deWitt), 188–189
  Stonehenge, 2000 BC (Cornwell), 31
  Stormy Weather (Jiles), 127
  Valley Forge (Gingrich), 119
gruesome
  The Company of Liars (Maitland), 128
  My Name Is Mary Sutter (Oliveira),
      120
  Valley Forge (Gingrich), 119
  See also violent

H
hard boiled
  Bernhard Gunther mysteries (Kerr),
      191–192
  The Silver Pigs (Davis), 190–191
Harlem Renaissance, 144
haunting
  Bloodroot (Greene), 64–65
  The Dovekeepers (Hoffman), 168–169
  Half of a Yellow Sun (Adichie), 58
  The Living (Dillard), 136
  Map of the Invisible World (Aw), 71–72
  Matterhorn: A Novel of Vietnam
      (Marlantes), 123
  Mudbound (Jordan), 132
  The Poisonwood Bible (Kingsolver), 59
  The Power of One (Courtenay), 57
  The River Wife (Agee), 131
  Tree of Smoke (Johnson), 123

  The Voyage of the Short Serpent (du
      Boucheron), 79–80
  Year of Wonders: A Novel of the Plague
      (Brooks), 42–43
heart wrenching
  Doc (Russell), 113
  The Heretic's Daughter (Kent), 125
  The Maid: A Novel of Joan of Arc
      (Cutter), 95–96
  Moloka'i (Brennert), 128–129
  My Name Is Mary Sutter (Oliveira),
      120
heartwarming
  Love Comes Softly (Oke), 166–167
  Rainwater (Brown), 131–132
  The Well and the Mine (Phillips), 60
  The Whistling Season (Doig), 62, 136
historical fantasy, 199–200
historical fiction
  appeal of, 8–10
  benchmark authors of, 5–7
  history of, 1–2
  organizing, 10–11
  subgenres of, 13
  twentieth-century authors of, 2–4
historical mysteries, 189–196
homespun
  Jim, the Boy (Earley), 126
  Love Comes Softly (Oke), 166–167
  That Old Ace in the Hole (Proulx), 135
  True Sisters (Dallas), 136
  The Whistling Season (Doig), 136
humorous, 212–213
  The Amazing Adventures of Kavalier
      and Clay (Chabon), 171
  Doc (Russell), 113
  Flight (Alexie), 154
  The Help (Stockett), 53–54
  The March (Doctorow), 120
  The Sisters Brothers (deWitt),
      188–189
  That Old Ace in the Hole (Proulx), 135
  Tipping the Velvet (Waters), 174–175
  An Unfinished Season (Just), 135
  West of Here (Evison), 62–64
  The Whistling Season (Doig), 62

I

immediacy
The First Man in Rome (McCullough),
33–34
The Fruit of Her Hands (Cameron),
169–170
The September Queen (Bagwell),
197–198
Wilderness series (Donati), 207–208
immersive
Agincourt (Cornwell), 39
Bound (Gunning), 133
Corrag (Fletcher), 125
Dreams of Joy (See), 72–73
Fall of Giants (Follett), 51–52
The First Man in Rome (McCullough),
92–93
The Fort: A Novel of the Revolutionary
War (Cornwell), 43–44
The Heretic's Daughter (Kent), 44, 125
An Imperfect Lens (Roiphe), 130
In the Time of the Butterflies (Alvarez),
159–160
The Last Kingdom (Cornwell), 36
Niccolò Rising (Dunnett), 40
People of the Wolf (Gear and Gear), 30
The Rebellion of Jane Clarke (Gunning),
119
Remarkable Creatures (Chevalier),
129–130
The Rising Tide (Shaara), 52–53, 122
Rose of York trilogy (Worth), 140
The Whiskey Rebels (Liss), 45
insightful
Doc (Russell), 113
The First Man in Rome (McCullough),
92–93
I Should Be Extremely Happy in Your
Company (Hall), 48
The Last Wife of Henry VIII (Erickson),
103–104
Lionheart (Penman), 94–95
The Secret Bride: In the Court of Henry
VIII (Haeger), 98–99
inspirational
Love Comes Softly (Oke), 166–167

The Power of One (Courtenay), 57
Year of Wonders: A Novel of the Plague
(Brooks), 42–43
intriguing
The Confessions of Catherine de Medici
(Gortner), 105
Loving Frank (Horan), 87–88
The Painter from Shanghai (Epstein),
108–109
"it" books, 238

J

jargon filled
Master and Commander (O'Brian),
182–183
Jewish historical fiction, 167–172

K

King Arthur, 200–202

L

language, appeal terms regarding, 9
Latin America
Conquistadora (Santiago), 68–69
Invisible Mountain (de Robertis),
67–68
The Long Song (Levy), 66–67
The War of the End of the World
(Vargas Llosa), 69
Latino and Latin American historical
fiction, 157–161
learning from historical fiction, 137
leisurely
Avalon series (Bradley), 201–202
Beautiful María of My Soul (Hijuelos),
160
The Boleyn Inheritance (Gregory),
102–103
The Confession of Katherine Howard
(Dunn), 103
Corrag (Fletcher), 125
The Day the Falls Stood Still
(Buchanan), 61
The First Man in Rome (McCullough),
33–34
The Given Day (Lehane), 133

leisurely (cont.)
 In the Shadow of the Cypress
  (Steinbeck), 150
 In the Time of the Butterflies (Alvarez),
  159–160
 Inés of My Soul (Allende), 157–158
 Islam Quintet series, The (Ali),
  205–206
 The Lacuna (Kingsolver), 158–159
 The Living (Dillard), 136
 Maisie Dobbs novels (Winspear),
  195–196
 Map of the Invisible World (Aw), 71–72
 New York (Rutherford), 134
 The Other Boleyn Girl (Gregory),
  86–87
 Patriot Hearts (Hambly), 119
 A Plague of Doves (Erdrich), 156–157
 Remarkable Creatures (Chevalier),
  129–130
 The Republic of Vengeance (Waters),
  175–176
 Sarai (Smith), 164–165
 The Well and the Mine (Phillips), 60
 When Christ and His Saints Slept
  (Penman), 37–38
 The Whistling Season (Doig), 62, 136
 The White Queen (Gregory), 96–97
 Wilderness series (Donati), 207–208
 Wolf Hall (Mantel), 41
leisurely paced
 Under Heaven (Kay), 199–200
LGBT and nontraditional gender
  identity historical fiction, 173–176
library websites, 229–230
literary
 Bloodroot (Greene), 64–65
 *Charlotte and Emily: A Novel of the
  Brontës* (Morgan), 110
 The Given Day (Lehane), 133
 Half of a Yellow Sun (Adichie), 58
 The Heretic's Daughter (Kent), 125
 An Imperfect Lens (Roiphe), 130
 The Last Witchfinder (Morrow), 125
 Loving Frank (Horan), 87–88
 Matterhorn: A Novel of Vietnam
  (Marlantes), 123

 Percival's Planet (Byers), 130–131
 The Sisters Brothers (deWitt), 188–189
 That Old Ace in the Hole (Proulx), 135
 Tree of Smoke (Johnson), 123
location/place, 55–56. *See also* strong
  sense of place
lush
 *Abundance: A Novel of Marie
  Antoinette* (Naslund), 105–106
 Caleb's Crossing (Brooks), 154–155
 Claude and Camille (Cowell), 108
 Cleopatra's Daughter (Moran), 93
 Helen of Troy (George), 90–91
 The Lieutenant (Grenville), 76–77
 The Religion (Willocks), 81–82
 Tipping the Velvet (Waters), 174–175
lyrical
 All Other Nights (Horn), 120
 All the Pretty Horses (McCarthy),
  186–187
 Beautiful María of My Soul (Hijuelos),
  160
 The Blood of Flowers (Amirrezvani),
  70–71
 Bucking the Sun (Doig), 127
 Caleb's Crossing (Brooks), 154–155
 Christ the Lord: Out of Egypt (Rice),
  165–166
 Corrag (Fletcher), 125
 Dreams of Joy (See), 72–73
 The Heretic's Daughter (Kent), 125
 *I Should Be Extremely Happy in Your
  Company* (Hall), 48
 In the Shadow of the Cypress
  (Steinbeck), 150
 Inés of My Soul (Allende), 157–158
 Invisible Mountain (de Robertis), 67–68
 Islam Quintet series, The (Ali),
  205–206
 Jim, the Boy (Earley), 126
 A Lesson before Dying (Gaines),
  146–147
 The Lieutenant (Grenville), 76–77
 The Living (Dillard), 136
 The Long Song (Levy), 66–67
 My Name Is Mary Sutter (Oliveira),
  120, 128

The Poisonwood Bible (Kingsolver), 59
The Quickening (Hoover), 134
The Republic of Vengeance (Waters),
175–176
The River Wife (Agee), 131
Shanghai Girls (See), 150–151
Skeletons at the Feast (Bohjalian), 78–79
Some Sing, Some Cry (Shange), 146
Things Fall Apart (Achebe), 58
Under Heaven (Kay), 199–200
The Whistling Season (Doig), 62, 136

M

magical realism, 65–66
Flight (Alexie), 154
Fool's Crow (Welch), 155–156
Things Fall Apart (Achebe), 58
marketing the collection, 221–222
medicine, history of
The Company of Liars (Maitland), 128
A Fierce Radiance (Belfer), 129
Moloka'i (Brennert), 128–129
My Name Is Mary Sutter (Oliveira),
128
melancholy
Baker Towers (Haigh), 133
Middle Ages
The Last Kingdom (Cornwell), 36
The Pillars of the Earth (Follett), 36–37
When Christ and His Saints Slept
(Penman), 37–38
Middle East
The Blood of Flowers (Amirrezvani),
70–71
mind mapping, 18, 209
mood
appeal terms regarding, 10
moody
Gates of Fire: An Epic Novel of the
Battle of Thermopylae (Pressfield),
32–33
The Lacuna (Kingsolver), 158–159
Loving Frank (Horan), 87–88
The Rebellion of Jane Clarke (Gunning),
119
William Monk and Hester Latterly
mysteries (Perry), 192–193

moving
Abundance: A Novel of Marie
Antoinette (Naslund), 105–106
The All-True Travels and Adventures of
Lidie Newton (Smiley), 185–186
Baker Towers (Haigh), 133
The Ballad of Tom Dooley (McCrumb),
113–114
Bound (Gunning), 133
Charlotte and Emily: A Novel of the
Brontës (Morgan), 110
Claude and Camille (Cowell), 108
Doc (Russell), 113
The Dovekeepers (Hoffman), 168–169
Dreams of Joy (See), 72–73
Fool's Crow (Welch), 155–156
Gratitude (Kertes), 172
The Heretic's Daughter (Kent), 44
Hotel on the Corner of Bitter and Sweet
(Ford), 151–152
Invisible Mountain (de Robertis),
67–68
The King's Daughter: A Novel of the
First Tudor Queen (Worth), 97–98
A Lesson before Dying (Gaines),
146–147
The Long Song (Levy), 66–67
The Lost Memoirs of Jane Austen
(James), 111
The March (Doctorow), 46–47, 120
Mudbound (Jordan), 132
Pacific Glory (Deutermann), 121
A Plague of Doves (Erdrich), 156–157
The Postmistress (Blake), 50–51
The Power of One (Courtenay), 57
Rainwater (Brown), 131–132
Shanghai Girls (See), 150–151
Skeletons at the Feast (Bohjalian),
78–79
Tree of Smoke (Johnson), 123
True Sisters (Dallas), 136
Under Heaven (Kay), 199–200
Wilderness series (Donati),
207–208
multiple perspectives
Bloodroot (Greene), 64–65
The Dovekeepers (Hoffman), 168–169

mystical
  Avalon series (Bradley), 201–202
  Bloodroot (Greene), 64–65

N
Napoleonic Wars, 181–184
Native American historical fiction,
    152–157
New York
  *The Amazing Adventures of Kavalier
      and Clay* (Chabon), 63
  Among the Wonderful (Carlson), 63
  Call It Sleep (Roth), 63
  The Chosen (Potok), 63
  City of Dreams (Swerling), 63
  City of Promise (Swerling), 63
  Diamond Ruby (Wallace), 63
  East Side Story (Auchincloss), 63
  Elizabeth Street (Fabiano), 63
  The Godfather (Puzo), 63
  The Great Gatsby (Fitzgerald), 63
  Heir to the Glimmering World
      (Ozick), 63
  Maggie: A Girl of the Streets
      (Crane), 63
  Manhattan Transfer (Dos Passos), 63
  Martin Dressler (Millhauser), 63
  Morningside Heights (Mendelson), 63
  New York (Rutherford), 63
  Rules of Civility (Towles), 63
  A Star Called Henry (Doyle), 63
  The Street (Petry), 63
  A Tree Grows in Brooklyn (Smith), 63
  World's Fair (Doctorow), 63
nineteenth century
  *I Should Be Extremely Happy in Your
      Company* (Hall), 48
  The March (Doctorow), 46–47
  Sea of Poppies (Ghosh), 47–48
North America
  Bloodroot (Greene), 64–65
  The Day the Falls Stood Still
      (Buchanan), 61
  The Well and the Mine (Phillips),
      60–61
  West of Here (Evison), 62–64
  The Whistling Season (Doig), 62

nostalgic
  Beautiful María of My Soul (Hijuelos),
      160
  Bucking the Sun (Doig), 127
  The Day the Falls Stood Still
      (Buchanan), 61
  Jim, the Boy (Earley), 126
  The Whistling Season (Doig), 136

O
offbeat
  Measuring the World (Kehlmann), 130
online resources, 226–237
online services, 213–214, 223–225
outreach, 222–225

P
pace
  appeal terms regarding, 10
page turner
  The First Man in Rome (McCullough),
      92–93
  Helen of Troy (George), 90–91
  The Maid: A Novel of Joan of Arc
      (Cutter), 95–96
  See also compulsively readable; fast
      paced
Paris
  *Abundance: A Novel of Marie
      Antoinette* (Naslund), 77
  An American in Paris (Vandenburg), 77
  April in Paris (Wallner), 77
  The Book of Salt (Truong), 77
  City of Darkness, City of Light
      (Piercy), 77
  The Coral Thief (Stott), 77
  The Last Time I Saw Paris (Sheene), 77
  Les Misérables (Hugo), 77
  *Lydia Cassatt Reading the Morning
      Paper* (Chessman), 77
  Paris (Rutherford), 77
  Paris (Zola), 77
  The Paris Wife (McClain), 77
  Pictures at an Exhibition
      (Houghteling), 77
  A Place of Great Safety (Mantel), 77
  The Scarlet Pimpernel (Orczy), 77

The Secret Life of Josephine: Napoleon's Bird of Paradise (Erickson), 77
A Sentimental Education (Flaubert), 77
A Tale of Two Cities (Dickens), 77
The Three Musketeers (Dumas), 77
personal reading plans, 237–243
picaresque
    The All-True Travels and Adventures of Lidie Newton (Smiley), 185–186
    Outlander (Adamson), 187
    Sea of Poppies (Ghosh), 47
place/location, 55–56. *See also* strong sense of place
plot
    appeal terms regarding, 10
plot driven
    Gettysburg trilogy (Gingrich), 202
    The Hangman's Daughter (Pötzsch), 124–125
    In the Shadow of the Cypress (Steinbeck), 150
    Mudbound (Jordan), 132
    New York (Rutherford), 134
    The Pillars of the Earth (Follett), 36–37
    Rainwater (Brown), 131–132
    The Religion (Willocks), 81–82
    The Whiskey Rebels (Liss), 45
poignant
    Bucking the Sun (Doig), 0
    In the Time of the Butterflies (Alvarez), 159–160
    The King's Daughter: A Novel of the First Tudor Queen (Worth), 97–98
    The Lotus Eaters (Soli), 124
    Measuring the World (Kehlmann), 130
    On Agate Hill (Smith), 132
    Rainwater (Brown), 131–132
    An Unfinished Season (Just), 135
    The Well and the Mine (Phillips), 60
    The Whistling Season (Doig), 136
prehistory
    The Clan of the Cave Bear (Auel), 29
    People of the Wolf (Gear and Gear), 30
    Stonehenge, 2000 BC (Cornwell), 31
print resources, 225–226
programs, 222–225

R
read-arounds, 22–23
reader preferences, exploring, 15–18
reading flow charts, 215, 216
reading maps, 18–25, 209
reading profiles, 215, 217
reflective
    Jim, the Boy (Earley), 126
    Percival's Planet (Byers), 130–131
    Remarkable Creatures (Chevalier), 129–130
regional historical fiction, 213
    Baker Towers (Haigh), 133
    Bound (Gunning), 133
    The Given Day (Lehane), 133
    Heyday (Anderson), 135
    The Living (Dillard), 136
    Mudbound (Jordan), 132
    New York (Rutherford), 134
    On Agate Hill (Smith), 132
    The Quickening (Hoover), 134
    Rainwater (Brown), 131–132
    The River Wife (Agee), 131
    A Season of Fire and Ice (Zimpel), 134
    That Old Ace in the Hole (Proulx), 135
    True Sisters (Dallas), 136
    An Unfinished Season (Just), 135
    The Whistling Season (Doig), 136
Renaissance
    Agincourt (Cornwell), 39
    Niccolò Rising (Dunnett), 40
    Wolf Hall (Mantel), 40–41
resources for RA, 225–237
reviews, 232–233
romantic
    Amelia Peabody mysteries (Peters), 193–194
    At the Mercy of the Queen: A Novel of Anne Boleyn (Barnhill), 101
    Avalon series (Bradley), 201–202
    The Ballad of Tom Dooley (McCrumb), 113–114
    Beautiful María of My Soul (Hijuelos), 160
    The Boleyn Inheritance (Gregory), 102–103
    Claude and Camille (Cowell), 108

romantic (cont.)

The Constant Princess (Gregory), 100

The Day the Falls Stood Still
   (Buchanan), 61

Etta (Kolpan), 112–113

The Favored Queen: A Novel of Henry
   VIII's Third Wife (Erickson),
   101–102

A Fierce Radiance (Belfer), 129

Helen of Troy (George), 90–91

Heyday (Anderson), 135

Hotel on the Corner of Bitter and Sweet
   (Ford), 151–152

An Imperfect Lens (Roiphe), 130

Islam Quintet series, The (Ali),
   205–206

The Last Wife of Henry VIII (Erickson),
   103–104

The Lost Memoirs of Jane Austen
   (James), 111

Love Comes Softly (Oke), 166–167

Loving Frank (Horan), 87–88

The Other Boleyn Girl (Gregory), 86–87

Outlander series (Gabaldon), 204–205

Pacific Glory (Deutermann), 121

People of the Wolf (Gear and Gear), 30

Percival's Planet (Byers), 130–131

The Postmistress (Blake), 50–51

Rainwater (Brown), 131–132

The River Wife (Agee), 131

Rose of York trilogy (Worth), 140

The Secret Bride: In the Court of Henry
   VIII (Haeger), 98–99

The Silver Pigs (Davis), 190–191

Tea Rose trilogy (Donnelly), 198–199

The Time in Between (Dueñas), 121

To Be Queen: A Novel of the Early Life of
   Eleanor of Aquitaine (English), 94

Under Heaven (Kay), 199–200

The White Queen (Gregory), 96–97

The Widow of the South (Hicks), 121

Wilderness series (Donati), 207–208

romantic historical fiction, 197–199

S

science, history of

An Imperfect Lens (Roiphe), 130

Measuring the World (Kehlmann), 130

Percival's Planet (Byers), 130–131

Remarkable Creatures (Chevalier),
   129–130

sea stories, 181–184

sensual

Beautiful María of My Soul (Hijuelos),
   160

The Blood of Flowers (Amirrezvani),
   70–71

Conquistadora (Santiago), 68–69

Eve: A Novel of the First Woman
   (Elliott), 162–163

setting

appeal terms regarding, 9

See also strong sense of place

shelf talkers, 223

skills, honing, 11–12, 25, 180–181,
   212–213

slavery, 144

social media, 223–225, 239

sophisticated language

Sea of Poppies (Ghosh), 47

spare

Gratitude (Kertes), 172

The Memoirs of Mary, Queen of Scots
   (Erickson), 104

Tree of Smoke (Johnson), 123

speed-reading, 238, 245–247

stark

The Quickening (Hoover), 134

steamy

At the Mercy of the Queen: A Novel of
   Anne Boleyn (Barnhill), 101

Beautiful María of My Soul (Hijuelos),
   160

The Blood of Flowers (Amirrezvani),
   70–71

The Clan of the Cave Bear (Auel), 29

The Confession of Katherine Howard
   (Dunn), 103

The Religion (Willocks), 81–82

The September Queen (Bagwell),
   197–198

Tipping the Velvet (Waters), 174–175

story

appeal terms regarding, 10

storytelling style
  Conquistadora (Santiago), 68–69
  Etta (Kolpan), 112–113
  The First Man in Rome (McCullough),
    33–34, 92–93
  The Last Jew (Gordon), 170–171
  The Lieutenant (Grenville), 76–77
  Master Georgie (Bainbridge), 173–174
  Percival's Planet (Byers), 130–131
  The Quickening (Hoover), 134
  The Whistling Season (Doig), 62
strong sense of place
  Baker Towers (Haigh), 133
  Beautiful María of My Soul (Hijuelos),
    160
  Bloodroot (Greene), 64–65
  Bucking the Sun (Doig), 127
  Charlotte and Emily: A Novel of the
    Brontës (Morgan), 110
  Cleopatra's Daughter (Moran), 93
  Conquistadora (Santiago), 68–69
  Corrag (Fletcher), 125
  The Day the Falls Stood Still
    (Buchanan), 61
  Deep Creek (Hand), 149
  Doc (Russell), 113
  The Hangman's Daughter (Pötzsch),
    124–125
  In the Shadow of the Cypress
    (Steinbeck), 150
  Jim, the Boy (Earley), 126
  The Lacuna (Kingsolver), 158–159
  The Lieutenant (Grenville), 76–77
  The Living (Dillard), 136
  Map of the Invisible World (Aw), 71–72
  Master Georgie (Bainbridge), 173–174
  Moloka'i (Brennert), 128–129
  Mudbound (Jordan), 132
  New York (Rutherford), 134
  On Agate Hill (Smith), 132
  The Quickening (Hoover), 134
  Remarkable Creatures (Chevalier),
    129–130
  The River Wife (Agee), 131
  Roma: The Novel of Ancient Rome
    (Saylor), 80–81
  Sarai (Smith), 164–165

A Season of Fire and Ice (Zimpel), 134
Stormy Weather (Jiles), 127
Tea Rose trilogy (Donnelly), 198–199
That Old Ace in the Hole (Proulx), 135
Tipping the Velvet (Waters), 174–175
To Be Queen: A Novel of the Early
    Life of Eleanor of Aquitaine
    (English), 94
Under Heaven (Kay), 199–200
The Voyage of the Short Serpent (du
    Boucheron), 79–80
The Well and the Mine (Phillips), 60
West of Here (Evison), 62–64
The Wettest County in the World
    (Bondurant), 126
The Whistling Season (Doig), 62, 136
Wilderness series (Donati), 207–208
William Monk and Hester Latterly
    mysteries (Perry), 192–193
The Winter Palace: A Novel of Catherine
    the Great (Stachniak), 106–107
style
  appeal terms regarding, 9
surreal
  Under Heaven (Kay), 199–200
suspenseful
  Abundance: A Novel of Marie
    Antoinette (Naslund), 105–106
  All Other Nights (Horn), 120
  The Boleyn Inheritance (Gregory),
    102–103
  Bound (Gunning), 133
  City of Thieves (Benioff), 49–50
  The Company of Liars (Maitland), 128
  The Constant Princess (Gregory), 100
  Deep Creek (Hand), 149
  The Dovekeepers (Hoffman), 168–169
  The Favored Queen: A Novel of Henry
    VIII's Third Wife (Erickson),
    101–102
  A Fierce Radiance (Belfer), 129
  Fool's Crow (Welch), 155–156
  Gates of Fire: An Epic Novel of the
    Battle of Thermopylae (Pressfield),
    32–33
  Georgian Saga (Plaidy), 141
  Gratitude (Kertes), 172

suspenseful (cont.)
   The Hangman's Daughter (Pötzsch),
      124–125
   Heyday (Anderson), 135
   In the Time of the Butterflies (Alvarez),
      159–160
   Islam Quintet series, The (Ali),
      205–206
   Killing Rommel (Pressfield), 122
   The Last Jew (Gordon), 170–171
   The Last Kingdom (Cornwell), 36
   A Lesson before Dying (Gaines),
      146–147
   The Lost Memoirs of Jane Austen
      (James), 111
   The Lotus Eaters (Soli), 124
   Matterhorn: A Novel of Vietnam
      (Marlantes), 123
   The Memoirs of Mary, Queen of Scots
      (Erickson), 104
   Norman Trilogy (Plaidy), 139
   Outlander series (Gabaldon), 204–205
   Pacific Glory (Deutermann), 121
   Plantagenet Saga (Plaidy), 139–140
   Pompeii (Harris), 34–35
   The Postmistress (Blake), 50–51
   Queen Victoria novels (Plaidy), 141
   Queens of England series (Plaidy),
      138–139
   The Quick and the Dead (Eickhoff),
      123–124
   Rainwater (Brown), 131–132
   The Rebellion of Jane Clarke (Gunning),
      119
   The Rising Tide (Shaara), 52–53
   Rose of York trilogy (Worth), 140
   Sano Ichiro mysteries (Rowland),
      194–195
   Saxon Stories (Cornwell), 139
   Sea of Poppies (Ghosh), 47
   The Secret Bride: In the Court of Henry
      VIII (Haeger), 98–99
   Skeletons at the Feast (Bohjalian),
      78–79
   Some Sing, Some Cry (Shange), 146
   Stonehenge, 2000 BC (Cornwell), 31
   Stuart Saga (Plaidy), 140–141

   The Time in Between (Dueñas), 121
   Tudor series (Plaidy), 140
   Valley Forge (Gingrich), 119
   Wench (Perkins-Valdez, Dolen), 145
   The Wettest County in the World
      (Bondurant), 126
   The Whiskey Rebels (Liss), 45
   The White Queen (Gregory), 96–97
   The Winter Palace: A Novel of Catherine
      the Great (Stachniak), 106–107
swashbuckling
   Nathaniel Drinkwater series
      (Woodman), 183–184
   The Religion (Willocks), 81–82

T

taut
   My Name Is Mary Sutter (Oliveira),
      120
thought provoking
   Alexander the Great trilogy
      (Renault), 91–92
   The All-True Travels and Adventures of
      Lidie Newton (Smiley), 185–186
   Beautiful María of My Soul (Hijuelos),
      160
   Caleb's Crossing (Brooks), 154–155
   Claude and Camille (Cowell), 108
   The Confessions of Catherine de Medici
      (Gortner), 105
   Deep Creek (Hand), 149
   The First Man in Rome (McCullough),
      33–34
   Gates of Fire: An Epic Novel of the
      Battle of Thermopylae (Pressfield),
      32–33
   I Should Be Extremely Happy in Your
      Company (Hall), 48
   In the Shadow of the Cypress
      (Steinbeck), 150
   Inés of My Soul (Allende), 157–158
   Islam Quintet series, The (Ali),
      205–206
   The Lacuna (Kingsolver), 158–159
   The Last Witchfinder (Morrow), 125
   A Lesson before Dying (Gaines),
      146–147

A Plague of Doves (Erdrich), 156–157
The Quick and the Dead (Eickhoff),
    123–124
The Rising Tide (Shaara), 52–53
*Sinners and the Sea: The Untold
    Story of Noah's Wife* (Kanner),
    163–164
The Sisters Brothers (deWitt), 188–189
Things Fall Apart (Achebe), 58
Tree of Smoke (Johnson), 123
An Unfinished Season (Just), 135
Wanting (Flanagan), 75–76
The War of the End of the World
    (Vargas Llosa), 69
Wench (Perkins-Valdez, Dolen), 145
West of Here (Evison), 62–64
Wolf Hall (Mantel), 41
time periods
    Age of Enlightenment, 41–45
    ancient world, 31–35
    Middle Ages, 35–38
    nineteenth century, 45–48
    overview of, 27–28
    prehistory, 28–31
    Renaissance, 38–41
    twentieth century, 49–54
time sweep, 205–206
    West of Here (Evison), 62–64
time travel, 203–205
tone, 15
    appeal terms regarding, 10
topical historical fiction, 117–118
tracking reading, 239–240
twentieth century
    City of Thieves (Benioff), 49–50
    Fall of Giants (Follett), 51–52
    The Help (Stockett), 53–54
    The Postmistress (Blake), 50–51
    The Rising Tide (Shaara), 52–53
Twitter, 223

U
upbeat
    In the Shadow of the Cypress
        (Steinbeck), 150
    Maisie Dobbs novels (Winspear),
        195–196

V
Vietnam War
    The Lotus Eaters (Soli), 124
    Matterhorn: A Novel of Vietnam
        (Marlantes), 123
    The Quick and the Dead (Eickhoff),
        123–124
    Tree of Smoke (Johnson), 123
violent
    The Ballad of Tom Dooley (McCrumb),
        113–114
    The Conqueror: A Novel of Kublai Khan
        (Iggulden), 88–89
    Deep Creek (Hand), 149
    *The Fort: A Novel of the Revolutionary
        War* (Cornwell), 43–44
    Gettysburg trilogy (Gingrich), 202
    Helen of Troy (George), 90–91
    The Maid: A Novel of Joan of Arc
        (Cutter), 95–96
    Matterhorn: A Novel of Vietnam
        (Marlantes), 123
    The Poisonwood Bible (Kingsolver), 59
    The Power of One (Courtenay), 57
    Rainwater (Brown), 131–132
    The Religion (Willocks), 81–82
    The River Wife (Agee), 131
    The Sisters Brothers (deWitt), 188–189
    The War of the End of the World
        (Vargas Llosa), 69
    See also gory; gruesome
virtual services, 213–214

W
war, 117–118
well researched
    *Abundance: A Novel of Marie
        Antoinette* (Naslund), 105–106
    Alexander the Great trilogy
        (Renault), 91–92
    The Ballad of Tom Dooley (McCrumb),
        113–114
    Caleb's Crossing (Brooks), 154–155
    Christ the Lord: Out of Egypt (Rice),
        165–166
    The Confessions of Catherine de Medici
        (Gortner), 105

well researched (cont.)
A Fierce Radiance (Belfer), 129
The First Man in Rome (McCullough), 92–93
The Fort: A Novel of the Revolutionary War (Cornwell), 43–44
Gates of Fire: An Epic Novel of the Battle of Thermopylae (Pressfield), 32–33
Heyday (Anderson), 135
The King's Daughter: A Novel of the First Tudor Queen (Worth), 97–98
The Last Empress (Min), 89
The Last Witchfinder (Morrow), 125
Lionheart (Penman), 94–95
The Lost Memoirs of Jane Austen (James), 111
Loving Frank (Horan), 87–88
The Maid: A Novel of Joan of Arc (Cutter), 95–96
The Painter from Shanghai (Epstein), 108–109
The Rebellion of Jane Clarke (Gunning), 119
The Religion (Willocks), 81–82
The Time in Between (Dueñas), 121
The Widow of the South (Hicks), 121
well developed characters
Abundance: A Novel of Marie Antoinette (Naslund), 105–106
Agincourt (Cornwell), 39
Charlotte and Emily: A Novel of the Brontës (Morgan), 110
Cleopatra's Daughter (Moran), 93
The First Man in Rome (McCullough), 33–34, 92–93
The Heretic's Daughter (Kent), 44
I Should Be Extremely Happy in Your Company (Hall), 48
The Last Jew (Gordon), 170–171
The March (Doctorow), 46–47
Nathaniel Drinkwater series (Woodman), 183–184
Niccolò Rising (Dunnett), 40
The Other Boleyn Girl (Gregory), 86–87
Patriot Hearts (Hambly), 119

People of the Wolf (Gear and Gear), 30
The Pillars of the Earth (Follett), 36–37
The Postmistress (Blake), 50–51
Rise to Rebellion: A Novel of the American Revolution (Shaara), 118
The Rising Tide (Shaara), 52–53
Shanghai Girls (See), 150–151
Sinners and the Sea: The Untold Story of Noah's Wife (Kanner), 163–164
To Be Queen: A Novel of the Early Life of Eleanor of Aquitaine (English), 94
The War of the End of the World (Vargas Llosa), 69
When Christ and His Saints Slept (Penman), 37–38
Wolf Hall (Mantel), 41
See also character driven
well drawn characters
The Whiskey Rebels (Liss), 45
West, historical fiction set in, 184–189
whole-collection readers' advisory, 137, 209–219
witchcraft
Corrag (Fletcher), 125
The Hangman's Daughter (Pötzsch), 124–125
The Heretic's Daughter (Kent), 125
The Last Witchfinder (Morrow), 125
witty
Amelia Peabody mysteries (Peters), 193–194
Bernhard Gunther mysteries (Kerr), 191–192
Bucking the Sun (Doig), 127
Flight (Alexie), 154
The Last Witchfinder (Morrow), 125
The Long Song (Levy), 66–67
The Lost Memoirs of Jane Austen (James), 111
The March (Doctorow), 46–47
Measuring the World (Kehlmann), 130
Niccolò Rising (Dunnett), 40
Percival's Planet (Byers), 130–131
The September Queen (Bagwell), 197–198
West of Here (Evison), 62–64
Wolf Hall (Mantel), 41

World War II
Killing Rommel (Pressfield), 122
Pacific Glory (Deutermann), 121
The Rising Tide (Shaara), 122
Skeletons at the Feast (Bohjalian), 78–79
The Time in Between (Dueñas), 121

AUTHOR/TITLE INDEX

A

Absalom! Absalom! (Faulkner), 254

Absolutist, The (Boyne), 174

Abundance: A Novel of Marie Antoinette (Naslund), 105–106, 242

Accursed, The (Oates), 253

Achebe, Chinua, 11, 57, 58, 255

Across the Nightingale Floor (Hearn), 200

AD Chronicles (Thoene), 165–166

Adams, "Bruin" (James Fenimore Cooper Adams), 153

Adamson, Gil, 187

Adult Reading Round Table (ARRT), 227, 237

Adventures of Huckleberry Finn, The (Twain), 19

Age of Innocence, The (Wharton), 255

Agee, Jonis, 131

Agincourt (Cornwell), 5, 16, 39, 81, 241

Agony and the Ecstasy, The (Stone), 4

Alan Lewrie series (Lambdin), 183

Albany Trio (Kennedy), 126

Albright, Madeleine, 211

Aleichem, Sholem, 168

Alexander, Tasha, 194

Alexander the Great trilogy (Renault), 4, 91–92, 173

Alexie, Sherman, 154

Ali, Tariq, 205–206

All Other Nights (Horn), 120

All the King's Men (Warren), 256

All the Pretty Horses (McCarthy), 185, 186–187, 243

Allende, Isabel, 46, 65, 157–158

All-True Travels and Adventures of Lidie Newton, The (Smiley), 185–186

Alvarez, Julia, 159–160, 242

Amazing Adventures of Kavalier and Clay, The (Chabon), 21, 107, 171, 250

Amelia Peabody mysteries (Peters), 193–194

American by Blood (Huebner), 157

Amirrezvani, Anita, 70–71, 242

Ancient Egypt series (Moran), 80, 93

And Only to Deceive (Alexander), 194

And the Mountains Echoed (Hosseini), 238

Anderson, Kurt, 135

Andersonville (Kantor), 255

Angel with One Hundred Wings, The (Horch), 40

Angle of Repose (Stegner), 251, 255

Anton, Maggie, 169–170

Any Approaching Enemy (Worrall), 184

Anything for Billy (McMurtry), 74

Appelfeld, Aharon, 235

Archer, Jeffrey, 208

Archer's Tale, The (Cornwell), 17

ARRT Popular Fiction List, 237

Arruda, Suzanne, 56

At Swim, Two Boys (O'Neill), 175–176, 242

At the Mercy of the Queen: A Novel of Anne Boleyn (Barnhill), 101

Atlas of Impossible Longing, An (Roy), 253

Attila: The Gathering Storm (Napier), 89

Attila: The Judgement (Napier), 89

Attila: The Scourge of God (Napier), 89

Audiobooker, 233

Auel, Jean, 29, 30

Aurora Crossing (Schlesier), 156

Austin, Lynn N., 164

Autobiography of Henry VIII, The (George), 41

Avalon series (Bradley), 31, 201–202

Aviator's Wife, The (Benjamin), 252

Aw, Tash, 71–72

Away (Bloom), 171

B

Bagwell, Gillian, 197–198

Bainbridge, Beryl, 173–174

Baker Towers (Haigh), 133

Ball, John, 81

Ball, Margaret, 94

Ballad of Tom Dooley, The (McCrumb), 113–114

Balzac and the Little Chinese Seamstress (Dai), 72

Banks, Iain, 243

Barker, Pat, 242

Barnes, Margaret Campbell, 98, 102–103

Barnhill, Anne, 101

Barrett, Andrea, 46, 75–76

Barron, Neil, 226

Barry, Sebastian, 47

Bastard King, The (Plaidy), 139

Battle Won (Russell), 183

Baudolino (Eco), 34–35

Beautiful Fools (Spargo), 251

Beautiful María of My Soul (Hijuelos), 160–161

Becoming Marie Antoinette (Grey), 106

Belfer, Lauren, 129

Ben-Hur (Wallace), 167

Benioff, David, 49–50, 250

Benjamin, Melanie, 252

Bennett, Ronan, 59

Bennett, Vanora, 87

Berlin Trilogy (Rabb), 192

Bernhard Gunther mysteries (Kerr), 191–192

Bess Crawford mysteries (Todd), 196

Beyond the Sea of Ice (Sarabande), 30

Billy Budd (Melville), 182

Bilyeau, Nancy, 162

Binet, Laurent, 250

Birds without Wings (de Bernières), 49, 70, 206

Birth of Venus, The (Dunant), 6, 38, 70–71, 107

Bitter Sweets (Farooki), 148

Bitter Truth, A (Todd), 196

Black Caucus of the American Library Association Awards, 234

Black Hills (Simmons), 154, 243

Blake, Sarah, 50–51

Blogging for a Good Book, 214

Blood of Flowers, The (Amirrezvani), 70–71, 242

Bloodroot (Greene), 64–65

Bloom, Amy, 171

Blue Asylum (Hepinstall), 197–198

Bohjalian, Christopher, 78–79, 242, 251

Boleyn Inheritance, The (Gregory), 102–103

Bolitho stories (Kent), 184

Bombingham (Grooms), 147

Bondswoman's Narrative, The (Crafts), 144

Bondurant, Matt, 126

Bonhoeffer, Dietrich, 21

Book Group Buzz blog, 233

Book Lust (Pearl), xiv, 10–11

Book of Night Women, The (James), 66

Book Reporter, 233

BookBrowse, 232–233

Booklist Online, 233

BookPage, 233

Books and Authors, 227–228

Border Trilogy (McCarthy), 212

Borgia Duet (Plaidy), 3

Bostonians, The (James), 255

Boudica series (Scott), 34, 96

Bound (Gunning), 133

Boundless Deep, The (Brallier), 199

Boyden, Joseph, 155

Boyle, T. C., 88, 252

Bradford, Richard, 50, 62, 181

Bradley, Marion Zimmer, 31, 201–202, 243

Bread and Dreams (Ceely), 198–200

Brennert, Alan, 128–129

Brides, The (Gist), 162

Bridge of Scarlet Leaves (McMorris), 152

Bright's Passage (Ritter), 252

Bring Down the Sun (Tarr), 91

Bring Up the Bodies (Mantel), 41, 212, 235

British Crime Writers Association Dagger Awards, 234

Broken Paradise (Samartin), 161

Brooks, Geraldine, 42–43, 154–155, 242, 252, 253

Brother Cadfael mysteries (Peters), 179

Brown, Dan, 238
Brown, Sandra, 131–132
Buchanan, Cathy Marie, 61
Buck, Pearl S., 254
Bucking the Sun (Doig), 127, 252
Buddha in the Attic, The (Otsuka), 254
Building of Jalna, The (de la Roche), 206
Bunyan, John, 167
Burning Land, The (Cornwell), 88–89
Burns, Ken, 46
Butch Cassidy and the Sundance Kid (movie), 112
Butler, Octavia, 203
Buzan, Tony, 18
By Fire, by Water (Kaplan), 170–171
Byatt, Lucinda, 83
Byers, Michael, 130–131
Byrd, Sandra, 101

C

Cailiffs of Baghdad, Georgia, The (Stefaniak), 62
Cain at Gettysburg (Peters), 237
Cairo Trilogy (Mahfouz), 70, 255
Caldwell, Taylor, 2, 167
Caleb's Crossing (Brooks), 154–155
Call It Sleep (Roth), 168
Callanan, Liam, 253
Cameron, Michelle, 169–170
Cane (Toomer), 144
Cane River (Tademy), 146
Captain Alatriste adventures (Pérez-Reverte), 81–82
Captains and the Kings (Caldwell), 2
Captains Courageous (Kipling), 182
Captive of Kensington, The (Plaidy), 141
Captive Queen, The (Weir), 94
Card, Orson Scott, 165
Carey, Peter, 74–75, 112
Carr, Philippa, 3
Carter, Forrest, 153
Carter, Jimmy, 44
Carter, Stephen, 202
Cassandra and Jane (Pitkeathley), 111
Cataloochee (Caldwell), 65
Catastrophist, The (Bennett), 59
Cather, Willa, 142, 255

Cecil County (MD) Public Library, 214
Ceely, Jonatha, 198–200
Celestials, The (Shepard), 149
Century trilogy (Follett), 51
Ceremony (Silko), 153
Chabon, Michael, 107, 171, 202, 243, 250
Chadwick, Elizabeth, 37–38
Chain of Thunder, A (Shaara), 7
Chalice, The (Bilyeau), 162
Chance, Megan, 44
Change and Cherish series (Kirkpatrick), 166
Charles Edgemont novels (Worrall), 184
Charles Hayden novels (Russell), 183
Charlotte and Emily: A Novel of the Brontës (Morgan), 110
Charlotte Mecklenburg (NC) Public Library, 229
Chase-Riboud, Barbara, 45
Chesapeake (Michener), 59–60
Chevalier, Tracy, 12, 42, 114, 129–130, 242
Child of the Holy Grail, The (Miles), 202
Children of God (Russell), 23
Children of Henry VIII, The (Weir), 83
Chosen, The (Potok), 168
Christ the Lord: Out of Egypt (Rice), 165–166
Christie, Agatha, 189
Christmas Carol, A (Dickens), 203
Cities of the Plain (McCarthy), 187
City of Ash (Chance), 213
City of the Dead (Morson), 195
City of Thieves (Benioff), 49–50, 250
City of Women (Gillham), 251
Civil War, The (Burns), 46
Clan of the Cave Bear, The (Auel), 29
Clara (Galloway), 88
Clara and Mr. Tiffany (Vreeland), 84
Clash of Eagles, A (Smale), 236
Claude and Camille (Cowell), 108
Claudius the God and His Wife Messalina (Graves), 34
Clavell, James, 42, 253
Cleopatra's Daughter (Moran), 80, 93
Clifton Chronicles (Archer), 208
Clotel; or, The President's Daughter: A Narrative of Slave Life in the United States (Brown), 144

Cloud Atlas, The (Callanan), 253
Coal Black Horse (Olmstead), 50
Cocaine Blues (Greenwood), 243
Cold Mountain (Frazier), 12, 46, 60
Collector of Worlds, The (Trojanow), 76–77
Collins, Wilkie, 189
Color of Lightning, The (Jiles), 156–157
Color Purple, The (Walker), 254
Commoner, The (Schwartz), 89
Company of Liars, The (Maitland), 128
Confession of Katherine Howard, The
   (Dunn), 103
Confessions of Catherine de Medici, The
   (Gortner), 105
Connecticut Yankee in King Arthur's Court,
   A (Twain), 203
Conqueror, The: A Novel of Kublai Khan
   (Iggulden), 88–89
Conquistadora (Santiago), 68–69, 158
Conrad, Joseph, 59, 182, 252, 255
Consequences (Lively), 253
Conspirata (Harris), 28
Constant Princess, The (Gregory), 41, 100
Cooper, James Fenimore, 254
Coplin, Amanda, 250
Corban Loosestrife novels (Holland), 36
Cords, Sarah Statz, 225
Corelli's Mandolin (de Bernières), 22, 173,
   250
Cornwell, Bernard, 5, 16, 17, 28, 31, 36,
   39, 43–44, 81, 88–89, 137, 139, 241
Corrag (Fletcher), 125
Count of Monte Cristo, The (Dumas), 1
Country of Bad Wolfes (Blake), 68, 159
Country of Pointed Firs, The (Jewett), 181
Court of Henry VIII series (Haeger), 103
Courtenay, Bryce, 57
Courts of Love, The (Plaidy), 138
Cousins' War series (Gregory), 6
Cove, The (Rash), 234
Covenant, The (Michener), 58
Cowell, Stephanie, 108
Crane, Stephen, 182, 254
Crocodile on the Sandbank (Peters), 193
Crooked Letter, Crooked Letter (Franklin),
   234, 253
Cross, Donna, 24

Crossing, The (McCarthy), 187
Crown, The (Bilyeau), 162
Crown of Dust (Volmer), 186
Cry, the Beloved Country (Paton), 57–58
Crystal Cave, The (Stewart), 181, 201
Cutter, Kimberly, 95–96
Cyrus Barker and Thomas Llewelyn
   mysteries (Thomas), 192–193

D

Da Vinci Code, The (Brown), 238
Dalager, Stig, 254
Dallas, Sandra, 60–61, 136
Dancing at the Chance (Cameron), 199
Dante Club, The (Pearl), 180
Dark Monk, The (Pötzsch), 124
Darkening Field, The (Ryan), 192
Daughter of Fortune (Allende), 46
Daughter of Joy: A Novel of Gold Rush
   California (Levy), 149
Daughters of the Stone (Llanos-Figueroa),
   68–69
Daughters of the Witching Hill
   (Sharratt), 79
David J. Langum, Sr. Prize for American
   Historical Fiction, 234
Davis, Lindsey, 190–191
Day after Night (Diamant), 79
Day the Falls Stood Still, The
   (Buchanan), 61
Days of Splendor, Days of Sorrow (Grey),
   106
de Bernières, Louis, 22, 49, 70, 206, 250
de la Roche, Mazo, 206
Dean, Debra, 50, 243, 250
Dear and Glorious Physician (Caldwell),
   2, 167
Death at the Crossroads (Furutani), 195
Deep Creek (Hand), 149
Derby Day (Taylor), 189
Deutermann, Peter T., 53, 121
Devils' Queen, The (Kalogridis), 105
Devoto, Pat Cunningham, 53–54
deWitt, Patrick, 188–189
Diamant, Anita, 12, 79
Dickens, Charles, 42, 203, 254
Dillard, Annie, 136, 253

Dinesen, Isak, 76
Disappeared, The (Echlin), 147
DiSclafani, Anton, 251
Distant Mirror, A (Tuchman), 37
Doc (Russell), 113, 188–189
Doctorow, E. L., 46–47, 49, 120, 242, 250
Doig, Ivan, 62, 127, 136, 142, 252
Donati, Sara, 207–208, 243
Donn, Linda, 61
Donnelly, Jennifer, 52, 198–199, 243
Doomsday Book, The (Willis), 204, 243
Douglas, Lloyd C., 167
Dovekeepers, The (Hoffman), 168–169
Downie, Ruth, 191
Doyle, Arthur Conan, 189
Dragon Scroll, The (Parker), 195
Drawn to the Earl (Sharpe), 234
Dray, Stephanie, 93
Dreamers of the Day (Russell), 24
Dreaming the Bull (Scott), 96
Dreaming the Eagle (Scott), 34, 96
Dreaming the Hound (Scott), 96
Dreaming the Serpent (Scott), 96
Dreams of Joy (See), 72–73
du Boucheron, Bernard, 79–80
Duchess of Aquitaine: A Novel of Eleanor
    (Ball), 94
Dueñas, María, 121
Dunant, Sarah, 6, 38, 40, 70–71, 107, 241
Dunn, Suzannah, 101, 103
Dunnett, Dorothy, 2, 40
Durham, David Anthony, 28, 33
Duty to the Dead, A (Todd), 196

E

Earley, Tony, 60, 126, 251
Earth's Children series (Auel), 29
Earthsong Trilogy (Mackey), 29–30
Ebsco's NoveList and NoveList Plus
    databases. *See* NoveList and
    NoveList Plus
Eco, Umberto, 34–35
Edge of Eternity (Follett), 51
Edgerton, Clyde, 53
Education of Little Tree, The (Carter), 153
Edwards, Selden, 204–205
Eickhoff, Randy Lee, 123–124

*Eighty Days: Nellie Bly and Elizabeth
    Bisland's History-Making Race
    around the World* (Goodman), 252
Elegant, Simon, 200
Eleventh Stack blog, 214
Eliot, George, 254
Elliott, Elissa, 162–163
Elyot, Amanda, 91
Emerson, Kate, 180
Emily's Ghost (Giardina), 110
Emperor: The Gates of Rome (Iggulden),
    92–93, 242
Empire (Saylor), 205
Empress (Shan), 89
Empress Orchid (Min), 89
Engelmann, Karen, 253
English, Christy, 94
English Passengers, The (Kneale), 73
English Patient, The (Ondaatje), 78
Epstein, Jennifer Cody, 84, 108–109
Erdrich, Louise, 153, 156–157
Erickson, Carolly, 86, 101–102, 103–104,
    106, 137, 180
Esquivel, Laura, 66, 158
Essex, Karen, 107
Etta (Kolpan), 112–113
Eve: A Novel of the First Woman (Elliott),
    162–163
Evison, Jonathan, 62–64
Eye of the Fleet, An (Woodman), 184
Eye of the Leopard, The (Mankell), 58

F

Face of a Stranger, The (Perry), 192
Fair and Tender Ladies (Smith), 65
Fair Blows the Wind (L'Amour), 181, 201
Fall of Giants, The (Follett), 51–52, 64, 205
Farming of Bones, The (Danticat), 67
Fast, Howard, 3
Faulkner, William, 254
*Favored Queen, The: A Novel of Henry
    VIII's Third Wife* (Erickson),
    101–102
Fiction_L, 229–230
Fierce Radiance, A (Belfer), 129
Figures in Silk (Bennett), 87
Final Storm, The (Shaara), 122

Fire from Heaven (Renault), 4, 91–92, 173
First Americans series (Sarabande), 30
First Light (Thoene), 165–166
First Man in Rome, The (McCullough), 33–34, 92–93
Fisher, Susan, 48, 250–251
Five Quarters of the Orange (Harris), 22
Fixer, The (Malamud), 168
Flanagan, Richard, 107
Fleming, Thomas J., 203
Fletcher, Susan, 125
Flight (Alexie), 154
Floating Life, A (Elegant), 200
Flora (Godwin), 251
Follett, Ken, 12, 36–37, 51–52, 205, 242
Follow the River (Thom), 30
Fool's Crow (Welch), 155–156
For Whom the Bell Tolls (Hemingway), 21
Ford, Jamie, 151–152
Ford, Mackenzie, 51
Ford, Michael Curtis, 33
Forest Lover, The (Vreeland), 7, 107, 241
Forester, C. S., 183
Forsyte Saga, The (Galsworthy), 206–207
Fort, The: A Novel of the Revolutionary War (Cornwell), 43–44
Founding, The (Harrod-Eagles), 80, 207–208
Fowler, Therese Anne, 251
Franklin, Ariana, 38
Franklin, Miles, 73
Franklin, Tom, 253
Frazier, Charles, 12, 46, 60
Freeman (Pitts), 234
Freshwater Road (Nicholas), 53, 144
Frey, James, 83
Frida (Mujica), 88
Fruit of Her Hands, The (Cameron), 169–170
Funeral Games (Renault), 91–92, 173
Furst, Alan, 180, 243
Furutani, Dale, 195

G
Gabaldon, Diana, 180, 197, 204–205
Gael, Juliet, 110
Gaines, Ernest, 146–147

Galloway, Janice, 88
Game of Kings (Dunnett), 2
García Márquez, Gabriel, 65
Garden of Evening Mists, The (Tan), 236
Gardner, Laurien, 100, 101, 102
Gates, Henry Louis, Jr., 144
Gates of Fire: An Epic Novel of the Battle of Thermopylae (Pressfield), 32–33
Gates of Rome, The (Iggulden), 86
Gates of the Alamo, The (Harrigan), 186
Gathering of Old Men, A (Gaines), 144
Gauld, Tom, 162
Gear, Kathleen and Michael, 30
Gemmell, David, 28
Genreflecting: A Guide to Popular Reading Interests (Orr and Herald), 225
George, Margaret, 41, 90–91, 93, 104
Georgian Saga (Plaidy), 141
Germanicus Mosaic, The (Rowe), 190–191
Gettysburg (Gingrich), 202
Gettysburg trilogy (Gingrich), 202–203
Ghosh, Amitav, 47, 251
Giardina, Denise, 110
Gibbons, Kaye, 142
Gift of Rain, The (Tan), 71–72
Gifts of War (Ford), 51
Gillham, David, 251
Gingrich, Newt, 44, 119, 202–203
Girl in Hyacinth Blue, The (Vreeland), 7, 107
Girl with a Pearl Earring (Chevalier), 12, 42, 107
Girzone, Joseph F., 167
Gist, Deeanne, 162
Given Day, The (Lehane), 133, 242
Glancy, Diane, 48, 156
Glass-Eye, the Great Shot of the West (Adams), 153
Glorious Cause, The (Shaara), 118
Gloss, Molly, 61, 242
Gods and Generals (Shaara), 7
Gods and Kings (Austin), 164
God's Country (Everett), 188
Godwin, Gail, 251
Gogol, Nikolai, 254
Golden, Arthur, 12, 254
Golden Heart Award, 234

Golden Mean, The: A Novel of Aristotle and Alexander the Great (Lyon), 92
Golem and the Jinni, The (Wecker), 250
Goliath (Gauld), 162
Gone for Soldiers (Shaara), 46
Goodman, Matthew, 252
Goodreads, 239
Gordon, Noah, 170–171
Gortner, C. W., 105
Gould's Book of Fish (Flanagan), 107
Govier, Katherine, 109
Grace Hammer (Stockbridge), 180
Grail Quest trilogy (Cornwell), 5, 17
Grapes of Wrath, The (Steinbeck), 126, 256
Gratitude (Kertes), 172
Graves, Robert, 28, 34, 254
Gray, Francine du Plessix, 106
Gray, Juliana, 180
Great Divorce, The: A Dream (Lewis), 167
Grecian, Alex, 193
Greene, Amy, 64–65
Greene, Graham, 255
Greenlanders, The (Smiley), 78
Greenwood, Kerry, 189, 243
Gregory, Philippa, 6, 12, 25, 38, 41, 86, 86–87, 100, 102–103, 104, 114, 137, 180, 221, 241
Grenville, Kate, 76–77
Grey, Juliet, 106
Grey, Zane, 184
Gruen, Sara, 251
Guernsey Literacy and Potato Peel Pie Society, The (Shaffer), 51
Guests on Earth (Smith), 251
Gulliver's Travels (Swift), 73
Gunman's Rhapsody (Parker), 74–75, 113
Gunning, Sally, 45, 119, 133
Guns of the South, The (Turtledove), 203
Guterson, David, 60
Guthrie, A. B., 255
Gwenhwyfar: The White Spirit (Lackey), 201
Gypson, Katherine, 231

H

Haeger, Diane, 87, 98–99, 103
Haigh, Jennifer, 133

Half Broke Horses (Walls), 243
Half of a Yellow Sun (Adichie), 58
Hall, Brian, 48, 251
Hall, Radclyffe, 173
Halter, Marek, 165
Hambly, Barbara, 119
Hand, Dana, 149
Hangman's Daughter, The (Pötzsch), 124–125
Haque Family trilogy (Ali), 206
Hardy, Thomas, 255
Harrigan, Stephen, 186, 235
Harris, Joanne, 253
Harris, Robert, 28, 34–35
Harrod-Eagles, Cynthia, 80–81, 207–208
Haruf, Kent, 250
Havah: The Story of Eve (Lee), 163
Hawaii (Michener), 31, 59, 205
Hawthorne, Nathaniel, 255
Healing, The (Odell), 143
Heart of a Lion (Morris), 164
Heart of Darkness (Conrad), 59, 182, 252, 255
Heart of the Lion, The (Plaidy), 95
Hearts of Horses, The (Gloss), 242
Heat and Dust (Jhabvala), 255
Heaven Tree Trilogy, The (Peters), 37
Hegi, Ursula, 24, 49
Helen of Troy (George), 90–91
Help, The (Stockett), 53–54, 117, 143, 212
Hemingway, Ernest, 182
Hennepin County (MN) Library, 230
Henry II series (Penman), 17, 35
Henry V (Shakespeare), 17, 39
Herald, Diana Tixier, 225
Here Be Dragons (Penman), 35
Heretic, The (Weinstein), 170
Heretic Queen, The (Moran), 80
Heretic's Daughter, The (Kent), 44, 125, 242
Heretic's Wife, The (Vantrease), 240
Hesse, Hermann, 255
Heyday (Anderson), 135
HHhH (Binet), 250
Hibbert, Eleanor (Plaidy), 3
Hickey, Elizabeth, 107, 108
Hicks, Robert, 121

Hidden Diary of Marie Antoinette, The (Erickson), 106
Higginbotham, Susan, 97
High Wind in Jamaica, A (Hughes), 181
Hijuelos, Óscar, 160–161
Hill, Lawrence, 242
Hillenbrand, Laura, 211, 251
Historical Fiction II: A Guide to the Genre (Johnson), xiii, 10, 225
Historical Fiction Notebook, 231–232
Historical Novel Society, 229
Historical Novel Society International Award, 234
Historical Novels.info, 228
Historical-Fiction.com, 231
Hitler's Pope: The Secret History of Pius XII (Cornwell), 21
Hitler's War (Turtledove), 181
Hoffman, Alice, 168–169
Holland, Cecelia, 31, 36, 94, 95, 137
Hollands, Neil, 215, 217, 218
Holmes, Marjorie, 167
Holt, Victoria, 3
Holy Thief, The (Ryan), 192
Homecoming (Schlink), 253
Homer and Langley (Doctorow), 250
Hooper, Brad, xiv
Hoover, Michelle, 134
Horan, Nancy, 87–88, 252
Horatio Hornblower series (Forester), 183
Horch, Daniel, 40
Horn, Dara, 120
Hornet's Nest, The (Carter), 44
Horse Goddess, The (Llywelyn), 30
Hosseini, Khaled, 238
Hotel on the Corner of Bitter and Sweet (Ford), 21, 151–152, 213
Hound of the Baskervilles, The (Doyle), 189
House at Tyneford, The (Solomons), 198
House Made of Dawn (Momaday), 153
House of the Spirits, The (Allende), 65–66, 67
How to Tame Your Duke (Gray), 180
Howarth, William. *See* Hand, Dana
Hoyt, Elizabeth, 235
Hugo, Victor, 255

Hummingbird's Daughter, The (Urrea), 66
Hundred Secret Senses, The (Tan), 150
Hunter, Seth, 184
Hurston, Zora Neale, 255

I

I, Claudius (Graves), 28, 34, 254
I, Quantrill (McCoy), 114
I Am Forbidden (Markovits), 236
I Should Be Extremely Happy in Your Company (Hall), 48, 155, 251
Iggulden, Conn, 86, 88–89, 92–93, 114, 137, 242
Illuminator, The (Vantrease), 37, 161
Immigrants, The (Fast), 3
Immigrants series (Fast), 3
Impeachment of Abraham Lincoln, The (Carter), 202
Imperfect Lens, An (Roiphe), 130
Imperial Women (Buck), 254
Imperium (Harris), 28
Impressionist, The (Kunzru), 148
In the Company of the Courtesan (Dunant), 6, 40, 241
In the Garden of Beasts: Love, Terror, and an American Family in Hitler's Berlin (Larson), 210, 211, 251
In the Memory of the Forest (Powers), 21
In the Shadow of the Crown (Plaidy), 138
In the Shadow of the Cypress (Steinbeck), 150
In the Time of the Butterflies (Alvarez), 67, 159–160, 242
Incidents in the Life of a Slave Girl (Jacobs), 144
Indian Clerk, The (Leavitt), 175, 254
Inés of My Soul (Allende), 68, 157–158
Inferno (Brown), 238
Infinity in the Palm of Her Hand (Belli), 163
Inhabited Woman, The (Belli), 69
Inheritance (Chang), 151
Innocent Traitor (Weir), 83
Instance of Fingerpost, An (Banks), 243
Into the Wilderness (Donati), 207, 243
Investigations of Captain Korolev (Ryan), 192

Invisible Bridge (Orringer), 21–22, 25, 172
Invisible Man (Ellison), 144
Invisible Mountain, The (De Robertis),
	67–68, 159
Ironfire (Ball), 81
Ishiguro, Kazuo, 72–73
Islam Quintet series, The (Ali), 205–206
Italian Woman, The (Plaidy), 105
Ivanhoe (Scott), 1–2

J

Jade del Cameron mysteries (Arruda),
	196
Jakes, John, 47, 52
James, Henry, 255
James, Syrie, 111
James Fenimore Cooper Award, 235
Janissary Tree, The (Goodwin), 194
Japrisot, Sebastian, 250
Jesus Chronicles (LaHaye), 165
Jewett, Sarah Orne, 142, 181
Jhabvala, Ruth Prawer, 255
Jiles, Paulette, 127
Jim, the Boy (Earley), 60, 126, 251
*Joan: The Mysterious Life of the Heretic
	Who Became a Saint* (Spoto), 96
Joheved (Anton), 169
Johnny Got His Gun (Trumbo), 255
Johns, Linda, 223–225
John's Story: The Last Eyewitness
	(LaHaye), 165, 242
Johnson, Arleigh, 231
Johnson, Charles, 48
Johnson, Denis, 123, 252
Johnson, Sarah, xiii, 10, 225, 232
Jones, Ben, 251
Jordan, Hillary, 132, 242
Joshua (Girzone), 167
Journey in Blue (Dalager), 254
Just, Ward, 135, 242
Just Jane (Moser), 111
Justin de Quincy mysteries (Penman),
	179

K

Kadare, Ismail, 24
Kalogridis, Jeanne, 105

Kamil Pasha series (White), 193
Kanawha, West Virginia, Library, 23
Kanner, Rebecca, 163–164
Kantor, MacKinlay, 255
Katharine, the Virgin Queen (Plaidy), 100
Kay, Guy Gavriel, 199–200, 243
Kearsley, Susanna, 204
Kehlmann, Daniel, 130
Keneally, Thomas, 172
Kent, Alexander, 184
Kent, Kathleen, 44, 125, 242
Kept (Taylor), 189
Kerr, Philip, 191–192
Kertes, Joseph, 172
Kidnapped (Stevenson), 182
Killer Angels, The (M. Shaara), 7
Killing Rommel (Pressfield), 52–53, 122
Kindred (Butler), 203
King Bongo (Sanchez), 161
King Must Die, The (Renault), 34
King's Coat, The (Lambdin), 183
King's Damsel, The (Emerson), 180
*King's Daughter, The: A Novel of the First
	Tudor Queen* (Worth), 97–98
King's Grace, The (Smith), 98
King's Pleasure, The (Loft), 100
King's Witch, The (Holland), 95
Kingsolver, Barbara, 12, 59, 158–159,
	242, 252
Kipling, Rudyard, 182
Kirkpatrick, Jane, 166
Kneale, Matthew, 73
Known World, The (Jones), 145
Kolpan, Gerald, 112–113
Kondazian, Karen, 113
Kristin Lavransdatter (Undset), 78, 255
Kydd (Stockwin), 184
Kydd Sea Adventures (Stockwin), 184

L

Lackey, Mercedes, 201
Lacuna, The (Kingsolver), 158–159
Lady Emily Ashton mysteries
	(Alexander), 194
Lady in the Tower, The (Plaidy), 138
Lady Julia Grey mysteries (Raybourn),
	194

Lady of the Roses (Worth), 97
Lady Raised High, A (Gardner), 101
LaHaye, Tim F., 165, 242
Lambdin, Dewey, 183
L'Amour, Louis, 184, 185
Larson, Erik, 210, 251
Last Empress, The (Min), 89
Last Full Measure, The (Shaara), 7
Last Jew, The (Gordon), 170–171
Last Kingdom, The (Cornwell), 36, 139
Last Town on Earth, The (Mullen), 42–43, 253
Last Wife of Henry VIII, The (Erickson), 103–104
Last Witchfinder, The (Morrow), 44, 125
Lavinia (Le Guin), 199
Lawgiver, The (Wouk), 236
Le morte d'Arthur (Mallory), 200
Leatherstocking Tales (Cooper), 153, 254
Leavitt, David, 175, 254
Lee, Harper, 255
Lee, Tosca Moon, 163
Lee at Chattanooga: A Novel of What Might Have Been (McIntire), 203
Lehane, Dennis, 133, 191–192, 242
Leonardo's Swans (Essex), 107
Lerner, Eric, 114
Les Misérables (Hugo), 255
Lesson before Dying, A (Gaines), 146–147
Let the Dice Fly (McCullough), 93
Levy, Andrea, 66–67
Lewis, C. S., 167
Libertus Mysteries (Rowe), 190–191
LibraryThing, 239
Lieutenant, The (Grenville), 76–77
Life Class (Barker), 242
Life Studies (Vreeland), 108
Life Together (Bonhoeffer), 21
Light between Oceans, The (Stedman), 250
Light in the Ruins, The (Bohjalian), 251
Light on Lucrezia (Plaidy), 3
Like Water for Chocolate (Esquivel), 66
Lily of the Nile (Dray), 93
Lily Theater, The (Wang), 72
Lionheart (Penman), 94–95
Liss, David, 42, 45
Literature Map, 23–24

Little Balloonist, The (Donn), 61
Little Bee (Cleave), 56
Little Big Man (Berger), 185
Little Book, The (Edwards), 205
Little Stranger, The (Waters), 253
Live by Night (Lehane), 191–192
Lively, Penelope, 253
Living, The (Dillard), 136, 213
Llywelyn, Morgan, 30
Loft, Norah, 100
London (Rutherford), 80
London, Jack, 182
Lone Ranger, The (TV show), 153
Lonesome Dove (McMurtry), 185
Long, Long Way, A (Barry), 47
Long Song, The (Levy), 66–67
Lord Jim (Conrad), 255
Lord of the Silver Bow (Gemmell), 28
Lost Memoirs of Jane Austen, The (James), 111
Lotus Eaters, The (Soli), 49, 124
Love Comes Softly (Oke), 166–167
Love in the Time of Cholera (García Márquez), 65
Love Medicine (Erdrich), 153
Loving Frank (Horan), 87–88, 252
Lucky Billy (Vernon), 112–113
Luncheon of the Boating Party (Vreeland), 7, 107
Lust for Life (Stone), 4
Lymond Chronicles series (Dunnett), 2
Lyon, Annabel, 92

M

Mackey, Mary, 29–30
MacLean, Sarah, 235
Mad Desire to Dance, A (Wiesel), 22
Madame Serpent (Plaidy), 105
Mademoiselle Boleyn (Maxwell), 87
Madonna of the Seven Hills (Plaidy), 3
Madonnas of Leningrad, The (Dean), 22, 50, 243, 250
Mahfouz, Naguib, 70, 255
Maid, The: A Novel of Joan of Arc (Cutter), 95–96
Maisie Dobbs novels (Winspear), 195–196

Maisie Dobbs (Winspear), 196

Maitland, Karen, 128

Malamud, Bernard, 168

Malinche (Esquivel), 158

Mallory, Thomas, 200

Malouf, David, 73–74

Mambo King Plays Songs of Love, The (Hijuelos), 160

Man of Property, The (Galsworthy), 206–207

Mandrakes from the Holy Land (Megged), 176

Mantel, Hilary, 38, 40–41, 86, 242

Map of Love, A (Soueif), 255

Map of the Invisible World (Aw), 71–72

March, The (Doctorow), 46–47, 120, 242

March Violets (Kerr), 191

Marcus Didius Falco mysteries (Davis), 190–191

Mark of the Lion, The (Arruda), 56, 196

Marlantes, Karl, 123

Mary, Queen of France (Plaidy), 99

Mary, Queen of Scotland and the Isles (George), 104

Mary Magdalene (Taylor), 163

Master, The (Toibin), 254

Master and Commander (O'Brian), 182–183, 243

Master Georgie (Bainbridge), 173–174

Masters of Rome series (McCullough), 86, 92–93

Matterhorn: A Novel of Vietnam (Marlantes), 123

Matthews, Anne. *See* Hand, Dana

Maxwell, Robin, 87

Mayor of Casterbridge, The (Hardy), 255

Maytrees, The (Dillard), 253

McBride, James, 250, 254

McCann, Colum, 252

McCarthy, Cormac, 111, 186–187, 243

McCoy, Max, 114

McCrumb, Sharyn, 113–114

McCullough, Colleen, 33–34, 74, 86, 92–93, 114

McKenzie, Nancy, 202

McMurtry, Larry, 62, 111, 187

Measuring the World (Kehlmann), 130

Medicus (Downie), 191

Meely LaBauve (Wells), 65

Melville, Herman, 182

Memoirs of a Geisha (Golden), 12, 70, 254

Memoirs of Cleopatra, The (George), 93

Memoirs of Hadrian, The (Yourcenar), 255

Memoirs of Helen of Troy, The (Elyot), 91

Memoirs of Mary, Queen of Scots, The (Erickson), 104

Mercy, A (Morrison), 145, 254

Mercy of a Rude Stream series (Roth), 168

Mercy Seller, The (Vantrease), 79–80

Meridian (Walker), 144

Merlin the Enchanter series (Stewart), 181, 201

Michener, James, 31, 58, 59–60, 167, 205

Middle Passage (Johnson), 48, 212

Midshipman Bolitho (Kent), 184

Midwife of Venice, The (Rich), 170

Miles, Rosalind, 201–202

Mill on the Floss, The (Eliot), 254

Million Little Pieces, A (Frey), 83

Million Nightingales, A (Straight), 143

Min, Anchee, 89

Mina (Ceely), 198–199

Mind Map Book, The (Buzan), 18

Miracle at St. Anna (McBride), 22, 250

Missouri Book Challenge, 215

Mistress of the Art of Death (Franklin), 38

Mists of Avalon, The (Bradley), 31, 201–202, 243

Mitchell, David, 252–253

Moby Dick (Melville), 182

Molly Murphy mysteries (Bowen), 196

Moloka'i (Brennert), 128–129

Momaday, N. Scott, 153

Moment in the Sun, A (Sayles), 64

Monkey Bridge (Cao), 147

Montana Trilogy (Doig), 62

Moonstone, The (Collins), 189

Morgan, Jude, 110

Morgan, Murray, 213

Morgan's Run (McCullough), 74

Morland Dynasty series (Harrod-Eagles), 80–81, 207–208

Morrison, Toni, 145, 254

Morrow, James, 44, 125
Morson, Ian, 195
Moser, Nancy, 111
Moving Pictures (Immonen), 210
Mr. Midshipman Hornblower (Forester), 183
Mudbound (Jordan), 132, 242
Mujica, Barbara Louise, 88
Mullen, Thomas, 42–43, 253
Murder in the Tower, The (Plaidy), 140
Murphy, Louise, 253
Murphy's Law (Bowen), 196
Musashi (Yoshikawa), 255
Museum of Human Beings (Sargent), 154
My Ántonia (Cather), 255
My Brilliant Career (Franklin), 73
My Career Goes Bung (Franklin), 73
My Dream of You (O'Faolain), 173
My Enemy's Cradle (Young), 210, 251
My Lady of Cleves (Barnes), 102–103
My Name Is Mary Sutter (Oliveira), 42–43, 120, 128, 242
Myself, My Enemy (Plaidy), 3, 138

N

Napier, William, 89
Narrative of the Life of Frederick Douglass, an American Slave, Written by Himself (Douglass), 144
Naslund, Sena Jeter, 105–106, 242
Nathan Peake novels (Hunter), 184
Nathaniel Drinkwater series (Woodman), 183–184
National Jewish Book Award, 235
Native Son (Wright), 144
Nefertiti (Moran), 80
Nemirovsky, Irene, 250
New York (Rutherford), 7, 25, 51–52, 134, 241
New York Times Sunday Book Reviews, 233
News from Paraguay, The (Tuck), 160
Niagara Falls All over Again (McCracken), 171
Niccolò Rising (Dunnett), 40
Nicholas, Denise, 53
Nick Zuliani mysteries (Morson), 195

Night Soldiers (Furst), 243
Night Train, The (Edgerton), 53
No Less Than Victory (Shaara), 122
No Woman So Fair (Morris), 165
Norman Trilogy (Plaidy), 139
North and South (Jakes), 52
NoveList and NoveList Plus, 25, 27, 210, 212, 213, 228, 237
Now Read This III: A Guide to Mainstream Fiction (Pearl and Cords), 225
Nun, The (Hornby), 199

O

O, Pioneers (Cather), 185
Oates, Joyce Carol, 253
Obasan (Kogawa), 152
O'Brian, Patrick, 181, 182–183, 243
October Horse, The (McCullough), 93
Oke, Janette, 166–167
Old Man and the Sea, The (Hemingway), 182
Oliveira, Robin, 42–43, 120, 128, 242
Oliver Twist (Dickens), 1
Olmstead, Robert, 50
Olson, Georgine, 238–239, 245–247
On Agate Hill (Smith), 132
O'Nan, Stewart, 253
Once and Future King series (White), 200–201
Ondaatje, Michael, 78
One Day in the Life of Ivan Denisovich (Solzhenitsyn), 256
One Hundred Years of Solitude (García Márquez), 65
One Last Look (Morrow), 76
O'Neill, Jamie, 175–176, 242
Only Time Will Tell (Archer), 208
Open Boat, The (Crane), 182
Orchardist, The (Coplin), 250
Orr, Cynthia, 225
Orringer, Julie, 25
Other Boleyn Girl, The (Gregory), 6, 12, 38, 86–87
Other Queen, The (Gregory), 104
Otsuka, Julie, 117, 254
Our Lives Are the Rivers (Manrique), 69, 160

Out of Africa (Dineson), 76
Outlander (Adamson), 187
Outlander (Gabaldon), 180, 197, 204
Outlander series (Gabaldon), 197, 204–205
Owl Killers, The (Maitland), 79
Ox-Bow Incident, The (Clark), 185

P

Pacific Glory (Deutermann), 53, 121
Painted Kiss, The (Hickey), 107
Painter from Shanghai, The (Epstein), 71, 84, 108–109
Pargeter, Edith. *See* Peters, Ellis
Paris (Rutherford), 7
Paris Wife, The (McLain), 212
Parker, I. J., 195
Parker, Robert B., 113
Pasha, Kamran, 95
Passing (Larsen), 144
Passion of Artemisia, The (Vreeland), 7, 107
Patchett, Ann, 252
Patriot Hearts (Hambly), 119
Paxson, Diana, 201–202
Pearl, Matthew, 180
Pearl, Nancy, xiv, 9, 10–11, 225
Pears, Iain, 107–108
Penman, Sharon Kay, 17–18, 35, 37–38, 94–95, 97, 179
People of the Book (Brooks), 242, 252
People of the Wolf (Gear and Gear), 30
Percival's Planet (Byers), 130–131
Pérez-Reverte, Arturo, 81–82
Perkins-Valdez, Dolen, 145
Perry, Anne, 189, 192–193
Persian Boy, The (Renault), 91–92, 173
Personal Recollections of Joan of Arc, The (Twain), 96
Peters, Elizabeth, 193–194
Peters, Ellis, 37, 179
Phillips, Gin, 60, 253
Piano Tuner, The (Mason), 71–72
Pikes Peak Library District, 23
Pilgrim's Progress, The (Bunyan), 167
Pillar of the Sky (Holland), 31
Pillars of the Earth, The (Follett), 12, 36–37, 205, 221, 242

Pinkerton's Secret (Lerner), 114
Pirate Latitudes (Crichton), 181
Pitkeathley, Jill, 111
Pitts, Leonard, Jr., 234
Plague of Doves, A (Erdrich), 156–157
Plaidy, Jean, 3, 95, 98, 99, 100, 105, 137, 138–141, 231
Plain Jane (Gardner), 102
Plainsong (Haruf), 250
Plantagenet Prelude (Plaidy), 139
Plantagenet Saga (Plaidy), 95, 139–140
Pleasures of Love, The (Plaidy), 138
Plot against America, The (Roth), 202
Poe, Edgar Allan, 189
Poisonwood Bible, The (Kingsolver), 12, 59, 242, 252
Poland (Michener), 78
Polished Hoe, The (Clarke), 66–67
Pompeii (Harris), 34–35
Pope, Dudley, 183
Porter, Katherine Anne, 47–48, 251
Portrait, The (Pears), 107–108
Postmistress, The (Blake), 21, 50–51, 212
Potok, Chaim, 168
Pötzsch, Oliver, 124–125
Power of One, The (Courtenay), 57
Prague Winter: A Personal Story of Remembrance and War, 1937-1948 (Albright), 211
Prayer for the Dying, A (O'Nan), 253
Prayers for Sale (Dallas), 60–61
President's Daughter, The (Chase-Riboud), 45
Pressfield, Steven, 32–33, 39, 52–53, 86, 92, 122
Pride of Carthage: A Novel of Hannibal's War (Durham), 33
Pride of Carthage (Durham), 28
Prince and the Pauper, The (Twain), 255
Princeling, The (Harrod-Eagles), 208
Princes of Ireland, The (Rutherford), 36, 78
Printmaker's Daughter, The (Govier), 109
Proulx, Annie, 64, 135
Pushing the Bear: A Novel of the Trail of Tears (Glancy), 156

Q

Queen Jezebel (Plaidy), 105
Queen of Camelot (McKenzie), 202
Queen of Subtleties, The (Dunn), 101
Queen Victoria novels (Plaidy), 141
Queen's Lover, The (Gray), 106
Queen's Mistake, The (Haeger), 87, 103
Queens of England series (Plaidy), 3,
    138–139
Queen's Rival, The (Haeger), 87
Queen's Secret, The (Plaidy), 138
Quick and the Dead, The (Eickhoff),
    123–124
Quickening, The (Hoover), 134
Quiet American, The (Greene), 255
Quinn, Julia, 180
Quo Vadis (Sienkiewicz), 167, 255

R

RA for All blog, 23
Rabb, Jonathan, 192
Ragtime (Doctorow), 49
Railroad Stories, The (Aleichem), 168
Rainwater (Brown), 61, 131–132
Raj Quartet (Scott), 70, 255
Ramage (Pope), 183
Rash, Ron, 234
Rashi's Daughters trilogy (Anton),
    169–170
Raybourn, Deanna, 194
Read On . . . Historical Fiction (Hooper),
    xiv
*Readers' Advisory Guide to Genre Fiction,
    The* (Saricks), xiii, 9, 226, 237
Readers' Advisory Guide to Nonfiction
    (Wyatt), 18, 23, 210
*Readers' Advisory Service in the Public
    Library* (Saricks), 4, 214
Reading List, The, 235
Reading the Past, 232
Rebellion of Jane Clarke, The (Gunning),
    45, 119
Rebels of Ireland, The (Rutherford), 78
Red and the Black, The (Stendhal), 256
Red Badge of Courage, The (Crane), 254
Red Queen, The (Gregory), 25
Red River (Tademy), 146

Red Sky at Morning (Bradford), 50, 62, 181
Red Tent, The (Diamant), 12, 169
Redeeming Love (Rivers), 167
*Redlaw, Half-Breed; or The Tangled Trail: A
    Tale of the Settlements* (Badger), 153
Reeducation of Cherry Truong, The (Phan),
    147–148
Religion, The (Willocks), 81–82
Reluctant Queen, The (Plaidy), 138
Remarkable Creatures (Chevalier),
    129–130, 242
Remember Ben Clayton (Harrigan), 235
Remembering Babylon (Malouf), 73–74
Renault, Mary, 3–4, 34, 173
Republic of Vengeance, The (Waters),
    175–176
Return of Little Big Man, The (Berger), 74
Ricci, Nino, 166
Rice, Anne, 165–166
Rice Mother, The (Manicka), 71
Rich, Roberta, 170
Richard Sharpe novels (Cornwell), 5
Riders of the Purple Sage (Grey), 185
*Rise to Rebellion: A Novel of the American
    Revolution* (Shaara), 43–44, 118
Rising Tide, The (Shaara), 7, 17, 52–53,
    122, 241
RITA Award, 235
Ritter, Josh, 252
River of Smoke, A (Ghosh), 47
River of Stars (Kay), 200
River Wife, The (Agee), 131
Rivers, Francine, 164, 167
Rob Roy (Scott), 2
Robe, The (Douglas), 167
Robertis, Carolina de, 67–68
Rogue by Any Other Name, A (MacLean),
    235
Rohweder, Roger, 228
Roiphe, Anne, 130
Roma Sub Rosa series (Saylor), 190
Roma: The Novel of Ancient Rome (Saylor),
    80–81, 205
Roman Blood (Saylor), 190
Romancing Miss Brontë (Gael), 110
Romantic Times Reviewers' Choice
    Awards, 235–236

Rope Eater, The (Jones), 181, 251
Rosa (Rabb), 192
Rose of York trilogy (Worth), 140
Rose without a Thorn, The (Plaidy), 138
Rosnay, Tatiana de, 253
Roth, Henry, 168
Roth, Philip, 202
Rowland, Laura Joh, 194–195
Roy, Anuradha, 253
Royal, Priscilla, 180
Rules of the Wolf (Blake), 159
Running Vixen, The (Chadwick), 37–38
Russell, Mary Doria, 20, 23–24, 39, 113,
    188–189, 250
Russell, S. Thomas, 183
Russian Concubine, The (Furnivall), 71
Russka (Rutherford), 107, 205
Rutherford, Edward, 6–7, 25, 36, 51–52,
    78, 80, 107, 134, 205, 241
Ryan, William, 192

S
Sackett series (L'Amour), 185
Sacred Hearts (Dunant), 6
Sacred Place, The (Black), 147
Sails on the Horizon (Worrall), 184
Sally Hemings (Chase-Riboud), 45
Samurai mysteries (Furutani), 195
Sankaran, Vanitha, 109
Sano Ichiro mysteries (Rowland),
    194–195
Santiago, Esmeralda, 68–69
Sapphire's Grave (Gurley-Highgate), 146
Sarabande, William, 30
Sarah (Card), 165
Sarah (Halter), 165
Sarah's Key (Rosnay), 253
Sarai (Smith), 164–165
Saricks, Joyce, xiii, 9, 214, 226, 237, 240
Sarum (Rutherford), 7, 205
Savannah; of, A Gift for Mr. Lincoln
    (Jakes), 47
Saving Private Ryan, 53
Saxon Stories (Cornwell), 5, 28, 36, 139
Sayers, Dorothy, 189
Sayles, John, 64
Saylor, Steven, 80–81, 190, 205

Scarlet Letter, The (Hawthorne), 2, 255
Schindler's List (Keneally), 172
Schlesier, Karl H., 156
Schlink, Bernard, 253
Schwartz, John Burnham, 89
Scott, Manda, 34, 96
Scott, Paul, 70, 255
Scott, Walter, 1–2
Sea of Poppies (Ghosh), 47, 251
Seabiscuit (Hillenbrand), 251
Season of Fire and Ice, A (Zimpel), 134
Seattle Public Library, 217–218, 232
Sea-Wolf, The (London), 182
Second Son, The (Rabb), 192
*Secret Bride, The: In the Court of Henry
    VIII* (Haeger), 87, 98–99
Secret Eleanor, The (Holland), 94
Secret Sharer, The (Conrad), 182
Secret Trial of Robert E. Lee, The (Fleming),
    203
Secrets of Jin-Shei, The (Alexander), 200
See, Lisa, 12, 72–73, 150–151, 242, 254
September Queen, The (Bagwell), 197–198
Servant's Quarters, The (Freed), 57
Shaara, Jeff, 7, 17, 43–44, 46, 52–53, 118,
    122, 241
Shaara, Michael, 7
Shadow and Light (Rabb), 192
*Shadow of the Swords: An Epic Novel of the
    Crusades* (Pasha), 95
Shadows of the Pomegranate Tree (Ali), 205
Shaffer, Mary Ann, 51
Shakespeare, William, 39
Shan, Sa, 89
Shane (Schaeffer), 185
Shange, Ntozake, 146
Shanghai Girls (See), 72, 150–151, 242
Sharpe, Joanna, 234
Shelf Renewal, 233
ShelfTalk, 215, 232
Shepard, Karen, 149
Shinju (Rowland), 195
Ship of Fools (Porter), 47–48, 251
Shipping News, The (Proulx), 56, 142
Shoemaker's Wife, The (Trigiani), 198
Shoes of the Fisherman, The (West), 162,
    167

Shogun (Clavell), 42, 253

Short-Straw Bride, A (Witemeyer), 162

Shosha (Singer), 255

Siddhartha (Hesse), 255

Sideways Award or Alternate History, 236

Sienkiewicz, Henryk, 167, 255

Silent in the Grave (Raybourn), 194

Silko, Leslie Marmon, 153

Silver Chalice, The (Costain), 162

Silver Pigs, The (Davis), 190–191

Simmons, Dan, 154, 243

Sin Killer (McMurtry), 62, 187

Singer, Isaac Bashevis, 255

*Sinners and the Sea: The Untold Story of
Noah's Wife* (Kanner), 163–164

Sisters Brothers, The (deWitt), 188–189

Sixth Wife, The (Dunn), 104

Skeletons at the Feast (Bohjalian), 78–79,
242

Skid Road: An Informal Portrait of Seattle
(Morgan), 213

Sleep, Pale Sister (Harris), 253

Slouka, Mark, 250

Smale, Alan, 236

Smiley, Jane, 185–186

Smith, Anne Easter, 98

Smith, Duncan, 228

Smith, Jill Eileen, 164–165

Smith, Lee, 132, 251

Snow Falling on Cedars (Guterson), 60,
213

Snow Flower and the Secret Fan (See), 12,
254

Snow Mountain Passage (Houston), 186

Soli, Tatjana, 49, 124

Solzhenitsyn, Aleksandr, 256

Some Danger Involved (Thomas), 192–193

Some Sing, Some Cry (Shange), 146

Someone Knows My Name (Hill), 145, 242

Song of the Nile (Dray), 93

Song Yet Sung (McBride), 254

Sophie Brody Award, 236

Sophie's Choice (Styron), 21, 210

Sophie's Dilemma (Snelling), 166

Soueif, Ahdaf, 255

Soul Thief, The (Holland), 36

Source, The (Michener), 167

Spanish Bride, The (Gardner), 100

Spanish Match, The (Pursell), 162

Spargo, R. Clifton, 251

Sparrow, The (Russell), 23

Spies of Warsaw, The (Furst), 180

Spoto, Donald, 96

Spratford, Becky, 214, 230–231

Spur Awards, 236

Stachniak, Eva, 106–107, 242

Stagecoach (movie), 153

Star Shines over Mt. Morris Park, A
(Roth), 168

Starbuck Chronicles (Cornwell), 5

State of Wonder (Patchett), 252

Stedman, M. L., 250

Steel Wave, The (Shaara), 122

Stegner, Wallace, 251, 255

Steinbeck, John, 256

Steinbeck, Thomas, 150

Stendhal, 256

Stevenson, Robert Louis, 182

Stewart, Mary, 201

Stockbridge, Sara, 180

Stockett, Kathryn, 53–54, 117

Stockholm Octavo, The (Engelmann), 253

Stockwin, Julian, 184

Stolen Crown, The (Higginbotham), 97

Stone, Irving, 4, 114

Stone Heart (Glancy), 48

Stonehenge, 2000 BC (Cornwell), 31

Stones from the River (Hegi), 21–22, 49

Stormy Weather (Jiles), 127

Strickler, John, 228

Stuart Saga (Plaidy), 140–141

Sudden Country, A (Fisher), 48, 187,
250–251

Suite Française (Nemirovsky), 22, 250

Sultan's Seal, The (White), 193

Summer We Got Saved, The (Devoto),
53–54

Sun over Breda, The (Pérez-Reverte), 82

Sunne in Spendour, The (Penman), 97

Susannah Morrow (Chance), 44

Sweet Thunder (Doig), 62

Sword in the Stone, The (White), 201

Sword of Avalon (Paxson), 201

Sword Song (Cornwell), 28

T

Tailor-Made Bride, A (Witemeyer), 162
Take, Burn or Destroy (Russell), 183
Tale of Two Cities, A (Dickens), 2, 42, 254
Tales of the Otori, The (Hearn), 200
Tan, Twan Eng, 236
Taras Bulba (Gogol), 254
Tarr, Judith, 91
Taylor, D. J., 189
Tea Rose, The (Donnelly), 52, 198–199, 243
Tea Rose trilogy (Donnelly), 52, 198–199
Ten Thousand, The (Ford), 33
Tendering in the Storm, A (Kirkpatrick), 166
Testament (Ricci), 166
Tevye the Dairyman (Aleichem), 168
Thackeray, William Makepeace, 256
That Old Ace in the Hole (Proulx), 64, 135
Their Eyes Were Watching God (Hurston), 144, 255
Theophilos (O'Brien), 162
Thief of Shadows (Hoyt), 235
Thieftaker (Jackson), 199
Thing about Thugs, The (Khair), 148
Things Fall Apart (Achebe), 11, 56, 58, 255
Thoen, Bodie, 165–166
Thom, James Alexander, 30
Thomas, Will, 192–193
Those Who Save Us (Blum), 22
Thousand Autumns of Jacob de Zoet, The (Mitchell), 252–253
Thread of Grace, A (Russell), 20, 21, 24, 39, 78–79, 250
Three Day Road (Boyden), 155
300 (Miller), 33
Tides of War: A Novel of Alcibiades and the Peloponnesian War (Pressfield), 39
Time and Again (Finney), 203
Time in Between, The (Dueñas), 121
Time Machine, The (Wells), 203
Time of Terror, The (Hunter), 184
Time Traveler's Wife, The (Niffenegger), 203
Tipping the Velvet (Waters), 174–175
To Be Queen: A Novel of the Early Life of Eleanor of Aquitaine (English), 94
To Die For (Byrd), 101

To Kill a Mockingbird (Lee), 255
Tobacco Road (Caldwell), 126
Todd, Charles, 196
Toibin, Colm, 254
Tolstoy, Leo, 255
Train Dreams (Johnson), 252
Transatlantic (McCann), 252
Treasure Island (Stevenson), 182
Tree Bride, The (Mukherjee), 148
Tree of Smoke (Johnson), 123
Trigiani, Adriana, 198
Trott, Barry, 217
True Grit (Portis), 185, 186
True History of the Kelly Gang, The (Carey), 74–75, 112
True Sisters (Dallas), 136
True Story of Hansel and Gretel, The (Murphy), 21, 253
Trumbo, Dalton, 255
Tsarina's Daughter, The (Erickson), 180
Tuchman, Barbara, 37
Tucker's Reckoning (Compton and Mayo), 236
Tudor Rose, The (Barnes), 98
Tudor series (Plaidy), 3, 140
Tudors, The (HBO series), 41
Turtledove, Harry, 181, 203
Twain, Mark, 96, 203, 255
Two from Galilee (Holmes), 167

U

Unbroke Horses (Jackson), 237
Unbroken: A World War II Story of Survival, Resilience, and Redemption (Hillenbrand), 211
Uncle Tom's Cabin (Stowe), 1
Under Enemy Colors (Russell), 183
Under Heaven (Kay), 199–200, 243
Under the Poppy (Koja), 175
Undset, Sigrid, 255
Uneasy Lies the Head (Plaidy), 3, 98
Unfinished Season, An (Just), 135, 242
Unreal Life of Sergey Nabokov, The (Russell), 174
Unspoken (Rivers), 164
Until the Dawn's Light (Appelfeld), 235
Urrea, Luis, 66

V

Valley Forge (Gingrich), 44, 119
Vanity Fair (Thackeray), 256
Vantrease, Brenda Rickman, 37, 161
Vernon, John, 112–113
Very Long Engagement, A (Japrisot), 21, 250
Victoria Victorious (Plaidy), 138
Virtues of War, The: A Novel of Alexander the Great (Pressfield), 92
Virtues of War, The (Pressfield), 86
Visible World, The (Slouka), 250
Voyage of the Narwhal, The (Barrett), 46, 75–76
Voyage of the Short Serpent, The (du Boucheron), 79–80
Vreeland, Susan, 7, 84, 107, 108, 114, 241

W

W. Y. Boyd Award for Excellence in Military Fiction, 237
Walker, Alice, 254
Wallace, Lewis, 167
Walls, Jeannette, 243
Walter Day novels (Grecian), 193
Walter Scott Prize, 236
Wanting (Flanagan), 75–76
War and Peace (Tolstoy), 2, 255
War in Heaven (Williams), 167
War of the End of the World, The (Vargas Llosa), 69
War That Came Early series, The (Turtledove), 181
Warlord Chronicles (Cornwell), 5
Warren, Robert Penn, 256
Water for Elephants (Gruen), 251
Water Ghosts (Ryan), 150
Watermark (Sankaran), 109
Waters, Paul, 175–176
Waters, Sarah, 174–175, 253
Waverly (Scott), 2
Way West, The (Guthrie), 185
Wayward Muse, The (Hickey), 108
Wecker, Helene, 250
Weinstein, Lewis, 170
Weir, Alison, 83–84, 94, 114
Welch, James, 155–156

Welcome to Hard Times (Doctorow), 188
Well and the Mine, The (Phillips), 60, 253
Well of Loneliness, The (Hall), 173
Wells, H. G., 203
Welsh Princes trilogy (Penman), 35
Wench (Perkins-Valdez, Dolen), 145
West, Morris, 167
West of Here (Evison), 62–64
Western Heritage Awards (Wrangler Award), 237
Western Saga (Guthrie), 255
Wettest County in the World, The (Bondurant), 126
Wharton, Edith, 255
What Do I Read Next? A Reader's Guide to Current Genre Fiction, 25, 226
What Happens in London (Quinn), 180
When Angels Wept: A What-If History of the Cuban Missile Crisis (Swedin), 236
When Christ and His Saints Slept (Penman), 17, 35, 37–38
When the Emperor Was Divine (Otsuka), 21, 117
When the Lion Feels (Smith), 56
When We Were Orphans (Ishiguro), 73
WhichBook, 24
Whip, The (Kondazian), 113
Whiskey Rebels, The (Liss), 42, 45
Whistling Season, The (Doig), 62, 136
White, Jenny, 193
White, T. H., 200–201
White Earth, The (McGahan), 75
White Queen, The (Gregory), 6, 96–97, 241
White Serpent, the Shawnee Scourge; of Indian Heart, the Renegade (Gardner), 152
Whiteoaks of Jalna (de la Roche), 206
Widow of the South, The (Hicks), 121
Wild Life (Gloss), 61
Wild Swans: Three Daughters of China (Chang), 151
Wilderness series (Donati), 207–208
William Monk and Hester Latterly mysteries (Perry), 192–193
Williams, Charles, 167
William's Wife (Plaidy), 138

Williamsburg (VA) Regional Library, 217, 230, 231
Willis, Connie, 243
Willocks, Tim, 81–82
Winding Road, The (Harrod-Eagles), 80–81
Wine of Violence, The (Royal), 180
Winspear, Jacqueline, 195–196
Winter of the World (Follett), 51
Winter Palace, The: A Novel of Catherine the Great (Stachniak), 106–107, 242
Winter Sea, The (Kearsley), 204
Witch of Cologne, The (Learner), 169
Witemeyer, Karen, 162
With Blood in Their Eyes (Cobb), 234, 236
Wives of Henry VIII series (Gardner), 101
Wolf Hall (Mantel), 38, 40–41, 221, 242
Wolves of Andover, The (Kent), 44
Women, The (Boyle), 88, 252
Woodman, Richard, 183–184
Work Song (Doig), 62
World without End (Follett), 36
WorldCat, 24
Worrall, Jay, 184

Worth, Sandra, 97, 97–98, 140
Wright, David, 218
Wyatt, Neal, 18, 22–23, 210, 240

Y
Yard, The (Grecian), 193
Yashim Togalu mysteries (Goodwin), 194
Year of Wonders: A Novel of the Plague (Brooks), 42–43, 253
Year the Horses Came, The (Mackey), 29–30
Yiddish Policeman's Union, The (Chabon), 202, 243
Yonahlossee Riding Camp for Girls The (DiSclafani), 251
Yoshikawa, Eiji, 255
Young, Sara, 251
Your Next 5 Books, 217–218
Yourcenar, Marguerite, 255

Z
Z: A Novel of Zelda Fitzgerald (Fowler), 251
Zimpel, Lloyd, 134

CPSIA information can be obtained at www.ICGtesting.com
Printed in the USA
LVOW08s1809301214

420952LV00013B/318/P